Learning the Art of Helping

Building Blocks and Techniques

Second Edition

Mark E. Young
University of Central Florida

Merrill
Prentice Hall

Upper Saddle River, New Jersey
Columbus, Ohio

Library of Congress Cataloging in Publication Data

Young, Mark E.
   Learning the art of helping : building blocks and techniques / Mark
E. Young.– 2nd ed.
     p. cm .
   Includes bibliographical references and index.
   ISBN 0-13-018396-2
   1. Counseling. 2. Psychotherapy. I. Title
BF637.C6 Y583 2001
158' .3–dc21

                                            00-040217

Vice President and Publisher: Jeffery W. Johnston
Executive Editor: Kevin M. Davis
Editorial Assistant: Christina M. Kalisch
Development Editor: Hope Madden
Production Editor: Linda Hillis Bayma
Production Coordination: WordCrafters Editorial Services, Inc.
Design Coordinator: Diane C. Lorenzo
Cover Designer: Thomas Borah
Cover art: ©SuperStock
Production Manager: Laura Messerly
Director of Marketing: Kevin Flanagan
Marketing Manager: Amy June
Marketing Services Manager: Krista Groshong

This book was set in ITC Century Schoolbook Light by Carlisle Communications, Ltd. It was
printed and bound by R.R. Donnelley & Sons Company. The cover was printed by Phoenix
Color Corp.

10 9 8 7 6
ISBN 0-13-018396-2

To my sons and daughters:
Joseph, Angela, Melissa and Peter.
Your love helps me every day.

About the Author

Mark Young is a professor at the University of Central Florida. He received his doctorate from Ohio University in 1985. He has trained helpers for more than 15 years and has worked in community mental health, private practice, college counseling centers, and corrections for more than 20 years. His professional writing has focused primarily on therapeutic methods and techniques and counseling couples. If you have comments or suggestions on what you have read, please send e-mail to *meyoung @mail.ucf.edu.*

Preface

An overarching metaphor is used in this book: that learning the art of helping is a journey. It is described as a journey with a beginning but no real endpoint. Those who embark on this quest find it to be a lifelong process of discovery rather than a destination. There is always more to learn about human behavior and the process of change.

Let us take the metaphor one step further. Let us suppose that two people are traveling to a foreign country to learn more about that country. One person is an engineer and the other is a historian. As they travel together, the engineer notices and responds to the bridges and buildings, while the historian looks for monuments and clues to the great events of the past. If you were the tour guide for these two people, you would want to know something about each person's interests in order to accommodate them on the trip. Learning words and phrases that incorporate engineering feats or historical situations might increase interest and make each learner feel that his or her field is important. Similarly, in your journey to become a helper, you will bring along your life experience, family history, and cultural background, as well as your biases and prejudices, your likes and dislikes. At every stage, you will test your new learning against what you already know. You will accept most readily those things that mesh with your present way of looking at the world.

Not every learning environment can achieve this kind of tailor-made curriculum. Your teachers will probably not have time to think about the background you bring to this new experience. But you can be responsible for your own learning and integrate new thoughts with what you already know through the process of reflection. In every chapter, there are opportunities to stop and reflect and to engage in additional learning activities. The decision to present the material in this way is based on the philosophy that people carry with them a set of assumptions about the world that affects what they learn and how they assimilate new learning. Reflecting on new material helps you integrate it with what you already know. It lays bare your prejudices and untested assumptions. In addition, new material becomes connected to the storehouse of information you have already collected and the skills that you already possess.

Reflection means thinking about new learning through writing, contemplation, or discussion with others. It is particularly important to reflect on issues that cause you emotional distress, that clash with what you already know, and that you have trouble grasping. Reflection is a skill that will serve you well in difficult situations on the journey to becoming a professional helper. Helping is filled with difficult diagnostic, ethical, and practical problems. By incorporating a reflective process early in your journey, you will avoid many of the pitfalls caused by making snap judgments.

There are several effective methods for reflecting. They include discussion with a small group, bouncing your ideas off another person, or e-mailing fellow learners and teachers. One of the best ways to learn to reflect is through the use of a journal. A journal is not simply a collection of emotional reactions. It should include your feelings about the material, but it should also contain a serious consideration of alternative viewpoints or competing voices. In other words, use reflection when you find yourself at a crossroads between two points of view. Learn to state your current thinking on a particular topic and then write down an alternative viewpoint as well. For example, you may have learned that giving advice is very helpful in dealing with friends and families. In this book, it is rather strongly stated that you should consider retiring that skill for the time being because it is not very effective and can, at times, be dangerous. Perhaps you could write a bit on the virtues of each argument before blindly accepting my premise or rigidly sticking to your own point of view. See if there is a way to integrate these divergent positions.

A Japanese exercise called the *pillow technique* illustrates good reflective thinking. Each corner of the pillow represents an area to ponder when a controversy arises. The exercise begins when you identify two contrasting viewpoints on a topic: *A* is true or *B* is true. For example, *A* = Giving advice is extremely helpful, *B* = Giving advice is not helpful. In reflecting on the issue, move methodically from one corner of the pillow to the next, giving each point of view due consideration. In the first corner, think of all the reasons you believe that giving advice is extremely helpful. In the second corner, think of all the reasons why giving advice is *not* helpful. At the third corner, think of all the reasons why neither *A* nor *B* is true, and finally, in the fourth corner, list all the reasons why *A* and *B* might both be true.

Of course, it is not necessary to go through this entire process when you reflect on the material in this book. But it should be a conscious process for which you set aside time. That is why journal starters have been included in each chapter. If you wish, you may choose one of the starters and write a new journal entry for each chapter. Alternatively, you may choose to write in your journal when you experience a conflict or wish to test a new idea. Try to write about things that interest, excite, or trouble you. Share your writings with others and reflect together.

Organization of the Book

This book contains 15 chapters and teaches 22 basic building-block skills and several more advanced skills. Chapters 1 and 2 introduce you to the book and its organization and approach. Chapter 3 delves deeply into the therapeutic relationship, perhaps the most important ingredient for producing change. Chapters 4, 5, and 6 teach the basic helping skills, including nonverbal skills, opening skills, reflecting, and advanced reflecting. Chapter 7, a chapter new to this edition, is an overview of basic assessment techniques to collect data and gain a clearer picture of the client and the client's problems. Chapter 8, "Challenging Skills," teaches how to give feedback and how to confront inconsistencies in the client's story. Chapter 9 adds goal-setting skills so that you can narrow down the list of client issues and focus on the most important ones. Chapter 10, "Solution Skills," describes techniques to assist clients in creatively solving problems. In essence, Chapters 4 through 10 present the key skills or basic building blocks you will need to facilitate change in a person seeking help. These skills are fundamental and must be practiced until they become second nature.

The final five chapters of the book are organized around curative or *therapeutic factors*. These are the "megaskills" that helpers from different persuasions commonly use to enhance client growth. In this book, we describe six such factors. The first is the therapeutic relationship, which is covered in Chapter 3. It is so important that we decided to address this early in the book. The remaining curative factors are enhancing efficacy and self-esteem (Chapter 11), practicing new behaviors (Chapter 12), lowering and raising emotional arousal (Chapter 13), activating client expectations, hope and motivation(Chapter 14), and new learning experiences (Chapter 15). In the discussion of each of these therapeutic factors, you will learn standard helping techniques such as role-playing, relaxation, and reframing. Although these techniques are more advanced, once you have established the foundation with the building blocks, you will be ready to construct these more elaborate methods.

Acknowledgments

In my own journey, many people have taught and inspired me to be a better person and a better helper. I must acknowledge my teachers: Rajinder Singh, J. Melvin Witmer, Harry Dewire, and James Pinnell. I must also mention my friends who have encouraged me in my writing: Sam Gladding, Gerald Corey, and Jeffrey Kottler. My best source of learning continues to be my students. I was helped in this edition of the book by Samantha White, Anna Doyan, Liza Leite, and Scott Rasmus.

I appreciate the feedback from my friends and collaborators at the Ohio State University, Paul and Darcy Granello, and I recognize the helpful comments of those who reviewed various drafts of the manuscript: Julia Madden Bozarth, Illinois State University; Carroy Ferguson, University of Massachusetts–Boston; John Lewton, University of Toledo; Debbie Newsome, Wake Forest University; Ken Norem, Texas Tech University; Norman Stewart, Michigan State University; and Michael Taleff, Pennsylvania State University.

I would like to thank my editor, Kevin Davis, for his confidence and his high expectations, which helped to make this book so much better. I am also grateful for the work of Hope Madden at Prentice Hall, who helped to edit this manuscript and manage its production. Finally, I recognize the contribution of my wife Jora, who is both my most demanding critic and my staunchest supporter.

Discover the Companion Website Accompanying This Book

The Prentice Hall Companion Website: A Virtual Learning Environment

Technology is a constantly growing and changing aspect of our field that is creating a need for content and resources. To address this emerging need, Prentice Hall has developed an online learning environment for students and professors alike—Companion Websites—to support our textbooks.

In creating a Companion Website, our goal is to build on and enhance what the textbook already offers. For this reason, the content for each user-friendly website is organized by topic and provides the professor and student with a variety of meaningful resources. Common features of a Companion Website include:

For the Professor—

Every Companion Website integrates **Syllabus Manager**™, an online syllabus creation and management utility.

- **Syllabus Manager**™ provides you, the instructor, with an easy, step-by-step process to create and revise syllabi, with direct links into Companion Website and other online content without having to learn HTML.
- Students may logon to your syllabus during any study session. All they need to know is the web address for the Companion Website and the password you've assigned to your syllabus.
- After you have created a syllabus using **Syllabus Manager**™, students may enter the syllabus for their course section from any point in the Companion Website.
- Clicking on a date, the student is shown the list of activities for the assignment. The activities for each assignment are linked directly to actual content, saving time for students.
- Adding assignments consists of clicking on the desired due date, then filling in the details of the assignment—name of the assignment, instructions, and whether or not it is a one-time or repeating assignment.

- In addition, links to other activities can be created easily. If the activity is online, a URL can be entered in the space provided, and it will be linked automatically in the final syllabus.
- Your completed syllabus is hosted on our servers, allowing convenient updates from any computer on the Internet. Changes you make to your syllabus are immediately available to your students at their next logon.

For the Student—

- **Topic Overviews**—outline key concepts in topic areas
- **Electronic Bluebook**—send homework or essays directly to your instructor's email with this paperless form
- **Message Board**—serves as a virtual bulletin board to post—or respond to—questions or comments to/from a national audience
- **Chat**—real-time chat with anyone who is using the text anywhere in the country—ideal for discussion and study groups, class projects, etc.
- **Web Destinations**—links to www sites that relate to each topic area
- **Professional Organizations**—links to organizations that relate to topic areas
- **Additional Resources**—access to topic-specific content that enhances material found in the text

To take advantage of these and other resources, please visit the *Learning the Art of Helping* Companion Website at

www.prenhall.com/young

Brief Contents

Contents

9 Goal-Setting Skills   197

10 Solution Skills   217

Helping as a Personal Journey

Mark Young and Darcy Granello

1

earning to be a professional helper is a journey that takes years. It is a personal journey because you must be committed to understanding yourself as well as your clients. It is not enough to be skilled; at every turn, you face self-doubt, personal prejudices, and feelings of attraction, repulsion, and frustration. Helpers typically experience self-doubt when clients encounter complex and unfamiliar problems—attraction and repulsion because of the helpers' needs and prejudices based on cultural conditioning. All helpers become frustrated at times when clients fail to reach the goals expected of them. All of these reactions can be roadblocks on our journey if they interfere with our ability to form a solid client/helper relationship or when we see the client as a reflection of ourselves rather than as a unique human being. This journey requires that we simultaneously try to focus on the client while keeping a strict watch on our own tendencies to judge, to boost our egos, or to force our viewpoint on others.

The Reflective Practitioner

In this book, we teach one method of dealing with the dilemma of understanding the client and monitoring the self. This is an approach called the *reflective practitioner*. Being a reflective practitioner means that you make a commitment to personal awareness of your automatic reactions and prejudices by taking time to think back on them and perhaps recording them in a journal or discussing them with a supervisor or colleague. If you are engaged in a course of study to become a professional helper, you will probably be confronted with many new learning experiences. If you undertake the challenge of becoming a reflective practitioner, we suggest that you allow yourself to register surprise and all the other emotions as you encounter these novel situations. Later, take time to think back on what you know and what you have learned previously. Through reflecting, you will able to maximize your growth as a helper. When new information comes in, you will be prepared to integrate it with what you already know through the process of reflection. The process of reflection seems to imbed this knowledge more firmly, especially at times when you feel that so much is being thrown at you.

Being a reflective practitioner also means asking for feedback from others and reflecting on how you can work more effectively in a particularly difficult situation (Schön, 1983). Many times in your training, you will become defensive, rationalizing your mistakes, discounting the giver of feedback, or blaming the client for a lack of progress. These are natural reflexes to the threat of feeling uncertain or incompetent. The reflective practitioner is one who examines and reflects upon critical incidents and strong personal feelings in the course of supervision, rather than defending oneself with rationalizations or blaming others. Traditionally, helpers have sought supervision to aid in this reflective process. Lawrence LeShan (1996) reports that his own mentor still seeks supervision, even though she is in her 80s, indicating that the reflective process can be helpful at all stages on the journey to becoming a helper.

There are many ways to help solve this prime dilemma of focusing on the client and then reflecting on yourself. Among these are having a supportive group of co-workers with whom you can discuss your personal reactions, entering a counseling relationship as a client, and keeping a personal journal. All of these provide opportunities for reflection. A helper may rely on all three of these at various times.

As you read this book, we will offer several opportunities to develop this reflective habit. In every chapter, we have included "Stop and Reflect" sections that ask you to consider your reaction to cases or situations. You will also have the opportunity to receive feedback from your fellow students and to reflect on your own progress based on their input. Finally, we have included suggested journal questions at the end of each chapter. These questions are meant to stimulate your reflection on what you are presently learning, but do not feel that answering these questions is your only journaling option. Choose another question or record your reaction to practice sessions each week.

Let us practice reflecting through an inventory of your present attitudes about helping. The key step is to record your answers and then think back on what it might reveal about you. Rather than writing what might impress your teacher or fellow students, in this self-assessment, respond as honestly as possible. Toward the middle of this course and again at the end, you may wish to review this inventory, reflect on it in writing, and determine if your attitudes have changed. For the time being, answer the questions and then write down a reflection or two about what you notice in your answers. Remember that the "Stop and Reflect" sections have no right or wrong answers. They ask for personal reactions to specific topics and hopefully stimulate your thinking. They can make your learning more interactive if you take the time to respond honestly, providing an opportunity to decide whether you agree or disagree with a particular presentation. You may or may not wish to share your answers with others during a class discussion, but by putting your answers on paper, you can take a step back and look at your thoughts from a more objective viewpoint. You may find that your implicit viewpoints about human nature, your attitudes about helping, and your personal values come into sharper focus. Before you can change, you must first become aware of these basic attitudes that you bring to the helping relationship.

Stop and Reflect

1. Write *A* or *D* next to each of the following statements indicating whether you agree or disagree. Note as well any thoughts that may clarify or qualify your responses.

   A a. In most cases, clients come to me for help because they are in a crisis. They need leadership. In order to help, I should generally be active and directive, providing guidance and advice. *At first until alliance develops!*

   A b. Clients may have different values about families, religious principles, and what is important in life. It is not up to me to change clients' values.

   A c. The relationship between helper and client must be a good one. Without "good chemistry," the counseling process will be difficult, if not impossible.

   D d. I must remain at a professional distance. Caring too much about a client makes me lose my objectivity. *Can care but maintain professionalism*

   A e. People are responsible for their own problems. I must get clients to work on themselves, rather than blaming others.

   D f. If I have not been through an experience personally, I cannot help another person deal with it.

   D g. I should never disclose anything personal to a client; the client's issues should be paramount.

2. Answer the following questions:
   As a helper, which do you think you are most likely to focus on helping a client to change? (You may circle more than one.)
   a. A client's feelings
   b. A client's thoughts and perceptions
   c. A client's behaviors

   Why? *All 3 thoughts lead to feeling which leads to behavior*

When talking with a client about a problem, which do you think are most likely to interest you?
a. The history of the problem
b. The present difficulties caused by the problem
c. The client's future goals

Why?_____

_____

_____

Do you think a helper is more responsible for helping a client adjust to the difficulties in the world or for changing the society that breeds these problems?

Why?_____

_____

_____

3. Describe briefly a specific circumstance in which you actually displayed each of the following helper characteristics:
Empathy (the ability to put yourself in the shoes of another, to understand the other person's subjective reality):

_____

_____

_____

Positive regard (the ability to respect another person, even though you may not like what he or she has done):

_____

_____

_____

Genuineness (the ability to be honest and open with another person, even though what you have to say might be difficult to express):

_____

_____

_____

Courage to confront (the ability to bring up inconsistent thoughts, feelings, and behaviors displayed by the client and the willingness to address "touchy subjects"):

_____

_____

_____

4. The following are some difficult situations helpers face. Rank-order them from 1 to 5, depending on how uncomfortable you might feel in each case. In this ranking, 5 is the most difficult and 1 is the least difficult.
   - A client is considering suicide.
   - A client is suffering from the death of a loved one.
   - A client is struggling over whether to get an abortion.
   - An adolescent client is trying to decide whether he is gay or straight.
   - A married client is having an affair.
5. Stop and Reflect: As you look back on your answers, what life experiences have probably shaped your answers? What areas of personal growth are likely to emerge in your training? Which answers were the most difficult to record? Where were you stumped? Where were you confident?

How a Helper Develops: Perry's Stages

Susan has known for a long time that she wants to work with people. During her teenage years, a school counselor helped her cope during her parents' divorce. Since then, she has always hoped to work in a helping profession. She is finally sitting in her first course, a techniques class where she will begin her formal training. Suddenly, she is filled with a combination of excitement and apprehension. What if she can't do it? What if she says the wrong thing in front of the class or to a fragile client? She is confident in her abilities to memorize facts from the textbook and to select the best answers in multiple-choice exams, but can she really learn and demonstrate her skills? Is she in the wrong place?

Three weeks into the class, Susan is still nervous. When her professor calls on her to practice a role-play, her stomach is in knots. She feels light-headed as she makes her way to the front of the classroom. She fears that she will forget the skills she has just learned, that she will make a mistake, that her mind will go blank, and that she will appear foolish to her classmates and professor. Beginning a new course of study can be simultaneously exciting, overwhelming, and intimidating. Maybe you have even watched an experienced professional at work and thought, How does he or she know what to say? How will I ever know the right answers? Perhaps you also feel apprehensive as you read this, wondering whether you will ever learn to make effective interventions.

The desire to learn the "right" answers and to make the "right" interventions, and the nervousness that accompanies it, are a natural part of the process of becoming a helper. It may be helpful to know that students often progress through a series of developmental stages and that this tendency to want answers immediately is normal. Let us begin with an overview of the developmental stages that you can expect to experience during your training. The stages of cognitive development presented here are based on the work of Perry (1970), who studied undergraduate students during a 20-year period. Later research found that Perry's stages are also applicable to graduate students learning a new profession (Simpson, Dalgaard, & O'Brien, 1986). By recognizing these stages as they arise, you may be able to avoid some of the discouragement that may accompany learning new skills when you realize that you are on the expected path. You may also be able to identify some ways to get beyond the thinking patterns that are holding you back.

The Dualistic or "Right/Wrong" Stage

The first stage is a dualistic or absolutist position that can also be called the "right/wrong" stage. It is characterized by the belief that a helper's responses to a client are either right or wrong. In the beginning, trainees often believe that there is only one right way to respond to a client's statement or situation. This black/white, success/failure way of thinking increases the internal pressure and makes helpers overly concerned with their own performance. Moreover, they may fail to listen fully to their clients because they are thinking about what they are going to say next. They may feel that by planning their next statement, they will be able to construct a better response. Actually, they are losing the train of the interview. Students in this stage often ask for direct feedback with questions such as "Was that right?" "How long should I wait before giving advice?" and, "What should I have told the client when she asked me that question?"

The Multiplistic Stage

As you learn the therapeutic building blocks presented in the early chapters of this book, you will recognize that there are actually many possible responses to each statement a client makes. Eventually, you will become comfortable with the knowledge that there is no one right answer at any moment in the helping process. Because of the diversity in clients' backgrounds, experiences, and worldviews, what is "right" for one client is not helpful at all to another. For example, a client considering leaving her boyfriend might say something like this:

"I think that I should get out of the relationship, and then other times I think that I should stay. Everyone is giving me advice. What do you suggest?"

You might react in several different ways.

You could respond with a question: "What aspects of the relationship make you question whether you should continue it?"
You could respond with a reflection of feeling: "You feel overwhelmed and confused, and you would like someone to guide you."
You could respond with a confrontation: "On the one hand, you are saying that you are confused by all the advice; on the other hand, you want me to give my viewpoint. How will another viewpoint help?"

Each of these responses could be helpful, depending on the client's unique situation. When you discover that there are several "right" answers to the same client statement, you will have moved into a multiplistic way of thinking. In fact, at the multiplistic stage, all interventions and techniques may seem equally appropriate. You may find yourself feeling overwhelmed by so many possibilities and wonder what differentiates a good response from a great one.

Students at this stage often report being frustrated and defensive with supervisors who "correct" them because they do not yet know how to select the most helpful course of action. All roads seem to be equally valid. For example, a student may pose a series of probing questions to a client. The supervisor might point out, in turn, that the questions made the client feel interrogated and that the best idea would have been to identify and reflect the client's feelings. The student at the multiplistic stage knows that questioning can be a valid approach, but he or she does not yet understand when this approach is most appropriate and therefore concludes that a mistake has been made. Students at this stage may feel that because there are many possible "right" responses to a given situation, there is no organized system in helping. In fact, the students' ideas may seem just as valid as the instructor's. Here are some common statements students make at this phase of development, indicating their confusion when confronted with several helpful responses:

"I watched Albert Ellis on film. He was very effective, and he didn't do any of the things you taught us."

"I can't see why you told me not to ask so many closed questions when you told Ximena that it was all right with her client."

"I thought you said that we weren't supposed to give advice, and now you're saying that I should have given this client more direction."

The Relativistic Stage

When you have gained some experience through study and practice, you will move into a relativistic stage. At that stage, you will recognize that although many types of responses may be appropriate, depending on circumstances, some are relatively better than others. You will become more skilled at choosing from the many possibilities based on the available information and on the goals for the session.

Let us reconsider the client we discussed earlier who was asking for help with a relationship problem. The client said, "I think that I should get out of the relationship, and then other times I think that I should stay. Everyone is giving me advice. What do you suggest?" We identified three different possible helper responses, each of which leads in a different direction. The interventions and possible client reactions are as follows:

Question: "What aspects of the relationship make you question whether you should continue it?"

Response: The client will probably discuss the good and bad points of the relationship.

Reflection of Feeling: "You feel overwhelmed and confused, and you would like someone to guide you."

Response: The client will talk about feelings and may indicate why she feels so helpless.

Confrontation: "On the one hand, you are saying that you are confused by all the advice; on the other hand, you want me to give my viewpoint. How will another viewpoint help?"

Response: The client may respond with anger at the helper's perception that she is maintaining her confusion by asking people for advice. The client may also begin to explore her lack of confidence in her own decisions.

Obviously, none of these responses is glaringly wrong, but each will take the session in a different direction. When you reach the relativistic stage, you will judge a response as good or bad, depending on whether it takes the session in the direction you want to go. You will have moved past a belief in right or wrong answers and toward an understanding that your choice of responses will have particular repercussions. This will happen when you have the knowledge and self-confidence to make effective choices among a wide variety of interventions and techniques. As contrasted with the dualistic stage, you will probably not be so concerned with your own performance, and you will be better able to think about the effects of certain responses on the client and their effectiveness in reaching the desired goals. Achieving the relativistic stage takes time. By becoming a reflective practitioner, you can speed this process along; however, it has been our experience that you may not become a comfortable resident of the relativistic stage until long after this course is over.

The main value of thinking about stages of development is that it can help you recognize that your struggles are part of a normal progression. In the beginning, try to focus less on grades and "right" answers. Instead, keep your focus on the effects your interventions are having on your clients. Listening to feedback and reflecting on it and self-correcting based on the feedback will be the most helpful tools to spur your development as a helper.

The Development of Expertise

Another way of thinking about helper development is that it is a matter of developing expertise or mastery. This definition is more skills oriented than Perry's cognitive system. The concept of levels of expertise is a commonsense approach that has been around for centuries, especially in the skilled trades. For example, we often hear of a master carpenter, master plumber, or master electrician.

The term "master counselor" or "master therapist" has also been used among helpers. For example, one of the professional organizations has a video series of master therapists. It has long been known that expertise in helping does not come solely from university degrees or from years of experience. Becoming a master is probably the result of training, experience, mentoring, and a passion and zeal for the profession that keeps one a lifetime learner.

Robert Hoffman and his associates (1995) have studied the concept of expertise and concluded that mastery comes after a long period of hands-on experience, perhaps even 10 years, during which one gains at least 50,000 bits of information (Hoffman, et. al., 1995). It is understandable that expertise in helping also takes a lengthy apprenticeship because of the vast differences among clients and the immense amount of knowledge needed to assess, diagnose and treat various disorders and problems. Hoffman and his colleagues use traditional "guild" terminology from the trades to divide expertise into seven stages. In Table 1.1, you will see this concept applied to the development of expertise in helping (Young, 1998).

Implications of the Concept of Expertise to Training Helpers

The first piece of disappointing news is that one cannot master the art of helping in one semester or even two years of training. Sometimes it is overwhelming when you realize how much there is to know. Although becoming a master in the helping arts is a lifetime journey, we sometimes expect to have some measure of competence quickly. Those feelings may elude you for quite some time. Take comfort in the small victories when your instructor or fellow students notice your progress—even if it is hard for you to see.

A second implication is that, despite what state legislatures allow, a new helper is probably not able to handle all of the day-to-day decisions independent of super-

Table 1.1.
"Guild" Terminology for Helper Development (Based on Hoffman et al., 1995)

Naivette	One who knows nothing about the practice of counseling or psychotherapy—a layperson. This term was coined by Hoffman to identify a person who is completely naive to the trade.
Novice	The word novice means one who is new. The novice is a new trainee who is on probation, for example, someone beginning the first class in basic counseling skills but not yet accepted into the program.
Initiate	A person who has been selected for a program and has begun introductory training—a new student in his or her first semester.
Apprentice	A student still undergoing instruction but who is beyond the introductory level. The apprentice is fully immersed in the practice of counseling and works as an assistant. Students in practicum and internship experiences are apprentices. In the trades, apprenticeship lasts from 1 to 12 years.
Journeyman	Journeyman means one who can do a day's work unsupervised. A journeyman works on orders from his or her supervisor. In the counseling field, this period may last 2 to 3 years after graduation before the supervisor or the licensing state allows the person to work independently.
Expert	An expert is an exceptional journeyman who is highly thought of by his or her peers, whose diagnostic and counseling skills are exceptionally accurate, and who can quickly and effectively deal with normal counseling situations. In addition, the expert is one who can handle "tough cases" and may have some particular area of expertise based on considerable experience with a particular type of problem—for example, substance abuse, crisis intervention, domestic violence, and so on. Expert status is by no means inevitable. Some helpers stay at the journeyman stage for life.
Master	A master therapist is one of a select group of experts who are qualified to teach others. A master is one whose judgments and practices become standards for others to follow. One way to identify a master is that he or she is regarded as an expert by other experts. Frequently, this is because the master is thought of as "the expert" in a particular area within the field.

Source: Young, M. E. (1998). Skills-based training for counselors: Microskills or mega-skills? *Counseling and Human Development, 31,* 2. Reprinted with permission of Love Publishing.

vision after two years of education and two more years of supervised experience. A journeyman still needs ongoing contact with an expert or master counselor. Supervision is a vital part of the journey because it provides a forum for you to reflect.

Third, people enter this training with varying levels of expertise. A significant number are already journeymen when they register for basic counseling skills training (McLennan, 1994). If you are in this situation, you may feel that your time is being wasted going back over the basic skills. I have frequently taught basic skills to students who have been working as helpers for several years. Invariably, the more experienced students eventually feel that the course has been extremely valuable. They report that it was beneficial to reexamine their basic positions on important questions such as "Under what circumstances should I give advice?" If you already have some helping experience, you may find that on-the-job training has not been systematic and that this course can help fill in the gaps. You may also discover that your experience allows you to make connections not available to you the first time you learned these skills. If you feel that this course is repetitious, ask your instructor for more challenging assignments. Also, with your instructor's permission, find ways to help other members of your training group by giving them detailed feedback. Encourage them to reflect on their learning. You will be learning supervision skills as you do so.

The Challenge of Development

Although the major shifts in your thinking may follow some of the predictable stages of development described by Perry or in the discussion of expertise, there are a number of other challenges that arise. During the initial period of instruction, you will encounter frustration and feelings of incompetence that accompany helping skills training, so much so that many students feel like throwing in the towel. By encountering these common issues now, you may be able to recognize them when they arise and you will deal with them more effectively.

Taking Responsibility for Your Own Learning

Helping skills training requires you to perform skills in front of other people in practice situations. To receive the maximum benefit from practice sessions, you must open yourself up to feedback and suggestions. There is a strong tendency to compare oneself with others and to view training as a competition. Although that may have been a good strategy in some classes, it can be a detriment in learning helping skills because it may keep you from practicing in front of others and receiving the information you need. For example, you may appear to be ahead or behind your classmates as you learn a particular skill in this book. If the class moves ahead, you may need to continue to work on that skill by practicing with fellow students, watching videotapes of your performance, reading, or getting special help from the instructor. You must take responsibility for educating yourself and request the training that you need, rather than seeing the process of learning as a "mug and jug" phenomenon, in which the teacher pours from the jug of knowledge into the student's mug. You must move from teacher-directed learning to student-directed learning (Caffarella, 1993). In your training, this may mean that you face embarrassment if you are honest about what you do not know or cannot do. Although you may be able to keep your difficulties hidden for a little while, eventually you will be alone with a client and you will need these skills to really be of help.

Finding a Mentor

One of the best ways to learn the helping skills is to watch effective models and to receive feedback from teachers. It is a challenge, however, to find experienced helpers who have the time to act as mentors. Once I watched one of my own teachers in a session with a client. I remember saying to myself, "He acts like being with that person is the most important thing in the world." Although I had read about "eye contact," "empathy," and "unconditional positive regard," when I saw the quality of his presence, I grasped, for the first time, how powerful such attention can be. How few are the times when someone really stops to listen.

Teachers and supervisors are important throughout the journey, especially in the beginning, and you must seek them out. As time goes on, it is true that one learns to have more faith and confidence in one's own judgment and abilities (Skovholt & Ronnestad, 1992). Even then, supervision and mentoring are essential for self-assessment and reflection.

Finding the Perfect Technique

Beginning helpers are extremely anxious about learning specific techniques and interventions. They gather techniques and tricks of the trade at workshops, hoping that one will be the magic pill that cures all clients. When you feel anxious or ineffective, it is normal to experience a desire to learn every technique available and assume a sort of "cookbook" approach to helping. There is nothing wrong with learning all you can. It is unlikely, however, that you will find a perfect technique that will work for every client. The pursuit of a perfect technique or magic pill is characteristic of dualistic or "right/wrong" thinking. In the relativistic stage, you will evaluate a technique to see if it is best for a specific client, with a particular problem, in a particular situation.

In Limbo

As you begin the process of learning to help, you may find that you abandon your "pre-training" natural helping style. Although beginning helpers are often naturally therapeutic, they typically find that they must temporarily set aside their old ways of helping. You may find that the new techniques and interventions feel artificial or "not like me" at first. Do not be surprised to hear yourself say, "I used to know what to do when a friend was upset. Now that I've begun to study helping, I no longer know what to say." Even your attempts to regain your old self seem awkward and artificial. It is a little like the centipede that was asked how she could coordinate those hundred legs and walk. Once she started thinking about it, she couldn't do it. As you consciously learn the helping process, it may seem hard to be natural. One reason this happens is that helping training invariably asks helpers to focus on the client, rather than on the client's problems. This is really unnatural to us because we have always spent most of our helping efforts on figuring out clever problem-solving strategies. The good news is that this feeling passes as you see that your efforts to understand the client have a beneficial effect. Over time, you will find that you are able to integrate the old "therapeutic friend" with the new "therapeutic helper."

Accepting Feedback and Being Perfect

Your willingness to accept feedback will be another indicator of developmental change. As we have said, students in the dualistic stage accept feedback but feel discouraged when they "do it wrong." In the multiplistic stage, they may be defensive in the face of feedback and attempt to justify their actions, rather than listening to critiques and suggestions. As you gain confidence and see how different responses take clients in different directions, it is easier not to take such criticism personally. The risk in the relativistic stage is that you may be too hard on yourself, demanding perfection when you are just beginning. Try to focus on your strengths, build on what you are doing well, and learn from feedback.

I experienced a similar crisis when I turned from full-time helper to textbook writer. Although I was confident in my approach to clients, I was sensitive about how my writing would be seen by others. I frequently see writers who are extremely afraid to show their work to others. Writing and engaging in a therapeutic relationship are both very personal forms of self-expression and so we are tempted to hide our work and avoid any damage to self-esteem.

Following Ethical Guidelines

Becoming sensitive to ethical issues early on will help in your later training, but there is an even more important therapeutic issue. First, by establishing clear guidelines, clients feel safer in the therapeutic relationship. Second, we can avoid potential damage caused by well-intentioned blunders. We are quite familiar with medical problems caused by inappropriate treatment. However, we may fail to recognize that clients can be harmed by inappropriate advice, emotionally arousing techniques, and subtle messages of contempt when we fail to fully understand their backgrounds. The Hippocratic challenge to all practitioners of the healing arts is *primum non nocere, first, do no harm.*

Ethical guidelines have been proposed by virtually every professional organization in the helping professions. These guidelines and references can be found in recent publications, and updated versions are available online. Ethical guidelines and codes largely deal with your work environment; however, similar issues will arise in your training group. The following are some guidelines you may wish to adopt as a group during your class. Optimally, you should discuss these thoroughly, so that everyone is in agreement on how to approach these situations. On the other hand, rules are inadequate to deal with every problem that arises. In many cases, it will be necessary to talk with your instructor about how to handle these conflicts when things become complicated.

Guideline 1

Do not reveal to anyone outside of the class disclosures made by students during role-play situations and associated discussions.

This guideline should include spouses as well as friends. Although there may not seem to be any serious harm, forming these boundaries will set up an atmosphere of trust and allow for more freedom for all participants. It may be your first experience in keeping professional secrets. Try thinking of it as a sacred trust, similar to the seal of the confessional taken by Catholic priests. Disclose these secrets in your training situation only when necessary to help another student or to further your own learning in discussions with the instructor.

Guideline 2

Avoid giving advice. This is a practical suggestion as well as an ethical guideline. From the practical standpoint, you may find that giving advice, especially early on, can damage the relationship and slow down client progress. From the ethical perspective, are you really competent and knowledgeable enough to give advice? Could your advice be dangerous to a person's relationships or his or her academic or professional life? Could it undermine the client's self-confidence? These concerns suggest that you might wish to resist giving advice during this part of your training and develop some alternative skills.

Guideline 3
Do not impose your values on others. Avoid making value judgments on a person's lifestyle, life experiences, or philosophy of life. Similar to giving advice, your judgments may be based on inadequate knowledge, may reflect your own limited experiences, or may communicate contempt or lack of acceptance of the other person. Learning to be sensitive to the cultural differences and unique experiences of clients helps us to avoid the trap of subtly communicating that a person's values and worldview are unacceptable.

Guideline 4
Be careful with feedback to clients and to fellow students. Give feedback only when asked and package it in a way that the other person can accept. Give only specific and constructive feedback. Giving vague and very negative feedback can be damaging. Give feedback on areas where the person wants more information. Sometimes when you are frustrated by a client's lack of movement, you might be tempted to become too confrontational. Before confronting one of your clients, consider whether you are doing this to help the client or to reduce your own feelings of powerlessness. In other words, consider whose needs the confrontation and feedback are meeting.

Guideline 5
Stay mainly with the techniques described in the book or those taught by your instructor. Using an unfamiliar and potentially harmful method should only be attempted with the guidance and permission of your teacher or supervisor. A powerful technique may have an equally powerful negative effect when misapplied. Generally speaking, reading about a technique or seeing it demonstrated at a workshop is not sufficient training.

Guideline 6
Notify your instructor or supervisor at once if a member of your training group or a client is contemplating suicide or is considering harming others.

Even if you are relatively sure that the probability of violence is low, it is vital that you discuss this with someone in authority. This is good training for your later work when you must learn to consult when an ethical or clinical problem arises.

Although many of the issues described in these guidelines will not surface in your training group, it is important to be prepared. Talk with your group about how you might handle specific situations. Make sure everyone is in agreement to abide by the ethical guidelines.

Other Challenges

The Work Environment for Helpers at the Turn of the Century
The work settings of helpers at this point in history are dramatically different from those 50 years ago. These environments dictate, to some extent, which helping skills

will be most utilized. Specifically, at the mid-century mark, psychoanalysis was the accepted paradigm. At that time, clients might have been seen over a period of several years, with sessions two or three times per week. Today, the typical client in a private practice, college counseling center, drug treatment center, hospital, or community counseling setting is seen for only 6 to 10 sessions. Compared to the 1950s, the sessions today are aimed more at achieving specific goals, rather than focusing on the past. Much of this emphasis has been due to the managed-care revolution in health care, but there has also been a general disillusionment among helpers about the efficacy of long-term work.

In the 1950s, school counselors focused almost entirely on career testing and career counseling as well as scheduling. Today, school counselors are much more concerned with the psychological problems of students and dealing with disruptive and violent behavior. They require keen diagnostic and crisis management skills and work more with parents and families and on a short-term basis. In summary, whether you work in a community, university, private practice, hospital, or school, you will more than likely be challenged to become a brief, present-oriented, and goal-directed helper.

Individual Differences

If you are a member of a minority group or a female, have a disability, are one of the first in your family to attain higher education, or are going through a particularly stressful life stage (i.e., getting married or divorced, leaving home, having children), this can add an additional challenge to the process of becoming a helper. Students facing outside stressors may also have difficulty maintaining the flexible schedule that is required (Gaff & Gaff, 1981). Specifically, consider how the following differences may have an impact:

Minority students may lack same-race peer interactions and minority role models (Cheatham & Berg-Cross, 1992). Female students raised in traditional families may have difficulty trusting in an internal authority (Bernard, 1981; Marx, 1990). Some male students may not be as attuned to relationships and feelings as their female counterparts. Hypermasculine upbringing may cause male trainees to seek solutions quickly, before understanding the client. They may fail to recognize such feelings as fear and helplessness in themselves and may therefore have difficulty recognizing them in others.

Such considerations should serve to illustrate that development is not the same for each person, rather than discouraging those with special situations. An individual's progress cannot be confined to a timetable (Barrow, 1987), nor is it necessarily a linear, step-by-step process. Sometimes you may feel that you are taking two steps forward and one step back Allow yourself time to develop and move at your own pace. Development is not a competition with your classmates; it is a personal journey.

The Perfect Helper

When Do I Quit "Developing"?

Your development as a professional helper does not end with graduation; it is a lifelong process toward mastery. Academic training will give you the skills, but practice, supervision, networking, and experience will make you a helper. Neither a Ph.D. nor a certificate from a training institute will mean that you have become the perfect helper. Students develop during their training and this does not stop when they finish their formal training. In fact, interviews with professionals possessing more than 20 years of experience revealed that these helpers believed most of their development occurred after graduation (Skovholt & Ronnestad, 1992). Equipped with diplomas, but not a lot of work experience, new professionals may feel the effects of the "imposter phenomenon." Beginning helpers also tend to see themselves as frauds who are vulnerable to being found out (Harvey & Katz, 1985). Those professionals who have been out of school more than 10 years speak of a deeper authenticity in their work, the reassurance of accumulated wisdom, and the ability to make individual and personalized interventions with their clients. Do you have to wait 10 years until you can be a good helper? No—you can be the best helper you can be at your particular stage. Keep learning, keep receiving supervision, and do not pretend you know more than you do. One of the best books on this topic is *Finding Your Way as a Counselor* by Jeffrey Kottler (1996). It is a collection of stories by practicing counselors about the issues they face as they develop. Besides making us feel that we are not alone, the writers give us help in thinking about how to get over these hurdles we continue to face.

To address ongoing developmental needs, the concept of lifelong learning is essential for helpers. Our knowledge of new techniques, advances in research in the field, new client populations, and emerging social issues can be updated through workshops, professional journals, classes, study groups, and conventions. The foundation you receive in your formal training is important. But it is not enough. Some of the most important things you learn will be those that help you make contact with the needs, dreams, feelings, and viewpoints of your clients.

Who Can Be an Effective Helper?

Questioning whether you are really cut out for a job is to be expected when you enter a new field. Are you similar to the professionals you know? What must you know and what abilities must you possess going in? Although there is no one personality configuration that defines the perfect helper, various writers have looked at specific traits that lead to effective helping. They have also looked at the beliefs and attitudes most conducive to learning and working in the profession. Knowing more about these may help you because many of these qualities can be acquired.

The Legacy of Rogers

The writings of Carl Rogers (1967) have provided much of the framework for the core facilitative conditions that many see as the necessary ingredients for change and growth. More than anyone else, Rogers talked about therapeutic attitudes. Rogers believed that clients would move toward growth and positive outcomes if the helper provided the right environment. This environment, he felt, was more a reflection of the helper than an outcome of prescribed techniques or interventions. He considered three personal characteristics to be essential for a helper: congruence, positive regard, and empathy.

Congruence *Congruence* is the ability to be completely genuine with another person. Congruency means that there is consistency between what a person feels and says and how he or she acts. When we are congruent, we are not afraid to take risks and to spontaneously share reactions and thoughts with clients. If we are congruent, we react to clients in the here and now and do not hide behind the facade of the professional role. A simple example of incongruence is when our verbal and nonverbal messages conflict. Suppose you tell a client that you will provide support on the phone during a period of crisis, but then you do not regularly return phone calls. The nonverbal action comes across more clearly than the verbal message. A helper who is incongruent is not trusted.

Positive regard It is not that helpers must approve of every client behavior. Rather, the helper must respect the personhood of each client and believe that all persons have inherent worth. Hazler (1988) wrote about finding unconditional positive regard while working with a prison population. He described the insight that occurred when he was able to differentiate the prisoners (as real, valuable persons who had hopes and dreams and goals) from their crimes (which were brutal). A helper who works from unconditional positive regard never rejects a person, although he or she may reject that person's actions.

Empathy *Empathy,* or empathic understanding, is the ability to understand another person's feelings or worldview. Responding to another's feelings can be called *emotional empathy,* whereas taking the time to reflect an understanding of a person's motives, intentions, values, and thinking might be called *cognitive empathy.* Helpers suspend their own judgment as they learn the subjective worldview of their clients. Rather than evaluating the content of client statements, the purpose is to simply understand the client's feelings, beliefs, experiences, and goals. Rogers believed that through empathy, clients feel understood and are empowered to solve their own problems. Again, the habit of reflecting is an important activity we can employ to monitor our tendency to judge rather than to empathize.

Courage to Confront

The effective helper has the supportive qualities that Rogers mentions, but he or she is also able to "go for the jugular." Clients come to a helper for more than support. Sometimes the job of a helper is to make the client aware of painful realities. Helpers may be forced to show the client their annoying interpersonal behaviors and be willing to risk the client's anger when delicate issues need to be addressed. Effective helpers are not so dependent on the client's approval that they will fail to bring up touchy subjects. As one moves from dualistic to relativistic thinking, it is easier to think about the client's best interests and not be so focused on oneself.

Other Research on Effective Helping

In the writings of 14 different authors, we found 55 characteristics, attitudes, and beliefs of effective helpers. We have tried to consolidate these into five key elements (Combs, Avila, & Purkey, 1971; Corey, Corey, & Callanan, 1997; Gladding, 2000; McConnaughy, 1987; Patterson & Eisenberg, 1983; Spurling & Dryden, 1989; Truax & Carkhuff, 1967).

First and foremost, an effective helper has a *positive view of other people.* He or she accepts people who are different and is not judgmental about other people's lifestyles, values, cultures, and religions. He or she wants to help others and believes that people have the desire to change. The helper must be able to communicate his or her nonjudgmental attitude as well as warmth and caring.

Second, the effective helper has *good self-esteem and is a secure and mentally healthy person*. He or she is not attracted to helping in order to experience power over others or to feel superior to those with more serious problems. He or she seeks cooperation rather than control. Effective helpers appreciate themselves but know their limitations, too. They are able to examine themselves critically. They have the courage to look at themselves under a microscope. They make personal growth integral to their lifestyles.

Most writers agree that the effective helper has *good self-care skills*. Many who are attracted to this profession want to help others, but soon find that in order to do so they must make certain that they have something to give. It is easy to become emotionally "bankrupt" and "burned out" if one does not develop techniques for stress management, time management, relaxation, leisure, and personal self-renewal. The effective helper has a stable and fulfilling personal life with close family and friends to provide support as a buffer to the stress of helping.

The effective helper is both *creative and intellectually competent,* a renaissance person, who appreciates both the science and the art of helping. The effective helper has specialized knowledge of human relationships, human motivation, and human development and understands how to create change. Those who remain vital in the profession have "insatiable curiosity" to learn and grow in their skills and knowledge (Spurling & Dryden, 1989). Creativity and flexibility are equally vital. Helping requires one to devise innovative ideas with different clients in different situations. A helper must be able to deal flexibly with ambivalence, unfinished business, and moral dilemmas. He or she has to allow clients to work through difficult situations without moving them to premature decisions.

When Moreno, the founder of psychodrama, was once asked what the most important quality was for a group leader, his unexpected response was "*courage.*" This fifth characteristic of an effective helper has two facets: First, the helper must be able to listen unflinchingly to stories of great pain. Like a physician who sets a broken arm, he or she must be able to look with a detached eye at human destruction and see where the healing can be started. Second, the helper's job requires risk taking and action, without the security offered by other sciences. Individuals who believe that they can control every circumstance and that there is a procedure and a solution for every crisis have a difficult time as helpers. For example, there are no psychological tests that accurately predict a person's tendency to be violent. Helpers' decisions must be based on experience, training, and even intuition. Because human behavior is relatively unpredictable, effective helpers must be able to live with that uncertainty.

What Can You Bring to a Client?

There is no one set of personal qualities that makes an effective helper. There is room in the profession for many types of individuals, each of whom brings significant strengths and simultaneously must be aware of the limitations of his or her own personality style. The example of a former student may help to illustrate this. Maria, a graduate student, got under my skin sometimes because she had little patience for long theoretical discussions and did not like studying anything that did not have immediate application. She seemed to roll her eyes when the discussion became too intellectual. She was practical and concrete and liked people who were "down-to-earth."

She wanted to solve problems and make a difference in the lives of children. It seemed to me that sometimes she tended to be too quick to come to closure with adult clients when they became stuck or were indecisive. Sometimes she pushed them to make decisions and seemed insensitive to their turmoil.

However, Maria now works effectively as a school counselor. Her particular strength is that she knows how to manage crises. She instantly grasps what has to be done and takes bold and concrete steps to accomplish it. She has excellent judgment and is indispensable to her school because she knows how to take quick action and exudes calm and poise in times of confusion. Maria's case illustrates that each of us brings strengths to the helping role. Much depends on knowing our own abilities and finding an environment where they can be put to good use.

As you consider the characteristics of effective helpers that we have identified, remember two things. First, many of the characteristics can be developed. They are not necessarily inborn. Second, each person brings unique characteristics to the helping profession and, as in Maria's case, the challenge is to find a place where these will help others. Do not look at the characteristics of effective helpers in order to identify those you do not have. We are not trying to produce clones. A client will have a relationship with you, not a set of skills. By focusing on your strengths, you will have much to bring to a client.

Stop and Reflect

The characteristics of effective helpers identified by the experts are listed in brief form in the following statements. Answer the accompanying questions as truthfully as possible, because your answers may point out areas you may wish to address later in your training. Which of these qualities do you presently possess and on which do you want to improve? For those skills you need to develop, think for a moment about what you might do to challenge yourself. What extracurricular activities might help you to grow?

Positive View of Humankind
You believe that most people are basically good and are striving for self-improvement. You enjoy people and believe that people can change.

How true is this for you?
How can you grow?

Stable and Mentally Healthy
You have good self-esteem and are basically a secure, mentally healthy person. You may not be able to make a completely unbiased self-assessment, but friends and family can give you feedback on your coping ability.

How true is this for you?
How can you grow?

Good Self-Care Skills
You do not become overly involved with those you are helping. You know your limits and are able to set boundaries to protect yourself from burnout.

How true is this for you?
How can you grow?

Intelligent and Psychologically Minded

You are an intellectually curious person who is interested in the psychological world of other people. You can appreciate both a scientific and an artistic approach to learning about helping.

> How true is this for you?
> How can you grow?

Creative

You are a creative person in some aspect of your life. You are not rigid or inflexible in your attitudes. You are not bothered by many prejudices about people, cultures, religions, and family customs that differ from your own.

> How true is this for you?
> How can you grow?

Courageous

You have enough courage to examine your own personal problems and to seek help and guidance for yourself when you need it. You are willing to admit that you need to change and grow. You are able, for the most part, to deal with the cruelties that other people inflict on each other without being so disturbed that it disrupts your own life or your ability to help.

> How true is this for you?
> How can you grow?

Summary and Suggestions

Entering a new field of knowledge brings about uncertainty and challenges us to remain open and nondefensive. Knowing that learning the art of helping follows some predictable stages should allow us to be less self-critical when we face the normal developmental hurdles. At every step, however, reflection is needed so that we can separate our clients' goals from our own personal wishes.

Learning the art of helping is a long journey and everyone travels at a different rate, bringing unique traits and differing gifts. Although experts have identified characteristics of effective helpers, including self-acceptance, cooperation, and the ability to reach out to others, there is not just one kind of person who can practice the helping arts. The core conditions of Carl Rogers remain a legacy to beginning helpers. They remind us that our job is to be personally honest, to have a positive regard for our clients, and to convey empathy.

You might find it helpful to consider some methods for reflection, self-assessment and self-improvement that other students have found conducive to their own learning and development.

- Many have found it helpful to keep a journal of their thoughts and feelings during this course. Identify your fears and moments of success and then look back from start to finish to see how far you have come. Especially when you are stuck or have trouble progressing, write down your frustrations and then talk them over with your instructor.
- Consider getting together on a regular basis with other students to practice new

skills and to provide support for each other.

- You may want to keep a record of unrealistic thoughts, self-criticisms, and exaggerated expectations that you may be holding for yourself. Are you focusing enough on what you do well or is self-criticism becoming a barrier to growth?
- Think about recording your practice sessions and writing down all of your responses. Identify each of your responses and think about how it affected the client.

By now you might be thinking that learning to help is a long journey requiring much of the learner. It is that, but it is also a voyage of personal discovery and an opportunity to encounter and appreciate other people at a level of intimacy that few professions allow. As you begin, remember the adage of the mountain climber: Don't look at the summit; keep your attention on your next step. One day you'll get to the top, but right now appreciate where you are.

Exercises

1. In groups of three, discuss your reasons for wanting to become a professional helper. What are your expectations and concerns?
2. Think of a time when you learned a new skill (e.g., playing tennis or learning to sew). What stages did you go through? How did you improve? Were you self-critical at first? If

so, what effect did your negative thinking have? Can you identify any particular thoughts that you had during that time? Discuss them with classmates and see if you can relate your previous experience to what you might encounter as you learn helping skills.

Homework

Homework 1

Make an appointment with a professional who has been working for only a few years (say 1–5). Ask him or her the following questions and react briefly in writing to each one of them. (Be sure to add a couple of questions of particular interest to you.)

1. Does another helper supervise you? If so, what do you value about these sessions?
2. Are there any particular helpers you admire?
3. When do you feel least confident in your job?
4. To what theoretical orientation do you subscribe?
5. What kinds of professional reading do you do?
6. Do you benefit from conferences?

7. Did you notice any big "jumps" or stages in your ability to help?
8. Other questions . . .

Homework 2

Review your resume or your past work history, whether paid or volunteer. Include jobs you held in organizations in high school or college if your work history is short. List your jobs and, under each, write significant learnings you gained about working with other people, both clients and co-workers. Even if your job was not in a helping capacity, did you find ways to help others? Has helping been a regular part of your work life or is it a new development? Summarize your learnings in a final paragraph.

Journal Starters

Think about starting a personal journal that chronicles your experiences on the journey to becoming a helper. Development of expertise is sometimes described as gaining knowledge, skills, and attitudes in a particular domain. Through this book, your lectures, and other courses, you are definitely gaining knowledge and skills. The journal, on the other hand, allows you to reflect on your own attitudes about helping and to react personally to what you are learning. Such reflection is the basis for modern approaches to assessment such as the portfolio. By looking back over your work, you can gauge your own development and think about future goals. A journal is not just a record; it should be re-read and thought about.

You can use a computer, purchase a blank notebook, or develop a three-ring binder to construct a journal that allows you to add other information such as important articles, poems, pictures, and so on. Bring your reflections to class or share them privately with your instructor. Because this class invites so much personal growth, your instructor may ask you to complete journal entries several times during the semester. Try to be as honest as you can; think about what you share, too, not only in a journal but with your classmates. Is it possible to share too much about a particular topic that might overwhelm others? Whether you are asked to share some of your journal or not, approach it with complete honesty and edit it later. Sometimes I suggest that students write everything down and then remove or black out those portions they want to keep private before they hand in their assignment.

The following are two stimulus sentences you can use to provide a warmup for your journaling. Each chapter contains several of these starters. Because these are warmups, continue writing, even if you feel that you have departed from the original stimulus sentences. Feel free to modify them or to create your own.

1. Thinking about my previous relationships with significant others in my life, what are the best and worst parts of my personality? How might these show up in my relationships with clients? What fears do I have about my abilities?
2. Reviewing times in my life when I have not been as successful as I wanted to be, how did I react? What helped me to overcome the problem? How can I best deal with setbacks in my basic skills training? What feelings do I have as I start this process?

For more journal ideas and activities, refer to Chapter 1 in *Exercises in the Art of Helping.*

References

Barrow, J. C. (1987). Is student development "dissonance roulette"? *Journal of College Student Personnel, 28* 12–13.

Bernard, J. (1981). Women's educational needs. In A. W. Chickering (Ed.), *The modern American college* (pp. 256–278). New York: Jossey-Bass.

Caffarella, R. S. (1993). Self-directed learning. *New Directions for Adult and Continuing Education, 57,* 25–35.

Carkhuff, R. R. (1969). *Counseling and human relations: Selection and training* (Vol. 1). New York: Holt, Rhinehart, & Winston.

Cheatham, H. E., & Berg-Cross, L. (1992). College student development: African Americans reconsidered. *College Student Development, 6,* 167–191.

Combs, A. W., Avila, D. L., & Purkey, W. W. (1971). *Helping relationships: Basic concepts for helping professions.* Boston: Allyn & Bacon.

Corey, G., Corey, M. S., & Callanan, P. (1997). *Issues and ethics in the helping professions* (4th ed.). Monterey, CA: Brooks/Cole.

Cormier, W. H., & Cormier, L. S. (1991). *Interviewing strategies for helpers.* Pacific Grove, CA: Brooks/Cole.

Gaff, J. G., & Gaff, S. S. (1981). Student-faculty relationships. In A. W. Chickering (Ed.), *The modern American college* (pp. 642–657). New York: Jossey-Bass.

Gladding, S. (2000). *Counseling: A comprehensive profession* (4th ed.) Upper Saddle River, NJ: Merrill/Prentice Hall.

Harvey, C., & Katz, C. (1985). *If I'm so successful, why do I feel like a fake? The imposter phenomenon.* New York: St. Martin's Press.

Hazler, R. J. (1988). Stumbling into unconditional positive regard. *Journal of Counseling and Development, 67,* 130.

Hoffman, R. R., Shadboldt, N. R., Burton, A. M., & Klein, G. (1995). Eliciting knowledge from experts: A methodological analysis. *Organizational Behavior and Human Decision Processes, 62,* 129–158.

Kottler, J. A. (1993). *On being a therapist.* San Francisco: Jossey-Bass.

Kottler, J. A. (Ed.) (1996). *Finding your way as a counselor.* Alexandria, VA: American Counseling Association.

LeShan, L. (1996). *Beyond technique: Psychotherapy for the 21st Century.* Northvale, NJ: Jason Aronson.

Marx, S. D. (1990). Phase I: On the transition from student to professional. *Psychotherapy in Private Practice, 8*(2), 57–67.

McConnaughy, E. A. (1987). The person of the therapist in psychotherapeutic practice. *Psychotherapy, 24,* 303–314.

McLennan, J. (1994). The skills-based model of counselling training: A review of the evidence. *Australian Psychologist, 29,* 79–88.

Patterson, L. E., & Eisenberg, S. (1983). *The counseling process* (3rd ed.). Boston: Houghton Mifflin.

Perry, W. G., Jr. (1970). *Forms of intellectual and ethical development in the college years.* New York: Holt, Rinehart, & Winston.

Rogers, C. R. (1967). *Person to person: The problem of being human.* Moab, UT: Real People Press.

Shöen, D. A. (1983). *The reflective practitioner: How professionals think in action.* New York: Basic Books.

Simpson, D. E., Dalgaard, K. A., & O'Brien, D. K. (1986). Student and faculty assumptions about the nature of uncertainty in medicine and medical education. *Journal of Family Practice, 23*(5), 468–472.

Skovholt, T. M., & Ronnestad, M. H. (1992). Themes in therapist and counselor development. *Journal of Counseling and Development, 70,* 505–515.

Spurling, L., & Dryden, W. (1989). The self and the therapeutic domain. In W. Dryden & L. Spurling (Eds.), *On becoming a psychotherapist.* London: Tavistock/Routledge.

Sue, D. W., Arredondo, P., & McDavis, R. J. (1992). Multicultural counseling competencies and standards: A call to the profession. *Journal of Multicultural Counseling and Development, 20,* 64–88.

Truax, C. B., & Carkhuff, R. R. (1967). *Toward effective counseling and psychotherapy: Training and practice.* Chicago: Aldine.

Young, M. E. (1998). Skills-based training for counselors: Microskills or mega-skills? *Counseling and Human Development, 31,* 2.

The Nuts and Bolts of Helping

2

The purpose of this chapter is to orient you to this book and to the way in which we will be teaching the helping process. We will provide some important definitions of the terms that we will be using. In addition, we want to introduce you to the basic skills, or "building blocks," that we will be teaching you in later chapters. We plan to show that these building blocks are the basic elements that make up more complicated counseling techniques that you also will be learning. Because beginning helpers often question how basic skills fit into the larger picture, we will present the theoretical concept of "common or therapeutic factors," which is a way of organizing helping techniques based on what we are trying to achieve. We end the chapter by taking you through the process of a basic helping session. After reading and completing the exercises in this chapter, you should have a framework that will help you organize your learning.

Defining Some Important Terms

What Is Helping?

Helping is a broad term that encompasses all of the activities we use to assist another person, whether we have a professional relationship or not. For example, a school administrator who takes time to listen to a crying first grader can utilize helping skills. A foster parent can learn to listen to the child and to the biological parents. A teacher's aide in a sixth-grade classroom can take a nonjudgmental stance when a child talks about why homework is late. Husbands and wives can help each other. Helping does not require a contract or a professional, confidential relationship. Helping only requires a person desiring help (a client), someone willing and able to give help (a helper), and a conducive setting (Hackney & Cormier, 1988). You can learn helping skills and use them whether you are on the way to becoming a professional or you simply want to help those with whom you live and work.

While *helping* is the overarching term, different settings and different contracts between helper and client mean that there are a variety of ways that the helping can be defined (see Figure 2.1). To the newcomer, this can be confusing. In the next sections, we will clarify some of the most common terms, including *interviewing, counseling,* and *psychotherapy.*

Is Interviewing Helping?

According to the simplest definition, *interviewing* is a conversation between an interviewer and an interviewee. During the conversation, the interviewer gathers and records information about the interviewee. The purpose of the interview may be to

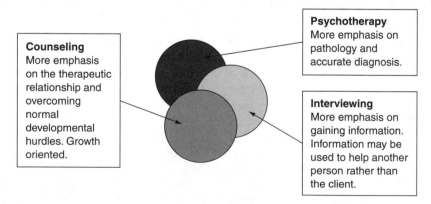

Figure 2.1
Different Emphases Among Psychotherapy, Counseling, and Interviewing
Despite these differences, there are many common theoretical underpinnings as well as common skills. The area overlapped by all three circles represents this shared base.

help an interviewee or to make a decision about that person. For example, many counseling centers hire intake interviewers who talk with clients and then assign them to the appropriate counselor or refer them to another service or treatment facility. Employers interview applicants for jobs and for promotions. Normally, interviewing involves one or two sessions. There is no long-term relationship.

Interviewing is not simply a mechanical procedure best accomplished by a computer. It usually has a purpose beyond completing a file folder. An interview may be used to help make a decision about an applicant for a job, for a promotion, or for entrance into a special training program; to determine the appropriateness of counseling for an individual; or to assess some skill, as in an oral examination in graduate school. Interviewing is an art whose medium is the relationship. A skilled interviewer knows how to quickly develop a working relationship with an interviewee in order to obtain the most relevant information for the decision-making process.

An interview may also be used to test the interviewee's skills, poise, or ability to think in a "live" setting. For example, some companies use a "stress interview" to determine which of their employees can operate best under pressure. The interviewee is "grilled" and even treated disrespectfully to gauge his or her reaction. Many people think that this kind of interview is unethical, but the point is that an interview can provide an opportunity to observe the reaction of a student or employee in a contrived situation similar to actual situations that he or she may encounter.

In summary, interviewing is not necessarily helping and the interviewee is not necessarily a client of the interviewer. At times, an interview can lay the groundwork for helping by establishing a working relationship and collecting needed information. However, interviews are also conducted in a wide variety of settings to further the goals of companies, agencies, or institutions, rather than the interests of the interviewee.

What Are Counseling and Psychotherapy?

Counseling and *psychotherapy* are professional helping services provided by trained individuals who have contracts with their clients to assist them in attaining their goals. Counselors and psychotherapists use specific techniques to persuade, inform, arouse, motivate, and encourage their clients. Sessions with a counselor or psychotherapist take place on a regularly scheduled basis, usually weekly, and last about one hour. A therapeutic relationship will last several months or even several years. Although counselors and psychotherapists may help clients deal with emergencies, they also try to empower clients to address persistent problems in living and make changes in their lives that will lead to overall improvement rather than momentary relief.

In the literature and in practice, the words *counseling* and *psychotherapy* are now used interchangeably. Historically, however, different professional groups, including mental health counselors, social workers, psychiatrists, psychologists, and marriage and family therapists, have tended to prefer one or the other, and many people, including clients, are confused by the two terms.

Between 1920 and 1950, psychotherapy was mainly practiced with clients troubled by mental disorders. *Mental disorders* are defined as severe disturbances of mood, thought, and behavior for which there are specific diagnostic criteria. Examples include Major Depression, Schizophrenia, and Anxiety Disorders. The criteria are outlined in *DSM-IV,* the American Psychiatric Association's catalog, which is the bible of mental disorders (1993). Even today, these are the only problems that most health insurance companies recognize as reimbursable. From the beginning, the processes of assessment, diagnosis, and treatment planning have been integral aspects of psychotherapy.

Counseling was invented as psychotherapy for "normal people," beginning in the 1960s. Medical terminology was shunned by counselors, along with words such as *treatment* and *diagnosis.* Counselors believed in seeing each individual as a unique person, rather than a diagnostic label. For that reason, personality tests and other assessment activities were minimized in practice because they tended to categorize clients. Counseling was focused more on the counselor/client relationship as the medium for change.

Today, the distinctions between counseling and psychotherapy have blurred. Now, counseling includes helping people with mental disorders as well as those experiencing normal developmental problems. Modern counselors routinely use assessment tools, learn diagnostic methods, and engage in treatment planning. By the same token, professionals such as psychologists and marriage and family therapists who prefer the term *psychotherapy* or *therapy* also help clients with difficulties such as adolescent adjustment, marital issues, and the transition to college or work— what we might call "normal problems." Although some may still feel there are good reasons to make distinctions between the terms *counseling* and *psychotherapy,* they will be used interchangeably in this book. Both will refer to the contractual and professional relationship between a trained helper and a client.

How Is Professional Helping Different from Friendship?

As you learn the art of helping, you will be able to provide friends with a listening ear, a caring attitude, and emotional support, enhancing your relationships and aiding those you care about. There is, however, a difference between friendship and a professional helping relationship; each is built on a distinct contract. A friendship is based on the assumption that we are there for each other—a two-way street. In a professional helping relationship, it is the client's issues that are discussed and the client's welfare that is paramount. In exchange, the helper receives compensation for professional services rendered. Consider this analogy: You mention to your friend, who is a dentist, that you have a toothache. She may suggest you take some aspirin and that you make an appointment with a dentist as soon as possible. Despite her professional capabilities, she probably won't pull out her dental equipment and start drilling in the living room. Although the comparison doesn't hold completely, counseling can also be a painful process best accomplished in a more professional setting. For example, a professional helper is required to identify and articulate issues not normally broached in a friendship, from sex to painful childhood memories. Moreover, the professional helper is committed to hours of listening, confidentiality, responsibility for the outcome, and disregard for whether the client ultimately likes him or her. The helper's concern, as a professional, is to do a good job, not to maintain a relationship for its own sake.

One reason for drawing the distinction between a professional helping relationship and a friendship is that it is easy to make mistakes in both settings when you begin learning helping skills. You might be tempted to use elaborate techniques on your friends when all they are asking for is support. On the other hand, you might find yourself treating a client as a friend. Remember that with friends you have no contract to initiate change, but rather an opportunity to care, to show concern, and to provide support. In the helping relationship, you have a contract to help the client make specific changes in his or her life, not to make a new friend, enjoy each other's company, or discuss the weather, your family, or your favorite hobby. What makes this difficult is that we have learned our natural helping skills in the context of our friendships and family relationships. It is easy to find ourselves being sociable and sympathetic, rather than thinking about how to help the client. In the next chapter, we will focus more on the characteristics of the therapeutic relationship.

What Can You Expect from a Helping Relationship?

Beginners' hopes about what can be achieved in a professional helping relationship are often very grand. When, inevitably, they are dashed, naturally there is disappointment. In this section, we will identify some common unrealistic beliefs about the helping process that many struggle with, and we will examine the corresponding more reasonable expectations.

> **Unrealistic Belief:** I must help clients solve all of their problems.
> **Reasonable Expectation:** If all goes well, I may make a good-sized dent in a problem or two and the client will continue to progress when the relationship ends.

Most agencies and private practitioners find that, on average, helpers and clients see each other for 6 to 10 sessions. Most clients do not expect long-term relationships, and they come to a helper to deal with specific problems. Indeed, contrary to our expectations, clients who have even just a session or two with a helper are often very satisfied with the results. Helpers must not become disappointed when they want more changes than the client wants.

> **Unrealistic Belief:** If the client is not motivated, it is my fault.
> **Reasonable Expectation:** Although I can stimulate clients to consider making changes, I cannot force them.

It is estimated that nearly a third of helpers' clients today are involuntary referrals by courts, government agencies, or others. Although clients can be forced to attend sessions, helping is a voluntary relationship. Ethically, we cannot attempt to coerce clients to change. We can supply the opportunities for change, but the client must meet us halfway.

In the real world, some clients are genuinely opposed to changing their lifestyles, even self-destructive ones. Others know that they need to change but require encouragement. The art of helping involves getting clients to envisage and consider a different kind of life and persuading them to change. For example, when an alcoholic client is sent by the court for treatment, the helper's job is twofold. First, the helper must intensify the client's awareness of the negative consequences of drinking; second, the helper must help the client to see the advantages of sobriety. However, even with detoxification and Alcoholics Anonymous, the odds are less than even that the client will stop drinking.

> **Unrealistic Belief:** If I care about my clients or have good practical experience, that is enough.
> **Reasonable Expectation:** Besides caring and practical experience in the helping field, I must learn all the skills I can.

No matter how good our intentions are, caring about another person is not a substitute for professional knowledge of how to help him or her. A caring physician is, of course, better than one who is indifferent, but the physician must also be well trained and kept fully abreast of his or her specialty through continuing education. Similarly, caring will enhance your helping skills, but it cannot replace them.

Some helpers believe that they are already fully trained. They have practical skills gained in the helping field and they go on for formal education merely to "have their ticket punched." This is a potentially dangerous attitude. When we see the wide variety and severity of client problems and the new treatments that are cropping up everywhere, it is unreasonable to believe that we can ignore skills training in our formal education or that we can ever really be finished learning.

Unrealistic Belief: If I am a good helper, my client will never need help again.
Reasonable Expectation: If I am successful, the client may consult me again when a similar problem arises.

It is unrealistic to expect that clients will be "cured" in a single encounter with a helper. A family doctor model is a better analogy for the helping relationship. Such a relationship can be revived if the client needs help at a later developmental stage.

Unrealistic Belief: If I am effective with one client, I will be effective with every client.
Reasonable Expectation: I will not be the best match for every client.

Even famous therapists have found that they are not effective with every person who consults them. There are many reasons why a helping relationship may not succeed; some are not under the helper's control. The client may perceive a mismatch because the helper is not of his or her gender, race, or social class. The client may instantly dislike the helper because the helper reminds him or her of someone in the past. It is easy to feel rejected and disappointed if a client does not wish to continue the helping relationship, especially if you feel positive about it.

Unrealistic Belief: It is unacceptable to make a mistake.
Reasonable Expectation: I am a fallible human being who can learn from my mistakes.

If you attend workshops and seminars, you will see well-known counselors and psychotherapists showing videos of their amazing successes. In *The Imperfect Therapist* (1989), Jeffrey Kottler and Diane Blau have suggested that we can learn just as much from our failures, but we rarely talk about them. It is both ego protection and a fear that we are incompetent that keeps us from discussing our mistakes with colleagues, supervisors, and teachers. However, if we do not examine these missteps, we are likely to repeat them.

Unrealistic Belief: Sometimes I feel incompetent; therefore, I am not competent.
Reasonable Expectation: There will be many times in my training and work as a helper when I will feel incompetent. It goes with the territory.

No matter how long you have worked as a helper, clients will surprise you. They have problems you have never heard of and problems your supervisor has never encountered. This can be either an assault on your self-esteem or a reminder that you need to keep learning. Although you need to keep abreast of changes in the field and reach the highest level of training that you can, neither a Ph.D. nor a certificate from a training institute will prepare you for everything. Feeling incompetent should motivate you to learn more about a client and his or her problems, but it should not paralyze you. You can seek supervision or possibly refer your client, if an honest appraisal of the situation suggests that this would be in the client's best interest.

Stop and Reflect

Learning the art of helping is a personal journey that asks you to examine your own ideas and reflect about what you are reading. Try to use the "Stop and Reflect" sections, such as this one, to jot down your thoughts and reactions and to share them with another classmate or small group. You will certainly find other points in the book where your own ideas are challenged. Learn to pause at those moments and contrast the two positions. If you can begin this habit now, you are well on your way to becoming a reflective practitioner.

Begin by considering each of the following questions about friendship and helping:

- Have you ever given help to a friend that was not well received or that changed the friendship? Discuss with a small group.
- Some people think that our mobile, stressful society has led to a lack of community and has separated us from our extended family. If friendships and family relationships were closer, do you think that professional helping would be needed?
- What would you do if a friend told you that he or she was contemplating suicide? Think about your answer and then discuss it with the class. In what other situations do you think that a professional helper might have an advantage?
- When you look for friends, do you look for someone who is similar to you? Does this search for similarity mean that it is harder to make contact with someone who is quite different? How could one's preference for similar people be a handicap in a helping profession?

What Makes Helping Work?

Every system of counseling and psychotherapy has a slightly different answer to this question and each theory has its own set of techniques to produce change. Unfortunately, there are now between 100 and 460 systems of counseling and psychotherapy (Corsini, 1981; Herink, 1980; Parloff, 1979). In response to this confusion, many practitioners have adopted an *eclectic,* or integrative, point of view. *Eclecticism* can be defined as selecting what is best from many theories and also selecting "what works." As Paul (1967) stated, the task is to ascertain "what treatment, by whom, is most effective for this individual with that specific problem (or set of problems) and under which set of circumstances" (p. 111).

In recent years, eclectic, or integrative, approaches have been developed that attempt to reconcile the differences in the various theories, or at least try to take what is best from several points of view (Norcross, 1986; Young, 1992). One survey showed that as many as 75% of practicing counselors could be defined as eclectic (Young,

1990). Surveys of other professions, including psychologists and social workers, show similar results (Jayartne, 1982; Norcross & Prochaska, 1982; Smith, 1982).

Therapeutic Factors

There are several approaches to eclecticism, but one that merits a deeper examination is called *common curative or therapeutic factors.* Therapeutic factors are the activities that seem to be used by all effective helpers. For example, a positive, supportive, and confiding relationship between client and helper is considered to be a necessary condition for helping by nearly all theoretical positions.

The lifetime work of Jerome Frank (1971, 1981) showed how different theories rely on common therapeutic factors for their effectiveness. Although helpers seem to be utilizing different techniques, they are actually drawing on similar methods. Frank described six common therapeutic factors that seem to cut across all theoretical persuasions (Frank & Frank, 1991):

1. Maintaining a strong helper/client relationship
2. Increasing the client's motivation and expectations of help
3. Enhancing the client's sense of mastery or self-efficacy
4. Providing new learning experiences
5. Raising emotional arousal (in this book, we also discuss lowering emotional arousal through relaxation and other methods)
6. Providing opportunities to practice new behaviors

Jerome Frank's therapeutic factors provide the basis for organizing much of the third part of this book.

Therapeutic factors are a way of understanding that many different theories and techniques seem to be effective because they are actually drawing on similar methods; however, this knowledge does not provide us with a starting point in our own journey. Which skills should we learn first? Over the last few decades, writers and educators have generally agreed upon a similar set of basic, "generic" helping skills, forming a good starting point regardless of the setting where the helper works or the theory that he or she follows. The second part of the book is devoted to teaching these basic skills, or building blocks.

Basic helping skills are normally taught as small units called "microskills" (Ivey, 1971). Individual skills often seem so insignificant, however, that students may experience difficulty in learning them. They have trouble seeing the big picture when they learn first one piece and then another. In this section, we want to help you to understand how all of the specific skills of helping fit together. With this structure in the back of your mind, it may be easier to learn these building blocks one by one.

Therapeutic Building Blocks

Therapeutic building blocks is the phrase we use to describe the fundamental components of the helping interview, such as asking open-ended questions or maintaining eye contact. These building blocks are like the elements of the periodic table we all learned in high school chemistry. There are both simple elements like carbon and more elaborate elements like uranium. The therapeutic building blocks represent the simplest behaviors used to create change. There are simple building blocks like paraphrasing and more complex ones like confrontation. In this book, we identify 22 building blocks. They represent the combined wisdom of many theorists and helpers over time. Although 22 may seem to be an overwhelming number, 10 of the building blocks are quite simple (we call them invitational skills) and very easy to master. The building block skills are divided into six categories (see Table 2.1). Each category represents an important helping activity.

Invitational Skills (10 Skills—Chapter 4)

Invitational skills are the basic means by which the helper invites the client into a therapeutic relationship. These skills encompass all the subtle verbal and nonverbal messages that helpers send to encourage a client to open up without applying pressure. For example, imagine how you would feel if the helper constantly checked her watch or looked out the window. You may think that paying attention is only polite, but it is also a skill. Learning to keep your focus on the client with eye contact and body posture are two of the invitational behaviors you will learn and practice in Chapter 3.

Reflecting Skills (2 Skills—Chapter 5)

Whereas invitational skills invite clients to tell their stories, reflecting skills let them know that you have heard their stories. Reflecting skills are condensed versions of

Table 2.1
The Building Block Skills

Skill Category	Building Blocks
Invitational Skills	**Nonverbal skills**
	Eye contact
	Body position
	Attentive silence
	Voice tone
	Gestures and facial expressions
	Physical distance
	Touching
	Opening Skills
	Door openers
	Minimal encouragers
	Open and closed questions
Reflecting Skills	Paraphrasing
	Reflecting feelings
Advanced Reflecting Skills	Reflecting meaning
	Summarizing
Challenging Skills	Giving feedback
	Confrontation
Goal-Setting Skills	Focusing on the client
	Boiling down the problem
Solution Skills	Giving advice
	Giving information
	Alternate interpretation
	Brainstorming

the facts and emotions the client has conveyed. The helper shares these "snapshots" of the client's story to let the client know that he or she is being understood both in terms of content and at the affective level. When clients feel understood, they disclose more deeply and the important issues begin to surface.

Advanced Reflecting Skills (2 Skills—Chapter 6)

Advanced reflecting skills help a client move even deeper than the reflecting skills. They include reflecting meaning and summarizing. Advanced reflecting skills are hunches that helpers make and repeat to their clients to see whether they understand the unique impact of their clients' problems beyond the basic facts and feelings. For example, the loss of a job is not just the change in economic status and feelings of loss. Depending on the person, losing a job may also be seen as a sign of failure or evidence of incompetence.

Challenging Skills (2 Skills—Chapter 8)

Whereas invitational skills, reflecting skills, and advanced reflecting skills encourage deeper self-examination, challenging skills push clients to recognize discrepancies in their statements. Challenging skills identify incongruities in a client's story and may give information on client strengths and weaknesses. For example, a client who says that he wishes to stop smoking but does not follow any of the suggestions by the helper might be challenged about the discrepancy between words and behavior. Challenging skills can strain the relationship, but they may also remind clients that the helping relationship is a work project, not a social encounter. Giving feedback and confrontation are fundamental challenging skills.

Goal-Setting Skills (2 Skills—Chapter 9)

Up to this point, the aim of the skills has been to encourage the client to disclose in as much depth and breadth as possible. Goal-setting skills, however, begin to narrow the focus. Goal-setting skills keep the client focused on his or her own issues and ask the client to identify the most crucial areas. For example, helpers encourage clients to talk about how they can change, rather than focusing on how to change others. The second key helping skill in this area is "boiling down the problem," which involves shaping a client's vague or unrealistic goals into specific and achievable targets. These building blocks are fundamental skills needed to develop short- and long-term goals for the helping relationship.

Solution Skills (4 Skills—Chapter 10)

Once tentative goals have been collaboratively established, solution skills are employed to help achieve those goals. Solution skills outline alternatives for action and press the client to consider new possibilities. Giving advice is a commonly misused solution skill whose advantages are usually outweighed by its drawbacks. Other solution skills include giving information, using alternative interpretation, and brainstorming.

The Importance of Building Blocks

We have said that one of the problems confronting most beginning helpers is that they learn elementary skills in isolation and cannot see how they fit into a grand scheme. They do not understand how flashy theory-based techniques such as

Gestalt's "empty chair" relate to the "baby steps" they are learning in class. They begin making fun of their own tendencies to say "Um Hmm . . . ," and "What I hear you saying is . . . ." They secretly yearn to do what famous therapists do in training films: have a tremendous impact on clients.

Just as in basketball or baseball, every helper needs to practice the fundamentals. In sports, when fundamentals are mastered, they are linked into more complex movements, or plays. Without solid fundamentals, the plays are less effective. An example of this principle is shown in the film *The Karate Kid.* When he begins to study karate, the student, Daniel, is put to work sanding wood, painting, and waxing cars. At one point, he rebels and angrily confronts his teacher for having wasted his time. Daniel wants to be Bruce Lee. In a moving scene, the teacher shows him how each of the seemingly unrelated tasks is a fundamental move in the art of karate. Through repetition, the movements become second nature; when combined in a combat situation, they form an impenetrable defense. Your training in the helping skills will be very similar. You will learn basic helping movements, many of which will seem awkward and repetitive. However, when they are properly learned and put in proper sequence, they form more elaborate and elegant techniques. The "art" of helping develops when the basics have become second nature.

Consider another example. When you first began to drive a car, you probably learned about the functions of various parts of the car, for example, the brake pedal, the gas pedal, the steering wheel, and the gear shift lever. You might have learned to accelerate, brake, and steer as separate activities before you put them all together in your first attempt at driving. The more you drove, the more automatic some functions became. You probably don't even remember pressing the gas pedal down during your last outing. If you learn to accelerate smoothly early in your driver training, that skill may stay with you, even when you are attempting more complex maneuvers. In the same way, practicing the basic building blocks until they become automatic will provide a foundation for the more complicated techniques you learn later.

Stages of the Helping Process: A Road Map

Figure 2.2 shows the stages of the helping process over time. The diagram shows five helper tasks that occur more or less sequentially from the first session to the last. This five-part structure is based on the work of several different writers (Dimond & Havens, 1975; Dimond, Havens, & Jones, 1978; Ivey & Mathews, 1986). The arrows show the typical progression of a client problem and the activities of helper and client through the process. The name for each stage reflects the helper activity *and* the expected client response. For example, in the first stage, relationship building and opening up, the helper engages in nonverbal activities to build a trusting relationship. The helper does this primarily by using invitational, reflecting, and advanced reflecting skills. As a result, the client opens up and discloses more fully. Most helpers find that they use a session or two in the beginning just for building the therapeutic relationship and allowing time for the client to open up. As its central position suggests, relationship building interacts with all the other stages because the strength of the relationship helps to move the helping process forward and empowers the methods and techniques used later on. For example, a strong therapeutic relationship allows a client to disclose more easily in the assessment stage.

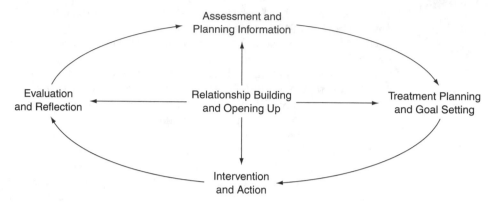

Figure 2.2
Stages of the Helping Process

In the second stage, assessment and providing information, the helper collects information and the client provides it through answers to questions or data from intake forms or tests. In this book, assessment skills are covered briefly, although we have not included them in the therapeutic building blocks. They are discussed in Chapter 7. The reason for not saying more about assessment in this book is that these skills, although important, tend to sidetrack us from our central purpose, which is to learn the fundamentals of a helping relationship. Normally, your course of study will include an entire course on assessment. Many helpers might spend an entire session on collecting background data and some might spend a session or two conducting more in-depth evaluations using tests. However, assessment can occur throughout the helping process when a new problem emerges and the helper takes some time from the session to collect needed information

The third stage in the helping process is treatment planning and goal setting. Not all helpers like to set clear identifiable goals for the helping relationship. Some prefer to let each session unfold. In any case, treatment planning has become a necessity today because most insurance companies and managed-care companies require detailed plans. In practice, the helper normally sets up a few key goals with the client's help. From the client's side, goal setting helps him or her identify some direction and think about something beyond the immediate crisis. These goals may be somewhat different from the helper's treatment plan because they may continue when the helping relationship has been terminated.

Next, in the intervention and action stage, the helper identifies and implements helping techniques to accomplish each of the treatment goals. The helper does this based on his or her theoretical background, training, and expertise. The client is expected to take action to aid in this process. The degree to which this is successful depends largely on two things: the strength of the client/helper bond and the extent to which the goals are really important to the client. It is often in this stage that a helper realizes that a client's unique makeup and background determine how effective a technique will become. If the helper implements a technique that is repugnant to the client, is mysterious, or seems to miss the mark, progress will be slowed. Again, the helper must return to the therapeutic relationship to see if client and helper are on the same page or whether the client feels that the helper is imposing treatment on him or her.

In the evaluation and reflection stage, the helper invites the client to think about the progress being made and together a joint decision is made about whether to continue the helping relationship. As the client reflects, the helper also shares his or her evaluation of progress. Often, the evaluation is a kind of celebration of their mutual success.

Evaluation is the last stop in the stages of the helping process depicted in Figure 2.2. Once a problem has been resolved, the cycle either begins again with a new problem or leads to termination of the relationship. The stages of the helping process become clearer in a case example described in the words of the Jane, a counselor, whose client Barbara was referred by her daughter because of depression.

Relationship Building and Opening Up: The Heart of Helping

Jane: "Barbara is 68 years old with gray hair, somewhat slim but apparently in good physical condition. Barbara's husband died six months ago and although she felt that she had handled the first three months well, recently she had become depressed and apathetic about life. She reminded me a lot of my grandmother, and I felt an urgency to help her when I realized how much her depression was interfering with her life. She had recently started taking antidepressant medication, but her doctor had insisted that she also receive counseling. Barbara had never seen a counselor before, so I took some time to explain the process to her. She was skeptical that anything would help, so I spent about half of the first session listening, reflecting, and getting to know her better. I told her a little bit about myself because I sensed that we would not be successful unless she trusted me. Near the end of the session, I told her that we would be working on the feelings of depression that she was experiencing and I told her about the techniques we might use. We also discussed the issue of confidentiality and I explained that I could not even discuss our sessions with her daughter without her permission. This seemed to alleviate some of her tension because Barbara saw asking for help as a weakness and was afraid that others would judge her for being depressed. We signed an agreement for treatment that outlined the limits to confidentiality and the fees. By the end of the session, Barbara seemed more hopeful about progress, but the work of dealing with her depression was still before us."

At the heart of the helping process is the therapeutic relationship, which provides the core conditions or supports for the other activities of the helper. The relationship is the glue that holds the entire process together. The relationship has a special place in Figure 2.2 to emphasize its central role in the helping process. In relationship building, the helper uses invitational skills to allow the client to open up, to convey understanding, and to create a safe environment. This is exactly what Jane did with Barbara during their first session. Jane tried initially to allay any misgivings that Barbara might have had by giving her information, developing a personal relationship, and dealing with Barbara's real concern that entering a helping relationship was a sign of weakness. It is obvious in this case that if the relationship were not firmly established, assessment would be extremely difficult.

Assessment and Providing Information

Jane: "When I first saw Barbara, I was a little bit surprised to see that she was well groomed, alert, and talkative. Her depression seemed to have started about three months after the death of her second husband, Carl. I took a complete history of Barbara's life and noted a number of losses. Barbara's mother died when Barbara was 20 years old. She had her only daughter at age 28. The next year, she lost a baby through a miscarriage, whose complications left her unable to have more children. Barbara's first husband subsequently died during military training. In addition to the death of her second husband, Barbara was now coping with financial problems. Carl's will had named her as the sole beneficiary, but his children were contesting the will. The family problems and the lack of money were both sources of worry.

"One of the things I did in the very first session was to assess her suicide risk. Barbara denied any suicidal thoughts. She said, 'Sometimes I wish I were dead, but I would never kill myself.' Barbara had strong religious beliefs against suicide, did not own a gun, and her depression was not so severe that I was worried about her taking her own life. I did call the family physician and asked him to limit the number of antidepressant pills that were issued to Barbara each week to reduce the possibility of an overdose. I diagnosed Barbara's problems as mild depression stemming from grief and associated stress, with only a small risk of suicide.

"One of the things that I noticed was that any time Barbara identified something she was doing well, she discounted it and seemed to exaggerate the minor deficiencies in her performance. For example, she still went to church twice a week but she was very discouraged over the fact that it often took her 15 minutes to decide what clothes to wear in the morning. Barbara agreed to keep a journal of her 'negative thoughts' so that we could deal with them in future sessions."

Assessment and providing information is the second stage of the helping process. As is apparent in Barbara's case, much of the assessment stage is inseparable from the relationship-building stage because helpers are observing their clients and collecting information from the moment that they first meet. This process continues throughout the helping relationship, but most of the background data pours in during the first few sessions. Some agencies ask that assessment forms be completed and a preliminary diagnosis be made during the first session. This approach has an important drawback: It fails to take into account that a therapeutic relationship must be established before there is trust and a contract for helping. Figure 2.2 illustrates this premise. The relationship is drawn at the center of the diagram and is connected to each part of the process. Clearly, when the relationship is well established, assessment is more complete and easier to accomplish because clients are much better able to freely disclose information about the problem and about themselves.

Assessment includes formal and informal ways that helpers collect information about clients, among them paper-and-pencil tests, client reports, and helper observations. Collecting background data helps us determine whether the services available are appropriate for a particular client and ensures that we are not missing a serious mental disorder such as schizophrenia, a substance abuse problem, or suicidal or violent behavior. Beyond this, assessment is the organizing of data on the client's problem, providing baseline data and relevant history. Chapter 7 addresses these issues more fully.

Treatment Planning and Goal Setting

Jane: "In the second session, I started off by giving Barbara a summary of what I had learned so far. She had three major problems: feelings of depression that interfered with her life, financial problems, and disruption of family relationships caused by the fight over the will. We both agreed that there was little she could do at the present time to work on the money issues or deal with her husband's children. Instead, we decided to focus efforts on reducing her feelings of depression. In order to do this, I asked Barbara to think about what she would be doing if the depression lifted and what she would be feeling and thinking. This was easy for her. Barbara said, 'I would be able to play golf again. I would get dressed early every morning, and I would not have these negative thoughts going around in my head.' Using Barbara's ideas, we hammered out some goals for the next few sessions. First, we agreed that we would reduce the negative self-talk that Barbara was complaining about because this probably caused or made the depression worse. Second, Barbara would become more physically active to help her get back to her old routine. Barbara resisted playing golf because she was afraid that friends would notice her depression, and she wanted to appear normal. I encouraged her to accept the fact that being depressed was a normal reaction to the loss of a spouse and that she did not have to expect so much of herself right now. I hoped that by acting 'normal,' Barbara would start to feel 'normal.' "

Once a helper has gained an understanding of the client's problem and the important background issues, it is time to identify the helping goals. Here, Barbara and Jane have identified two goals: reducing Barbara's negative self-talk and increasing her physical activity. In this book, we advance the theory that goals, such as those set by Barbara and Jane, are a collaborative construction of helper and client. Although, goals do not necessarily have to be defined behaviorally, if the desired outcomes are observable, it is easier to know when they have been achieved. In the goal-setting phase, professionals draw up treatment plans that state agreed-upon goals and the interventions that will be used to achieve them. This plan instills hope in the client and invites his or her participation as a team player.

Intervention and Action

Jane: "The third session was spent in going over the negative thoughts that Barbara had recorded. When summarized, they seemed to have two persistent themes: 'I should not be depressed,' and 'I am a burden on everyone by being depressed.' These seemed to reflect Barbara's tendencies to be a perfectionist and her fear of relying on others. We discussed the fact that Barbara even felt that she was a burden to me. During the session, we identified some ways of countering her negative thinking by examining the flaws in her negative conclusions. She readily admitted that the thoughts were not logical, but she did not know how to stop them. We suggested that she combat these thoughts in a two-step process. First, stop the thought when she noticed it; second, replace the thought with one that was more constructive. For example, when the thought came up, 'I am a weakling for being depressed,' she was to argue back, 'Feeling this way is a natural part of grieving. I am not perfect; no one is.' We decided to check on how effective these replacement thoughts were at the next meeting. She was to practice 'stopping and inserting' over the next week. During the previous session, I had encouraged Barbara to begin playing golf one time per week as an experiment. I explained that she might not feel 'normal,' but that the exercise would help to reduce the depression. She reluctantly agreed to try it, but at this session Barbara admitted that she had not done so yet."

During the intervention and action stage, professional helpers utilize more advanced skills and ask clients to take active steps to reach their goals. The client is invited to do something to begin solving the problem. In the case of Barbara, Jane taught Barbara how to identify negative self-statements and replace them. Once again, she directed Barbara to continue physical exercise and indicated that she would check on Barbara's progress on both goals at the next meeting. As is typical, Jane met with mixed success in getting Barbara to take action. Note again in Figure 2.2 that the relationship occupies a central position and is connected to the intervention and action stage. In the case of Barbara and Jane, you might see how important a trusting, confiding, therapeutic relationship is to the implementation of techniques. At this stage, if Barbara does not have confidence and trust, she will not wholeheartedly engage in the activities suggested by Jane. Barbara is also more likely to complete homework assignments because Jane is expecting her to do so.

Evaluation and Reflection

Jane: "We spent about five sessions working on Barbara's negative thinking and increasing her physical exercise. Although her physician decided to discontinue the antidepressant medication because of severe dizziness, Barbara's depression gradually lifted over this time. I asked Barbara to evaluate her progress after about two months of counseling. She said, 'Well, I am back to doing most of the things I used to do. I am still very sad sometimes when I think about Carl. I still have trouble making decisions. That is not totally over. I guess I won't be happy until that is resolved. I am still afraid to be around people too much because I don't want them to see how I feel.' Because Barbara focused on the missing elements only, I felt that I should also ask her to give herself a pat on the back for having reduced her depression and increased her physical activity. She was reluctant to do this, but admitted that things were substantially improved. I continued to see Barbara for three more months. The last month was mainly follow-up to make certain that changes were lasting and to reassure her that support was available."

Helpers regularly ask their clients to evaluate by reflecting on the progress made toward the treatment goals. Some time in each session is devoted to gauging the effectiveness of specific techniques and homework. Evaluation also occurs during the final sessions when the helper and client—like Jane and Barbara—review and celebrate the resolution of problems. When client and helper agree that the goals have been reached, either new goals are set (completing the circle in Figure 2.2) or the relationship is terminated.

Stop and Reflect

Let us think back for a moment to the case of Jane and Barbara. Jot down your answers to the following questions and discuss them with classmates or your training group.

Relationship Building and Opening Up
Jane was reminded of her grandmother when she first saw Barbara. Because Jane seemed to care about her own grandmother, this created a motive to help Barbara. Can you think of some situations that might arise between Barbara and Jane where Jane's feelings might not have been productive? In your own experience with different age groups, think about whether you feel more comfortable working with children, adults, or older people. Which group will create the biggest challenge for you? Discuss some past experiences that might account for this.

Assessment and Providing Information

One of the first issues Jane assessed was Barbara's suicide potential. All helpers have to make judgments about this in the first few sessions, even those who work with young children. Because assessing suicide and violent behavior is not an exact science, how do you think you might handle a situation in which you are not certain about a particular client's suicidal intentions?

Treatment Planning and Goal Setting

In the case of Jane and Barbara, they both agreed that Barbara needed to deal with her depression, but it was Jane who suggested the goal of increasing physical exercise. Some feel that the helper's job is to accomplish the client's agenda. Others feel that the helper's expertise and a diagnosis should be the basis of the goals. For example, some would say that because Barbara was depressed, she needed medication and a certain kind of therapy, whether Barbara wished to deal with her depression or not. Who do you think should set the goals in the helping relationship: the helper, the client, or both?

Intervention and Action

In thinking about which techniques to use, Jane mainly focused on cognitive techniques: identifying and replacing negative thoughts. Barbara only reluctantly agreed to the procedure. How do you think you might deal with a client's lack of motivation to work on a problem or do homework assignments? What might you say?

Evaluation and Reflection

In this stage, Jane highlighted Barbara's successes, but Barbara focused on the fact that she was not 100% back to normal. Why do you think Barbara made this statement? Could she be fearing the termination of the helping relationship? What other issues might be behind her unwillingness to recognize success? How do you think you might deal with her fears about termination or other reasons for her reluctance to celebrate success?

Summary

Helping, counseling, and *psychotherapy* are all terms that have been used to describe the professional relationship that identifies problem issues and brings about positive change. Helping skills are best used within a professional relationship that includes a trained helper and a client seeking help. There are limits to how much one can employ helping skills with personal friends and family.

In this book, you will be learning 22 basic helping skills, or building blocks. When combined and elaborated, these building blocks form more complex techniques. It is important to take the time to practice the fundamental skills and gain mastery of them, even if they seem overly simple or awkward.

A therapeutic relationship has special characteristics that differentiate it from other relationships. Among these are a contractual relationship between helper and client. In the case of Jane and Barbara, we emphasized how crucial this relationship is in accomplishing the goals of the helping relationship. Each of the other stages of helping—assessment and providing information, treatment planning and goal setting, intervention and action, and evaluation and reflection—is dependent on the quality of the client/helper bond.

As you learn the helping process, understand that you will encounter expected hurdles along the way. It is not merely an intellectual exercise involving memorization and taking tests. Unlike other courses you have taken, your ability to read and understand the textbook will probably not be sufficient to ensure success. You will need to demonstrate the skills taught in the textbook. For those who are "book smart," this might create anxiety. For those who learn best in a "hands-on" environment, this may be a refreshing change.

Finally, let us warn you against comparing yourself with others. Each person has a separate timetable for learning new skills. Some of us are so cognitively oriented that it takes longer. If you run into trouble, ask your instructor for help. Watch videos demonstrating basic helping skills. Most of all, practice and get feedback from your instructor and classmates. Experience has shown that students with a desire to help can learn the requisite skills in time, but it is a personal journey and each person's timetable is different. To learn helping skills, you must be patient with your own pace, watch good models, and practice whenever possible.

Exercises

Exercise 1

To get a better idea of the helping process, let us examine the five stages shown in Figure 2.2. Think about a problem that you are experiencing. It can be a small problem you are now facing or an issue from the past that you can pretend is an issue today. Jot down your answers to the following questions about each stage of the helping process.

a. Relationship building and opening up: How important would it be for a helper to be warm and inviting; or would you prefer a more businesslike atmosphere?

_____

_____

How long do you think it would take before you trusted a helper enough to disclose something extremely personal?

_____

_____

What sort of personal characteristics would you want in a helper?

_____

_____

b. Assessment and providing information: What important issues would a helper have to find out about you, your family, your environment, your goals, your cultural and religious background, and your history before he or she could help you?

_____

_____

_____

_____

How would you feel about spending the first session answering questions about your problem?

_____

_____

_____

How might you respond to the helper's request that you take complete tests or inventories?

_____

_____

c. Treatment planning and goal setting:
Imagine yourself without the problem.
What would you be doing, thinking, or
feeling that you are not experiencing now?

———————————————————————

———————————————————————

———————————————————————

Can you turn your problem into a goal?
For example, rather than stating the problem, "I bite my fingernails," transform it
into a future scenario, such as "I would like
to have attractive nails that I would not be
ashamed of in public."

———————————————————————

———————————————————————

———————————————————————

d. Intervention and action:
What kind of approach by a helper would
you object to? What kind of help would you
like? If your problem does not fit well with
these questions, describe your general preferences if you were going to receive help on
any problem. Respond briefly to each of the
following interventions a helper might use:

Advice about how to solve your problem

———————————————————————

Writing in a journal _____

Just someone to listen (no advice) _____

Keeping a record of specific behaviors

———————————————————————

Role-playing your problem _____

Entering group therapy _____

Bringing a family member with you _____

An assignment to say "no," more often

———————————————————————

Other _____

e. Evaluation and reflection:
How would you know that you had definitely completed your goal?
How would you be thinking, feeling, and
acting when you had accomplished it?

———————————————————————

———————————————————————

———————————————————————

Homework

Homework 1

Go over the list of unrealistic beliefs about
helping and the corresponding reasonable expectations given in this chapter. Identify two
or three that you think might create difficulties for you in the helping relationship. Do you
agree with the author's conclusions? Write a
paragraph about each belief giving your reactions and indicate how you might deal with
that belief if it should arise in your interaction
with a client. Alternately, identify some of the
beliefs you have about helping that you think
are realistic.

Homework 2

You will sometimes hear helpers talk about being "overinvolved" with clients, and they may
sometimes suggest that you "keep a professional distance." What kinds of behaviors do you
think would indicate that a helper was too involved in a client's life? What limits should the
helper set in the relationship? Does this necessarily mean that the helper should not care
about a client? What ethical guidelines do professional helpers rely on to determine whether
the professional relationship has become too
close? Write down your reaction to these questions in a page or two.

Journal Starters

1. In this chapter, you read about the case of Jane and Barbara. What do you imagine it would be like to work with someone much older than yourself? How would you feel about working with someone who is very depressed or who has a serious mental disorder?

2. Think about some key friendships in your life. What is it that has made them so important for you? Compare you feelings of closeness in your friendship with your feelings about favorite teachers you have known. Can you gain something from relationships in which you are not emotionally close to someone?

3. *Rescuing* is sometimes defined as doing more than 50% of the work in a helping relationship. Have you ever helped someone who did not put forth much effort to help themselves? How did you end up feeling? As you think about that, how do you think this affected your relationship with that person? Is it difficult to imagine working with someone who may not really want to be helped?

For more journal ideas, as well as more practice with the nuts and bolts of helping, refer to Chapter 2 in *Exercises in the Art of Helping*.

References

American Psychiatric Association. (1993). *The diagnostic and statistical manual of mental disorders* (4th ed.). Washington, DC: Author.

Corsini, R. J. (Ed.). (1981). *Handbook of innovative psychotherapies.* New York: Wiley.

Dimond, R. E., & Havens, R. A. (1975). Restructuring psychotherapy: Toward a prescriptive eclecticism. *Professional Psychology, 6,* 193–200.

Dimond R. E., Havens, R. A., & Jones, A. C. (1978). A conceptual framework for the practice of prescriptive eclecticism in psychotherapy. *American Psychologist, 33,* 239–248.

Frank, J. D. (1971). Psychotherapists need theories. *International Journal of Psychiatry, 9,* 146–149.

Frank J. D. (1981). Therapeutic components shared by all psychotherapies. In J. H. Harvey & M. M. Parks (Eds.), *Psychotherapy research and behavior change* (pp. 175–182). Washington, DC: American Psychological Association.

Frank, J. D., & Frank, J. B. (1991). *Persuasion and healing* (3rd ed.). Baltimore: Johns Hopkins University Press.

Hackney, II., & Cormier, L. S. (1988). *Counseling strategies and interventions* (3rd ed.). Upper Saddle River, NJ: Prentice Hall.

Herink, R. (1980). *The psychotherapy handbook: The A to Z guide to more than 250 different therapies in use today.* New York: New American Library.

Ivey, A. E. (1971). *Microcounseling: Innovations in interviewing training.* Springfield, IL: Thomas.

Ivey, A. E., & Mathews, J. W. (1986). A metamodel for structuring the clinical interview. In W. P. Anderson (Ed.), *Innovative counseling: A handbook of readings* (pp. 77–83). Alexandria, VA: American Counseling Association.

Jayartne, S. (1982). Characteristics and theoretical orientations of clinical social workers: A national survey. *Journal of Social Services Research, 4,* 17–30.

Kottler, J., & Blau, D. (1989). *The imperfect therapist.* San Francisco: Jossey-Bass.

Korchin, S. J. (1976). *Modern clinical psychology.* New York: Basic Books.

Lambert, M. J. (1986). Implications of psychotherapy outcome research for eclectic psychotherapy. In J. C. Norcross (Ed.), *Handbook of eclectic psychotherapy* (pp. 436–462). New York: Brunner/Mazel.

Norcross, J. C. (1986). Eclectic psychotherapy: An introduction and overview. In J. C. Norcross

(Ed.), *Handbook of eclectic psychotherapy* (pp. 3–24). New York: Brunner/Mazel.

Norcross, J. C., & Prochaska, J. O. (1982). A national survey of clinical psychologists: Affiliations and orientations. *Clinical Psychologist, 35,* (1), 4–6.

Parloff, M. B. (1979, February). Shopping for the right therapy. *Saturday Review,* 135–142.

Paul, G. L. (1967). Strategy of outcome research in psychotherapy. *Journal of Consulting Psychology, 31,* 109–119.

Smith, D. S. (1982). Trends in counseling and psychotherapy. *American Psychologist, 37,* 802–809.

Smith, M. L., & Glass, G. V. (1977). Meta analysis of psychotherapy outcome studies. *American Psychologist, 32,* 752–760.

Witmer, J. M. (1985). *Pathways to personal growth.* Muncie, IN: Accelerated Development.

Young, M. E. (1990). Theoretical trends in counselling. *Guidance and Counselling, 8,* 1–16.

Young, M. E. (1992). *Counseling methods and techniques: An eclectic approach.* New York: Merrill/Macmillan.

The Therapeutic Relationship

3

In the beginning was the relationship.
Martin Buber

In the last chapter, we talked about the high expectations we have for ourselves in the helping relationship. We also highlighted the differences between a therapeutic relationship and a friendship. But what is so special about this helping relationship? In this chapter, we will dig a little bit deeper into the mystery of the interaction between client and helper, discussing briefly why helpers and researchers place so much emphasis on it. More practically, we will also talk about how you can build such a relationship with another person. Finally, we turn to the issue of mistakes that can be made in the helping relationship and the knotty problems of transference and countertransference. Before addressing these important issues, let us take a look at a real client's recollections about her counselor.

I came to counseling because my husband was having an affair and I was devastated over the impending breakup of my marriage. I was anxious, depressed, and having trouble eating and sleeping. I was like a zombie at work. I heard that Jim was the best therapist in the area so I called to make an appointment. Jim was a minister who also had a degree in counseling. Although I am not a Christian, I am very spiritually oriented and I wanted someone who could understand that side of me. In many ways, Jim fit perfectly my ideas of what a helper should be. He was older than me by 25 years, had gray hair, and I had heard that he had been happily married for many years to another therapist in the area. I had also heard that he studied with some famous teachers. My expectations were high and I was desperate.

At our first meeting, Jim got up to greet me at the door, shook my hand warmly with both of his, ushering me into his crowded office. Then, I had one of the most powerful experiences of my life. He listened to me for the next half-hour as though nothing else in the world was more important. I had talked to a few friends about the situation, but he seemed to make me feel that there was all the time in the world and I sensed that all my problems were no burden to him. Although I cried through much of the first session, Jim remained calm and at the end offered some hope. First, he asked me the question, "What holds you together?" I then talked about my spiritual beliefs. It made me realize that I could rely on that to help me through this crisis. Later, he commented, "I don't think it is time to give up on this yet." Having that light at the end of the tunnel made a lot of difference. I was able to hold on for a few weeks while things sorted themselves out.

Once, I came to a session and found that there was a mix-up in communication and only a half-hour of my session remained. I was upset because I really needed to talk to someone. I was bursting with sadness and anger. That night I dreamt that I was sitting in Jim's waiting room and everybody else was allowed to go in except me. Even though it wasn't his fault, I felt displaced. When we talked about it in the counseling session, Jim said, "I guess it was hard for you to face another rejection." This really helped me become aware of how discarded and unwanted I felt in my relationship with my husband. I also felt sick to my stomach when I realized how dependent I had become on my therapist.

As time went on, I became stronger and was able to handle my problems much better. Knowing Jim was there was a great comfort sometimes. At other times, I was frustrated that when I needed to talk to him, it was still three or four days until our session. For some irrational reason, it made me mad that he was not available when I called.

After four or five months, Jim told me one day that he thought I had become too dependent on the relationship and that we needed to reduce our sessions to once per month. I agreed that things were better and silently assented to this new arrangement. After that session, I met a friend for lunch and as we went through the buffet line, I took three knives, three forks, three spoons, and four napkins. I was so disoriented by powerful feelings, I could hardly concentrate. Part of me saw Jim's reducing our sessions as a form of confidence in me. But I also felt suddenly adrift. It took six months or so before I was able to really get back on solid ground and feel a sense of confidence.

I feel that I owe Jim a debt that I can never adequately repay. He helped me survive during the lowest period of my life. I don't idealize him any longer but I recognize his caring and his undivided attention as one of the things that pulled me through.

                                                                                              Alicia B.

The Importance of the Therapeutic Relationship in Creating Change

The real experiences of clients like Alicia B. help us to see that the person of the helper and the relationship with the client can be powerfully important in a client's life. Helpers, too, have long recognized the vital role of a therapeutic working alliance in achieving success (Belkin, 1980; Fiedler, 1950). Most theorists from behaviorists (Kanfer & Goldstein, 1986) to Carl Rogers (1957) have emphasized that without a strong therapeutic alliance, the goals of therapy cannot be reached. As much as 30% of improvement in psychotherapy clients has been linked to this factor (Lambert, 1986).

The importance of the chemistry between client and counselor, however, is probably even more significant when we ask clients why they drop out in the first few sessions. Often, it is due to feeling uncomfortable with the helper, not liking the helper, or deciding that the helper is not capable of helping. So, although the power of the therapeutic relationship is key to creating improvement, it is also vital that this environment be created immediately. If the helper does not instill confidence and communicate warmth and acceptance in the first few sessions, a client's fragile hopes may be dashed, and he or she will give up on the relationship or even give up on gaining professional help altogether.

The central importance of the relationship in the helping process is portrayed in Figure 3.1, which shows the six therapeutic factors we introduced in chapter 2. The therapeutic relationship is shown at the center of the diagram to suggest that the other factors depend, to a large extent, on the power of the relationship for their effectiveness. It is also true that the stages of the helping process—relationship building and opening up, assessment and providing information, treatment planning goal setting, intervention and action, and evaluation and reflection—all require the existence of a strong, cooperative relationship between helper and client (see Figure 2.2). In order to gain full and accurate assessment information, for example, the client must feel safe enough to disclose the good, the bad, and the ugly. In this chapter, you will learn skills to enhance the relationship, so as to maximize the effectiveness of the other therapeutic factors and to identify and reduce impediments to the relationship that can lead to client dropout and slower progress.

Figure 3.1
Six Common Therapeutic Factors

The Unique Characteristics of a Therapeutic Relationship

Professional helping has as its basis a special therapeutic relationship involving a trained helper and a client wanting help. The most effective helping relationships have the following attributes that differentiate them from other relationships. In the previous chapter, we talked about the difference between friendship and a helping relationship. Keep this difference in mind as you look over this list.

The purpose of the relationship is the resolution of the client's issues. Compared to other relationships, the helper/client dyad is unbalanced in favor of the client. Even if the client invites it, the helper does not ask for or receive support from the client. It is a one-way street where the helper is the giver. The helper's own issues are dealt with outside of the client's hour.

There is a sense of teamwork as both helper and client work toward a mutually agreed-upon goal. The client can draw strength from the fact that the helper is there to provide support for change in the mutually decided direction. Just as a friend might become your ally in quitting smoking or maintaining an exercise program, the client feels the helper's presence as a constant nudge to grow.

There is a contract specifying what will be disclosed to others outside of the relationship. Safety and trust are established, allowing honest disclosure by the client and feedback from the helper. Unlike a friendship at work, confidences with a family member, or feelings shared with a neighbor, the client begins to realize that secrets will not circulate. As the client experiences this safety, he or she begins to discuss deeper and deeper issues. At times, the helping relationship requires the helper to give the client honest feedback or nonjudgmental information about the client's behavior.

There is an agreement about compensation for the helper. Although some helpers may be volunteers, most receive credit or money for each client hour. Even the volunteer may benefit by listing the work experience on his or her résumé. At the beginning of the relationship, helper and client discuss compensation. Help from a professional is usually not a gift but a fee-for-services relationship.

There is an understanding that the relationship is confined to the counseling sessions and does not overlap into the participants' personal lives. As a general rule, helpers try to devote regularly scheduled times to a client. Crises are exceptions to the rule, but nearly all helpers have a system for dealing with emergent problems. Most helpers give out a 24-hour crisis hotline number rather than their home phone number. They do not interact socially with clients when it can be avoided so that objectivity is not strained by other considerations.

As a contractual relationship, the relationship can be terminated at any time. A unique aspect of the helping relationship is that once the client has reached the identified goals, the helping relationship is put on hold until some future help is needed. The relationship can be ended by either party at any time. Generally, the helper does this only if the client is not making progress or if the helper's employing agency places time limits on the relationship. If the client is not making progress or the helper identifies a particular problem best handled by an expert (e.g., substance abuse or sex therapy), the helper may end the relationship by referring the client elsewhere.

How Can a Helper Create a Therapeutic Relationship?

So far, we have looked at the therapeutic relationship from the account of a client and heard about its importance and special characteristics. But how can a helper create this special experience? Before looking at our suggestions, remember that you probably already know some of the ways to make a relationship work. You may have found that people naturally seek you out for help already. It is important to recognize your natural abilities and not discount them as you eliminate some behaviors and try out new ones.

Relationship Enhancers

Take a look at Table 3.1, an adaptation of a chart designed by Frederick Kanfer and Arnold Goldstein (1986, p. 21). In the first column, the authors identified key relationship enhancers or helper behaviors that improve the quality of the therapeutic relationship. They include some nonverbal skills such as posture, as well as empathy, expertness and credibility, and self-disclosure. These behaviors lead to the emotional qualities or relationship components in column 2: liking, respect, and trust. In other words, the relationship enhancers in the first column create a favorable emotional climate for helping. The relationship consequences in column 3 naturally follow from the relationship components in column 2. They are communication, openness, and persuasibility. If we like, respect, and trust someone, there is a free flow of information and the person's comments hold more weight. Finally, the hoped-for outcome in column 4 is therapeutic change. Because our focus in this section is on creating and enhancing the therapeutic relationship, let us look at each of the four relationship enhancers (column 1) in more detail.

Table 3.1
Relationship Enhancers

Relationship Enhancer	Relationship Component	Relationship Consequence	Outcome
Physical closeness, posture, and warmth (invitational skills)	Liking ⟶	Communication	
Helper empathy (reflecting and advanced reflecting skills)			
Helper expertness and credibility	Respect ⟶	Openness ⟶	Change
Helper self-disclosure and good helper/client match	Trust ⟶	Persuasibility	

Source: Adapted from Kanfer, F. H., & Goldstein, A. P. (1986). Introduction, Figure 2.1. In F. Kanfer & A. Goldstein (Eds.), *Helping people change: A textbook of methods.* (p. 21). New York: Pergamon.

Physical Closeness, Posture, and Warmth

In the next chapter, you will learn the basic skills associated with physical distance, posture, creating a warm atmosphere for helping, and other body language skills. These nonverbals invite the client into a safe relationship and lead to greater openness. Although these may seem like small things, they can be powerful in all kinds of interpersonal situations. Let us assume that you are going for two different job interviews. In the first case, the interviewer greets you by shaking your hand. Her voice is friendly and informal. When you arrive at her office, she smiles and welcomes you, then she sits down in a chair next to you, turning it around so she can face you directly. Contrast this scenario with another office in which a secretary ushers you into the interviewer. The interviewer greets you from behind her desk. She spends much of the session staring at a file and making notes as she asks direct questions about your history. Under which circumstances are you likely to feel the most comfortable and to open up about your past? In which situation are you most able to get across the information you would like the potential employer to know? If one of these interviewers were to ask you to say something very personal about yourself, to whom would you be most likely to disclose? Although interviewing is not necessarily a helping relationship, even in this circumstance it is easy to see how powerful the small nonverbal enhancers can be in eliciting greater communication, openness, and persuasiblity.

Empathy

The word *empathy* is derived from the German word, *Einfhlung,* which means "feeling oneself into" another person's experience. Empathy means that you grasp the facts, the feelings, and the significance of another person's story; more important, empathy involves the ability to convey your accurate perceptions to the other person. There is a vast literature on the importance of empathy. Although much of it focuses on the helping relationship, empathy has been found to be a vital aspect of other interpersonal situations. Marriage counselors have found that basic empathy training for distressed couples is among the most potent interventions for communication problems (Young & Long, 1998). Empathy training has been found to be an essential in good leadership (Gordon, 1986). Stephen Covey, in *The Seven Habits of Highly Effective People* (1990), recommends seeking "first to understand then to be understood" as one of the ingredients of personal success regardless of your profession.

Recent news events have focused on alienated adults and teenagers who seem to lack any recognition of the feelings and needs of others. The book, *Emotional Intelligence,* by Daniel Goleman (1995) suggests training in emotional awareness as the long-term cure for this condition in our society. Goleman's research shows that awareness of one's own emotions and those of others is among the most important predictors of success, mental health, happy families, and friendships. In summary, beyond its uses in helping, developing the skills of empathy can have a positive spillover into other areas of a person's life.

Helper empathy   The special thing about empathy in the helping relationship is that, here, the term encompasses the experiences of both client and helper. Empathy is not empathy, in this situation, if the helper has not communicated understanding to the client. If the helper hears the story only superficially or appears judgmental, even if he or she is accurate about the facts, the client does not experience the helper's empathy. Empathy occurs when the client feels and may even say, "That's it! That's how I feel!" If we further analyze this statement, it could be said that a client experiences empathy when the helper communicates that he or she understands the facts, the emotions, and the special meanings of the client's story.

Empathy and differences   Empathy is a crucial skill in overcoming cultural, gender, and other differences between client and helper. Empathy means taking a "tutorial stance" rather than an authoritarian position when we are confronted with a person's life experience that clashes with our own. A tutorial stance means the helper becomes a learner, seeking to understand the client—recognizing that the helper must learn from the client what it is like to be that person.

Racism and prejudices about various cultural groups can be seen as a form of narcissism or self-absorption. We become so attached to our own perspective that we have no tolerance for those who do not share it. Of course, we all come to an interpersonal situation with cultural "baggage" and a worldview that contains prejudices of one kind or another. These will show up in our verbal and nonverbal messages. Clients recognize our attitudes not only from the things we say, but also by body language that may signal subtle disapproval.

Empathy is a first step in getting us off our ethnocentric narcissism and signals to clients that we are trying to "feel ourselves into" their world, rather than attempting to convert them to our perspective. Although empathy provides a doorway to the inner life of another person, is it really ever possible to enter the world of another completely, leaving behind the vestiges of our own beliefs? Probably not. However, it is important that our clients recognize that we are struggling to understand, that we care enough to try.

What empathy isn't   *Empathy is not merely supporting or agreeing with the client.* Consider the following story related by a school counselor:

> Last week, I saw 17-year-old Monique, a young woman who has been accepted to college with a full scholarship. She has a keen intellect and is especially good in math. She has always preferred older men, and now she has become pregnant by a man, David, who is 15 years older than she is. Recently, she found out that he was lying to her about his relationships with other women and that he had even lied to her about his job, saying that he was an architect when, in fact, he is a paraprofessional in an architect's office. Her parents have told her she cannot remain at home with a child to raise. Although David will support her, she is afraid of him because she has heard he can become violent. Monique is also afraid to stay with him and feels that if she has a child with him, they will be bonded forever. She is considering an abortion because she feels that she misjudged him and cannot see a good future for herself or the child.

This situation presented a dilemma for the helper because, although she could empathize with the client's situation, she felt that, by empathizing, she was supporting the client's decision to obtain an abortion. Many helpers are afraid to empathize with a client for fear of taking sides. In fact, empathy can help clients examine their feelings at a deeper level and make decisions that are more consistent with their own feelings and values. You can communicate understanding about the circumstances that spawned the problem without supporting or agreeing with the client's subsequent action.

Empathy is not pretending to understand. In the next chapters, you will learn some techniques to help you communicate empathy to clients. You will discover, however, that empathy is not effective if it is not sincere. Clients pick up on the nonverbals as well as what you say. Merely saying the prescribed formula will not help the client, if you truly do not understand the situation. The best advice for the beginning helper is to be patient. Spend as much time as you need to hear the story before you tell the client that you understand.

Empathy is not taking on your client's problems. For the most part, helper fears about being overwhelmed by the client's problems are unfounded. Empathic people try to understand another person's pain in order to relieve it (Johnson, 1990). Consequently, it may be natural to fear that problems are "catching" and that by entering another person's world too deeply, we may become depressed ourselves. Although it is impossible not to be affected in some way by great pain, you learn over time to deal with it within the session and not let it hamper your time with the next person or carry over into your personal life. The great therapist Frieda Fromm-Reichmann (1960) claimed that we must be like skin divers able to go to the depth of a client's problems but also able to surface when we need to.

Empathy is not a one-time behavior. Although empathy is especially important in the relationship building and opening up stage of the helping process, empathy is crucial throughout. As the relationship develops, the client may disclose more and more deeply. For example, as marriage counseling progresses, instead of talking about the problems the kids are having at school, a couple might begin to examine their attitudes about child rearing and their disagreements about how to discipline. These very personal topics might require the helper to empathize at a deeper level, trying to understand their perspectives and how these were shaped by their own families.

Expertness and Credibility

For the relationship to gel, the helper must first qualify for the job (Yalom, 1985). In other words, it is important for the client to perceive the helper as a competent professional. Writers have called this client perception *credibility* (Sue & Zane, 1987) or *expertness* (Barak, Patkin, & Dell, 1982; Heppner & Dixon, 1986; Strong, 1968). Client expectations of competence are increased by objective evidence of competency: the helper's office, therapeutic rituals, reputation, and even the certificates and diplomas hanging on the walls (Frank, 1961; Loesch, 1984).

If a client perceives the helper as an expert, the client is also more likely to be attracted to and respect the helper. Ultimately, experts are more persuasive (Corrigan, Dell, Lewis, & Schmidt, 1980; Strong, 1968). In a review of the literature, Heppner and Dixon (1986) indicated that objective evidence of training as well as certain helper behaviors and "prestigious cues" affect ratings of helper expertness by their clients. These behaviors and cues include (1) appearing confident, organized, and interested and (2) nonverbal behaviors associated with attentiveness. Using interpretive statements and psychological jargon was also found to increase ratings of expertness. Although the latter may seem phony, they are consistent with Frank's

(1961) idea that one of the ways that helpers influence clients is to induct them into a therapeutic ritual and set of procedures. According to Frank, the office setting, the ritual, and the therapeutic procedures all help to reassure the client and to combat the demoralization that has caused the client to seek help. How would you feel, for example, if you were facing a serious lawsuit and you found that your attorney's office was a disorganized room behind a convenience store?

The issue of competence does have a dark side. The client may overestimate and idealize the helper's powers. He or she may attribute success to the helper, rather than to his or her own efforts. Although helpers are uncomfortable with the admiration of clients, it may be difficult and perhaps counterproductive to discourage the client's attraction, at least in the beginning. Sheldon Kopp (1978) uses a metaphor to explain this. Kopp compares the client to Dorothy in *The Wizard of Oz,* who sees the helper as a powerful sorcerer (Oz) hidden behind a screen. Because of the client's confidence in the sorcerer's power, he or she is empowered to go out and kill the wicked witch. Here, killing the wicked witch symbolizes the client's efforts to follow treatment plans and make necessary changes. It is only at a later stage that the client is ready to see the helper as just a person behind a curtain. A client may have to go through the process of therapy before realizing that the source of strength, like Dorothy's, has been there, within himself or herself, all the time. If the client does not eventually abandon this magical view of the helper, the client will not be able to take responsibility for the change process and will instead wait for the wave of the helper's wand. As Alicia B.'s story in the beginning of the chapter suggests, however, faith in the helper is useful, especially when the client has lost faith in himself or herself.

Some helpers find this kind of talk disturbing because it implies that the helper should try to present a powerful but possibly phony image. This certainly could have harmful effects for both client and helper. Helpers are not sorcerers and should not try to feed their egos in the helping process. On the other hand, some helpers have the mistaken impression that they should do nothing to communicate credibility and expertness to clients. Dressing informally and being overly casual may make the helper, but not the client, feel more comfortable. Perceptions of expertness lead to positive outcomes, including faith and trust in the process of helping and faith is powerful medicine.

Credibility and cultural difference Sue and Zane (1987) identify credibility as a crucial relationship issue in helping someone who is culturally different. Although knowledge of the client's culture lends credibility to a helper who is dealing with someone from a different background, other factors are also important. Sue and Zane distinguish between ascribed and achieved credibility. *Ascribed credibility* is the status given to the helper by the client that is often due to sex, age, experience, and similarity of life experiences and attitudes. For example, in some cultures, an older person is ascribed more credibility than a younger person.

Achieved credibility refers to the helper's skills and demonstrated abilities. If the helper cannot be ascribed much credibility with an individual from a different background, he or she may be able to achieve it over time. For example, a helper who is not recovering from alcohol or substance abuse will be ascribed very little credibility by clients in treatment programs for these problems. Because the helper has never been addicted, clients are skeptical about how much he or she really knows. If the helper possesses special knowledge and skills, however, it may be possible to achieve some measure of acceptance, even without a history of personal addiction.

According to Sue and Zane, the helper can achieve credibility by conceptualizing problems in a way that is congruent with the client's beliefs and values. For example, it has been suggested that framing a problem as medical, rather than psychological, is more acceptable to a Hispanic client (Meadow, 1982). It has also been suggested that African American clients prefer educational and practical strategies for dealing with problems to methods that focus only on feelings (Parker, 1988). However, prejudging a client's values and beliefs or making a treatment plan based on a single characteristic such as race, ethnicity, or religion without a complete understanding of the client's background and unique personality is a serious mistake (Wohl, 1995). Counselors lose credibility when they fail to take into account the full complexities of the person and try to simplify a client by identifying him or her as a member of a particular culture, socioeconomic group, sex, or age.

A significant issue in dealing with those who are culturally different is that the helper may not have much ascribed credibility coming from outside of the client's ideas of what a helper should be. Therefore, the helper must work hard during the initial phase of the relationship to achieve credibility. Early studies suggested that as many as 50% of Asian American clients did not return after the first session (Sue & McKinney, 1975). This is probably true of clients from many different backgrounds who encounter culturally different helpers. When clients don't return, we can only speculate about their reasons, but it seems obvious that many clients have concluded at the first session that they have not been understood or that they cannot be helped. One way that a helper can achieve credibility under these circumstances is to do something tangible to help the client as soon as possible.

Credibility and gender   *Sex* refers to basic physiological differences between men and women; *gender* refers to the roles that each sex is taught (Taylor, 1994). Each culture has different expectations for men and women, boys and girls. Some of these ideas about gender are described in the following discussion. Much of this review is contained in a manuscript by Granello (1999) and is summarized here.

In the United States, women are expected to be caregivers, as well as nurturing and dependent. Women are expected to behave nonaggressively or to suppress their aggressive impulses (Maccoby & Jacklin, 1974; Pearson, West, & Turner, 1995). Women have also been trained to be the ones who maintain relationships and to see relationships as valuable to personal happiness (Workman, 1993). Robbins (1983) states that women have been conditioned to believe that a man should be the focus of their world if they want to receive affection and attention themselves.

Men, on the other hand, are expected to be strong and in control of themselves and of the environment at all times (Bem, 1975; Block, 1973; Scher & Stevens, 1987). They are conditioned to believe that they must achieve, compete, control their feelings, and follow the rules (Workman, 1993). It is understandable, therefore, that men are viewed as more dominant, practical, and decisive than women (Broverman, Vogel, Broverman, Clarkson, & Rosenkrantz, 1972; Freudenberger, 1990; Good, Dell, & Mintz, 1989, Heilbrun, 1976).

In summary, the dominant culture has historically portrayed men as more powerful, credible, and influential than women. Consequently, in the past, clients of both sexes most often preferred male helpers. We now see consistent evidence that both men and women prefer helpers of the same sex. Nelson (1993) also found that helpers prefer same sex clients. Nelson sees this as evidence that in general, we prefer people who are similar to ourselves. However, is having a same-gender helper always the best idea? This might actually perpetuate male stereotypes if men were to be counseled only by other men. Nor does it always seem best to allow clients to choose the gender of the helper because some women might choose male helpers when exposure to a good female role model would be more useful. At this juncture, a clear answer to this dilemma is unavailable.

In general, training programs teach helpers to address the issues of gender and cultural differences directly with clients throughout the therapeutic relationship. Training should also allow the helper to examine his or her own assumptions about gender and to engage in some consciousness-raising activities. Whether the helper is male or female, he or she can uncover these assumptions about credibility and expose them to the light of day (Devoe, 1990).

Unfortunately, many helpers are not aware of their gender or cultural biases. When asked, many helpers believe that their own behavior toward a client is not affected by gender or cultural differences. Because we do not feel prejudiced, we assume that our behavior is not influenced by cultural norms. Periods of supervision, consciousness raising, and scrupulous reflection are nearly always necessary before we can see our own automatic patterns of relating.

Self-Disclosure

In the first place, it is hypothesized that personal growth is facilitated when the psychotherapist is what he is, when in the relationship with his client, he is genuine and "without" front or facade, openly being the feelings and attitudes which at the moment are flowing in him. We have coined the term "congruence" to try and describe this condition. By this we mean that the feelings the therapist is experiencing are available to him, available to his awareness, that he is able to live these feelings, be them, and able to communicate them if appropriate. (Rogers, 1972, p. 129)

Helper self-disclosure occurs when the helper relates personal information verbally or nonverbally to the client. The preceding quote from Carl Rogers emphasizes one very positive effect of self-disclosure by the helper, namely, that the client begins to see the helper as an honest and open person. Rogers' quote also contains a caution. Self-disclosure by the helper must be "appropriate." In other words, the helper must consider what kinds of disclosure will be helpful to the client. Self-disclosure is not initiated to develop a social relationship or to allow the helper to ventilate feelings.

The jury is still out on how valuable self-disclosure may be in the long run (Watkins, 1990). One reason is that there are all kinds of disclosures, ranging from the superficial "I have a master's degree," to the personal "I once had a drinking problem." Consequently, it has been difficult for researchers to give a blanket endorsement to self-disclosure. Still, helper self-disclosure has been shown to increase trust in the relationship (Johnson & Matross, 1977; Jourard, 1971), deepen client self-disclosure, and encourage expression of feelings (McCarthy, 1982; Nilsson, Strassberg, & Bannon, 1979; Sermat & Smythe, 1973). Clients have reported that self-disclosure by the helper is extremely valuable (Knox, Hess, Petersen, & Hill, 1997).

It appears that moderate levels of self-disclosure are better than highly personal or only mildly personal disclosures (Bannikotes, Kubinski, & Purcell, 1981). Too much self-disclosure can be a serious mistake. One of the best discussions of this is contained in Kottler & Blau's book, *The Imperfect Therapist* (1989). According to the authors, "Whether the therapist's ignorance, insensitivity or narcissism are at fault, more than a few clients have been chased out of treatment because they felt negated by the repeated focus on the therapist's life" (p. 137). Kottler and Blau go on to say that clients are "frightened away" because helpers who talk about themselves make the client feel less important. Clients with low self-esteem do not want to hear about the successes of others. Helpers may lose their authority as transference figures and might be less able to influence the client through modeling. Finally, the client becomes bored with the repetition of therapist stories and anecdotes. The mistake here is that the helper simply spends too much time in self-disclosure. Taking too much time for helper self-disclosure may put more stress on a client who already feels overburdened. Kottler and Blau contend that the saddest aspect of this situation is that the helper is usually unaware of the problem. To give a concrete example, a couple recently came to me for premarital counseling. They had been dissatisfied with a previous therapist because "She didn't seem interested in us. Instead, she spent the whole hour talking about her relationship with her husband and how they handled their differences. It was a waste of time and money."

Common mistakes in helper self-disclosure   The following are some examples of other common errors in self-disclosure made by helpers. The purpose of self-disclosure is to help the client realize that he or she is not alone or that his or her experience is normal. However, if the helper's story is vastly different from the client's, self-disclosure may have the opposite effect. In addition, self-disclosure shifts the focus onto the helper. Once disclosure is made, it is imperative that the helper shift the focus back onto the client.

Mistake 1: The helper's self-disclosure is too deep. The client has to react to the helper, rather than focus on parallels between the two stories.
Situation: The client expresses that she feels like a failure because she is going through a divorce.
Inappropriate Disclosure by the Helper: "When I was going through my third divorce, I thought that there was something wrong with me. After all, I am supposed to help other people with their problems. So I went into therapy for over a year."
Appropriate Disclosure by the Helper: "I have been through divorce myself and I can relate to those feelings. I guess they are pretty common."
Mistake 2: Self-disclosure is poorly timed. When a person has gone through a traumatic event, it is a poor time to get him or her to focus on the helper's story. Rather, they should be encouraged to disclose more.
Situation: The client's mother died last week. (In this case, the client cannot really appreciate or focus on another person's story.)
Inappropriate Disclosure by the Helper: "I know just how you feel because my mother died about five years ago after a long illness. It was a long time before I got over it."
Appropriate Disclosure by the Helper: "I don't know exactly what you are going through, but I know a little bit about what it means to lose someone that close. I can guess that this whole thing has been very painful for you."

Mistake 3: The helper's self-disclosure does not match the client's experience.

Situation: The client has received a basketball scholarship to go to college. No one in her family has ever gone to a university. She is having trouble achieving satisfactory college board scores for admission.

Inappropriate Disclosure by the Helper: "Once I wanted to go to a prep school that cost $20,000 per year. But I had to go to one that cost a lot less because my family couldn't afford it."

Appropriate Disclosure by the Helper: "I can relate to your story in that I have had some goals in my life that I wanted that badly. It must be frustrating to be almost there and run into this new hurdle."

Matching Helper and Client

Chances for success in the helping relationship are maximized when there is a good match between helper and client. We sometimes use the mystical term "chemistry" to describe a good fit in a relationship. On the other hand, a poor match can create problems that take time away from achieving the therapeutic goals.

Let us look first at problems caused by a poor match. Elkind (1992) suggested that "lack of fit" can be due to differences in stage of life between helper and client. Sometimes clients want older, "wiser" helpers, whereas others may find a better match with someone closer in age. Mismatches can occur when the client brings issues or life experiences of which the therapist has no knowledge. For example, a Viet Nam veteran may find it difficult to relate to a therapist who was born after the war. Personality differences can also cause mismatches. Clients who are very practical and concrete may not relate to a helper who wants to explore ideas and possibilities. Extroverted helpers may find introverted clients difficult to reach. Introverted clients may find extroverts annoying. As we discussed earlier, gender is a consideration in matching clients, too. Finally, Elkind identifies mismatches that occur as a result of differences in theoretical orientation or life philosophy. For example, a feminist client might have difficulty accepting the premises of a traditional psychodynamic approach. Some religious ideas might clash with assertiveness training or ideas about the marital relationship.

The major difficulties in helper/client match occur when the client and helper come from widely different cultural backgrounds or when the client is a member of a special population that the helper has difficulty relating to. Special populations include, but are not limited to, ethnic minorities; war veterans; the elderly; those from a distinct socioeconomic stratum, such as the homeless; those with serious or chronic illness and pain; prison inmates; gay and lesbian people; children of alcoholics; nonChristians; ex-convicts; and those with physical or mental disabilities (Campbell & Witmer, 1991).

Now that we have talked about poor matches, what can a helper do to create a better match? Kanfer and Goldstein (1986) identify several characteristics researchers have discovered that contribute to good matches. First, the helper and the client agree on the roles and obligations of each person in the helping relationship. When the expectations of helper and client are congruent, a better match is obtained. Helpers can create a better match between client expectations and the content of the sessions by explaining the process and structure of the helping process. Some helpers use a handout that discusses fees, confidentiality, access to records, and other common concerns.

Second, a match is improved when both the client and the helper have a positive feeling about success, beginning with the first meeting. Helpers can instill hope without false reassurance and select clients who they feel that they can help.

Third, a better match is obtained when clients and helpers come from similar cultural, economic, social, and racial backgrounds. Finally, clients tend to prefer individuals who are similar to them in attitudes, personality, and ethnicity (Atkinson, Poston, Furlong, & Mercado, 1989), and helpers also seem to prefer clients who are similar to them.

How to handle mismatches   This discussion may seem trivial to helpers who work in agencies where the system does not allow the option of matching helper and client. Clients are assigned to whomever is next on the list. The question then becomes not how to avoid mismatches but how to deal with them. If you are an African American counselor in a primarily white college counseling center, does this mean that you will be ineffective? No, but you will certainly have to find ways of addressing mismatches when they occur.

A mismatch can be minimized when the helper has specific knowledge about the client's background. Besides training in specific areas of knowledge about special populations, helpers need to examine their personal and cultural attitudes toward special populations. The helper must possess or adopt attitudes of empathy (rather than sympathy), tolerance for ambiguity, open-mindedness, and an openness to experience (Corey, Corey, & Callanan, 1988). In addition, Sue (1981) asserts that helpers who are skilled in dealing with special populations possess the following attributes:

1. They understand their own value systems and basic assumptions about human behavior and are able to appreciate that the views of others will differ. Helpers may be unaware, for example, how their therapeutic training and views of mental health are based on several strictly Western assumptions. Some of these assumptions include an emphasis on individualism versus duty to family and society, an emphasis on independence and a neglect of client support systems, a focus on changing the individual rather than the system, and a neglect of history and a focus on immediate events (Pedersen, 1987).
2. They understand that special populations have been shaped by social and political forces that may have also been important in shaping client attitudes and values.
3. They understand the worldview of the client, are able to share it in some way, and constantly strive to avoid being culturally encapsulated.
4. They are truly eclectic, using skills, methods, and techniques and forming goals that are congruent with the views, values, lifestyles, and life experiences of special populations.

In most cases, client expectations and differences can be explored by the sensitive helper and resolved if the client is able to see the helper as accepting and competent. It is important to address the differences directly, when it seems appropriate, and to ask the client how he or she feels about being helped by someone who is different. Many of these approaches require self-disclosure on the part of the helper. On the other hand, it is not necessary or even advisable to try to overcome all mismatches when they are identified. An appropriate referral, if available, can sometimes save time for both the helper and the client.

Stop and Reflect

Harry Dewire, a therapist in Dayton, Ohio, told me the following story about counseling a couple who had recently emigrated to the United States from Hong Kong. Because they did not speak English well, a Chinese translator was hired to be present during the sessions. Near the end of the first hour, it seemed that the translator was going beyond Dr. Dewire's statements and his simple reflections were turning into long paragraphs in Chinese. The couple left the session quite satisfied and smiling, promising to return. They even jotted down a few notes. When Dr. Dewire quizzed the translator about what he had said, the translator replied, "What you did was all right, but they came to you because you are an older and wiser person. If you didn't tell them how to handle their situation, they would have felt that the session was wasted. So, I gave them some advice on your behalf."

- Suppose you were confronted with Dr. Dewire's situation. How do you think that you might handle the counseling situation with someone from a completely different culture? Should the helper adapt to the clients' expectations or should the clients be inducted into the helper's way of doing things?
- Dr. Dewire's clients had expectations about helping based on a culture that looks to elders for wisdom. When you think about a helping relationship, what are your expectations? How would you expect to be treated? How would you have reacted to a helper who doled out advice in the first session?
- Dr. Dewire's story tells us that in the very first encounter, a client's cultural background can be a significant factor. In the United States, it is likely that many clients gain their ideas about the counseling relationship not from personal experience, but through television and movies. Can you think of some presentations of the counseling relationship in the media that might be priming clients for the wrong experience?
- How likely is it that you will be faced with a language barrier or see a deaf client who signs? Do you think that it is important for every helper to speak a second language or to learn an alternative form of communication such as signing?

Other Factors That Help or Strain the Therapeutic Relationship

In the previous section, we discussed helper behaviors that can enhance the therapeutic relationship. Here, we will talk about some other factors that affect the relationship. Among these are the environment where helping takes place, the therapeutic blunders that we can try to avoid, and the issues of transference and countertransference.

Facilitative Office Environment

The helper's office should be quiet, comfortable, orderly, and well lit. Most professionals and clients prefer soft lighting to bright fluorescence. Decorating that is comfortable rather than clinical is helpful, especially at the beginning of a therapeutic relationship.

Sigmund Freud called his office a "consulting room." In other words, it should not be the therapist's living room nor should it look like a laboratory. The office should not be merely an outgrowth of the helper's personality but a work place. Generally, it is recommended that the helper face away from the desk so that there are no obstacles between client and helper (Pietrofesa, Hoffman, & Splete, 1984). Side tables are useful for a clock and the indispensable boxes of facial tissue.

Not all helpers today have the ideal facilitative environment. School counselors see students in the hallways and in the lunchroom in five-minute snatches some times. Other helpers work in cubicles without soundproofing. Many work out of their cars, doing home visits and actually conducting sessions in their clients' homes. For them, the issues of distractions and privacy must be dealt with creatively. Many have traveling "helper kits" that can be unpacked to create a "therapeutic space," including clocks, tissues, and play equipment for working with children.

Distractions

Noise from outside can interfere with the session, disrupting a delicate moment or giving the client the feeling that he or she may be heard by persons outside. A "Quiet Please" sign or one that says "Session in Progress" should be placed on the outside of the door. In some cases, it may be necessary to purchase a mechanical white-noise or ocean-sound device that can act as a "sound blanket." Position office seating to provide the most freedom from glaring lights, noise, and the possibility of being overheard.

Other disturbances to be avoided during the session include knocking on the door and phone calls (Benjamin, 1969). Beier & Young (1998), in their classic book on therapeutic communication, *The Silent Language of Psychotherapy,* make the point that a helper communicates the importance he or she places on the relationship by the way in which these distractions are handled. If you were a client, how would you feel if I answered the phone during our sessions and ate a bag of potato chips? What would you conclude?

Schmoozing

Schmoozing is a Yiddish word that is nearly the equivalent of our English phrase "shooting the breeze." It refers to discussions between the client and the helper that are merely social and apparently unrelated to the client's problems. However, schmoozing has value at some points in the therapeutic relationship: It allows for a truly human encounter between client and helper. Sometimes the client is curious about the helper's personal life. Where this curiosity does not endanger the helper's safety and privacy, schmoozing can help client and helper develop a better relationship. At other times, useful information about the client's hobbies and special abilities comes to light in this way. Schmoozing is too easily abused to be encouraged wholesale. Like story telling and self-disclosure, it may place too much focus on the helper rather than on the client. Schmoozing puts helping on a social level and, if overused, may distract us from the major purpose of the session, which is to help the client find solutions.

Therapeutic Faux Pas

Faux pas is a French term meaning "false steps" or "wrong turns." It is better to think of faux pas not as mistakes, but as detours that can be corrected later.

The Therapeutic Relationship
61

Thomas Gordon (1986) identified 12 such "wrong turns," known as the "dirty dozen," that may occur in the development of a helping relationship. These are listed—with examples—in Table 3.2.

Gordon feels that there are two general messages communicated by the 12 roadblocks. First, they communicate that the client is incapable of solving his or her own

Table 3.2
Roadblocks to Communication

1. **Ordering, Directing, Commanding**
   You must do this.
   You cannot do this.
   I expect you to do this.
   Stop it.
   Go apologize to her.
2. **Warning, Admonishing, Threatening**
   You had better do this, or else . . .
   If you don't do this, then . . .
   You better not try that.
   I warn you, if you do that . . .
3. **Moralizing, Preaching, Imploring**
   You should do this.
   You ought to try it.
   It is your responsibility to do this.
   It is your duty to do this.
   I wish you would do this.
   I urge you to do this.
4. **Advising, Giving Suggestions or Solutions**
   What I think you should do is . . .
   Let me suggest . . .
   It would be best for you if . . .
   Why not take a different approach?
   The best solution is . . .
5. **Persuading with Logic, Lecturing, Arguing**
   Do you realize that . . .
   The facts are in favor of . . .
   Let me give you the facts.
   Here is the right way.
   Experience tells us that . . .
6. **Judging, Criticizing, Disagreeing, Blaming**
   You are acting foolishly.
   You are not thinking straight.
   You are out of line.
   You didn't do it right.
   You are wrong.
   That is a stupid thing to say.

7. **Praising, Agreeing, Evaluating Positively, Buttering Up**
   You usually have very good judgment.
   You are an intelligent person.
   You have so much potential.
   You've made quite a bit of progress.
   You have always made it in the past.
8. **Name-Calling, Ridiculing, Shaming**
   You are a sloppy worker.
   You are a fuzzy thinker.
   You're talking like an engineer.
   You really goofed on this one!
9. **Interpreting, Analyzing, Diagnosing**
   You're saying this because you're angry.
   You are jealous.
   What you really need is . . .
   You have problems with authority.
   You want to look good.
   You are being a bit paranoid.
10. **Reassuring, Sympathizing, Consoling, Supporting**
    You'll feel different tomorrow.
    Things will get better.
    It is always darkest before the dawn.
    Behind every cloud there's a silver lining.
    Don't worry so much about it.
    It's not that bad.
11. **Probing, Questioning, Interrogating**
    Why did you do that?
    How long have you felt this way?
    What have you done to try to solve it?
    Have you consulted with anyone?
    When did you become aware of this feeling?
    Who has influenced you?
12. **Distracting, Diverting, Kidding**
    Think about the positive side.
    Try not to think about it until you're rested.
    Let's have lunch and forget about it.
    That reminds me of the time when . . .
    You think you've got problems!

Source: Adapted from Gordon, T. (1986) *Leadership effectiveness training.* (pp. 60–62). New York: Random House.

problems. Second, they communicate that the client needs another person to solve the problem for him or her. Both are disempowering messages that take the responsibility for change away from the client and place it in the hands of the helper. Besides these 12 major detours, Wolberg (1967) has identified some other helper responses that can weaken or disrupt the therapeutic relationship. These include:

Exclamations of Surprise

Client: "I spanked the living daylights out of my kids last night."

Helpful: "What led you to do this?"

"You must have been really frustrated to have resorted to that. What other things might you have done?"

Not Helpful: "You what?!"

"That's awful!"

Being Punitive

Client: "I don't think that you are giving me the help I need."

Helpful: "You feel stuck, that you are not making any progress."

"What kind of help do you think would be useful to you at this time?"

Not Helpful: "Then I will just refer you to someone else."

"You are not making progress because you are not working on the problem."

Giving False Reassurance

Sometimes clients want us to give them hope that the helping process will be successful. This can backfire if the helper makes promises that cannot be kept.

Client: "Will I ever get over this completely and be normal?"

Helpful: "First, tell me how you would like your life to be. What would normal look like to you."

"Right now, you are feeling unsure about whether you can conquer this problem. I am hopeful that we can make a significant change if we work together."

Not Helpful: "Of course you will."

" I think that you are normal now!"

"You will be better in six weeks. I guarantee it."

Psychobabble and Premature Interpretations

Psychobabble is a word describing the overuse of psychological terminology. When the helper identifies a technical term for every issue, the client feels that his or her problems are trivialized or that they have become clinical syndromes. Premature interpretations is suggesting deep meanings before adequate data have been collected to support these interpretations.

Client: "My father was an alcoholic and my mother seemed to tolerate it. We lived in denial our whole lives."

Helpful: "Tell me more about what you mean by denial."

"Tell me something about your family relationships."

Not Helpful: "That's because your mother was co-dependent and that makes you ACOA (adult child of an alcoholic)."

"That is why you are a dependent personality."

Probing Traumatic Issues when the Client Strongly Resists

Respecting the client's wish to avoid a topic can be handled by noting it, reflecting, and suggesting that it can be put off until later. Damage to the relationship can take place when the helper mercilessly pursues a topic. It is often a question of timing. Sometimes it is best to nurture the relationship and address the topic later.

Client: "I don't want to talk about sex."

Helpful: "It is a painful subject for you."

"All right, we can come back to that another time if you want."

Not Helpful: "We have to talk about it sometime."

"Then, let's talk about your past sex life."

Transference and Countertransference

If we look closely at the relationship components and relationship consequences, in columns 2 and 3 of Table 3.1, we can see that as the relationship develops, a sort of intimacy grows. There is an openness, liking, respect, and trust that is being developed. This kind of therapeutic intimacy is generally seen as a positive state of agreement and mutual caring. It creates favorable conditions for change (Rogers, 1957) and increases client involvement and compliance with treatment.

However, intimacy also tends to elicit strong feelings—feelings that may have had their genesis in previous relationships. *Transference* and *countertransference* are terms that originated among psychoanalysts to denote these powerful feelings that develop when client and helper bond. As client and helper grow closer, a client may experience the same emotions of self-doubt, fear of abandonment, and other residue from parental or love relationships. This is the so-called *transference reaction.* On the other hand, the helper may also see the client as a reflection of a past or present relationship or may experience strong emotions for the client. This is called *countertransference.* When the helper finds that the client's progress is stymied by the relationship itself, the helper must be trained and willing to examine the therapeutic relationship itself as a living model of the client's social world. When the helper finds personal needs spilling over into the therapeutic setting, he or she needs to consult with a supervisor and deal with these issues privately.

Stop and Reflect

It is said that we make first impressions in less than four seconds. So, it is possible to experience transference reactions immediately on meeting an individual, that is, without having a close relationship. Most of us are familiar with automatic feelings of liking or disliking a person on sight. These emotional reactions are most likely due to experiences with a similar person in the past, and they may be vague and impressionistic, in other words, unreasonable. One simple way to categorize such reactions is to label them positive, neutral, or negative.

As an experiment, take a look around at your classmates and mentally note your feelings for each one—especially for those you have never met before this class or know only slightly. Write a one-word description of your emotional reaction or place a + or − next to each one to quantify your feelings. If there is neither attraction nor a negative feeling, write N for neutral. You may think that it is unfair to assign a value to your feelings without taking into account the fact that you do not really know all of your classmates well. That is true, but these impressions, like all first impressions, can be powerful. As mentioned earlier, we experience these first impressions within the first four seconds and act on them whether or not they are valid. Are there any real reasons for the positives and negatives you recorded? Are they the result of experiences with similar people? Think about the names of your classmates. Does any evoke an emotional reaction? If you had to choose two people in the class to play your parents in a role-play, whom would you choose? Are you transferring any of your experiences with your parents to these people in your other interactions?

What Is Transference?

Transference is a client's carryover of feelings from past relationships into a new one—the client/helper relationship. Relationship-building activities, such as listening and providing conditions of safety, increase feelings of intimacy and enhance the possibility of transference. Clients' feelings can be described as positive, ranging from liking to sexual attraction, or negative, ranging from suspiciousness to hatred (Watkins, 1986). Negative transference reactions are thought to be an important reason for treatment failures (Basch, 1980) because clients often drop out of therapy rather than face them.

Although it may be impossible to avoid transference altogether (Gelso and Carter, 1985), in many helping relationships, transference never endangers the relationship or the client's progress. For others, it is vital to examine the therapeutic relationship as a first step in setting other relationships straight. A client may experience such strong feelings toward the helper that they become a roadblock that must be overcome in order for treatment to continue. When issues of transference interfere with the attainment of goals, they must be dealt with, either in an isolated fashion or in conjunction with other relationship problems the client may be experiencing.

Psychodynamic Conceptions of Transference

Some believe that transference is caused by unfinished business from the past. This notion is central to psychoanalysis, which asserts that issues surface from the unconscious because they are unresolved. Freud believed that resolution of transference was the most important aspect of therapy because it allowed the client to address emotional issues about parents and siblings.

One alternative viewpoint that has emerged is to conceptualize transference as a set of cognitive distortions, rather than as unresolved conflicts or unfulfilled needs (Sullivan, 1954). These distortions are learned patterns of thinking, not unlike the irrational ideas that have been described by Albert Ellis (1985). Still, there is a common thread that binds the modern viewpoint to the psychoanalytic idea. In both conceptualizations, the client is seen as focused on the outside (external causes of behavior) versus the inside (self-direction). The client is thinking about the attributes of the helper, rather than focusing on self-awareness. Hero worship may even damage self-esteem if one compares oneself in a negative way to the helper (Singer, 1970).

To summarize, on the one hand, the client may have distorted ideas about the helper and the helping relationship that should be addressed. These may appear as inflated expectations about the helper, believing that he or she will solve all of the problems single-handedly. Alternately, the client may have strong negative feelings for the helper, especially when overblown expectations are not met. Watkins (1986) has identified five major transference patterns that are based on the concept of transference as cognitive distortion. Table 3.3, adapted from Watkins, shows these patterns along with the client's attitudes and the helper's reaction to them.

Countertransference: Dealing with the Helper's Feelings

Countertransference is defined as the helper's strong emotional reactions to a client. To give an example of this, consider this true story that a practicum student tells about one of her first clients:

> My client is a 35-year-old woman who owns her own business. She showed up for her first session five minutes late. When I came to the waiting room, she complained loudly that she had been waiting for 10 minutes and then followed me to my office in a huff. Although I was pretty sure that she had been late, not me, I was on the defensive from the beginning, and

Table 3.3
Major Transference Patterns

Client Behaviors/Attitudes	Counselor Experiences
Counselor as Ideal	
Compliments counselor profusely	Feels pride, satisfaction, and all-competent
Imitates counselor	
Wears similar clothing	Experiences tension, anxiety, confusion, anger, and frustration
General idealization	
Counselor as Seer	
Ascribes omniscience and power to the counselor	Experiences "God complex" and self-doubt
Views counselor as expert	
Sees self as incompetent	Feels incompetent and pressure to be right and live up to client's expectations
Seeks answers, solutions, and advice	
Counselor as Nurturer	
Experiences profuse emotion and sense of fragility	Experiences feelings of sorrow, sympathy, depression, despair, and depletion
Cries	
Feels dependent, helpless, and indecisive	Has urge to soothe, coddle, and touch
Desires to be touched and held	
Counselor as Frustrator	
Feels defensive, cautious, guarded, suspicious, and distrustful	Feels uneasy, on edge (walking on eggshells), tense, hostile, and hateful
Tests counselor	Withdraws and becomes unavailable
	Dislikes and blames client
Counselor as Nonentity	
Shifts topics	Feels overwhelmed, subdued, taken aback, used, useless
Lacks focus	
Is voluble and desultory	Experiences resentment, frustration, and lack of recognition
Meanders aimlessly	
	Characterizes self as a nonperson

I felt very uncomfortable and intimidated by her. As I watched the tape, I saw the many un-reasonable demands she made. For example, she said that she needed to change seats with me because there was too much glare in her eyes. She criticized the decorating and quizzed me about whether or not I had read the notes of the previous counselor. I watched myself on the tape just back down and become silent. I talked this over with my supervisor, who also noticed my passive behavior. I think that I reacted this way partially because this was my typical behavior with my previous boyfriend. Although he was not violent, he was ver-bally explosive and I learned to become quiet and back off during his rages. Now I am doing the same thing with this client.

As this story suggests, dealing with countertransference is not a skill utilized by the helper in the presence of the client. This is primarily an ethical and supervisory issue. However, because countertransference can seriously disrupt the client/helper bond, it merits discussion in this chapter on the therapeutic relationship.

Countertransference is an issue not fully appreciated by the beginning helper. When intellectualizing about the therapeutic relationship, one can hardly imagine the powerful feelings that some clients may elicit. In practice, helpers need ongoing supervision to monitor the tendency to be too helpful and to deal with feelings of sex-ual attraction, as well as fear and insecurity. Anger is one of the most common issues (Fremont & Anderson, 1986).

Some helpers try to deal with their own feelings simply by disclosing everything to the client. Such disclosure is a mistake if motivated by the helper's need to relieve his or her own discomfort: The therapeutic relationship is based on a contract that implicitly agrees that the helper should disclose information only if it is beneficial to the client. The therapeutic relationship is not a friendship, nor is it a two-way street. It involves a helper and the person being helped. The helper agrees to set his or her own needs aside and to do what is best for the client. Table 3.4 describes common helper emotional reactions, based on information collected by Corey, Corey, and Callanan (1988). The essential point apparent in the table is that countertransfer-ence issues are generally emotional reactions to clients, which can lead to certain be-haviors on the part of the helper. Instead of helping the client achieve mutually de-rived goals, the helper develops a second (you might say unconscious) agenda that changes the helper's view of the client as a contractual partner in the therapy process. The helper has come to see the client as a project, as a sexual object, as a friend, or even as a reflection of the self.

Countertransference is as common as transference, and most helpers regularly fall prey to these feelings. A great deal of the unethical behavior in which helpers in-dulge is probably due to the strong emotions elicited in the therapeutic relationship, which make us forget our "asocial," contractual role. This is one reason why a super-visory relationship is so crucial for every helper. The supervisor's role is to appeal to the helper's professional sense and to remind the helper to act in accordance with therapeutic goals.

Dealing with Transference from a Client

A client's strong emotional reactions to the helper may be the result of transference or may be honest reactions to the helper's behavior. In both cases, the task of the helper is the same: to help the client gain more awareness and to non-defensively ex-plore the source of these feelings. As an example, let us look briefly at how a helper can react therapeutically when a client expresses strong feelings of anger.

Table 3.4
Common Patterns of Countertransference

Counselor Emotional Response to Client	Counselor Behavior	Client Seen As
Paternal/maternal nurturing	Overprotective	Fragile
	Failure to challenge	
Fear of client's anger	Reduction of conflict	Aggressor
	Attempts to please	
Disgust, disapproval	Rejection	Needy
		Immoral
Need for reassurance	Socializing	Friend
Need for liking	Failure to challenge	
Anxiety	Avoidance of emotionally charged topics	
Insecurity		
Feelings of identification	Advice giving	Self
	Overinvolvement	
	Failure to recognize client's uniqueness	
Sexual	Seductive behavior	Sexual object
Romantic	Inappropriate self-disclosure	Romantic partner
	Reduced focus on presenting problems	
	Inappropriate exploration of sexual topics	
Frustration	Extreme confrontation	Product
Anger	Scolding	Success
	Criticizing	

Step 1: Convey acceptance of the client's remarks but don't retaliate.
Dealing with an angry client is one of the most difficult and delicate issues in helping. One reason is that it tends to evoke anger in the helper. Retaliation or a defensive response can be perceived by the client as a weakness, as an admission of guilt, or as a punishment. The client's anger may be triggered by frustration over lack of progress or by the perception that the helper is unfriendly, inept, or destructive. After having expressed this hostility, the client may be concerned about angering or hurting the helper or may fear abandonment.

Example:
Client: I don't think we're getting anywhere. When are we going to deal with the real issues? I'm sick of coming in here and paying all this money.
Helper: I can tell you're angry. I'm glad you had the courage to be so honest. I can't think of anything that will be of more help to you than dealing with this issue.

Step 2: Explore the client's feelings.   Following an expression of hostility toward the helper, the client may retreat, fearing punishment, losing control, or hurting the helper. Exploration of a client's hostile feelings involves continuing to encourage the expression and labeling of feelings while trying to clarify the source of the anger.

Example:
Client: I don't think this is working, and I am tired of coming in here and being told that it is all my fault.

Helper: What made you feel that it was all your fault?

or

Helper: Do you have the sense that I am blaming you for not changing?

or

Helper: You wish I would be more supportive.

Step 3. Use the experience to help the client to find new and better ways of expressing feelings and meeting his or her needs. If the helper can avoid blaming or shaming the client, the client's expressions of strong emotions such as anger can be used to examine the client's interpersonal life. Clients who exhibit excessive anger or who are indirect or revengeful may be alienating others and thereby engaging in self-defeating patterns. Dealing with transference by listening and exploring has the effect of making clients aware of these patterns, but they still may need assistance either individually or in a structured group to learn new and more productive ways of behaving.

Summary

In this chapter, we discussed the therapeutic relationship as a keystone in the process of change. In the stages of the helping relationship, the relationship is seen to empower all of the other activities that a helper uses to aid a client, including assessment, goal setting, intervention, and evaluation. There are a number of helper behaviors that can enhance the relationship, including nonverbals such as physical closeness, posture, and warmth. In addition, empathy, expertness and credibility, self-disclosure, and a good helper/client match can make the helping relationship stronger. The attribute of empathy was discussed in some detail because it seems to be a foundational skill, as well as an attitude that allows us to enter more deeply into relationships.

There are also issues and behaviors that can strain the budding alliance. Among these are the 12 roadblocks of Thomas Gordon, a number of therapeutic faux pas, a poor office environment, and the challenges of transference and countertransference.

Some time was taken in this chapter to deal with the issue of how to handle differences between client and helper when they seem to weaken the relationship. Extreme differences in culture, socioeconomic status, family background, and ethnic origin have their primary impact early in the session. Unless the therapeutic bond is forged quickly, there may be slow progress or clients may simply drop out. Although it may be impossible to cross all the barriers between people, because of the changing nature of our world, the helpers of tomorrow must possess the skills, knowledge, and attitudes that help them appreciate different people, different families, and different cultures.

One of the subtle points of this chapter is that a helping relationship is not a social relationship. It is more important that there be a working alliance than a friendship. The social skills of making clients feel comfortable, talking about the weather, and being a friendly person can reduce anxiety in the beginning stages, but the helping relationship should not be constrained by the social forces of politeness and cultural tendencies to avoid certain topics for fear of embarrassment or controversy. Entering a helping relationship requires you to boldly go where few have gone before, using the relationship as the fuel to explore more and more deeply into the mystery of another person.

Group Exercises

Group Exercise 1

Take a look at the list of six characteristics of a therapeutic relationship described in the beginning of this chapter. Compare a therapeutic relationship to a friendship or a relationship with a favorite teacher. What are the similarities and differences? Discuss this in a small group.

Group Exercise 2

Barriers to Communication

Divide into groups of three to five students. The instructor will assign each group one of Thomas Gordon's roadblocks in Table 3.2. (Roadblocks 4, 7, 10, and 12 are especially effective.) Each group is to put together a presentation that demonstrates its roadblock to the class in a role play between a helper and a client and then show helper behaviors that could enhance the relationship in that situation. Following each demonstration, the class can discuss the effects of the roadblock on the helping relationship. It is especially useful for the "clients" to describe what it felt like when the helper used one of these roadblocks.

Additional Exercises

Exercise 1: Case Study

In a small group, read and discuss the following example:

Ricardo is a counselor in private practice. The following is his discussion of a client who was referred for counseling by her family physician when she came to the medical office crying and needing to talk.

> The client began the therapeutic relationship with much enthusiasm and high expectations for achieving her goals. She was a 23-year-old only child who felt that she could not maintain a serious relationship. After a few weeks, her enthusiasm waned and she expressed disappointment in me as a helper. By this time, enough assessment had been done to identify this denouement as being similar to her history of intimate relationships. She began relationships with an idealized picture of her boyfriends and then was quickly disappointed. She came to the session one day indicating that she was angry that I had not been able to give her an earlier session. During her earlier phone call, she had said it was important but not urgent that she see me soon. She admitted that she expected me to know how upset she was and to set up an emergency appointment. When we examined our relationship, the client was able to pick out several times when she left hints and clues about her needs but failed to ask for things directly. I shared my feelings of surprise, being unaware of her real feelings. Naturally, this led to a discussion of how her behavior might have affected other relationships. It was a very significant insight when she realized that she was undermining relationships by her failure to send clear messages about her needs. In her case, this pattern of behavior could be traced back to her upbringing, which did not require that she state her needs and rewarded indirect suggestions. In therapy, she was able to learn some assertiveness skills and practice them in a group setting.

a. Do you think it was necessary to examine the client's past to help her with the problem in the helping relationship?
b. Is it possible that the client has a legitimate gripe and that Ricardo is "saving face" by making it the client's problem?
c. In a case such as this, how much responsibility should the helper take for the miscommunication about the client's needs. Would it have helped the client if the helper had apologized or assumed partial responsibility for the misunderstanding?

d. If you were Ricardo, how would you have handled the client's expression of anger?

Exercise 2

Part 1. Take a look at the common transference reactions in Table 3.3. Now, think back on the case of Alicia B. that introduced this chapter. Which of these reactions did she experience in her relationship with Jim?

Part 2. Have you ever experienced any of these feelings for someone in authority? Now, think for a moment about the concept of authority. You have probably heard it said that a person has "authority issues." How is this similar or different from a transference reaction discussed in this chapter? Discuss your findings with a small group.

Homework

Homework 1

Make a list of your five favorite teachers from elementary school to present. List the traits or qualities of these persons. Identify any similarities. Are there also glaring differences? Now, contrast them with some teacher or learning situation that was either very unpleasant or simply unhelpful. What do these experiences say about how you like to learn? Based on your experiences with teachers, what kind of helper do you think might be the best fit for you? What kind of helper is likely to "push your buttons" and elicit some of the feelings you have had in previous helping relationships? Summarize your reactions to this exercise in two or three paragraphs.

Homework 2

One of the most common countertransference reactions is to feel sorry for a client and help them too much. Another reaction is strong feelings of attraction for a client. Research the ethical codes of one of the helping professions. What guidelines can help you determine ethical action in such situations? In each case, what could be harmful about this particular countertransference reaction? In two or three paragraphs, discuss how you would handle each of the two situations, ethically and therapeutically.

Journal Starters

Remember that starters are designed to warm you up to the issues. You may take them in whatever direction you like. You need not answer all of them if they distract you from an important thought or stop the flow of ideas.

1. Think for a moment about an important friendship in your life; reflect on the ups and downs in the relationship and the stages that the relationship has gone through. What is it that makes this relationship special?
2. Consider the topic of anger in your journal. Look back over the past few months and think about times that anger has surfaced

in your life. Now, reflect about the ways in which anger was expressed in your family. Have there been times when anger has caused significant problems in your relationships? Has suppressing your needs and trying to be a "nice person" always been helpful? How do you think that you might deal with a client's anger as a helper? What about your own feelings of anger when they arise in the helping session?

For more journal ideas, as well as more practice with the therapeutic relationship, refer to Chapter 3 in *Exercises in the Art of Helping*.

References

Abadie, P. (1986). *A study of interpersonal communication processes in the supervision of counseling.* Unpublished doctoral dissertation, Kansas State University, Manhattan.

Abramowitz, S. I., & Abramowitz, C. V. (1976). Sex role psychodynamics in psychotherapy supervision. *American Journal of Psychotherapy, 30,* 583–592.

Alderton, S. M., & Jurma, W. E. (1980). Genderless/gender-related task leader communication and group satisfaction: A test of two hypotheses. *Southern Speech Communication Journal, 46,* 48–60.

Allen, G. J., Szollos, S. J., & Williams, B. E. (1986). Doctoral students' comparative evaluations of best and worst psychotherapy supervision. *Professional Psychology: Research and Practice, 17*(2), 91–99.

Atkinson, D. R., Poston, W. C., Furlong, M. J., & Mercado, P. (1989). Ethnic group preferences for counselor characteristics. *Journal of Counseling Psychology, 36,* 68–72.

Bannikotes, P. G., Kubinski, J. A., & Purcell, S. A. (1981). Sex role orientation, self-disclosure, and gender related perceptions. *Journal of Counseling Psychology, 28,* 140–146..

Barak, A., Patkin, J., & Dell, D. M. (1982). Effects of certain client behaviors in perceived expertness and attractiveness. *Journal of Counseling Psychology, 29,* 261–267.

Basch, M. F. (1980). *Doing psychotherapy.* New York: Basic Books.

Beier, E., & Young, D. M. (1998). *The silent language of psychotherapy: Social reinforcement of unconscious processes.* Chicago: Aldine de Gruyter.

Belkin, G. S. (1980). *Introduction to counseling* (2nd ed.). New York: Brown.

Bem, S. L. (1975). Sex-role adaptability: One consequence of psychological androgyny. *Journal of Personality and Social Psychology, 31,* 634–643.

Benjamin, A. (1969). *The helping interview.* Boston: Houghton Mifflin.

Block, J. H. (1973). Conceptions of sex role: Some cross-cultural and longitudinal perspectives. *American Psychologist, 28,* 512–526.

Broverman, I. K., Vogel, S. R., Broverman, D. M., Clarkson, F. E., & Rosenkrantz, P. S. (1972). Sex-role stereotypes: A current appraisal. *Journal of Social Issues, 28,* 59–78.

Campbell, J., & Witmer, J. M. (1991). *Working with special populations: Guidelines for treatment and counselor education.* Unpublished manuscript.

Cavanagh, M. E. (1982). *The counseling experience.* Monterey, CA: Brooks/Cole.

Corey, G., Corey, M. S., & Callanan, P. (1988). *Issues and ethics in the helping professions* (3rd ed.). Monterey, CA: Brooks/Cole.

Corrigan, J. D., Dell, D. M., Lewis, K. N., & Schmidt, L. D. (1980). Counseling as a social influence process: A review. *Journal of Counseling Psychology, 27,* 395–441.

Covey, S. (1990). *The seven habits of highly effective people: Powerful lessons in personal change.* New York: Fireside.

Devoe, D. (1990). Feminist and nonsexist counseling: Implications for the male counselor. *Journal of Counseling and Development, 69,* 33–36.

Elkind, S. N. (1992). *Resolving impasses in therapeutic relationships.* New York: Guilford.

Ellis, A. (1985). *Overcoming resistance: Rational-emotive therapy with difficult clients.* New York: Springer.

Fiedler, F. E. (1950). The concept of an ideal therapeutic relationship. *Journal of Consulting Psychology, 14,* 239–245.

Fine, R. (1975). *Psychoanalytic psychology.* New York: Jason Aronson.

Frank, J. D. (1961). *Persuasion and healing.* Baltimore: Johns Hopkins University Press.

Fremont, S., & Anderson, W. P. (1986). What client behaviors make counselors angry? An exploratory study. *Journal of Counseling and Development, 65,* 67–70.

Freudenberger, H. J. (1990). Therapists as men and men as therapists. *Psychotherapy, 27*(3), 340–343.

Fromm-Reichmann, F. (1960). *Principles of intensive psychotherapy.* Chicago: University of Chicago Press.

Gelso, C. J., & Carter, J. A. (1985). The relationship in counseling and psychotherapy: Components, consequences and theoretical antecedents. *Counseling Psychologist, 13,* 155–243.

Goleman, D. (1995). *Emotional intelligence: Why it can matter more than IQ.* New York: Bantam.

Good, G. E., Dell, D. M., & Mintz, L. B. (1989). Male role and gender role conflict: Relations to help seeking in men. *Journal of Counseling Psychology, 36*(3), 295–300.

Gordon, T. (1986). *Leadership effectiveness training, L.E.T.: The no-lose way to release the productive potential of people.* New York: Bantam.

Granello, D. (1999). *Gender issues in counseling.* Unpublished manuscript, The Ohio State University.

Heilbrun, A. B. (1976). Measurement of masculine and feminine sex role identities as independent dimensions. *Journal of Consulting and Clinical Psychology, 44,* 183–190.

Heppner, P. P., & Dixon, D. N. (1986). A review of the interpersonal influence process in counseling. In W. P. Anderson (Ed.), *Innovative counseling: A handbook of readings* (pp. 8–16). Alexandria, VA: American Association for Counseling and Development.

Johnson, D. W., & Matross, R. (1977). Interpersonal influence in psychotherapy: A social psychological view. In A. S. Gurman & A. M. Razin (Eds.), *Effective psychotherapy: A handbook of research* (pp. 395–432). Elmsford, NY: Pergamon.

Johnson, J. A. (1990). Empathy as a personality disposition. In R. C. Mckay, J. R. Hughes, & E. J. Carver (Eds.), *Empathy in the helping relationship* (pp. 49–64). New York: Springer.

Jourard, S. (1971). *The transparent self.* New York: Van Nostrand Reinhold.

Kanfer, F. H., & Goldstein, A. P. (1986). Introduction. In F. Kanfer & A. Goldstein, (Eds.)*Helping people change: A textbook of methods.* New York: Pergamon.

Kell, B. L., & Mueller, W. J. (1966). *Impact and change: A study of counseling relationships.* Upper Saddle River, NJ: Prentice Hall.

Knox, S., Hess, S., Petersen, D., & Hill, C. E. (1997). A qualitative analysis of client perceptions of the effects of helpful therapist self-disclosure in long-term therapy. *Journal of Counseling Psychology, 44,* 274–283.

Kopp, S. (1978). *If you meet the Buddha on the road, kill him!* New York: Bantam Books.

Kottler, J. A., & Blau, D. S. (1989). *The imperfect therapist.* San Francisco: Jossey-Bass.

Lambert, M. J. (1986). Implications of psychotherapy outcome research for eclectic psychotherapy. In

J. C. Norcross (Ed.), *Handbook of eclectic psychotherapy* (pp. 436–462). New York: Brunner/Mazel.

Loesch, L. (1984). Professional credentialing in counseling. *Counseling and Human Development, 17,* 1–11.

Maccoby, E. E., & Jacklin, C. N. (1974). *The psychology of sex differences.* Stanford, CA: Stanford University Press.

McCarthy, P. (1982). Differential effects of counselor self-referent responses and counselor status. *Journal of Counseling Psychology, 29,* 125–131.

Meadow, A. (1982). Psychopathology, psychotherapy and the Mexican-American patient. In E. E. Jones & S. J. Korchin (Eds.), *Minority mental health* (pp. 331–362). New York: Praeger.

Nelson, M. L. (1993). A current perspective on gender differences: Implications for research in counseling. *Journal of Counseling Psychology, 40*(2), 200–209.

Nilsson, D., Strassberg, D., & Bannon, J. (1979). Perceptions of counselor self-disclosure: An analog study. *Journal of Counseling Psychology, 26,* 399–404.

Parker, W. M. (1988). Becoming an effective multicultural counselor. *Journal of Counseling and Development, 67,* 93.

Pearson, J. C., West, R. L., & Turner, L. H. (1995). *Gender and communication* (3rd ed.). Dubuque, IA: Brown & Benchmark Publishers.

Pedersen, P. B. (1987). Ten frequent assumptions of cultural bias in counseling. *Journal of Multicultural Counseling and Development, 14,* 16–24.

Pietrofesa, J. J., Hoffman, A., & Splete, H. H. (1984). *Counseling: An introduction.* Boston: Houghton Mifflin.

Robbins, J. H. (1983). Complex triangles: Uncovering sexist bias in relationship counseling. *Women and Therapy, 2*(2–3), 159–169.

Rogers, C. R. (1957). The necessary and sufficient conditions of therapeutic personality change. *Journal of Consulting Psychology, 21,* 95–103.

Rogers, C. R. (1972). Client-centered therapy. In J. Huber & H. Millman (Eds.), *Goals and behavior in psychotherapy and counseling* (pp. 117–141). Columbus, OH: Merrill.

Scher, M., & Stevens, M. (1987). Men and violence. *Journal of Counseling and Development, 65,* 351–354.

Sermat, V., & Smythe, M. (1973). Content analysis of verbal communication in the development of a relationship: Conditions influencing self-disclosure. *Journal of Personality and Social Psychology, 26,* 332–346.

Singer, E. (1970). *Key concepts in psychotherapy* (2nd ed.). New York: Basic Books.

Sue, D. W. (1981). *Counseling the culturally different: Theory and practice.* New York: Wiley.

Sue, S., & McKinney, H. (1975). Asian Americans in the community mental health care system. *American Journal of Orthopsychiatry, 45,* 111–118.

Sue, S., & Zane, N. (1987). The role of culture and cultural techniques in psychotherapy. *American Psychologist, 42,* 37–45.

Sullivan, H. S. (1954). *The psychiatric interview.* New York: Norton.

Taylor, M. (1994). Gender and power in counselling and supervision. *British Journal of Guidance and Counselling, 22* (3), 319–326.

Watkins, C. E., Jr. (1986). Transference phenomena in the counseling situation. In W. P. Anderson (Ed.), *Innovative counseling: A handbook of readings.* Alexandria, VA: American Association of Counseling and Development.

Watkins, C. E., Jr. (1990). The effects of counselor self-disclosure: A research review. *Counseling Psychologist, 18,* 477–500.

Weiner, M. F. (1979). *Therapist disclosure: The use of self in psychotherapy.* Boston: Butterworth Press.

Wohl, J. (1995). Traditional individual psychotherapy and ethnic minorities. In J. F. Aponte, R. Y. Rivers, & J. Wohl (Eds.), *Psychological interventions and cultural diversity* (pp. 74–91). Boston: Allyn & Bacon.

Wolberg, L. R. (1967). *The technique of psychotherapy* (2nd ed.). New York: Grune & Stratton.

Workman, W. J. (1993). Relationship of counselor variables to preference for type of response in counseling. *Counselor Education and Supervision, 32,* 178–188.

Yalom, I. (1985). *Theory and practice of group psychotherapy.* New York: Basic Books.

Young, M. E., & Long, L. L. (1998) *Counseling and therapy for couples: An integrative approach.* Pacific Grove, CA: Brooks/Cole.

Invitational Skills

4

Yes, there is no doubt that paper is patient and as I don't intend to show this cardboard covered notebook . . . to anyone, unless I find a real friend, boy or girl, probably nobody cares. And now I come to the root of the matter, the reason for my diary: it is that I have no such real friend.

Anne Frank
(in Moffat & Painter, 1974, p. 15)

The entry in Anne Frank's diary that introduces this chapter reminds us of the great human need to be understood and to communicate. This need has been met in various ways through the ages such as through journaling and diaries, in religious confessionals, through confiding friendships, and by prayer. Last, but not least, the therapeutic relationship, described in the previous chapter, is specifically designed to invite the client to communicate openly by providing a nonthreatening atmosphere with the safeguards of confidentiality. The act of disclosing is a great relief and is the first step in the healing process.

James Pennebaker is the author of some of the most interesting research on the benefits of self-disclosure and confession (1989). He became interested in the phenomenon while talking to polygraph operators who gave lie detector tests to people suspected of crimes. These technicians told him stories of suspects who admitted their guilt under questioning and who even thanked the operators. Some operators said they had even received Christmas cards from some of those they helped to convict! Pennebaker found in his own research that college students who regularly wrote diaries about their most troubling experiences showed better immune-system responses and better health. Pennebaker's work exemplifies a growing body of evidence that opening up is good for the soul *and* the body.

Pennebaker's work underlines the fact that when clients come for help, they are seeking to explain themselves to a nonjudgmental listener (Pennebaker, 1990). Clients want to untangle the knots of traumas, miscalculations, and resentments that are troubling them. However, they do not simply want absolution; they desire to understand how things got so mixed up and how to deal with the unfinished business. The therapeutic relationship can provide the opportunity to heal the body and the mind if the helper can get out of the way and allow the client to open up and investigate all the nooks and crannies of the problem.

In this chapter, you will learn and practice the first building block: invitational skills. They include nonverbal skills and opening skills (see Table 4.1). Using these skills will allow you to convey to clients that you are listening to them and that you are concerned. Clients respond to this atmosphere by opening up and exploring their problems more fully. The invitational skills are especially useful early on in the helping session when they do not interfere with the client's recitation of the story. However, these skills are used throughout the entire helping process, session after session, as the helper listens to the client relate his or her progress, setbacks, and new problems as they emerge.

Listening to the Client's Story

Is there such a thing as "therapeutic listening?" Is it possible that merely giving someone your full attention is healing in and of itself? Some writers have called this *active listening,* a way of attending and encouraging without intruding on the client's telling of the story. A client's story can create tremendous pressure on the listener. We want to help, have an impact, and create a change. This tendency is what prompts friends to offer quick advice. Frequently, however, the best approach in the professional helping relationship is to allow clients to describe fully a situation to you and to themselves before jumping into an instant solution. If you think about it, the client has probably heard a lot of advice already. What makes you think that your ideas are likely to be any better than a close friend's? It is through listening to the client's story that client and helper are able to find the keys to change, not by attempting to solve the problem in the first few minutes.

Table 4.1
The Building Blocks for Invitational Skills

Nonverbal Skills	
Nonverbal skills are the use of attentive silence, eye contact, appropriate voice tone, body position, and nonverbal encouragers such as head nodding or hand gestures that invite the client to talk.	

Nonverbal Skill	Example
Eye contact	Direct eye contact with occasional breaks for client comfort
Facilitative body position	"Open" attentive body position, squarely facing the client
Appropriate use of silence	Allowing the client to fill in the "voids" in the conversation
Voice tone	Using a voice tone that reflects the client's and is appropriate in volume and rate and shows warmth and support
Gestures	Encouraging the client to open up with appropriate gestures and head nodding.

Opening Skills	
Opening skills are verbal encouragers. They ask the client to explore a little deeper but are not very invasive. They also reassure the client that you are following the story.	

Opening Skill	Example
Door opener	"Say some more about that."
Minimal encourager	"Uh, huh," "Okay," "Say some more"
Open question	"Could you tell me what has been going on?"
Closed question	"Is she your ex-wife?"

Therapists such as Sheldon Kopp (1978) have emphasized the importance of clients' "telling their tales." The tale is a full recitation of the problem from the client's unique perspective. It is the client's "story." Michael White, the Australian therapist, describes it as a "narrative." Hidden in each client's story are the keys to understanding how that person views the world. Helpers who take the time to let the client's story unfold will design helping interventions that fit the unique client and his or her special worldview.

Stop and Reflect

Many beginning helpers get stuck because they feel that they have heard the whole story in the first five minutes. They become nervous because they think that if they spend more time listening, they will end up covering old ground. They also anticipate the client's unspoken question, "What should I do?"

Consider the first few minutes of this actual counseling session between a thirty-year-old African American woman, Tia, and her counselor Renee. Tia is living with her mother and her four-year-old son.

"My mother wants everything done her way. I can't do anything right, even with my son. For example, I have to call her at the end of today's session and let her know I came. She thinks I need counseling. But really I just need to her to get off my back. I have a job possibility and it's walking distance from home. But my mother thinks that it doesn't pay enough. But I have to start somewhere and I think I would like it. If it weren't for her, I would probably be living on the street. But when I try to get more independent, it's like she doesn't want me to. There are so many things I want to do. I want to go to school, have my own place, but she just won't let me."

After the session, Renee met with her supervisor, Marcy, to discuss the case:

Renee: "I had a hard time in the session because I just wanted to tell her to take the job and move out. I also wanted to agree with her that her mother is overbearing."

Marcy: "Do you know enough yet to make that kind of statement to her?"

Renee: "I guess not, but I wanted to help her figure out what to do."

Marcy: "Resist the temptation to intervene until you know more about the situation and about her."

Renee: "So I just listen? For how long?"

- As you look back at Tia, what more would you like to know about her before you feel that you have enough information to help?
- What cultural, family, and religious factors are in the background of this client's story? How important are these things in understanding the client? What assumptions have you already made about Tia based on her background? How can you test them?
- In this situation, would you be tempted to find ways for the client to change her mother? Would you, like Renee, be tempted to give advice?
- Why is Marcy cautioning Renee to listen more? What other issues does Tia have besides her mother?
- What parts of Tia's story would you like to hear more about? Why do you think that would be helpful?
- What specific issues does Tia need to address in herself? Would encouraging her to take a job or move from her mother's house solve her problems?

Like Tia, some clients will open the floodgates of the story during the first session, pausing only to take a breath and perhaps ignoring most of the helper's comments. It often seems that a client wants to get the story told as completely as possible before he or she will allow the helper to make an intervention. For others, it is a grueling process as the client's story is extracted drop by drop. In either case, the role of the helper *seems* passive, waiting for the client to finish the tale. Actually, the helper is listening with full attention so as to understand the facts, the feelings, and the unique perspective of the client. Many client stories are as ironic and full of twists and turns as a Shakespearean comedy or tragedy. You cannot make a comment that a client will respect until you know the names of all the players and their relationships. It is difficult for many beginning helpers to listen to all of these details. They cannot see where the story is going, and their own personal anxiety and desire to help propel them to fall back on the skills they have used all of their life: praise and advice giving. The art of helping, however, requires the helper to place his or her own concerns on the back burner and to focus on the client's story, waiting until all the wrinkles have been explored.

Nonverbal Skills: Sending the Right Message as a Helper

Nonverbal communication is body language. We generally talk about seven categories: eye contact, body position, silence, voice tone, attentive facial expressions and gestures, physical distance, and touching. If we think about it, it is obvious that these nonverbals can add additional information to messages, but we often fail to recognize their power. Some writers have suggested that as much as 80% of communication takes place on the nonverbal level. Where emotions are concerned, nonverbals are even more important. For example, the difference between a written letter from a family member and his or her voice on the phone illustrates that most communication about emotions is nonverbal. It has been estimated that only 7% of emotions are conveyed by verbal means, whereas 38% are conveyed by the voice and 55% by the face (Mehrabian, 1972).

Nonverbals can be compared to the musical score in a movie. They can affect us tremendously, but we rarely notice their presence. For example, researchers studying couples communication were at first confused when they examined written transcripts of troubled marriages. Everything appeared normal. It was not until they watched the videotapes that they were able to see the subtle nonverbal signals of contempt such as "rolling of the eyes." Even very minor movements and expressions can set off an argument. For example, it has been found that a raised eyebrow takes only a sixth of a second but it can be detected at distances of over 150 feet (Blum, 1998).

A clue to the importance of nonverbal communication in daily life is illustrated by the fact that many important decisions are handled "in person." For example, we have a friend who spends thousands of dollars each year traveling to local offices of her company scattered around the state. If communication simply consisted of an exchange of words or data, all of her business could be transacted by e-mail, telephone, or written correspondence, but, in fact, these approaches are only the "next best thing to being there." To communicate fully, you have to be face to face. Think about the difference between telling a friend that you are concerned, then really communicating it by placing an arm around his or her shoulder.

There are many situations in life that require us to interact without all of the nonverbal clues; it is then that we become aware of their vital role in getting the message across. Have you ever participated in a conference call on the telephone? In face-to-face conversations, cues about when to speak and when to listen are communicated nonverbally. Without access to these signals, everyone talks at once or there are long periods of silence.

Nonverbal communication is also a powerful component of persuasion. The gestures and voice tone of famous orators such as Martin Luther King are evidence of this. Certainly the most persuasive communication takes place when we can see another person's face and when we are in the same room. It is much easier to say no to the salesperson on the phone than to the one who is standing right in front of you. The art of helping also relies on persuasive nonverbal messages to encourage the client to open up. Helpers use specific nonverbal behaviors to communicate listening, attention, openness, and safety.

Nonverbal Skills in the Helping Relationship

One maxim says that you can't *not* communicate. Our bodies are not very good liars (Archer & Akert, 1977). Folded arms and drooping facial muscles tend to give us away. Astute helpers learn to read the body language of their clients as clues to the depth and meaning of the client's problems. However, helpers must be aware of the signals that they are sending, too. The client is interpreting and reacting to the nonverbal messages of the helper. Clients react to helper nonverbals from the very first contact by voice tone on the phone and even by the arrangement of the office where client and helper meet.

This discussion brings up an important caution about nonverbal messages. They are *ambiguous.* A client whose voice seems monotonous and depressed may actually be suffering from a cold. Crossed arms may be a better signal that the air conditioning is too high than that the client is "closed." Because of the ambiguous nature of nonverbal communication, most helpers are cautious about interpreting a client's posture, facial expressions, or voice tone, or about drawing serious conclusions about a client's mental state from a single piece of data. On the other hand, we have no control over what conclusions clients may draw from inadvertent nonverbal signals that we as helpers send. For this reason, from the beginning, helpers try to present the most welcoming, nonthreatening, and facilitative nonverbals that encourage the client to talk and do not interfere with the client's telling of the story.

Eye Contact

Eye-to-eye contact is the first and most important indicator of listening. It conveys the helper's confidence and involvement (Ridley & Asbury, 1988). In Western culture, we normally associate lack of eye contact with dishonesty, indifference, or shame. One should also be cautious in making assumptions about eye contact made by clients from different cultural backgrounds. For example, some African American clients may have been trained to look away when listening (LaFrance & Mayo, 1976).

The helper uses a moderate amount of eye contact to communicate attention. Eye contact implies that the client and helper are sitting at the same level and facing each other squarely. Remember, however, that a fixed stare can be disconcerting and should be broken naturally and intermittently if the client becomes uncomfortable. Even more care needs to be taken when dealing with Asians and others who may be offended by direct eye contact. In some situations such as the military and with some cultural groups, direct eye contact can be considered an act of defiance, rude gesture, a sexual invitation, or a sign that you consider yourself to be superior. A rule of thumb is to maintain a moderate amount of eye contact while closely monitoring its effect on the client. If cultures seem to clash, it might be useful to discuss this with the client. Depending on the situation, it might be best merely to respect the client's own way of using eye contact and try and mirror it. Bringing it up might instead be distracting and make the client feel overly self-conscious.

Body Position

Actions speak louder than words. Posture may be the most often noticed aspect of body language, so it becomes important to have a "posture of involvement." A relaxed alertness communicates, "I am comfortable with myself and I have time to listen to you." A relaxed and attentive posture is one of the fundamental tools for putting the client at ease (Maurer & Tindall, 1983). Lounging or sprawling in the chair might add an air of informality, but it may also communicate that the level of the helper's involvement is minimal. It is suggested that the helper lean *slightly* forward because leaning forward conveys attentiveness. Helpers normally maintain an open posture— no crossed arms or legs. Open postures seem to relax the client and encourage less defensiveness.

Attentive Silence

In social settings, it is considered vital to keep the conversation flowing. A deadly silence is a disaster at a party, but helping does not follow the same rules. Allowing for small periods of silence gives the client moments for reflection and the helper time for processing. Silence is often the most appropriate response to a client's disclosure of loss. Words often seem somehow to deny the validity of a person's grief or are perceived as attempts to sweep feelings under the rug. At these times, the helper falls back on attentive silence in order to be present without interfering. Finally, the most powerful use of silence is to nudge the client to disclose. When there is a gap in the conversation, there is a pressure to talk to fill in the void. If the helper is able to endure this discomfort, brief periods of silence may prompt the client to open up more.

Voice Tone

A client's voice can give clues to his or her emotional state. We can tell from the client's voice which issues are the most painful and the sources of the greatest motivation and excitement. Similarly, clients respond to the helper's voice tone. Helpers attempt to show calm concern and empathy with their voices. In addition, they try to mirror the client's emotional tone. The helper does not try to *match* the intensity of the client's feelings but, instead, raises the voice slightly or gives emphasis to words that give the client the message that the importance of his or her experience has been understood. For example, suppose a client describes a situation in which he or she did not get an expected promotion. The helper may respond to the client's situation by saying, "You were really angry," or "You were *really* angry." In the second sentence, the helper's voice tone emphasized the word, *really* to reflect the intense feelings.

Facial Expressions and Gestures

All human beings express the six primary emotions of sadness, joy, anger, surprise, disgust, and fear with the same basic facial expressions regardless of culture (Ekman, 1975). However, human beings can also discern about 5,000 different facial expressions, many of which are culturally specific (Blum, 1998). Helpers pay close attention to facial expressions to see if these signals match the clients' words. Incongruities are clues to lack of self-awareness and conflict.

Originally, Freudian analysts were trained to avoid reacting to the client's expressions of emotion. By contrast, those trained in the client-centered approach of Carl Rogers felt that gestures and facial expressions by the helper should be genuine responses to the client. Facial expressions that convey the helper's reactions to the client's joy or sadness, anger or fear, excitement or boredom can serve as invitations to greater disclosure (Fretz, Corn, Tuemmler, & Bellet, 1979; Maurer & Tindall, 1983).

Gestures are communication tools we use to convey emotion or emphasize important points. At the two extremes, excessive movement may signal anxiety, whereas a motionless statue-like pose communicates aloofness. Fidgeting, playing with a pencil, drumming fingers, frequent shifting of body position, checking a watch, and other such movements can be read by the client as nervousness, impatience, or disinterest. The listener who is moderately reactive to the client's content and affect is more likely to be viewed as friendly, warm, casual, and natural. Specifically, this includes occasional head nodding for encouragement, a facial expression that indicates concern and interest, and encouraging movements of the hands that are not distracting.

Physical Distance

One's personal space or "bubble" varies considerably from culture to culture. You may have noticed that people from Northern Europe require more space during a conversation than do Southern Europeans or Middle Easterners. It has been said that some Italians, for example, are perfectly comfortable with a conversation that is almost nose to nose (4 inches or less).

Most one-on-one dialogues among Americans take place at a distance of 1 to 4 feet. Normally, about 3 feet is a comfortable space for personal interaction. In general, the smaller the physical distance, the more personal the interaction. Physical barriers such as desks increase distance and add a feeling of formality to the relationship. On the other hand, extremely close quarters can also feel intimidating and create anxiety. Stone and Morden (1976) suggest 5 feet (knee-to-knee sitting down) as an optimal distance between client and helper. Many helpers like to set up office chairs at about this distance, allowing the client to rearrange the chair in a comfortable way if it feels too close or too distant.

Touching

Touch has a long history in the helping professions, dating back to Freud's "pressure technique," which involved placing a hand on the client's forehead to encourage free association (Smith, Clance, & Imes, 1998). Although there is much to be said for the healing power of the human touch, certain taboos must be observed (Goodman & Teicher, 1988; Hunter & Struve, 1997). Touch can communicate caring and concern, especially during moments of grief (Driscoll, Newman, & Seals, 1988). Willison and Masson (1986) contend that research supports the appropriate use of touch, which can have a positive impact on clients. Holroyd and Brodsky (1980) recommend touch with socially immature clients to foster communication and bonding and with clients who are grieving, depressed, or traumatized as a way of showing support. They also encourage the use of touch as a greeting or at termination. In addition, touch may be used to emphasize or underline important points (Older, 1982).

Touch can also engender powerful sexual and transference reactions in the client (Alyn, 1988). For a client who has been sexually abused, a good deal of anxiety may be aroused and any kind of touch might be inappropriate (Hunter & Struve, 1997). Perhaps fears about physical contact are overblown in the literature, but many writers have cautioned that it is important to know the client well before initiating even the safest forms of touch, such as a pat on the shoulder or back. One guideline is to use touch only sparingly to communicate encouragement and concern, with the knowledge that even slight gestures may evoke sexual or fearful feel-

Table 4.2

Nonverbal Cue	Warmth	Coldness
Tone of voice	Soft	Hard
Facial expression	Smiling, interested	Poker-faced, frowning, uninterested
Posture	Lean toward other; relaxed	Lean away from other; tense
Eye contact	Look into other's eyes	Avoid looking into other's eyes
Touching	Touch other softly	Avoid touching other
Gestures	Open, welcoming	Closed, guarding oneself, and keeping other away
Spatial distance	Close	Distant

Source: David W. Johnson, *Reaching Out: Interpersonal Effectiveness and Self-Actualization,* 7/e, Copyright 2000. Reprinted with permission of Allyn and Bacon.

ings in the client. The helper must be prepared to recognize this reaction in the client and be willing to discuss it.

Fisher, Rytting, and Heslin (1976) established three useful guidelines for helper touch: (1) Touch should be appropriate to the situation, (2) touch should not impose a greater level of intimacy than the client can handle, and (3) touch should not communicate a negative message (such as a patronizing pat). It must be recognized here that there is a "pro-hug" school of thought among some helpers. A hug may be a special gesture at the end of the counseling relationship, but it may be experienced as forced intimacy when used routinely. An embrace may be seen as phony, and the helper may actually be seen as less trustworthy (Suiter & Goodyear, 1985).

Although touch has its dangers, the helper can still convey caring nonverbally by communicating warmth. Warmth is not a skill but a synthesis of nonverbal communications that can have a powerful effect on a client's willingness to open up. Warmth is difficult to define, but when it is present, we recognize it and respond by opening up. In Table 4.2, David Johnson (2000) shows how nonverbal messages can communicate either warmth or coldness.

Stop and Reflect

Differences in nonverbal communication can be a stumbling block in forming a relationship with someone from a different cultural background. We make assumptions about people based on the way they talk, look, or dress. In this section, Andrew Daire, who worked in a university counseling center, describes how talking about these perceived differences can lead to a better helping relationship and turn a negative first impression into a source of growth for helper and client.

> I was the only black counselor at a small, private, predominantly white institution in the South. Once I was called to the office to meet a new client named Ray. When I came downstairs, I saw a burly young man in western wear and cowboy boots who possessed a strong southern drawl. He seemed very guarded initially, which I attributed to his discomfort in talking about his relationship problems. Soon, I realized that we were not talking about the obvious differences between us, so I made the decision, to cautiously open a discussion about his upbringing and how it differed from my own.

During that first session, he talked about his father being a racist and then admitted that he had almost walked out the door when he saw that his counselor was black. Despite this first encounter, we were able to form a good counseling relationship and over the next nine sessions, we talked about his relationship issues as well as stereotypes and prejudice. When I saw my client for the first time, based on his clothing and accent, I expected him to be racist and I was tempted to pull back and not even address our differences. I now believe that treating him in that way would probably have reinforced his stereotypes and prejudice, rather than providing an opportunity for him to examine them. I also began to understand a little about the fears that drive the attitudes of people like Ray and his father. Most important, we were able to develop a relationship that helped him deal with the issues he had come to work on. Had I not brought up the impressions we shared of each other, he probably would not have come back after the first session.

- Have you ever thought about attitudes you might have about people from various parts of the country? Do certain accents lead you to make unfair assumptions about people? What do a New York, Appalachian, or English accent imply about someone?
- Have you ever thought of clothing as a form of communication? Clothing choice is a nonverbal that can be culturally influenced. Think about your own background. What customs can you identify in your own culture that help you decide what clothes to wear? Are certain colors best for certain occasions? Have you ever gone to a function and found that your dress is culturally inappropriate?
- What can you really tell about a person from his or her clothing? Is there a risk in "pigeonholing" people based on their clothing choice or the kind of car they drive?
- Think for a moment about your experience with people from different cultural backgrounds. Which cultural groups do you have the most experience with through friends or family? Which groups do you know the least about? How important do you think it is for a helper to experience a variety of cultural groups during his or her training? Do you think it is possible for a helper to cross over cultural lines, as Andrew did, and help someone who seems to be so different?
- In Andrew's story, both helper and client reacted to the nonverbals of the other person—clothing, accent, skin color, and probably many other tiny cultural differences—but they were hesitant to mention them. When do you think it might be important in a helping relationship to notice these and talk about them? When do you think it is best to ignore them? Discuss this with your classmates.

Opening Skills: Inviting Client Self-Disclosure

The best atmosphere for encouraging client self-disclosure is one that is free of coercion, manipulation, and "game-playing." The first step in creating this climate is to communicate to the client that you, the helper, are present intellectually and emotionally. Opening skills are verbal encouragers by the helper that can help create coercion-free environments. Unlike the nonverbal skills that indicate, "I am ready to listen," the opening skills say, "Tell me more." Opening skills include door openers, minimal encouragers, and open and closed questions.

Door Openers

A *door opener* is "a noncoercive invitation to talk" (Bolton, 1979, p. 40). The door opener is initiated by the helper, but the client determines the depth of the response. More than a passing social response or greeting, the door opener signals availability on the part of the listener and encourages exploration and discussion. By contrast, valuative or judgmental responses are door closers. A door opener is generally a positive, nonjudgmental response made during the initial phase of a contact. It may include observations by the helper such as the following:

> "I see you are reading a book about Sylvia Plath [observation]. How do you like it?"
> "You look down this morning [observation]. Do you want to talk about it?"
> "What's on your mind?"
> "Tell me about it."
> "Can you say more about that?"
> "What would you like to talk about today?"

Door openers are invaluable to helpers because they can be used to get clients to expand on what they have been saying, to begin conversations in the first place, and to allow helpers additional time to formulate a response.

Minimal Encouragers

Minimal encouragers are brief supportive statements that convey attention and understanding. Most of us are familiar with minimal encouragers from the media's image of the Freudian analyst behind the couch, stroking his beard and saying, "Mmhmm." Minimal encouragers are verbal responses that show interest and involvement but allow the client to determine the primary direction of the conversation. They are different from door openers in that they communicate only that the listener is on track. Such phrases reinforce talking on the part of the client and are often accompanied by an approving nod of the head. Examples of minimal encouragers include:

> "I see."
> "Yes."
> "Right."
> "Okay."
> "Hmm."
> "I've got you."
> "I hear you."
> "I'm with you."

Of course, these responses are not sufficient to help a client achieve the goals of therapy, but if they are *not* used frequently enough (especially in the beginning of the session), the client feels stranded and uncertain. Minimal encouragers tell the client, "I am present," but do not interrupt the story's flow.

Questions

Be patient toward all that is unresolved in your heart.
Try to love the questions themselves.
Do not seek the answers which cannot be given,
Because you would not be able to live them.
And the point is to live everything.
Live the questions now.
Perhaps you will then gradually without noticing it,
Live along some distant day into the answers.
Rainer Marie Rilke

The great poet's words underline our common tendency to think that questions provide the ultimate road to understanding. We fall back on questioning when silence fails or we feel uncertain about the direction of the conversation. Sometimes it is better to sit with our questions and wait for the answers to arrive.

Of all the opening skills, *questions* are the most easily abused. Excessive questions get in the way of listening, and the client may feel interrogated and evaluated. Questions can distract the client from the story that is emerging because a question is a demand. Research suggests that beginning helpers ask more questions than experienced ones (Ornston, Cichetti, Levine, & Freeman, 1968). Specifically, inexperienced helpers ask a lot of "why" questions. Asking a client, "Why did you begin smoking marijuana?" puts him or her on the defensive. On the other hand, if you ask a five-year-old why he or she stepped in the mud, the inevitable and truthful answer is, "I don't know." It is only when we become adults that we are able to come up with lengthy rationalizations for our past behavior. A few decisions that people make, such as buying a car or a house, may have been the result of a lengthy rational process. However, the best answer to most "why" questions is usually, "It seemed like a good idea at the time." This seems to be true even with important life decisions such as getting married or changing jobs. Over time, helpers learn to ask more open questions and determine the "why" of the client's behavior from the whole of the story, rather than from the client's quick answer to a question.

Sometimes questions are definitely needed to get at the hidden or painful aspects of the story. This became apparent in a recent demonstration session in which a client discussed the trauma and aftereffects of a serious two-car accident. The helper, using door openers, minimal encouragers, and appropriate nonverbals was able to get the client to talk about many of the important issues. However, the student helper failed to ask if the other victim of the accident had been killed or injured, which was the key to the client's shame and remorse about the incident. It is vital to get this kind of question answered, but clients often talk about a problem on a superficial level at first. The helper must delve and pry to get the important facts. The difficulty is in knowing which aspects of the story are likely to be important. In this incident, for example, it was the seriousness of the accident that needed to be explored. Many beginning helpers might ask about less relevant details. They might ask when the accident occurred, how bad the damage was to the cars involved, where the incident took place, and so forth. These are the sorts of questions that sidetrack the client from the important issues.

In summary, there is a tendency for beginners to ask too many questions. Yet, it is also important to get crucial information. Good questioning is an art and we will consider it in greater detail when we discuss the assessment stage of the helping process (Goldberg, 1998). For the time being, keep a close watch on the overuse of questions in the exercises and practice sessions.

Open and Closed Questions

There are two major categories of questions: open and closed. *Closed questions* ask for specific information and usually require a short factual response. Some closed questions can be answered with a "yes," or "no." Others convey information. There are certainly times when closed questions are necessary, for example, when it is important to get the facts straight—especially in emergency situations. At other times, closed questions are necessary to clear up confusion in the helper's understanding of the story. Often, the answers to closed questions will come out in the client's narrative if we just take the time to listen.

Compared to closed questions, *open questions* allow more freedom of expression. They open up general topics, rather than request specific information. Here are some examples of open questions. Consider how you might respond to them.

"Could you tell me about the kinds of problems you have been having?"
"Last week, we discussed your relationships with men. Would you mind going into that again?"
"Can you tell me what has been happening at school?"
"You say you have self-esteem problems. What do you mean by that?"

Now consider the following closed questions:

"How old are you?"
"What school do you go to?"
"Are you planning to go to college?"
"Would you describe your marriage as happy?"

The difference between the two question types is something like the comparison between multiple-choice and essay exams. Multiple-choice tests check your knowledge of the facts, but essays ask you to show a deeper level of understanding. Here are some pairs of open and closed questions that each explore a similar topic. Note the differences in the client's typical response to open versus closed questions.

Closed
Helper: "Are you getting along with your parents these days?"

Client: "Yeah. Pretty good."

Open
Helper: "Can you tell me how you and your parents have been dealing with your differences recently?"

Client: "Well, we haven't been, really. We're not fighting but we're not talking, either. Just existing."

Closed

Helper: "Are you married now?"

Client: "No, divorced."

Open

Helper: "Can you tell me a little about your personal relationships during the past few years?"

Client: "Well, I've been divorced for six months from my second wife. We were married for over seven years and one day she left me for this guy at work. Since then, I haven't really been up to seeing anyone."

As these examples suggest, open questions eventually elicit more information than closed questions, even though they may not seem as direct. Open questions also persuade the client to answer by giving the client the opportunity to refuse. They don't box the client in by forcing him or her to answer directly. When you feel the need to ask a closed question, try and transform it into an open one first.

Stop and Reflect

Are You an Opener?

This scale was developed by Miller, Berg, and Archer (1983) to identify individuals who are good listeners and are able to get others to disclose information about themselves.* If you score yourself as low on this scale, it does not mean that you cannot learn the basic helping skills in this book. Consider it to be a self-assessment of where you are right now, not what you can become. At the end of the book, write down your answers again to see what changes you have made. Be as honest as you can. Do not compare your score to other people—this scale was not devised for that purpose.

Rate each statement as it applies to you on a scale of 0–4 (4 = strongly agree; 0 = strongly disagree).

1. People frequently tell me about themselves.
2. I've been told that I'm a good listener.
3. I'm very accepting of others.
4. People trust me with their secrets.
5. I easily get people to "open up."
6. People feel relaxed around me.
7. I enjoy listening to people.
8. I'm sympathetic to people's problems.
9. I encourage people to tell me how they are feeling.
10. I can keep people talking about themselves.

Although the test does not have any guidelines as to what constitutes a high or low score, let us arbitrarily set 0–10 as a low score and 30–40 as a high score. People with high scores on the Opener Scale are more successful in eliciting self-disclosure, even in people whose self disclosure is normally low. High scorers are able to take the viewpoint of others (be empathic) more easily than low scorers. Purvis, Dabbs, & Hopper (1984) found that high scorers show more comfort, enjoyment, and attentiveness than low scorers and are more verbally and nonverbally engaged. What reaction do you have to your results? Some helpers falsely believe that everyone has these interests and skills. They are surprised to find that the opening abilities tapped by this scale are not as common as they thought. Discuss this idea with classmates or record your reactions in your journal.

*Used with permission of American Psychological Association.

Summary

Every client has a story to tell, and invitational skills let the client know that we are interested in that story. Invitational skills have two basic components: nonverbal skills and opening skills. Nonverbal skills are messages used by helpers to provide the right conditions for the client to open up. The skills are eye contact, body position, attentive silence, voice tone, facial expressions and gestures, physical distance, and touching. Opening skills are the verbal messages the helper sends to facilitate the client's disclosure. Opening skills include door openers, minimal encouragers, and open and closed questions.

Invitational skills are relatively simple to learn but they count for so much in the relationship between client and helper. Getting the relationship off on the right foot means establishing the norm that the client has free rein to explore his or her deepest issues in a nonjudgmental atmosphere. Besides their importance in the beginning, invitational skills are needed at all stages of the helping process. As each new issue comes to the surface, the helper relies on invitational skills and a nonjudgmental attitude to provide the atmosphere of warmth and safety that allows for the deepest exploration of the client's needs, fears, and dreams.

Group Exercises

Group Exercise 1: Practice and Feedback Session Using Invitational Skills

Some Notes on the Helper/Client/Observer Training Group

For many of the practice sessions in this book, we will be asking you to break into groups of three or four. Generally, this works in a circular fashion with person A counseling person B. Later, person B counsels person C, and person C counsels person A. Depending on how your instructor likes to work, you may be assigned to the same groups for all practice sessions, or you may frequently change groups. Practicing on fellow students is a method used in medical and dental schools as well as in the training of mental health professionals. One of its benefits is that you learn just as much in the client role as in the helper role. You learn how it feels to be

challenged or supported. You also get a feeling about what is too invasive or too superficial. On the other hand, in the role of observer, you are able to step out of the helping situation and look at the situation more objectively. All three roles are instructive. As a member of a practice group, you will be challenged ethically, too. Although you may be role-playing part of the time, some of the situations are real; you should have an agreement for confidentiality just as if it were an actual problem. It has been our experience that students respect this confidentiality and take it very seriously. Still, it needs to be explicitly discussed in each group.

Instructions for Group Exercise 1:
Break up into groups of four. One person is the helper, another the client, and two act as observers. Before the "session" begins, the helper

should take time to review the "Quick Tips" section. The client can decide on the topic, and the observers can look over their checklists. Observer 1 will use Feedback Checklist 1 to give the helper data on his or her nonverbal skills. Observer 2 will use Feedback Checklist 2 to rate the helper on opening skills. For 5–8 minutes, the helper invites the client to discuss one of the following topics:

- How I chose my present job
- A trip I took that was very important to me
- My relationship with a close friend
- A topic of the client's choice
- The problem of a friend or acquaintance whose role the client assumes

Feedback

At the end of the time period, the observers and client give feedback to the helper. The client is encouraged to give qualitative feedback that may include general impressions of the helper's manner. The client should indicate whether or not he or she felt genuineness, empathy, and respect from the helper. The observers will give feedback based on their checklists. The participants switch roles, giving each person a chance to experience, helper, client, and observer roles. The entire process will take about 45 minutes.

Quick Tips: Invitational Skills

- Once you have adopted a facilitative body position, take a deep breath and relax.
- Remember that the ball is in the client's court: Invite the client to talk and to tell the story.
- After an open question or two, use the first few minutes to listen to the client using minimal encouragers and head nodding.
- When a silence occurs, don't rush to fill the void. Wait for the client to do it first.
- Rely on door openers such as "Go on," "Say some more about that," rather than asking too many questions at first.
- Use closed questions sparingly but ask yourself if you have understood the most important facts. If you are unsure, stop the client and ask a closed question or two.

Feedback Checklist 1 (to be completed by Observer 1)
During the practice session, try to work through the checklist systematically, recording your comments for each skill as you observe it. The helper may want you to write these observations directly in his or her book. If you have time, start at the beginning and review each skill again to check your observations. When you are finished, write down any suggestions for improvement. Be as honest as possible so that the helper can benefit from feedback.

1. Draw a stick figure sketch of the helper's body position.

What does the body position convey? (circle all that apply)

Openness
Relaxation
Tension
Stiffness
Interest
Aloofness

Comments for improvement:

2. Evaluate the helper's ability to maintain appropriate eye contact (circle one).

Avoids
Occasional
Constant with breaks
Stares

Comments for improvement:

3. Circle all that apply as you listen to the helper's voice tone:

Too loud	Cold
Too soft	Soothing
Confident	Clipped
Hesitant	Interested
Moralistic or smug	Bored
Warm	Other

Comments for improvement:

4. Evaluate the helper's gestures and facial expressions (circle all that apply).

Gestures: Nervous movement
Occasional
Inviting gestures
Rigid
Nodding: Head nodding appropriate
Head nodding too frequent
Too infrequent
Expression: Helper's face shows concern and interest
Face shows disinterest
Face reflects client's feelings
Face is unchanging/masklike
Other (e.g., warmth or use of touch)

Comments for improvement:

Feedback Checklist 2 (to be completed by Observer 2)
You are to give feedback on the helper's use of minimal encouragers and questions. Your task is to write down everything the helper says during the interview. At the end, categorize each response, and give the helper feedback.

Categories: Door opener (DO), minimal encourager (ME), open question (OQ), closed question (CQ)

Helper Question or Statement	Category
1.	
2.	
3.	
4.	
5.	
6.	
7.	
8.	
9	
10.	
11.	
12.	
13.	
14.	
15.	

Feedback on the Use of Minimal Encouragers
Did the helper supply enough minimal encouragers during the initial two minutes of the interview to encourage the client? Were minimal encouragers used too often instead of door openers and open questions?

Feedback on the Use of Questions
1. Examine the closed questions with the helper. Based on the client's response, were they necessary or merely asked out of curiosity? How many "why" questions did you see?
2. Were there more open or closed questions? Does the helper need to increase the use of open questions or decrease the use of closed questions?

Group Exercise 2: Open versus Closed Questions

Each member of a small group (two or three students) should individually turn the following closed questions into open questions. Write your answers down and later get feedback from the group. Remember, an open question can expand a topic beyond the original closed question. For example, a closed question, "Are your parents still married?" can be "opened" by changing it to, "Can you tell me something about your family?" Share your open questions with others in a small group. Think how you might answer your own open questions. Does it give you room to expand and disclose?

- Where are you from?
- What is your problem?

- When did all of your problems begin?
- Do your Mom and Dad fight?
- Did you have fun on the class trip?

Additional Exercises

Exercise 1

View 10–15 minutes of a videotape that shows a client/helper interaction. While viewing, write down any observations you may have concerning the client's body posture, gestures, and movements. Afterward, discuss the relationship of these nonverbal messages to the client's concerns. Alternately, half of the class can observe the client and the other half can focus on the helper. Check the helper's invitational skills against the list in Table 4.2.

Exercise 2

Form dyads and sit facing each other with your eyes closed. Discuss your activities over the past week for about 5–8 minutes. In the class discussion that follows, take turns giving your reactions to the experience. What nonverbal behaviors did you and your classmates find it most difficult to do without?

Exercise 3

Set up a simulated office for a role-playing situation. Provide one chair for the client and another for the helper. Use a third chair to represent a desk if one is not available. Place the chairs about 10 feet apart and ask two participants to hold a conversation at that distance concerning a minor problem one of them is having. Ask the group to comment on how the distance has affected the conversation.

Next, allow the participants to move the chairs to a comfortable distance. Once the chairs have been moved and the participants are seated, measure the distance from knee to knee with a yardstick or tape measure and see if it is approximately 18 inches, an average distance for helpers and clients. Next, move the

chairs so close that the participants feel uncomfortable. Measure that distance. If participants from diverse ethnic backgrounds are members of the group, interesting variations can occur. Try the exercise with participants standing instead of seated. Some people will feel comfortable with an interpersonal distance of 6 inches or less!

Exercise 4

Conduct a group discussion on the implications of touching clients. What constitutes sexual touching? Whose needs are being fulfilled by touching? Is it all right for the helper's emotional needs to be met by hugging a client? Under what circumstances would a hug be beneficial or harmful? What about hugging in group therapy?

Exercise 5

Videotape two trainees, one of whom acts as the client and the other, the helper, for 15 minutes. The client discusses a minor problem he or she is having at work or at school. Focus the camera for half of the session on the helper's face and the other half of the session on the helper's whole body. Replay the tape and ask the helper to evaluate his or her own facial expressions, body position, and gestures.

Exercise 6

Form dyads. The leader or instructor will keep time and signal the completion of the activity at the end of two minutes. Maintain eye contact with your partner and assume the appropriate helper's posture while remaining completely silent. Afterward, discuss your personal reactions to this exercise with your partner and then with the larger group.

Homework

Homework 1

Record a television show or movie and replay it with the sound off. Try to see if you can guess emotional content by examining the characters' body language. Write a one-page reaction to this assignment.

Homework 2

Conduct a survey among a few friends or family members. How would they feel about being hugged or touched by a professional helper? Try to be objective and prepare a one-page summary of their answers and your conclusions.

Homework 3

In conversations with co-workers, family, and friends, instead of immediately responding to what they say, build in attentive silence and notice the effect. The purpose of the assignment is to observe the effect of silence on the communication of others. Make notes and report findings to the group. Write a one-paragraph reaction to this exercise.

Journal Starters

1. Many nonverbal skills such as touching, distance, and eye contact are learned in one's family of origin and reflect cultural values. Think for a moment about the rules about touching, eye contact, and personal space that you learned growing up. How might you unknowingly create a barrier by being too familiar or too aloof with a client? How will you be able to tell when your client is uncomfortable? What would be comfortable for you and what would you object to as a client?
2. Think about a secret that you have not shared with anyone. How do you think you would feel if a helper urged you to share this private information? Would it be easier to share it with a close friend? How do you think you would feel after sharing this information? What are your fantasies about what might happen if you disclosed this secret? Do you imagine the helper telling others, or is it simply disquieting to think about the secret? What kind of response would you expect if you told a close friend about this issue? Would any of these expectations affect your willingness to share the information with a professional helper?

References

Alyn, J. H. (1988). The politics of touch in therapy. *Journal of Counseling and Development, 66,* 155–159.

Archer, D., & Akert, R. M. (1977). Words and everything else: Verbal and nonverbal cues in social interpretation. *Journal of Personality and Social Psychology, 34,* 443–449.

Bolton, R. (1979). *People skills: How to assert yourself, listen to others, and resolve conflicts.* Upper Saddle River, NJ: Prentice Hall.

Blum, D. (1998). Face it! *Psychology Today, 31*(5), 32–70.

Driscoll, M. S., Newman, D. L., & Seals, J. M. (1988). The effect of touch on perception of helpers. *Counselor Education and Supervision, 27,* 113–115.

Ekman, P. (1975). Universal smile: Face muscles talk every language. *Psychology Today, 9*(4), 35–39.

Fisher, J. D., Rytting, M., & Heslin, R. (1976). Affective and valuative effects of an interpersonal touch. *Sociometry, 39,* 416–421.

Fretz, B. R., Corn, R., Tuemmler, J. M., & Bellet, W. (1979). Counselor nonverbal behaviors and client evaluations. *Journal of Counseling Psychology, 26,* 304–311.

Goodman, M., & Teicher, A. (1988). To touch or not to touch. *Psychotherapy: Theory, Research and Practice, 25,* 492–500.

Goldberg, M. C. (1998). *The art of the question.* New York: Wiley.

Holroyd, J., & Brodsky, A. (1980). Does touching patients lead to sexual intercourse? *Professional Psychology, 11,* 807–811.

Hunter, M., & Struve, J. (1997). *The ethical use of touch in psychotherapy.* Thousand Oaks, CA: Sage.

Johnson, D. W. (2000). *Reaching out.* Boston: Allyn & Bacon.

Kopp, S. (1978). *If you meet the Buddha on the road, kill him!* New York: Bantam.

LaFrance, M., & Mayo, C. (1976). Racial differences in gaze behavior during observations: Two systematic observational studies. *Journal of Personality and Social Psychology, 33,* 47–52.

Maurer, R. E., & Tindall, J. H. (1983). Effect of postural congruence on client's perception of helper empathy. *Journal of Counseling Psychology, 30,* 158–163.

Mehrabian, A. (1972). *Nonverbal communication.* Chicago: Aldine.

Miller, L., Berg, J. H., & Archer, R. L. (1983). Openers: Individuals who elicit intimate self-disclosure. *Journal of Personality and Social Psychology, 44,* 1234–1244.

Moffat, M. J., & Painter, C. (Eds.). (1974). *Revelations: Diaries of women.* New York: Vintage.

Older, J. (1982). *Touching is healing.* New York: Stein & Day.

Ornston, P. S., Cichetti, D. V., Levine, J., & Freeman, L. B. (1968). Some parameters of verbal behavior that reliably differentiate novice from experienced therapists. *Journal of Abnormal Psychology, 73,* 240–244.

Pennebaker, J. W. (1989). Confession, inhibition, and disease. In L. Berkowitz (Ed.), *Advances in experimental social psychology* (Vol. 22, pp. 211–214). New York: Academic Press.

Pennebaker, J. W. (1990). *Opening up.* New York: Guilford.

Purvis, J. A., Dabbs, J. M., & Hopper, C. (1984). The "Opener": Skilled user of facial expression and speech pattern. *Personality and Social Psychology Bulletin, 10,* 60–66.

Ridley, N. C., & Asbury, F. R. (1988). Does counselor body position make a difference? *School Counselor, 35,* 253–258.

Smith, E. W. L., Clance, P. R., & Imps, S. (1998). *Touch in psychotherapy.* New York: Guilford.

Stone, G. L., & Morden, C. J. (1976). Effect of distance on verbal productivity. *Journal of Counseling Psychology, 23,* 486–488.

Suiter, R. L., & Goodyear, R. K. (1985). Male and female counselor and client perceptions of four levels of counselor touch. *Journal of Counseling Psychology, 32,* 645–648.

Willison, B. G., & Masson, R. L. (1986). The role of touch in therapy: An adjunct to communication. *Journal of Counseling and Development, 64,* 497–500.

Reflecting Skills

5

The invitational skills you learned in the last chapter encourage the client to open up and send the message that you are willing to listen. Although invitational skills convey that you are present and available, they do not indicate a deep understanding of the client's world. Invitational skills are commonly used by friends, family, and acquaintances, as well as by helpers. Reflecting skills, on the other hand, are specialized interventions used by helpers to stimulate deeper exploration of the facts and feelings of a client's problem.

In general, reflecting entails repeating back to the client his or her own thoughts and feelings in a condensed way, using different words, and in a manner that communicates nonevaluative, nonjudgmental understanding. Consider the following client-helper exchange:

Phillipe (Client): "When I was 16, I stole a car with some other kids. We went joyriding and had an accident. The driver was drunk and one of the kids in the car was killed. Every time my own kid goes out on Saturday night, I think of that. I yell and scream and maybe I am too strict with him."

Joyce (Helper): "It is difficult for you to know whether you are being overprotective because you remember that incident and worry that the same thing might happen to him."

Phillipe: "Yes, sometimes I get really scared. My own parents didn't care what I did. I don't want to keep him at home all the time but I don't want him doing something stupid."

Joyce: "At times you are really fearful about what might happen and you're confused about how strict to be because of your own upbringing."

The reflecting skills go beyond invitational skills by bringing out a deeper level of the story—the emotional reactions of the client. To use a metaphor, recognizing the emotions adds color to the black-and-white facts. With the example of Phillipe and Joyce in mind, let us look at the four functions served by reflecting skills in helping:

1. *Reflecting is a verbal way of communicating empathy.* In Chapter 3, we discussed the concept of empathy or trying to "feel oneself into" another's experience. We indicated then that the helper tries to share a client's deeper experiences and that it is also important to convey this understanding to the client. Reflecting feelings communicates, "I hear your emotions as well as the facts." In the preceding example, Joyce does not have to say to Phillipe, "I understand what you are going through." Instead, she communicates his worry, confusion, and fear, trying to understand the situation through his eyes rather than a similar experience of her own.

2. *Reflecting is a form of feedback or a mirror that enables the person to confirm or correct the impression he or she is giving.* In Joyce's first response to Phillipe, she uses the word "worry." For a number of reasons, this word might not have exactly fit what he was trying to communicate. He might have responded, "No, I don't worry that the same thing will happen, I just get mad at him for not listening to me!" This demonstrates that a reflecting statement, even if inaccurate, can give the client an opportunity to clarify. In other words, beginning helpers should try to reflect without being concerned that every reflection is perfect. If the helper does not hit the bull's-eye, in many cases, the client will expand and explain the situation more clearly.

3. *Reflecting stimulates further exploration of what the client is experiencing.* Notice that when Joyce identifies his feelings of worry in the first reflection, Phillipe begins discussing his own upbringing and talks about the conflict between being overprotective and too lenient. This shows that accurate reflection has an opening effect, bringing out more facts and deeper feelings.

4. *Reflecting captures important aspects of the client's message that otherwise might remain camouflaged.* In Phillipe's opening statement, he makes no mention of the fact that he is scared or worried about his son. Many people have difficulty admitting to negative feelings such as fear and anger. Perhaps, at this first meeting, Phillipe does not wish to appear foolish in his concerns. It is the helper's reflection that extracts this feeling that is hidden in his first statement.

Reflecting Content and Reflecting Feelings

Every client message has two basic components: the factual content and the underlying feelings (see Figure 5.1). The feelings are often hidden and it is up to the helper to bring these to the surface, as Joyce does with Phillipe. However, the content—the facts about the situation—is also important and the client needs to know that this has been understood. In the following story, a helper describes a situation that brought home to him the distinction between reflecting content and reflecting the often-unexpressed feelings implicit in the client's statements.

> Once I ran a private practice in a small town. The house next door to my office was guarded by a huge German shepherd dog that frequently growled at my clients when they approached the front door. When I greeted my clients, I was always interested in how they framed their reaction. They often said, "That is the biggest dog I've ever seen." If I had responded to the content of the message, I might have said, "Yes, that is exceptionally large for a German shepherd," or, "Actually, I've seen bigger," or even, "Yes, he weighs over 100 pounds and is in excellent health!"

This example brings out that every communication has at least two dimensions: the content or perceptions of the event described and the unspoken set of feelings that underlie the content. In this case, the hidden emotional message concerned the fear that the dog evoked but which very few people felt comfortable in expressing. In our culture, many people are reluctant to express their feelings and much more comfortable talking about content or facts. However, because the content and the emotional side are equally important, a response that recognizes both will lead to the deepest communication of understanding. At the beginning of the helping relationship, clients find it more comfortable if the helper is able to reflect the content of their story. Later, a helper can show that he or she also grasps the underlying, or hidden, emotional side.

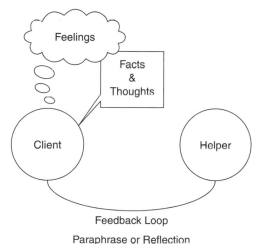

Feedback Loop

Paraphrase or Reflection
of Feeling

Figure 5.1
Facts and Feelings: The
Basic Components of the
Client's Message

Table 5.1
Two Building Blocks in Reflecting Skills

Skill	Examples
Paraphrase	"So this week has been very difficult, at work and at home."
	"It's not just your family ties, but also your friendships that have suffered."
Reflection of feeling	"It was a shock when they announced your promotion."
	"After all that had happened, you were wary about continuing your friendship."

Take another look at the lines in Figure 5.1 that connect helper and client. This is the feedback loop or helper's reflecting response to the client's story. If the helper paraphrases, he or she is reflecting the facts and the client's expressed thoughts. Alternately, the helper chooses a reflection of feeling to convey understanding of the emotional message. During a session, the helper makes a series of reflections. As the client responds to the reflections, the helper gets more information about the accuracy of paraphrases and reflections until the helper understands the whole message.

Two separate skills are used to reflect the two different aspects of the client's message. The first, paraphrasing, is primarily a reflection of content and the second skill reflects feeling. Table 5.1 shows the two building blocks of the reflecting skills. Each will be discussed in more detail in this chapter, along with opportunities for you to try out these skills in practice situations.

The Skill of Paraphrasing: Reflecting Content

In the discussion of invitational skills, you were warned not to ask too many questions at the beginning stages of the helping relationship. Questions, especially closed questions, can interrupt the flow of the client's story and make the client feel that he or she is under a microscope. However, it is important to have a clear grasp of the facts relating to the client's problem and also, at times, to repeat some important thought behavior or intention embedded in the client's statements. Paraphrasing is a reflecting skill that serves both purposes. The paraphrase is not a word-for-word reiteration. The paraphrase is a distilled version of the content of the client's message that restates the content in different words and in a nonjudgmental way. As a client tells his or her story, the paraphrase is used as a mirror to let the client know that you are following but does not pressure the client by asking a question. It is short and sweet and therefore does not slow the client down while he or she is disclosing. It does not take sides with the client by supporting his or her version of the story, but, rather, points out that this is the client's perspective.

How to Paraphrase

Paraphrasing involves two steps: listening carefully to the client's story and then feeding back to the client a condensed, nonjudgmental version of the facts and the client's thoughts. The second step in paraphrasing is collapsing the important information from a large volume of client material into a succinct summary. If the paraphrase goes on too long, it can fatally disrupt the client's story and he or she will not stay on track. Using a boxing analogy, the paraphrase is more like a jab. The helper gets in and out quickly. The paraphrase is actually a miniature version of the client's story. A good paraphrase keeps the client's story on track by mentioning only the important aspects, not issues that sidetrack the client. Here is an example of a conversation between a helper and a client in their first meeting. Notice how paraphrase assists the helper in understanding the facts of the story and also allows the client to feel the helper is on track:

Melvin (Helper): "So, what brought you in today?" (door opener)

Fred (Client): "Well, I am a teacher and I have been having some problems at school recently."

Melvin: "Okay, can you tell me about that?" (door opener)

Fred: "I have a group of sixth graders this year that are just wild. They won't listen and they constantly challenge me. I've sent more kids to the office this year than I can ever remember. I've sent notes home and scheduled a lot of parent conferences."

Melvin: "Uh-huh. Okay." (minimal encouragers)

Fred: "I guess you get a bad group sometimes. I've been teaching for 13 years and I am used to working with rowdy kids. But this year it seems like it's getting on my nerves even more."

Melvin: "So, first of all, it's a very difficult group to work with, even for someone with a lot of experience." (paraphrase)

Fred: "Right, but that's not all. This year, one of the teachers was fired during the first week for some unknown reason."

Melvin: "I see." (minimal encourager)

Fred: "That has left a lot of people upset. With that kind of support from the principal, I just don't know what this year is going to be like."

Melvin: "So, on top of the new students, you're dealing with a new atmosphere at work." (paraphrase)

Fred: "I guess this atmosphere isn't new. But it never really affected me before. I tried to stay out of all the politics and the complaining in the teachers' lounge. This year, all the teachers do is gripe. At meetings and after school, somebody is always talking about it."

Melvin: "So, for the first time, it's hard to escape the gossiping." (paraphrase)

Fred: "Yeah. And I am wondering if the gossiping is worse or if it is me. There are a lot of other things happening in my life."

Melvin: "You can't tell if things are different or if you are different this year." (paraphrase)

Fred: "That's it. That's what is so confusing."

Now that you have read the dialogue between Melvin and Fred, take a look at Melvin's reflections. Do you notice how Melvin does not repeat Fred's statements exactly? Melvin rewords Fred's statements to show that he grasps the essence. This is the art of distilling or collapsing the client's words into a brief statement.

When to Paraphrase

Paraphrases can be used early on in any helping session, as soon as the helper gets a grasp of the facts or, conversely, needs to clarify the facts. Paraphrasing should follow a sequence of opening and invitational skills. Figure 5.2 shows the typical sequence of a helper's using invitational skills and paraphrasing in the beginning of a session. The helper begins with door openers and minimal encouragers, perhaps going on to an open question before paraphrasing. Paraphrasing after every client statement might seem to make the helper's responses trivial. It is therefore better to wait until the client has gone on at some length. The entire sequence is aimed at getting the client to tell as much as possible about a particular aspect of the story, which we will call a topic. In the beginning, you might have the tendency to rush a client through a topic without discussing all the facts and feelings. More experienced helpers take time to ask open questions, check out key facts with closed questions, and paraphrase to make sure the story is being understood.

In the following conversation between a child and a school counselor, a paraphrase is shown in the normal progression of a topic:

Chris: "The teacher said I have to tell you what happened yesterday."

School Counselor: "Do you want to give me an idea about what went on?" (door opener)

Chris: "Well, I was walking around the playground, not really looking at anything, you know? I was bored."

School Counselor: "Yes; um-hmm." (minimal encouragers)

Chris: "And then these three second graders came around the corner and started calling me names. I said, 'Shut up.' And later I punched William in the nose. It was bleeding and he was crying but I didn't care because he is mean."

School Counselor: "So, you got into a fight with William. He got hurt but you don't think it was your fault." (paraphrase)

School Counselor: "Can you tell me more about why you don't think it was your fault?" (open question)

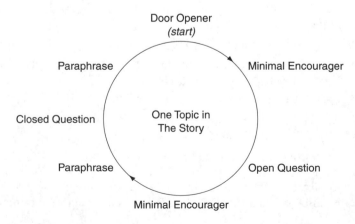

Figure 5.2
A Typical Sequence of Helper Responses in the First Few Minutes of a Session

Notice that the counselor's paraphrase is not just a restatement of what Chris said. It is a summary of the child's story, giving its essence in a nonjudgmental way. The paraphrase is brief and therefore does not interrupt the child unduly as he talks. It does not take sides by supporting one version of the story, but recognizes instead the child's perspective. It also identifies the child's thoughts, "you don't think it was your fault." We will look at these issues a little more as we consider some of the difficulties you might encounter in learning to paraphrase.

Common Problems in Paraphrasing

Simply Reciting the Facts

A common mistake is to simply list the major points the client has made in exactly the same way. The best way to illustrate this mistake is to take an example from Melvin and Fred's earlier dialogue. Following Fred's statement are two alternative paraphrases: The first one is copied from the actual dialogue and the second is a less effective paraphrase by Melvin that merely recites the facts.

Fred (Client): I guess this atmosphere isn't new. But it never really affected me before. I tried to stay out of all the politics and the complaining in the teachers' lounge. This year, all the teachers do is gripe. At meetings and after school, somebody is always talking about it.

Melvin (Helper): So, for the first time, it's hard to escape the gossiping. (paraphrase)

Melvin (Helper): It's not a new atmosphere, then, but now it is affecting you and although you try to escape, it's everywhere you go, at meetings and after school.

The problem with the second paraphrase is that it is too long and goes into too much detail. This means the client has to listen to your response and gets off track. Also clients seem to find it odd that someone has just repeated their own words right back to them.

Difficulty Hearing the Story

A second problem is caused by distractions. Of course, helpers must select quiet environments so that listening is not impaired by external noises. However, the biggest distractions come from "mental noise." You cannot grasp the client's message when you are listening to your own thoughts. Helpers sometimes experience internal noise when the client's story evokes a personal memory of a similar situation. Internal noise may interrupt because the client is expressing something you find distasteful or evokes moral outrage. When you find that you have lost track of the client's story because of mental noise, stop and request that the client repeat the last part again. Then respond with an appropriate paraphrase. Even though it is a distraction, it is better to stay on track than to miss the key elements of the story.

Worrying About What to Say Next

Worrying about what to say next is perhaps the biggest impediment to listening for the beginning helper. Worrying is another form of mental noise. Rather than responding to the client's statement, the helper is sidetracked by thinking about what his or her response ought to be. Because it is difficult to do two things simultaneously, when you become focused on your own thoughts, you lose track of the client's story. This happens to everyone at some time. The remedy is to focus more on what the client is saying. Focus your attention keenly on the client's story. One other help-ful hint is to remember that your job is to respond to the last thing the client said rather than come up with a new topic.

Being Judgmental and Taking Sides

Beginners are often too quick to take the client's side and agree that the problem is caused by other people. The tendency to be judgmental is often expressed in a par-aphrase. For example:

Rachel (Client): "At work, the other women ignore me because I don't go drinking with them on Friday night and they think I am the boss's favorite. The boss always compliments me on my work. I can't help it if they don't work as hard as I do."

Santiago (Helper): "Things aren't going very well at the job because your co-workers mistreat you."

With a judgmental paraphrase, the helper has essentially agreed that the co-workers are at fault. Shifting the blame to other people will not widen the client's per-spective. The following is a nonjudgmental response to Rachel's problem:

Santiago (Helper): "So, you see yourself as a hard worker but you don't have much of a connection with your co-workers."

A related error is being judgmental of the client as in this alternative scenario:

Rachel: "At work, the other women ignore me because I don't go drinking with them on Friday night and they think I am the boss's favorite. The boss always compli-ments me on my work. I can't help it if they don't work as hard as I do."

Santiago: "You're having trouble at work because you haven't been a team player." (judgmental)

Sometimes, helpers show a judgmental attitude when they try to sneak in a lit-tle free advice. In the previous example, there is a hidden message, "If you want to be liked, be more a part of the team." A nonjudgmental response would be:

Santiago: "So, you're saying that your boss appreciates you but, otherwise, you're not really liked at work." (nonjudgmental)

The purpose of a paraphrase is to make sure that you are understanding the facts, not to supply a solution or place blame.

Quick Tips: Paraphrasing

- Don't paraphrase too early. Wait until you have a firm grasp of the important details, then compress them into a short paraphrase.
- Early on, use minimal encouragers and door openers liberally to encourage the client to supply essential information.
- Don't repeat the client's exact words. Give a distilled version in slightly differ-ent words.
- Don't add a moral tone to your paraphrase.
- When you can, paraphrase the client's thoughts and intentions as well as the basic facts.

Stop and Reflect

Following are parts of three clients' stories. Try to paraphrase them. See if you can reflect the client's thoughts and intentions as well as the basic facts of the story. Leave out the client's feelings for now. Compare your paraphrases with those of your classmates and discuss any differences in your approaches.

1. "I had to tell one of my co-workers he couldn't go on the trip. He had not put in enough time with the company. I was forced to follow the rules. It wasn't really my fault and I couldn't do anything about it. When I told him, he didn't say much. He just walked away."

2. "I met this woman. She seems too good to be true. I don't know too much about her. We only met last week. But since then, everything I find out about her makes me feel more like she is 'the one.' I believe there is only one person out there for everyone, you know. But how can you be sure?"

3. "I called my husband's hotel room Tuesday night and when the phone picked up all I heard was the sound of a woman giggling. Then she hung up. I tried calling back and there was no answer. The next morning I called my husband's room again. He answered and I told him what had happened the night before. He said I must have dialed a wrong number. I guess I believe him. But we went through something similar before when he was younger. There was more than one woman then. I won't go through that again."

- Do any of these stories challenge your ability to be nonjudgmental?
- What feelings are aroused in you?
- Which one is the most challenging to remain nonjudgmental? Why?
- What might you be tempted to say that would indicate that you are taking sides?
- How well were you able to distill the client's story rather than reiterating the facts?
- Did you find it hard to leave out the feelings? Is there a time for listening to the facts of a story without reflecting the feelings?

The Skill of Reflecting Feelings

The building block of reflecting feelings involves essentially the same technique as paraphrasing. This time, however, the focus is on feelings rather than on content. Reflecting feelings involves expressing in one's own words the emotions stated or implied by the client. Feelings can be reflected from both verbal or nonverbal responses of the client.

A number of therapeutic events occur when feelings are reflected. For one thing, the client becomes more keenly aware of the emotions surrounding a topic. For example, the helper makes a reflection such as, "I can tell that you are terribly angry about that." The client's response may be one of surprise, "Yes, I guess I am." Because a reflection is done in a nonevaluative manner, it communicates understanding of feelings anger, guilt, and sadness—that the client may not be consciously aware of and that the client may feel he or she has no right to feel.

Another important effect is that reflection of feelings brings the client to deeper and deeper levels of self-disclosure. An accurate reflection focuses the client on emotions and teaches the client to become aware of and to report feelings. Even if the reflection is not quite accurate, the client will provide a correction that is more on target.

In addition, an accurate reflection of feelings has the almost magical power to deepen the relationship between client and counselor. Nothing transmits nonjudgmental understanding more completely. This is why this technique, which originated in the client-centered tradition of Carl Rogers (1961), has gained such wide usage. It taps the enormous healing properties of the therapeutic factor of enhancing the relationship. A beginning helper who can accurately reflect feelings can provide supportive counseling and understanding without any other tools.

Finally, reflecting feelings brings on feelings of genuine relief as the client gains some understanding of what he or she is feeling. Take, for example, the client who found his wife in bed with another man. He came to counseling crying about his loss of the relationship. He ran the gamut, on an emotional roller-coaster, from shock to disgust to affection to rage. Experiencing all of these conflicting emotions in one session can make anyone feel "crazy." Even though there were conflicting feelings, by the end, the client felt more in control simply because he had sorted out his feelings and labeled them. Untangling the emotional knots seems to be healing, even if no real action is taken. Somehow we can accept our feelings as normal reactions when we bring them to the surface. Reflecting feelings such as, "You feel so betrayed yet you still feel a bond of affection," can help to normalize what the client perceives as a deeply conflicting emotional experience.

Why It Is Difficult to Reflect Feelings

Reflecting feelings is one of the most valuable tools of the helper, but it is not an easy one to learn. Theodore Reik, the famous analyst, claimed that in order to hear these feelings one must learn to become sensitive to the unexpressed and listen with the "third ear." Referring to the fact that the client may not even be aware of these feelings, Reik said, "The voice that speaks in him speaks low but he who listens with a third ear, hears also what is expressed almost noiselessly, what is said *pianissimo*" (Reik, 1968, p. 165).

Feelings are often implicit in a client's statements and require hunches and guesses on the part of the helper to identify them. The reason is that our upbringing, family background, and culture affect the way we express emotions. For example, speaking in generalities, individuals with Appalachian and English roots may tend to express emotions in very subtle ways. Some native Americans, East Indians, and Europeans may come from cultures where open expression of feelings is rude or a sign of weakness. For example, a recent conference was held in Amsterdam on the "underexpression" of emotions as a mental health issue in Europe.

When a client's family background or culture is constantly sending the message, "Don't let anyone see your feelings," the job of helping is more difficult because the helper can only guess what the client is experiencing. Getting to feelings may require more time and effort and even then expression may seem faint by comparison. This can be frustrating when the client does not seem to respond to your reflections. For some clients, even a small crack in the voice may be quite an unusual expression and should be valued as a rather deep disclosure.

Gender also has a bearing on emotional expression. Men, more than women, have been trained to "never let them see you sweat." Big boys don't cry (see Kottler,

1997). Consequently, it may be difficult for some men to openly encounter strong feelings in the helping relationship. When they do occur, a man may feel weak or out of control. Feminine socialization, on the other hand, is more relationship oriented and is more likely to encourage the expression of emotions (Workman, 1993). However, women, too, are asked to repress certain emotions such as anger or even confidence that are not considered "ladylike."

How to Reflect Feelings

Like paraphrasing, reflecting feelings involves two steps. The first step is identifying the client's feelings; the second step is articulating the underlying emotions that you detect in his or her statements.

You can learn the first step in your practice sessions as you listen intently to a client's statements. Imagine how he or she feels in this situation, then try to label the feeling. The best way to do this is to think of yourself as the client, taking into account all the facts and also thinking about what you know about the client's personality and history. In other words, do not try to think about how *you* would feel in this situation; instead, become the client and think about how he or she might feel. For example, read the three client stories in the previous "Stop and Reflect" section. See if you can identify the main feelings. Take a look at the feeling words in Table 5.2 to see if another word is closer to what the client seems to be expressing. Don't forget that nonverbals are major clues to the client's feeling state. While reading and responding to vignettes in this book will be helpful, practicing with classmates will mean that you must pay close attention to the expressions as well as the words.

The second step in reflecting feelings is making a *statement* (not asking a question) that *accurately* mirrors the client's emotions. The client may not have actually shared the emotions; they may be hiding in the client's story. Although this sounds easier than the first step, it is actually more difficult because you must *accurately* express emotions in words.

In our experience, these two steps to reflecting feelings are often learned independently. Learning to identify feelings seems to be a precursor to actually reflecting them. Take some time to practice identifying feelings and then it will be easier to put them into words.

Reflecting feeling statements take two forms. The simple version of reflecting feelings is a helper statement with the structure, "You feel _____ ." As you look at the following interactions between helper and client, think about what the reflection of feelings brings to the client's story and to the relationship.

Latrice (Client): "You can imagine how everyone in the family reacted when grandpa got married six months after grandma's death."

Kendra (Helper): "It must have been quite a shock." (simple reflection of feelings)

After one or two reflections of feeling, a helper may then use a reflection of feelings that connects emotions and content. The format of this combination response is: "You feel _____ because _____ ." The first blank is a reflection of the client's feeling. The second blank explains the feeling by paraphrasing the content while, at the same time, showing the connection between the feeling and the content (Carkhuff, 1987). As the conversation between Latrice and Kendra continues, Kendra begins to understand and articulate the reason for Latrice's resentment and anger:

Latrice: "I was floored. I always thought that they had the perfect marriage."

Kendra: "You feel let down now that you have discovered that things were not as they seemed."

The reflection of feeling, "you feel let down," is connected to the paraphrase "now that you have discovered that things were not as they seemed." This last phrase is content. The connection is the word *because,* which demonstrates to Latrice that Kendra understands what has happened. Can you see that Kendra's statement is a mirror image of Latrice's? Does Kendra's reflection push Latrice to examine this situation a little more deeply?

Every reflection of feeling does not have to contain a paraphrase. Sometimes, it is sufficient to reflect the feeling using the simple, "You feel _____ ." When you understand the connection between feeling and content, you can then utilize the combined form to convey deeper understanding of the *reasons* for the client's feelings.

Students report that they often feel "phony" when they use a response such as, "You feel _____ because _____ ." The formula is merely a training tool that you can modify later when reflecting feelings has become second nature. Then, you will want to vary the way you reflect so that it feels natural to you and to the client.

Table 5.2
Feeling Words

Feeling	Mild	Moderate	Strong
Joy	at ease	glad	overjoyed
	pleased	happy	jubilant
	satisfied		elated
	content		
Sadness	down	glum	depressed
	sad	downhearted	dejected
	low		
	blue	melancholy	despondent
Anger	annoyed	angry	furious
	irritated	mad	outraged
	miffed		enraged
	ticked		
Guilt/shame	responsible	guilty	ashamed
	at fault	embarrassed	humiliated
	chagrined		mortified
Fear	apprehensive	anxious	frightened
	restless	scared	terrified
	uneasy	worried	panicked
	wary	afraid	
	insecure	nervous	
	on edge		
Disgust	offended	turned off	repulsed
	put off	disgusted	sickened
			revolted
			nauseated

Improving Your Feeling Vocabulary

To learn the first step in reflecting feelings, identifying feelings, it is important to recognize that emotions have many shades and variations. They also vary in strength. Thus, it is difficult to classify them in a way that fully captures their scope. Table 5.2 is an attempt to categorize feelings in a way that will help you recognize the basic emotions. They are like the primary colors in the light spectrum. The color analogy is used here because the emotions of clients are often mixed together, producing a completely unique hue. The primary emotions are listed top to bottom on the left-hand side of Table 5.2.

The emotions that have been identified as primary, or basic, are joy, sadness, anger, guilt/shame, fear, disgust, surprise, and interest/excitement. People around the world can recognize facial expressions of these emotional states whether they are from remote parts of New Guinea or New York City (Izard, 1977). They appear to have deep biological roots. In addition to the primary emotions, three other categories of emotions are indicated in the table: feelings of weakness and strength and feelings of general distress. Normally, the helper should be trying to identify the specific feeling that a client is experiencing. Sometimes though, especially in the beginning of a client's story, it is necessary to reflect a sense of general distress before honing in on the target feelings.

Feeling	Mild	Moderate	Strong
Surprise	perplexed	amazed	awed
	puzzled	bewildered	stunned
	stumped	baffled	astonished
		surprised	shocked
Interest/excitement	bored	amused	excited
	interested	curious	stimulated
		inspired	thrilled
		engaged	
Feelings Associated with Power and Confidence			
Weakness	unimportant	inadequate	worthless
	awkward	incompetent	helpless
	unsure	inept	dependent
		powerless	impotent
		weak	
Strength	able	confident	self-assured
	capable	strong	potent
		authoritative	powerful
		secure	
		competent	
Feelings of General Distress			
	upset	frustrated	distressed
	concerned	disturbed	pained
	troubled	perturbed	miserable
	bothered		anguished
			agitated
			overwhelmed

Across the top of Table 5.2, the emotions are categorized by intensity, much as colors can be described in terms of brightness. Besides finding precise words that suggest different intensities, you can qualify your reflections by using adjectives like "a little," "somewhat," and "very" to hone in on the client's exact feeling. In fact, some clients do not have large feeling vocabularies and it is better to say, "You were very angry," rather than, "You were filled with consternation."

You can utilize Table 5.2 to familiarize yourself with a wider variety of words. The more closely you express the exact shade of feeling, the more the client will sense that you understand his or her frame of mind.

Stop and Reflect

To consider further the distinction between content and feelings, take a look at a portion of a client's story and see if you can respond as a professional helper would, answering the related questions and comparing your responses with those of your classmates.

Teresa: "First, we went to the drugstore, then we went to the grocery; we went to two or three other places and ended up in a bad part of town. All because he wanted this particular kind of candy. I had a lot to do that day. And this wasn't the first time this kind of thing had happened. He's a lot of fun most of the time; other times, he is a pain! What can you do?"

- What might Teresa be feeling? (Identify as many emotions as you can.) Try and pinpoint her feelings using Table 5.2. Use qualifiers like "a little" or "very" as needed to try and get the right shade of emotion. Your answers and those of your classmates may vary because in a written example we cannot hear the client's voice tone to cue us in as to how strong her emotions are.

_____

_____

_____

- What nonverbals might give away her exact feelings?

_____

_____

_____

- Why do you think Teresa does not express her feelings about the situation in this part of her story?
- Try to summarize the content of Teresa's message (not the feelings) in a single sentence. Remember that the content includes thoughts, intentions, and facts that she relates.

_____

_____

_____

- Try to make a connection between what Teresa is feeling and the content of her story: Teresa feels _____ (emotion) because _____ (reason you identify from content).
- What facts about Teresa's cultural or family upbringing might affect her willingness to express her feelings about her friend?

_____

_____

_____

- Now think for a moment about your own upbringing, family background, and culture. What rules does your own family have about expressing emotions such as anger or sadness? How do you express affection? What would be the most difficult feelings for you to admit to a helper if you were a client?

_____

_____

_____

Common Problems in Reflecting Feelings

In many classes on helping skills, learning to paraphrase and reflect feelings takes up a large portion of the class time. These skills may take many weeks to develop. Following are a number of common problems that students encounter at the early stages. Under each problem are some suggested activities for dealing with that issue. If you find that you are having problems with one of these typical hurdles, let your instructor and fellow students know so that you can receive specific feedback during practice sessions.

Asking the Client, "How Did You Feel?"
Rather than using a reflecting statement, it is tempting to simply ask the client what he or she is feeling. One of the main benefits of a reflection is that it conveys empathy. When you ask a *closed question,* the client does not feel that you understand. He or she may feel misunderstood and may feel the need to clarify. Often, the client can't pinpoint the feeling when asked and the conversation stalls.

Waiting Too Long to Reflect
In the opening minutes of the helping session, utilize invitational skills to help elicit the client's story but don't wait too long. A common mistake is to wait 10 or 15 minutes before going on to reflect the client's feelings. It is better to reflect inaccurately than never to reflect at all. To avoid the mistake of waiting too long, work first on becoming proficient at identifying feelings. Make full use of the written exercises in this chapter. Look at exercises in previous chapters, read the client statements, and see if you can pick out the feelings. Also, watch television shows, particularly daytime dramas, to see if you can listen to people's statements and then reflect their feelings immediately after they speak, picking up on nonverbal as well as spoken cues.

Turning the Reflection into a Question

In the common error called, "Asking the client, 'How do you feel?' " we suggested that questions do not enhance an empathetic relationship. Often, you know what the client is saying, but you state it as a question. For example:

Santiago (Client): "I've had a very difficult time. My mother died about one month ago and now my dad is in the hospital with pneumonia. I'm here 2000 miles away and I can't get any time away from work."

Tori (Helper): "Are you feeling sad over the death of your mom and a sense of helplessness as you worry about your dad?"

Can you see how a client might respond with a simple "Yes" or "No"? The question suggests that the helper is confused, and it does not provide as many options to explore. Had the helper reflected the client's feelings with a statement, he or she could have said, "It must be a very helpless feeling for you to be so far away when you are worried about your dad and trying to deal with the sadness of your mom's death." Such a statement more effectively communicates understanding of the client's situation and is more compassionate. Rather than responding to a question, the client can go on to explore whatever issues seem important to him or her. If you have the tendency to turn statements into questions by raising your voice at the end of a sentence, let your fellow students know and see if they can alert you to this habit.

Combining a Reflection and an Open Question

In the early stages, it is tempting to add an open question after the reflecting statement. This confuses the client because he or she has been asked to do two things: respond to the reflection of feeling and answer the open question. For example, a helper might say, "You feel really alone since your wife died. Do you have any close friends?" Clients often respond by only replying to the open question rather than to the reflection of feeling. In this example, the client may go on to tell you about his close friends but fail to discuss his loneliness. If you have this tendency, try eliminating open questions altogether for a while in your practice sessions.

Focusing on the Wrong Person

A major aim of reflecting feelings is to make the client aware of his or her underlying emotions. Clients may lead us away from these emotions by focusing on other people and launching into long stories about them. Let us take a look at a couple of different ways the helper can respond to a client statement such as: "My best friend, Judi, and I are not as close as we used to be. Sometimes I think she just wants to neutralize our relationship. It seems like she has no time for me, like she doesn't care."

On the one hand, the helper can paraphrase in a judgmental way, focusing on the client's friend: "She neglects you." Or the helper can keep attention centered on the client: "You miss the relationship you used to enjoy so much."

Can you see how focusing on the other person can send a judgmental message about the friend? Because you do not know anything directly about the other person, such a statement is unfair and perhaps inaccurate.

Letting the Client Ramble

Many helpers tend to let their clients talk too long without responding. After all, it is not polite to interrupt. However, clients need paraphrases and reflections in order to know that their story is making sense to the helper. Because they are talkative or anxious, some clients leave little room for the helper to slow the pace and focus on a particularly important message. Beginning helpers need to give themselves permission to stop rambling clients and make reflections. Surprisingly, this often serves to reassure clients that each aspect of their story is being heard in a systematic way. Here is one example of a way that a helper politely requests a pause to verify that the right message is being received:

Helper: "Let me stop you here for a second and see if I understand correctly. You feel both angry and hurt that your friend is not spending time with you, but you are afraid to mention it because she may simply terminate the friendship."

Or,

Helper: "I'm sorry to interrupt, but let me tell you what I know so far. You resent the fact that you and your friend don't get together much anymore, but it is too scary to think about bringing it up."

A footnote to this discussion is that a helping relationship needs to have both people actively participating. By stopping the flow of the client's story to catch up, the helper is becoming involved with the client, creating a connection and *actively* listening, rather than becoming a "listening post."

Using the Word *Feel* Instead of *Think*

In the beginning, you may hear yourself or your classmates make a reflection along these lines, "You feel that your husband should have been more respectful of your need for privacy." This is not a reflection of feeling because the client's underlying emotions are not being identified. In this helper's statement, the word "think" may be substituted for "feel": "You *think* that your husband should have been more respectful of your need for privacy." If you can substitute the word "think" without changing the meaning, you have not reflected a feeling, rather you have paraphrased the client's thoughts which are part of the content. In the preceding example, a true reflection of feeling would be: "You feel angry (or hurt) because you think that your husband should have been more respectful of your need for privacy."

Some people use "feel" instead of "think" a great deal in their daily conversations. If you have this tendency, try to become aware of it and change your "feel" to "think" whenever you become aware of it. By being accurate in your word choice with clients, you are subtly teaching them to become aware of the differences between what happened and what is felt.

Undershooting and Overshooting

Undershooting and overshooting are two common mistakes in reflecting feelings (Gordon, 1975). *Overshooting* means that the helper has reflected a feeling that is more intense than the one expressed by the client. *Undershooting* is reflecting a feeling that is too weak to adequately mirror the client's emotion. Consider this client statement and three possible responses:

Client: "Becky told Mrs. Gordon that I was not a good typist, so she started giving the most interesting work to Ronaldo instead of me."

Helper: "You must have been mad enough to kill!" (overshooting)

Helper: "You were a little annoyed." (undershooting)

Helper: "You were angry." (accurate intensity)

Overshooting and undershooting are beginners' mistakes; this tendency normally corrects itself as you gain a larger feeling vocabulary. Like playing darts, you learn to hit the bull's-eye as you encounter your mistakes. Clients will let you know how accurate your reflections are. If you undershoot, you can raise the intensity a notch or lower it when you overshoot. If your feeling vocabulary seems limited at present, study lists of feeling words like those in Table 5.2. You may also try using qualifiers such as "a little angry," "somewhat angry," or "very angry" to convey various shades of emotional intensity.

Parroting

Parroting is another common mistake caused by an inadequate feeling vocabulary. Parroting means repeating back to the client the very same feeling words he or she has just used. For example, a client might say, "The whole party I planned was rather frustrating because no one came for the first hour and then people stayed past the time limit we had indicated in the invitation." The helper then responds (parroting): "You were frustrated that they disregarded your instructions." The paraphrase in this case is pretty good since it distills the facts. However, the feeling is an exact reproduction.

The tendency to parrot arises when the client seems to have beaten you to the punch and to have already expressed a feeling in his or her story. What do you do? The answer is to discern what other feelings the client might have experienced at the same time or to identify a feeling more accurate than the one the client has expressed. Forget about the feeling of frustration that the client has expressed and imagine what else you might have felt in that situation. Here are two possibilities:

Helper: "I'd guess you were also a little angry that they didn't seem to get the message after all the planning you put into it."

Helper: "If I had been in your shoes, I guess I might have felt a little hurt that very few of the people seemed to have honored my wishes."

Your Reflecting Statements Go On and On.

Sometimes helpers tend to continue to reflect and paraphrase, not in sentences, but in chapters. This is a kind of shotgun approach that waters down your effectiveness. The student thinks, "If I reflect several different things, one of them is bound to be right." Instead, try thinking of reflecting as a form of gambling, like playing poker. You must wait until you think you understand and then you place your bet on a single brief reflection, paraphrase, or combination. If you are wrong, the client will correct you and proceed to describe the accurate feeling, helping you to find the bull's-eye.

Summary

The reflecting skills are a quantum leap from the invitational skills because they do much more than encourage clients to tell their stories. The reflecting skills move clients to greater self-awareness and encourage the client to address deeper issues beneath the surface. They forge a bond between client and helper because the client senses that someone has taken the time to really understand.

Reflecting skills have two building blocks: paraphrasing, and reflecting feelings. Paraphrasing is a distilled version of the content of the client's message; reflecting feelings involves identifying and labeling the client's feeling, whether or not such feelings have been openly expressed. The feeling component of the message is often hidden because disclosure of feelings is bound by cultural and family rules.

The emotions that helpers identify when reflecting feelings have many nuances and variations. There are, however, some basic or primary feelings that helpers can consider when trying to accurately sense and communicate the client's unique emotional experience. Helpers need to improve their feeling vocabularies in order to convey understanding of the client's message. Labeling and reflecting feelings can be one of the most difficult processes to learn. There is a great variability in how quickly students learn to reflect feelings. Some come to it very naturally and quickly. Others take longer but can learn the skill eventually through persistence and practice.

Group Exercises

Group Exercise 1: The Alter-Ego Technique for Identifying Feelings

Identifying feelings precedes reflecting them. One of the best action methods for learning to identify feelings is the *alter-ego technique,* which comes to us from psychodrama (Moreno, 1958). The alter-ego technique asks the student to pretend that he or she is the client in order to imagine the client's feelings. This group exercise requires four members: the client, the helper, the alter ego, and the observer. It is in the role of alter ego that the student learns most about how to identify feelings.

The Client   The client discusses an experience with either positive or negative ramifications, such as a good or bad vacation, a relationship that ended abruptly, a missed opportunity, or another minor problem.

The Helper or Listener   The trainee who plays the part of the helper has little to do in this exercise. The job of the helper is to listen with appropriate body position, using only open questions and minimal encouragers, providing a focus for the client but rarely intervening.

The Alter Ego   The third student, an alter ego, stands behind the client and speaks for the client, identifying anything the client might be feeling but has left out. The alter ego speaks using the word "I" as if he or she were speaking for the client; "I am angry," "I am embarrassed," and so on.

The Observer   The fourth member of the group is an observer who records the alter ego's remarks on a blank sheet of paper. In the discussion phase, the client gives the alter ego feedback on the most accurate and the least accurate reflections and paraphrases. The observer should gently correct the alter ego if he or she forgets to speak as the client and lapses into "you feel" rather than "I feel . . . ."

Action Phase   Once roles have been assigned, the client tells his or her story to the helper/listener. The alter ego, standing behind the client, expresses underlying feelings in the client's story. The client should be directed to ignore the alter ego, except when the alter ego really hits the mark. At that point, the client should incorporate the alter ego's comment into his or her statements. For example, if the alter ego says, "I am angry and embarrassed," the client may then respond, saying, "I *am* embarrassed." The client always directs his or her response to the helper/listener, even when reacting to the alter ego. Although client and helper/listener may find this exercise frustrating, the alter ego learns to hear feeling, imagining himself or herself as another person.

Discussion Phase   After 5–8 minutes, the group members discuss their experiences and the observer gives the alter ego feedback. Members then exchange positions until everyone has had a chance to experience the role of alter ego.

Quick Tips: Reflecting Feelings

- You will probably need to use invitational skills and paraphrasing before you have enough information to reflect feelings. When you have heard enough of the client's story to grasp the emotional content, stop the client to make a reflection.
- If you don't know how the client is feeling, imagine yourself in the client's shoes. What would you be feeling if you were the client?
- Use different feeling words than those used by the client to avoid parroting.
- Don't agree with the client when he or she is placing blame on someone else. Convey that you understand the client's viewpoint without taking sides.

Group Exercise 2

The alter-ego technique is a good way to develop the initial skill of imagining oneself as the client and identifying thoughts and feelings. The next step is to incorporate the skill within the helping interview. Break into groups of three with a helper, client, and observer. During a 5–8-minute session, the client describes a small problem he or she has been having with a friend, a family member, or someone at work. The helper uses invitational skills, paraphrases, and, whenever possible, reflects feelings. The helper's goal is to reflect *at least three feelings* during the practice session.

The observer makes certain that the time limits are observed and, during the period, records every helper statement on the Feedback Check-

list. At the end of the time, he or she shares feedback with the helper. The client gives the helper feedback on which responses on the checklist were most accurate and which were least accurate. The client makes a check next to those that seem to "hit the mark." The group exchanges roles until everyone has had a chance to practice the role of helper and receive feedback.

Feedback Checklist: Reflecting Skills

Observer Name _____ Helper Name _____
During the session, the observer records the helper's responses verbatim (except minimal encouragers). After the session, the group categorizes the responses with the following symbols:
DO for door opener,
OQ for open question,
CQ for closed question,
P for paraphrase,
R for reflection of feelings, and
P/R for a combination paraphrase and reflection of feeling.

Category*	Helper Response	Client Feedback
_____ 1.	_____	_____
_____ 2.	_____	_____
_____ 3.	_____	_____
_____ 4.	_____	_____
_____ 5.	_____	_____
_____ 6.	_____	_____
_____ 7.	_____	_____
_____ 8.	_____	_____
_____ 9.	_____	_____
_____10.	_____	_____

*Do not include minimal encouragers.

Additional Exercises

Exercise 1: Practice in Identifying Feelings—*In Vivo* (Porter, 1996)

Form groups of four for this exercise. One student (the client) briefly describes a recent situation, or one in the more distant past, that

caused a strong emotional reaction—for example, being turned down for a job, breaking up with a girlfriend or boyfriend, or experiencing angry feelings toward a teacher or co-worker. During the description, the student who is relating the story is not to use any feeling words—

for example, "All day, I tried to talk to my boss but she kept cutting me off and avoiding me." The remaining three students listen to the story and write down the emotions they might have felt in this situation. Students then compare the feelings they identified.

Exercise 2: Practice in Identifying Feelings and Reflecting Feelings in Writing

Listed below are eight client statements. First, go through and identify the major feeling or feelings in each client statement. Then go back and write out a full reflection of feeling. If more than one feeling exists, reflect all of them.

a. "There I was, standing in front of the entire assembly, and I froze. Everyone was staring at me. My heart was pounding and I started to shake. I thought I was going to die right there on the spot. I can never show my face again after that."

_____

_____

b. "And for the third time in a row, he failed to show. What a jerk! My daughter looks forward to these outings with her father and I hate to see him treat her this way. Don't you think he is a jerk?"

_____

_____

c. "I can't wait to go to Europe with the French club. It's the opportunity of a lifetime! Yet, it is going to be expensive. In addition to the obvious things, I'm going to need spending money, too. I would have to bring my boyfriend something. I don't know how I am going to come up with all the money I need."

_____

_____

d. "The more I do, the more the boss seems to expect. He's never satisfied and is always finding fault. I think I should start looking for another job because I can't take it any more."

_____

_____

e. "I can't believe I trusted my sister-in-law. She is such a back-stabbing witch. I hate her. She'd start bad-mouthing my mother-in-law and get me going. Then after she got me saying negative things, I found out she was going back and repeating everything I said to her! Now my mother-in-law hates me."

_____

_____

f. "We just moved here and I'm working two jobs. But somehow I've got to find time to take my kids to their schoolmates' houses so they can get to know people and have some friends. I just don't seem to have time."

_____

_____

g. "My son keeps staying out late at night with his friends. He won't tell me where he goes. I'm afraid he'll get hurt. He's probably able to take care of himself. I don't know what to do."

_____

_____

h. "My boss just stays in her office doing her personal paperwork. She won't come out to help us and sometimes we get so busy. We get tired and then we get behind."

_____

_____

Homework

Keeping an Emotions Diary

Make a copy of Table 5.2 and keep it with some blank paper on a clipboard near your bed. Think about an emotion you experienced today. For example, if you felt angry at work, at school, or with family, record that feeling as the answer to the first question below. Fill out this diary for two successive days and then write a one-paragraph reaction recording your discoveries.

- What was the emotion? _____

- Think of a synonym for the emotion as you experienced it today. _____

- Describe the situation in which you experienced the emotion. _____

- Who was present when you experienced the emotion? _____

- What do you think caused your emotion? Do you blame other people for your emotion? Which of your personal values and beliefs might have given rise to this emotion? In other words, what did you say to yourself that seemed to spark this emotional response? _____

- How did you express the emotion? _____

- What societal rules come to mind when you think about expressing this emotion? _____

- Record any other thoughts you have about your experience today. _____

Journal Starters

1. Think about the expression of emotion in your own family. Do you think that some emotions are more allowable than others? How do you think your own family or ethnic background might affect your willingness to listen to a client's feelings?
2. Think about the following negative emotions: sadness/depression, anger, and fear. If a client expressed one of these feelings frequently and with great intensity, which ones would be the hardest for you to deal with?
3. Now that you have begun to practice some of the skills, how has this learning affected your feelings of confidence? Are you experiencing any of the anxiety or awkwardness that was predicted? If so, how are you coping with it? Do you have times when you feel comfortable with your work and other times when you lack confidence? What is different about these two times?

For more journal ideas, as well as more practice with reflecting skills, refer to Chapter 5 in *Exercises in the Art of Helping*.

References

Carkhuff, R. (1987). *The art of helping* (6th ed.). Amherst, MA: Human Resource Development Press.

Gordon, T. (1975). *PET: Parent effectiveness training.* New York: Wyden.

Izard, C. E. (1977). *Human emotions.* New York: Plenum.

Kottler, J. (1997). *The language of tears.* San Francisco: Jossey-Bass.

Moreno, J. L. (1958). *Psychodrama* (Vol. 2). New York: Beacon House.

Porter, S. (1996). Reflecting feelings. Unpublished manuscript.

Reik, T. (1968). *Listening with the third ear.* New York: Pyramid Books.

Rogers, C. R. (1961). *On becoming a person.* Boston: Houghton Mifflin.

Workman, W. J. (1993). Relationship of counselor variables to preference for type of response in counseling. *Counselor Education and Supervision, 32,* 178–188.

Advanced Reflecting Skills

6

It is not just what we inherit from our mothers and fathers that haunts us. It's all kinds of old defunct theories, all sorts of old defunct beliefs, and things like that. It's not that they actually live on in us; they are simply lodged there and we cannot get rid of them. I've only to pick up a newspaper and I see ghosts gliding between the lines.

Henrik Ibsen, *Ghosts*, Act 2

In the remake of the movie *Father of the Bride,* the bride-to-be calls off the wedding when her fiancé buys her a blender for the six-month anniversary of their meeting. The bride-to-be is tearful and angry because, for her, the blender is a sexist symbol. She interprets the present as an expression of his wish for her to take on a traditional female role—in the kitchen. Her husband-to-be responds with bewilderment because that is not what he intended.

This example illustrates two points about the perceived meaning of an event. First, each person's interpretations, values, and perceptions are unique. They are formed by the person's history, current needs, values, and worldview. Two people experiencing the same event will have different "takes" on its significance. As many cognitive therapists like to quote, "It is not what happens to us, but what we make of it." Second, the meaning of an event for an individual can be uncovered only with some deeper knowledge of that person. Had the fiancé understood that being independent and being recognized as more than wife and mother were very important to his future wife, he would have been able to anticipate her reaction to the gift of a blender! If a helper wants to really understand a client, he or she must be willing to go beyond content and feeling and uncover the deeper meaning that the client assigns to life events.

Advanced Reflecting Skills: Understanding the Client's Worldview

In this chapter, we will look at how a helper can identify and respond to the meanings of a client's story by using advanced reflecting skills. We will also look at summarizing, a way of binding together the parts of a story into a capsule account. Reflection of meaning is, by far, one of the most difficult skills to learn so we address it first.

Reflection of meaning is a significant step beyond paraphrasing and reflection of feeling because it taps the unique worldview of the client. The content of the story gives us an outline or picture in our minds about what has happened. The emotions give the story more color and help us see the feelings that the client is dealing with. The meaning of the story is that part that tells us why this event was so significant. It answers the question, "Why are you having these feelings about this content?"

Consider the case of Joan, who had been having problems at work for two years. Her co-workers had split into two factions that everyone on the job called "the redbirds" and "the bluebirds." There was considerable animosity because of a power struggle between the leaders of the two groups. Joan found herself allied with the bluebirds. During one of their after-work gripe sessions, she revealed that she knew one of the redbirds, Bob, had sought treatment for alcoholism. Bob had told her this several years ago when they were on good terms. Once this information leaked, Bob's boss called him "on the carpet" because the company was working on several government contracts, and Bob was investigated as a security risk. A couple of weeks later, Joan went to the company's employee assistance program (EAP) and asked for counseling. During the interview, she and the counselor (Lynn) had the following exchange.

Joan: "There is just so much turmoil. It used to be a good place to work. Now it's dog eat dog."

Lynn: "You are a bit sad that things have changed and there is so much competition." (reflection of feeling and paraphrase)

Joan: "Yes, that among other things."

Lynn: "Go on." (door opener)

Joan: "Well, Bob told me about his treatment for alcoholism one night when we were working late, sort of offhand. I even thought of him as a friend."

Lynn: "You're afraid of his reaction when he finds out that you leaked the information." (reflection of feeling and paraphrase)

Joan: "Not really. It just seems a nasty thing to do to someone who was trying to be friendly."

Lynn: "In other words, you are disappointed in yourself for having betrayed a confidence." (reflection of feeling and meaning)

Joan: "Yeah, that's the thing. I think I did it just to be part of the club. I don't like that about myself. I wish I were secure enough to have my own opinions about people."

Lynn: "It sounds like it has always been very important for you to be approved of and sometimes you find yourself doing something you don't agree with." (reflection of meaning)

If Lynn had merely paraphrased the story of Joan's problems at work, her thoughts, and her underlying feelings, they would have had a productive session. However, Lynn chose to dig more deeply, not only paraphrasing Joan's feelings about recent events but also looking at the underlying meaning—the perceptions and values her client attributed to the self, the office situation, and the other workers involved. Figure 6.1 shows that every client story, like Joan's, has several layers. As if peeling an onion, a client is likely to give us first the content of the story, then the

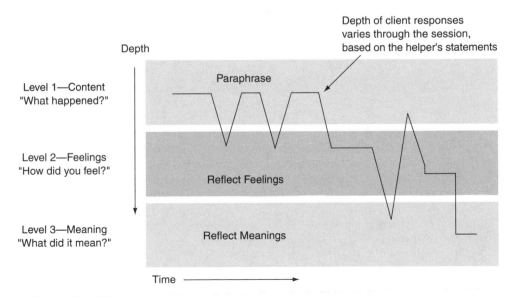

Figure 6.1
Levels of Disclosure

feelings it evokes, and, finally, its personal meaning. Sometimes the deeper feelings and meanings evoke embarrassment and shame, and much time and trust are needed before the full meaning of the story becomes apparent. In other words, as one goes deeper, the client may feel more threatened. However, if the client feels safe, the fullest version of the story can emerge. Notice how Lynn's understanding of Joan's disappointment in herself leads to a deeper response by Joan.

Levels of Disclosure

Why reflect meaning? It is clear that the events in Joan's story have a deeper significance than Joan herself is able to identify at first. Meaning is the background against which the client's story is played, but it needs to be noticed and brought into awareness. Why is it important for the helper to bring this deeper level of meaning to the surface? One reason is that the client takes these backdrop issues for granted. When the helper notices them, the client begins to realize their significance in shaping the story and that these meanings are part of the unique way he or she constructs the world.

In *Reality Isn't What It Used to Be,* Walter Truett Anderson (1990) points out that, as far back as Plato, we have marveled about how people from different backgrounds can have such different views of the same situation. One of Plato's great metaphors is the allegory of the cave. With apologies, I am extending it here to make a point. In Plato's story, people are living in a cave chained together so they must all face the cave wall. They never see the outside world, and their ideas about it are based entirely on the shadows they see reflected on the walls, which constitute their reality. Similarly, we are all caught up in the restrictions of our cultures and backgrounds, and we see other points of view as odd, misguided, or even ignorant.

Like the people in the cave, those who possess similar views and a similar culture see things the same way and reinforce each other's views. Only when we look at ourselves from outside our usual vantage point do we perceive the chains that are holding us within a narrow point of view. The helping relationship leads the client to look at himself or herself from a different perspective. The helper holds up a mirror to the client, "reflecting" rather than agreeing with what the client says. The helper lets the client get a good look at his or her own values and viewpoint about the self, others, and the world. When a client sees himself or herself through the eyes of another, he or she begins to envision how to make constructive changes. In Joan's case, by opening up to the meaning of the story, she begins to see that her actions were due, in part, to her long-felt need for approval. When she makes this connection, it paves the way to set a goal for becoming more self-directing.

Besides shifting the client's perspective, inevitably, reflecting meaning has the effect of getting the client to discuss even deeper issues than those brought out in the first version of the story. Can you see that Joan's next statements in her dialogue with Lynn might go into how she was raised, where her values came from, and other situations where she has disappointed herself? When meaning is not reflected, clients stay with more superficial topics.

Beginning helpers are often confused when the client's story seems to have run its course. They feel that once the basic facts are known, where else can the conversation go? Very often this is because the helper has not gone deeper into the story. Figure 6.1 shows the concept of depth in a client's story over time. According to this model, superficiality is the result of traveling too quickly in a horizontal direction, rather than going deeper or vertically. The depth that a client is willing to go is dependent on a number of factors. Among these are helper responses, client readiness and willingness, and some attributes of the therapeutic relationship. Questions and minimal encouragers do not increase the depth of the conversation. Instead, they keep the client at a more superficial level.

If the helper does not invite the client to reach deeper levels by reflecting feelings and meanings, the client will normally stay at level 1. Of course, some clients are very psychologically minded and will quickly discuss the deeper aspects of a problem. On the other hand, some clients are not very talkative and are uncomfortable with expressing feelings and uncovering personal issues. In that case, going deeper takes a much longer time, even if the helper is very inviting and uses reflecting skills. Finally, as we discussed in Chapter 3, clients are more likely to disclose deeply if the relationship with the helper is perceived as competent, trustworthy, and nurturing.

Obviously, the only factors that the helper can control are his or her own actions. The helper cannot always break through a client's reluctance to open up. To increase the likelihood of greater depth in the client's explorations, the helper must provide the best possible opportunity for a therapeutic alliance between client and helper. To do this, the helper must avoid the overuse of questions and must also use reflecting skills to deepen the client's story whenever possible.

Challenging the Client to Go Deeper: The Inner-Circle Strategy

In Joan's case, the helper used questions and reflections of meaning to get at the deeper levels of the story. Sometimes clients have difficulty recognizing that their stories have these deeper layers, and it is useful to challenge them to move from a superficial recounting to the area of personal meanings. Arnold Lazarus, the founder of multimodal therapy, uses what he calls an "inner-circle strategy" for getting clients to identify deeper, more personal issues (1981, p. 55). The helper draws a series of concentric circles labeled A, B, C, D, and E (see Figure 6.2), identifying ring A as issues that are very personal, normally disclosed to only the closest friends. At ring E are issues that are essentially public and might be discussed with almost anyone on first meeting. For example, at ring E is information about the client's appearance and occupation. At ring A are very personal issues such as sexual problems, anger and resentment toward people, negative views of the self, and secrets that the client feels are immoral or dishonest. Once the circles are identified, the client might be asked to write in the names of individuals, including the helper, who have access to the various rings from A to D. Lazarus likes to use the diagram to confront the client when counseling is too superficial. For example, the helper might say, "It seems to me that we are discussing issues that fall in the D or C category. The most effective work occurs at levels A or B. I am wondering if you do not feel comfortable talking about these deeper levels yet."

Stop and Reflect

We have been talking about the fact that the best information is forthcoming, and the most therapeutic relationships are developed, when clients reveal their deepest thoughts, feelings, and perceptions. Clients who venture to this level of disclosure are, however, risking a great deal. One way to realize this is to imagine yourself in the client's position. Think for a moment about what is unique about you. What would a person need to know about you before you would feel that he or she were sufficiently

Figure 6.2
Inner-Circle Strategy

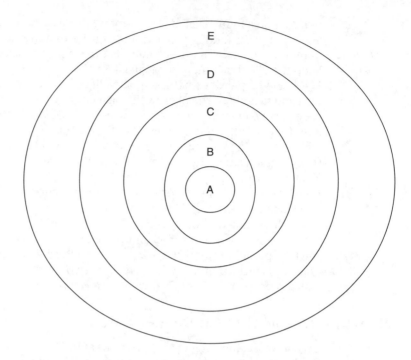

informed to help you? How long would you have to know someone before discussing your deepest secrets? Read each topic in the following list, and identify something relevant about yourself that you would be willing to discuss with a helper during the first session and something else that you probably would not discuss. Write down brief notes under each heading. What do you fear might happen if you disclosed the thoughts, feelings, and perceptions that you would prefer not to discuss.

Topic	I Would Disclose	I Would Not Disclose
Your family values and family history		
Your religion or spiritual beliefs		
Your history of intimate relationships		
Your personal dreams and ambitions		
Happy and unhappy childhood memories		
Physical limitations, disabilities, and illnesses		
Times when you were dishonest or unethical		

Draw an inner circle for yourself like the one in Figure 6.2 and write down the names of people who have access to the deeper issues in your life. Now think of one or two issues that you would not discuss with anyone, even a professional helper. What would stop you? Are there also issues at rings B and C that would be difficult but not impossible to discuss with a helper? What issues would you discuss only if there were safeguards of confidentiality? Share your inner circle with a small group of classmates if you feel comfortable in doing so. There is no need to discuss the issues at each of the levels. However, it might be interesting to compare the numbers of people who have access to the various levels. Who are these people and how did they gain access to this kind of trust?

Worldview and Values: The Sources of Meaning

Worldview is a term coined to refer to a person's view of self, others, and the world. Language, gender, ethnicity/race, religion/spirituality, age, differences in physical ability, socioeconomic status, and trauma all influence the development of one's worldview (Ivey, Ivey, & Simek-Morgan, 1997).

In counterdistinction to worldview, *values* are assumptions about what is right and wrong. By understanding a client's values, we begin to grasp his or her internal struggles and moral dilemmas. Values are a person's basis for self-evaluation and how they evaluate others as well. A client's values tell us about what the client expects of himself or herself, defining his or her ideals and aspirations and what is important. They are the internal guidance system of the individual (Young & Witmer, 1985).

The helper's job is to understand the client's worldview and values so that the client's viewpoint—and the meaning of his or her story—can be appreciated and an appropriate solution to the client's problems found. Following are examples of client statements that give a window to worldview or values:

View of Self
"I am essentially . . . (a good person) (evil) (selfish) (okay/not okay) (smart/dull) (damaged) (unlovable)."
"Nothing I do seems to work out."
"I always land on my feet."

Notice that these statements express general notions about the self, rather than defining specific abilities such as being a good piano player or having a good sense of direction.

Views of Others
"People are . . . (unreliable) (essentially good) (selfish) (trustworthy) (kind)."
"Men are all alike."
"People will take advantage of you if they can."
"White people are . . . ."
"Asians are . . . ."

Views of the Environment or the World in General
"It's dog eat dog."
"Life is a vale of tears."

"You can't get ahead."
"It's bad luck."
"God punished you."
"God rewarded you."
"Things always turn out for the best."
"Stuff happens!"

Values

"People should treat each other fairly."
"Men should be the providers."
"Family secrets should not be told to others."
"Conflict is bad."
"You should always try to do your best."

Helping a Client Whose Worldview Is Different from the Helper's

One of the biggest shocks to the beginning helper is dealing with someone whose worldview clashes sharply with his or her own. It is hard for the helper to remain neutral and nonjudgmental at first because it seems that the client is clearly mistaken or is operating from a distorted viewpoint. These are some general approaches that are helpful in dealing with clients who have a worldview that is distinctly different from that of the helper:

1. Especially at the beginning of the relationship, a helper should focus on listening rather than on telling. Recently, a famous radio psychologist told a welfare mother with three daughters that she should go back to work, even though she could not arrange good day care for her 3-year-old. Since this advice was offered in the first minute of the interview, the psychologist had not taken the time to assess the client's support system, the ages of the other children, or the importance the client placed on being a good mother. Anyone who offers advice so quickly is not respecting or understanding a client's worldview. Such advice is likely to be culturally insensitive, potentially damaging, and ultimately irrelevant to the client.

2. Helpers should expose themselves to knowledge and experiences that help them appreciate different cultures and special populations. At the minimum, helpers should have studied the culture and history of Asian Americans, African Americans, Hispanic Americans, and Native Americans (Sue & Sue, 1990). In addition, the counselor should probably have training in more than one language.

   Beginning helpers may feel overwhelmed when they realize the amount of information that they need to assimilate to become culturally sensitive. A rational approach to an overload of information is to accept that any helper cannot be prepared for all possible differences between helper and client. The best approach is a tutorial one. Let your client teach you about his or her background. Be open and sensitive and do not try to examine the client under the lens of the dominant culture or from your own moral perspective.

3. Helpers must be sensitive to nonverbal communication and to uses of language that might be offensive to special groups. Previously, we discussed the cultural differences in eye contact and physical distance. There are also dif-

ferences in the use of touch, gestures, facial expressions, and so forth. Although we cannot usually predict the effects of these differences, the helper must be open to discussing them and pay close attention when they seem to be interfering with communication.

4. Helpers must become sensitive to differences in emphasis on the role of the family among different cultures. Because families in North America are mobile and less than cohesive, we usually assume that becoming independent from the family of origin is a sign of maturity. However, in some Asian and Latino cultures, becoming independent of the family is not a valued goal of adulthood. One can learn from the client what a normal family is according to his or her background.

5. Helpers must recognize that the Western method of therapy may be unacceptable to some groups and that in many cases indigenous methods should be explored. For example, the World Health Organization recommends that Western medical personnel work jointly with traditional and folk medicine providers. Closer to home, a minister or priest in the African American or Mexican American communities may have more influence and insight than an external helper. Professional helpers need humility in dealing with unfamiliar situations and work in concert with natural support systems.

6. Helpers also need to examine their own personal and cultural attitudes. Because the world is shrinking and our society is changing, the prototype helper of tomorrow must possess or adopt attitudes of empathy (rather than sympathy), tolerance for ambiguity, open-mindedness, and an openness to experience (Corey, Corey, & Callanan, 1988). In addition, Sue (1981) asserts that helpers who are skilled in dealing with special populations understand their own value systems and basic assumptions about human behavior and can appreciate that the views of others will differ. They understand that different cultures have been shaped by different social and political forces than those that molded their own worldview (Pedersen, 1987). Most important, culturally effective helpers honor the worldview of the client, can share it in some way, and constantly strive to avoid the pitfall of believing that their own culture is superior and the right way of looking at life.

7. A final point is that helpers who hope to work effectively with those who are culturally different should become truly eclectic, using skills, methods, and techniques and forming goals that are congruent with the views, values, lifestyles, and life experiences of each client. Helpers must recognize that strategies and techniques useful with the majority population will probably need to be modified or even eliminated when dealing with someone from a different background.

Stop and Reflect

A helper is not always aware that his or her assumptions about good mental health are culturally bound. In this case, a counselor named Don was tempted to encourage a client to accept a Western concept of maturity, even though she comes from an Eastern culture. As you read the case, think how you might help such a client solve the problem in a way that is best for her.

Don was a counselor practicing in a small town near Denver, Colorado. He was born and raised in that area. One of his clients was a 25-year-old woman named Mira who had been born in the United States, although her parents were from northern India. She described the difficulties she was encountering with friends because she still lives at home. She was embarrassed because many raise their eyebrows when she tells them she is living at home. However, in her culture and family, any other living situation would be considered unacceptable before marriage. A previous helper had pushed her to move out of the house and told her, "If your parents don't like it, too bad."

- If the client were not from a different cultural background, aged 25, and still living at home, what assumptions might you make about her? Do you think you might be tempted to make these same assumptions about Mira?
- In talking about her previous counselor, what was Mira communicating to Don?
- What cultural values do you imagine Don might possess that would conflict with the client's upbringing?
- If you were Don, how might you begin helping this client? What more would you like to know about the client?

Jot down your answers to the questions raised here. Discuss them with your classmates.

Reflecting Meaning

Reflecting meaning denotes counselor attempts to restate the personal impact and significance of the event the client is describing. Meanings of events differ from person to person because of worldview and values. For example, much work was done in the 1960s and 1970s on the effect of stressful life events (Holmes & Rahe, 1967). If you have ever been in a stress workshop, you may have taken a "stress scale" that lists life events such as moving, changing jobs, divorce, and so on. Each event is given a weight based on its predicted impact on your life. Initially, it was thought that, by adding up the scores, one could anticipate how much stress a person would feel based on the number of changes during the past year. It turns out that it is not the events that predict your stress level but what meaning you place on them. For example, while divorce is highly stressful to most people, in highly conflictual relationships, it can lead to a reduction in stress. It is not really possible to know how an event has affected someone until you understand their basic worldview and values.

Because meaning is below the surface even deeper than feelings, meanings are harder to detect. The meanings are implicit in the client's story, but one must learn to read between the lines to unearth them. This sometimes means employing intuition or hunches. The more you know about a client, the greater the likelihood that your hunches will be correct. Therefore, helpers are encouraged to be patient using invitational skills, paraphrasing, and reflecting feelings to help the meanings emerge. Helpers generally use two methods to get at meaning in a client's story. First, helpers can *pose open questions* that ask the client to focus on the perceived significance and meaning of the story. Second, helpers can *reflect meanings* by listening carefully and taking educated guesses about why the story is important to the client.

Using Open Questions to Uncover Meaning

Open questions focusing on meaning can be useful, especially when a client is not very forthcoming. You are already familiar with open questions as a building block from Chapter 4. There, open questions were encouraged to delve deeper into some aspect of the client's story and to invite greater disclosure. Open questions can be employed to facilitate a client's identification and expression of meaning as well as to explore areas of content. Consider the following exchange between a client, Sonia, and a helper, Chris:

Sonia: "There was a big family problem because I didn't pick up my sister at the airport. Everyone in the family jumped on me. I guess I was wrong, but I was busy and no one seemed to understand. Now my Mom is mad at me and so is my brother."

Chris: "You feel confused about what happened." (reflection of feeling)

Sonia: "Yeah, and I am mad!"

Chris: "What is it about this situation that makes you so angry?" (open question focusing on meaning of the event)

Sonia: "My time isn't important. The family is important. My sister Camilla is important, but not me."

In this interaction, Chris correctly reflected a feeling of confusion, but Sonia added that she also felt angry. Getting at these seemed to pave the way for the client to expose more about the deeper significance of the problem. Because Chris could not quite identify the meaning in the client's statement, she used an open question to try to understand the deeper issue. The client responded by revealing the meaning of the event: This event reinforced her view that she is not an important part of her family.

How to Reflect Meaning

In Chapter 5, you learned to reflect feelings using the formula: "You feel _____ because _____." The first blank was to be filled in with the client's emotion and the second with paraphrased content—for example, "You feel angry because you didn't get the promotion." To reflect meaning, we use the same formula, but in this case, we place an accurate reflection of feeling in the first blank and a reflection of meaning in the second blank, as in the statement, "You feel disappointed in yourself because being a good daughter is an important value to you." Sometimes it may be necessary to include both a reflection of feeling and a short paraphrase of content in the first blank so that the client knows exactly which event you are referring to—for example, "You were excited (feeling) when you received your driver's license (paraphrase) *because* it meant you were becoming an adult (meaning)." The word "because" shows the connection between the content and feelings of the story and their relationship to the underlying meaning for the client. In other words, it is quite possible, as one goes deeper into the story, to shift among reflecting meaning, reflecting feelings, and paraphrasing as needed. They can be delivered alone or in combination.

Here are some examples of helper reflections of meaning. Assume that each reflection of meaning comes after a period of listening during a helping session.

Example 1

Client: "I don't know what to do now. Everything I worked for is going down the drain."

Helper: "You must feel pretty lost because the dream of having your own business was so important to you."

Here the helper reflects the feeling of being lost. The helper then ties this feeling with the unique meaning that the client's dream has died. The helper may only make a reflection like this when he or she has adequate knowledge of the client's hopes and ambitions from previous statements.

Example 2

Client: "My daughter isn't living right. She stays out late and now she's moved in with that boy and I don't have the heart to tell anyone where she's staying."

Helper: "You are ashamed about your daughter's living situation because you think you have failed as a parent to convey your values."

The helper reflects the client's feeling of being ashamed and briefly paraphrases by mentioning her "daughter's living situation" in a nonjudgmental way. Then, the helper connects the feelings to the underlying meaning: The client feels that she has failed.

Example 3

Client: "I never thought about being divorced. We were married for so long that I never really considered it. Since he left six months ago, I don't know how to act."

Helper: "You feel disoriented by your husband's leaving. Never in your wildest dreams did you expect to get divorced."

Here the helper reflects the client's specific feeling of shock and disorientation. The source or meaning of the shock is that the client had developed a worldview that did not include this possibility. The helper reflects this meaning by saying, "Never in your wildest dreams did you expect to get divorced." This variation of the client's own words is a bit risky, but if it is correct, the client might feel understood at a deeper level.

Reflecting meaning is one of the most difficult skills to learn. It requires that the helper think intuitively and it also means that the helper must fully comprehend the client's unique situation and values. Although we can guess what meaning most people might derive from a situation, as we saw in the case of Mira, to accurately reflect the meaning of an event, we must also have some understanding of its cultural context. The surest route to reflection of meaning is to patiently and persistently use the basic invitational and reflecting skills. These provide the best atmosphere for clients to tell their stories. The more fully we understand the content and feelings, the easier it will be to reflect the underlying meaning.

How to Summarize

Summarizing is the final reflecting skill among the building blocks. Summarizing pulls together everything a client has said in a brief synopsis of the session up to that point. The summary helps the client make some sense of the tangle of thought and feeling just evoked in the session. In other words, it serves a reflecting purpose, letting the client hear his or her own viewpoint in a more organized way. The summary ties some of the major issues that have emerged into a compact version of the story. It may include any of the following: (1) content, (2) major feelings, (3) meaning issues and themes, and (4) history or future plans. Of the reflecting skills, it could be considered the broadest brush, bringing together main content, themes, and feelings in the client's story by concisely recapping them. Summaries may be used at all points during a therapy session—beginning, middle, and end. Since summaries have different purposes, they can be divided into four types: focusing, signal, thematic, and planning.

Focusing Summaries

When used at the beginning of a session, a summary serves the function of a focusing statement. A *focusing summary* is an intervention that brings the discussion back to the major issues and themes, places the spotlight on the client's responsibility for the problem, and reminds the client of the goals. For example:

> "In the last few sessions, it seems like we have been dealing with two major issues. The first is the way that you are trying to renew your social network and find some supportive friends since your breakup with Alicia. The other issue is your mixed feelings about living back home with your parents."

Focusing summaries can even be used at a first session with a new client. For example:

> "Let's review what I know so far. Your mother called and made this appointment for you because you were arrested about a month ago for public intoxication. One of the conditions of your probation is that you receive help for your drinking problem. Your probation officer referred you to our agency. So you're here to do something about the problems you've been having with alcohol. Is this about right?"

Brammer (1973) points out that a focusing summary at the beginning gets the client on track immediately. Contrast this with the normal opening statements such as, "How have things been going this week?" or "What would you like to talk about today?" When a client begins the session by reacting to a focusing summary, he or she immediately begins talking about the key issues and goals.

Signal Summaries

In the middle of a session, the *signal summary* tells the client that the helper has digested what has been said and that the session can move on to the next topic. If the helper does not summarize, the client may feel that it is necessary to go over an issue several times until full understanding is communicated. A good time for a signal summary is when the client seems to have come to the end of a story and pauses. Client: "So that's about it . . . (pause)."

Helper: "Before we move on, let's just summarize where we've been so far. You have tried to get professional help for your daughter's drug problem and she has rejected it. Since she is an adult, there is not much force you can apply. This makes you feel helpless and when you see her, your relationship is very superficial because you can't talk about the drug issue without getting into a fight. You've always been the kind of person who likes to leap into action when a problem arises and here is a situation where there is little to do. That's what makes it especially frustrating." (summary)

Client: "Yes, but that's the way it is. Now I guess I need to talk about how I can go on with my life under these circumstances."

Helper: "Okay, let's talk about that." (door opener)

Thematic Summaries

A theme is a pattern of content, feelings, or meanings that the client returns to again and again (Carkhuff, 1987). The *thematic summary* is an advanced reflecting skill because it means that the helper has to be able to make connections among the content, emotions, or meanings expressed in many client statements or even during many sessions. When this kind of reflection is made, it often provides new information to the client, who may be unaware that the issue is resurfacing so often. Rather than signaling a transition to a new topic, the thematic summary tends to push clients to an even deeper level of understanding or exploration. Here are some examples of thematic summaries:

"There seem to be two issues that keep coming up. One of them is the anger you feel in a number of different close relationships (emotional or feelings theme) and the other is your sense that you haven't been able to reach your potential in your career (content theme)."

"As you have been talking, I seemed to notice a pattern and I'd like to check it out. You seem to want to end relationships when they begin to lose their initial excitement and romance (content theme)."

"From everything we've talked about over these past few weeks, one major issue seems to be that, over and over again, you hesitate to make a commitment to a career or to a relationship or to take any important action because you are afraid you might let your parents down by failing (meaning theme). Is this right?"

It is difficult to practice using thematic summaries because it presumes that you have seen a client over some time and usually for more than one session. It usually takes time for important themes to emerge. Identification of themes is an intuitive process. The helper must think back on the whole of his or her experience with the client and try to cull the big issues. Even though identifying themes is an advanced skill, we have included it here since it is possible you may notice these themes as you practice skills during this course. You may also have the opportunity to see advanced practitioners identify these themes in videotaped sessions.

Planning Summaries

Planning summaries entail a review of the progress, plans, and agreements made during the session. The planning summary brings a sense of closure and ends the session on a hopeful note. Here are two examples:

"Well, it seems like we've identified several things in this first session that we will want to pursue. First, you are unhappy with the way you tend to become overly dependent on your friends. You want to pursue your own interests. In fact, you want to get to know your self better. With this in mind, we thought about your entering a counseling group at the local mental health center. Besides that, you'd like to identify some goals for your career. That is something you and I can begin to work on right away. We'll set up an assessment program and talk more about this in the next several weeks. How does all this sound?"

"Let's recap what we have talked about so far. On the one hand, you have accomplished your financial goals but you are far from satisfied with your relationships with friends and family. You have said that this is because you are not very assertive. It sounds as if this is the area we need to discuss in our next session. What do you think?"

Stop and Reflect

Most writers agree that helpers should adapt the skills they use to the particular client. We have discussed some of the cultural differences that can affect the counseling relationship. However, there are also developmental considerations when applying these skills. In contrast to adults, what changes must be made in our approach to elementary school children? Following are a number of ideas from an article by Erdman and Lampe (1996). After each of the differences are some suggestions about how to modify your skills. Read through this list and then reflect on the questions at the end.

1. Children do not possess the same level of abstract reasoning as adults. Their moral reasoning might be at a different level as well. They do not always see the cause-and-effect relationship between their behaviors and the consequences. They don't always see alternative courses of action, and their ideas about time and the future are vague.

How to Modify Your Approach
Use specific, concrete examples, help the child think about real situations, and use counseling methods that are "hands on." Plans and goals should be short term and very simple.

2. Young children, according to Piaget, are egocentric—they are stuck on their personal reality. Essentially, they have trouble seeing another's point of view; consequently, they do not normally question their own actions or thoughts. A conflicting viewpoint is wrong.

How to Modify Your Approach
Small groups for young children help them to understand that their peers can have different ways of looking at things. A helper can begin to get a child to "decenter" by asking questions such as, "How do you think your friend feels when you do that?" or "How does your teacher react to that?"

3. Children may expect adults to make the rules, to lecture to them, and to punish them for misbehavior. Children become reticent in the presence of adults when they fear disapproval.

How to Modify Your Approach
From the outset, provide a permissive atmosphere where the child feels comfortable talking about any issue without fear of reprisal. Helpers need to take their time

before addressing the reason for the session while acknowledging the child's possible fears. The helper can try to change the child's perception of the helper as an authority figure by asking questions such as, "Do you think I can be of any help with this problem?" as opposed to, "Why did the principal send you to my office?"

Sometimes a tutorial approach can be helpful. Here, the helper turns the table on the child's expectations by asking him or her to become the teacher. For example, one school counselor asks children who speak another language to begin each session by teaching her a few words in their native tongue.

4. Children often express their feelings nonverbally, while adults talk more about their problems. Children pout or laugh rather than complain or compliment. In addition, their nonverbal communication may follow different rules. For example, depression in children may come to light through aggressiveness and negativity rather than crying or looking sad.

How to Modify Your Approach
Consider alternatives to verbal therapy such as therapeutic play, art or music therapy, puppet work, mutual storytelling, and even journaling. Helping children express their feelings in these nonverbal ways is analogous to an adult client opening up and discussing his or her feelings. In addition, the helper should not interpret emotional responses and misbehavior at face value but consider them to be nonspecific responses that could be indicative of several possible feelings.

- What is your immediate reaction to the idea of working with children as a helper?
- What differences have you noticed in talking to children that might mean you would have to adapt your basic helping skills?
- How would you feel if a child disclosed physical or sexual abuse during one of your sessions?
- How would feel about helping children with such serious problems on a daily basis?
- Discuss your reactions with a small group of fellow students.

The Nonjudgmental Listening Cycle

Why Is the Cycle Described as Nonjudgmental?

We have focused a great deal on the skills that a helper uses to understand a client's story. Beyond specific skills, however, the attitudes displayed by the helper can make a great difference in the willingness of the client to open up. Carl Rogers (1957), a pioneer in counseling and psychotherapy, identified positive regard as one of these important attitudes. Positive regard is, as the name suggests, not a neutral stance. The helper actively demonstrates a nonjudgmental approach to the client by showing respect and interest in the unique life of the client. It is a continual challenge to hold such an attitude, especially when we are confronted by clients who have perpetrated violence or engaged in self-defeating behaviors or have committed what we consider to be immoral acts. Positive regard means responding in an accepting and nondefensive way to others who are different in culture, language, ethnicity, and religion. The listening cycle is called "nonjudgmental" because the attitude of positive regard must be in place when the helping skills are being employed. Without this underpinning, the skills are perceived as cold and robotic. The client will feel dissected rather than understood.

When Do You Use Each Skill?

After they have completed their learning of the building-block skills, students frequently ask, "In what order should the skills be used? When will we know it is the right time to use a particular skill." Each individual tells his or her story in a particular way and at a particular pace, depending on his or her background, previous experiences with helpers, and present emotional condition. So, it is not possible to predict the exact order of the skills you will use. However, we can assume that, in general, helping sessions will follow a similar path through a client's story. We call this the *nonjudgmental listening cycle,* or just the *listening cycle,* to emphasize that it is a repeating pattern of basic listening skills. The nonjudgmental listening cycle is a way of conceptualizing a normal or average helping session during which you use most of the building blocks. The listening cycle is repeated with each major topic the client presents. It is used most often in the early part of the therapeutic relationship as you are trying to understand the client's story. Later, however, the helper institutes a listening cycle whenever the client opens a new topic, encounters difficulty, has a crisis, or needs to explain.

The building blocks can be thought of as a set of sequential procedures to be followed as each topic emerges, is discussed, and comes to closure. In our depiction, Figure 6.3, each topic forms a circle from open question to summary. The invitational skills open the topic and the reflecting and advanced reflecting skills move the discussion to deeper levels. A summary normally makes the transition from one topic to another or ends the session. Because each person and each helping relationship is different, this map of the average session should not be seen as the way every helping session must unfold. Instead, it is a guide for the trainee to follow as he or she is learning. A cycle like that shown in Figure 6.3 is typical of a discussion that would occur

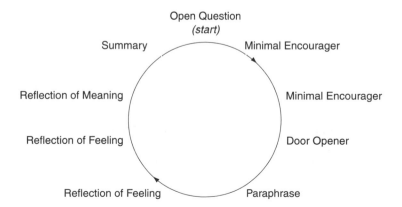

Figure 6.3
A Complete Nonjudgmental Listening Cycle Moving from Open Question to Summary

later in a helping session. It is deeper and more mature because it shows reflections of feeling and meaning. Early on, a client and helper move through several more superficial cycles, focusing initially on content issues. The helper normally uses open questions and paraphrases several times before finding an opportunity for a deeper discussion like that depicted in Figure 6.3.

Is the Nonjudgmental Listening Cycle All I Need to Know About Helping?

At this point, some students become restless to learn more advanced skills, thinking that their teachers are promoting the listening cycle as sufficient for all situations. The listening cycle is not the only set of skills used by helpers. Remember, however, that the listening cycle provides a pathway for the client to tell the story and builds openness and cooperation in the client-helper relationship. Without this foundation, the later processes of assessment, goal setting, and implementing techniques are much more difficult.

Following is an example of helper responses to client statements that represent a complete nonjudgmental listening cycle. It might take more than one such cycle to reach a summary. The session is condensed here to illustrate the major components in sequence:

1. Open question: "Would you tell me more about the accident?"
2. Minimal encouragers: "Okay," "Uh-Huh," "Yes;" "Can you tell me more about that?"
3. Closed question (important facts): "How badly were you hurt?"
4. Paraphrase: "So you had to be in the rehabilitation center for several weeks and you're still unable to work."
5. Reflection of feeling: "You're embarrassed about what has happened and a little afraid that people blame you."
6. Reflection of meaning: "Your identity has always been tied up with your job. Now that you cannot work for several months, it is hard to feel good about yourself."
7. Summary: "Though you're recovering on a physical level, there are several issues that continue to worry you, including how you might perform at your job and how other people will see you."

A Questioning Cycle Typically Found Early in Training

Figure 6.4 shows a relatively unproductive but common cycle, called a *questioning cycle,* typically found in the beginning of training. In this cycle, the helper starts with a good opening question and is able to paraphrase the content. Because the helper is unable to use reflecting or advanced reflecting skills yet, the helper utilizes a question to keep things moving. The question focuses the client back on content and the helper follows this with a series of questions or minimal encouragers. After several such cycles, the helper is tempted to give advice because he or she has understood essential facts and expects that the client is simply in need of direction. In fact, the discussion has not really scratched the surface.

One way of getting away from this kind of interaction is to respond to the client's last statement directly, using a minimal encourager, open question, or door opener. This will lead to reflections of feelings and meanings later on. Notice in the following

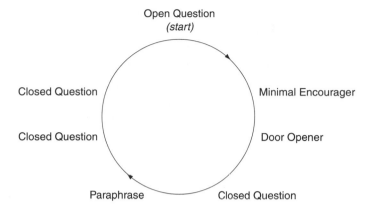

Figure 6.4
A Questioning Cycle Typically Found Early in Training

client-helper exchange how this questioning cycle takes the client off track because the helper's questions do not respond to the client's last statement.

Helper: "Tell me more about the accident."

Client: "It was horrible—what can I say? It was a financial problem, I felt terrible for months and there were the physical problems, too."

Helper: "Can you tell me more about the wreck itself?"

Client: "I ran into another car and that car hit some people on the sidewalk."

Helper: "How badly were you hurt?"

Client: "I had two weeks in the hospital with a broken femur and a broken ankle. I had to go to the rehab center for the month of May. I'm not walking yet without a cane. I don't know when I can go back to my job."

Helper: "Do you think you are getting better?"

Client: "Yes, but I am in no hurry to face people. I am a little afraid to see everybody."

Helper: "What is it like being out of work for so long?"

Client: "I am bored and I focus a lot on the pain in my legs."

Helper: "How much pain would you say you are in?"

Can you see that the helper's fifth question, "What is it like being out of work for so long?" is not responsive to the client's statement, "Yes, but I am in no hurry to face people. I am a little afraid to see everybody"? Here the helper has a golden opportunity to reflect the client's feelings of fear and embarrassment. Instead, the helper falls back on questioning, taking the client off track. When the helper is struggling to understand but cannot make a quick response, he or she is better off using a minimal encourager or a door opener as a delaying tactic. It is crucial that the helper respond to the client's last statement rather than ask a question that throws the discussion into a different topic. Following is an example of how responding to the client's last statement using minimal encouragers, reflecting feeling, and reflecting meaning in that sequence can deepen the client's self-examination.

Helper: "How badly were you hurt?" (closed question)

Client: "I had two weeks in the hospital with a broken femur and a broken ankle. I had to go to the rehab center for the month of May. I'm not walking yet without a cane. I don't know when I can go back to my job."

Helper: "So you had to be in the rehabilitation center for several weeks and you're still unable to work." (paraphrase)

Client: "Yes, but I am in no hurry to face people. I am a little afraid to see everybody."

Helper: "Go on." (door opener)

Client: "Well, I don't know what they are thinking."

Helper: "Okay." (minimal encourager)

Client: "I think that everyone blames me for what happened."

Helper: "You're worried that some of your friends will reject you because of the injuries to the other people."

Client: "I guess it is not rational."

Helper: "When you think about it, it doesn't seem sensible, but all the same, it worries you." (paraphrase and reflection of feeling)

Client: "Sure. I guess I would feel even worse if my own friends blame me."

Helper: "So it sounds like sometimes you blame yourself for what has happened." (reflection of meaning)

Summary

Reflecting feelings and content are important tools for communicating to a client that you understand the story, but for a client to deeply sense understanding from the helper, it is also important to identify and reflect the meanings behind the client's experiences. Meanings consist of the worldview and values that clients bring with them from their culture and from their experiences of life. Culture includes influences of family, religion, and ethnicity. Meaning is another way of describing why this story is so significant to the client.

The inner-circle strategy is a method described in this chapter to indicate to clients that they are not disclosing at the deepest levels, where the best helping occurs. It also helps us recognize that everyone maintains some secret areas. When we consider how scary it might be to expose these to others, we can begin to understand a client's need for a therapeutic alliance built on trust and time.

Reflections of meaning are helper responses that go beyond the superficial, getting at the implicit messages rather than the explicit. This means that the helper must use intuition to go beyond the surface of what the client says, extrapolating the underlying meanings. When the facts, feelings, and meanings of a client's story are reflected, he or she feels that the helper has understood at a very deep level.

The summary response is the second major skill described in this chapter. Summaries pull together the content, feelings, and meanings in a distilled form. Summaries serve to focus the client on the major issues, identify themes, signal a transition in the session, and provide a basis for planning the next steps.

The nonjudgmental listening cycle (NLC) is a way of explaining the sequence of skills that a helper normally employs in the first few hours of interaction. Understanding the NLC can help new learners decide which skills to use at various points in the initial stage of helping. By analyzing the NLC in transcripts or in classroom practice, a helper can determine if he or she is responding to the client's statements with deepening responses or shifting topics by the overuse of questions.

Group Exercises

Exercise 1

Form groups of three with a client, helper, and observer. The client is to pick a topic that evokes some deeper meaning such as:

> "My greatest ambition is . . ."
> "My biggest disappointment has been . . ."
> "Something I am not very proud of is . . ."
> "My ideas about divorce are . . ."
> "What I like about this country is . . ."
> "Something I would like to improve about myself is . . ."

The helper is to use minimal encouragers and open questions to keep things moving, but the main goal is to advance hunches about the personal meanings that lie behind the client's disclosures. The helper should review "Quick Tips: Reflecting Meaning" that follows and give reflections of meaning to the client's story.

The observer is to write down all helper responses on a sheet of paper. Later, the helper can record any useful feedback on this sheet and take this record home for further reflection. After 5 minutes or 10 attempts at reflection of meaning, the observer calls time. Together, look at the helper's responses and see how many of these are accurate reflections of meaning. The client, in particular, should give the helper feedback on key meaning issues that were missed. Group members should then change roles and continue until each person has had a chance to play the role of the helper.

Quick Tips: Reflecting Meaning

If you are having difficulty identifying the meaning behind the client's story, consider the following:

- Use the following plan in your practice sessions: Ask an open question to start, use minimal encouragers as you get the details, and then strive for reflection of feelings. Whenever possible, make a reflection of meaning.
- Ask yourself, "Why is this story important to the client?" "Why is he or she telling me this?" "What is it that bothers the client so much about the event?"
- Be patient! Wait until you have heard enough of the story to understand its importance, then reflect meaning.
- Think about the client's background, then tie in what you know about his or her unique viewpoint from previous topics.
- Are you responding to the last thing the client said or are you looking ahead to what you are going to say? If you stay with the client's statements, they will lead you to meaning.
- When you have established a good reflecting relationship and the client knows you understand the situation, take a risk and play your best hunch about some deeper underlying meaning.

Exercise 2

Look back in this chapter to the scenario of Joan and Lynn. After reading that dialogue again, write down a brief planning summary and share it with your classmates in a small group. Next, write down a focusing summary that you might use to begin the next session. Summaries should be about two or three sentences in length. They should contain a brief synopsis of the thoughts, feelings, and meanings expressed by the client. Use the following criteria to give each other feedback on the summaries:

- Was the summary no longer than two or three sentences?

- Did the summary essentially capture the major points?
- Did the summary include the key events, feelings, and meanings expressed?
- Is there a hopeful tone to the planning summary?

Quick Tips: Summarizing

- Use a summary when the client appears to be "stuck." This will tend to get things back on track.
- At the end of a summary, it is often useful to finish with a quick "checking question" such as, "Have I got that right?" or "Am I correct?"
- When you feel like asking a question, try summarizing to signal the client to move on to the next topic.
- Use a summary when the client is moving too quickly and you want to slow the session down.
- Try to finish every session with a planning summary.

Additional Exercises

Exercise 1: Identifying Meanings

In this exercise, you are asked to separately identify content, feelings, and meanings in a client's statement and then put them together in a response that reflects all three areas. Take into account that there may be more than one possible answer since, in practice, inflection or word emphasis would certainly change the meaning of these responses.

a. "I am extremely depressed and have been for about six months. I am now taking medication and things are a little better. But every day I go to the refrigerator and look in. I can't decide what to eat. In the morning, I can't decide what to wear. This isn't me. If a friend calls on the phone, I am not sure what I will talk about, so I dread anyone calling. How long do you think this is going to last? Never has anything like this happened in my family. I feel so bad that my daughter has to come and take care of me. She has a life, too. I even feel like I am burden to you."

Paraphrase the situation (content):

_____

_____

_____

_____

Identify the client's feelings about the situation:

_____

_____

Client's underlying meanings or unspoken assumptions (why is this important?):

_____

_____

_____

_____

Your reflection of meaning (content + feeling + meaning):

_____

_____

_____

_____

b. "I am a 31-year-old construction worker. Lately, I've had thoughts of hitting my child, Barbie. She is 'the light of my life.' But she doesn't mind me. I have to yell and scream. My wife and I don't seem to see eye-to-eye on how she should be raised. Maybe we don't agree on a lot of things. When I tell my daughter something, my wife rolls her eyes and belittles me. So, of course, Barbie won't do what I say. I tried to talk to my wife but she won't listen any better than my daughter does. Now, I was brought up with a belt. But only when I needed it. I don't necessarily think she has to be spanked, but she needs to learn to mind. I am embarrassed when I have to take her to my mom's house or anywhere else because she won't listen."

Paraphrase the situation (content):

_____

_____

_____

_____

Identify the client's feelings about the situation:

_____

_____

Client's underlying meanings or unspoken assumptions:

_____

_____

_____

_____

Your reflection of meaning (content + feeling + meaning):

_____

_____

_____

_____

c. "My main problem is that I am overweight. I know that. And I want to lose weight. Look at the television and magazines. Everybody's skinny! I guess I am supposed to go along with the crowd. But my husband doesn't realize that I have tried everything. He never says it, but I know he doesn't find me attractive anymore. But is a slim body all that is important? How about love? If I lost weight, what would I have to do next? Dress some particular way? He says he is concerned about my health, but do you believe that? Last week, my 7-year-old son and I went to the mall and one of his classmates was there. In front of everyone, the other kid said to my son, "You have a big fat mom!" Children can be so cruel. And his mother didn't even correct him. Don't you think she should have?"

Paraphrase the situation (content):

_____

_____

_____

_____

Identify the client's feelings about the situation:

_____

_____

Client's underlying meanings or unspoken assumptions:

_____

_____

_____

_____

Your reflection of meaning (content + feeling + meaning):

_____

_____

_____

_____

Exercise 2

Once your training group has completed the first typescript (see Homework 2), you will have a way to look at the nonjudgmental listening cycle.

Make a list of all of the skills you used, in order, during your taped practice session. Can you discern a cycle from open question to minimal encouragers to paraphrases to reflection of feelings and meaning? Do you stick with a topic long enough to get at deeper feelings and meanings, or do you tend to go into a questioning cycle? Get feedback from your training group, your instructor, or a classmate about how you can deepen your nonjudgmental listening cycles.

Exercise 3

Form groups of four. Each member is to write down a three- or four-line statement that a fictitious client might give as a summary of a presenting problem. It should be written in the first person, as follows: "I am having trouble getting my children to mind me. That's not all. I've been very depressed and I'm not going to be able to pay my bills this month. What am I supposed to do?" When writing the example, students should remember to include enough information so that a reflection of meaning is possible. The trainer or leader reads each one anonymously and the training group takes turns giving a reflection of meaning using the formula, "You feel _____ because _____. " A good response to the preceding problem might be, "You are feeling overwhelmed because everything is coming apart all at once." The trainer or leader asks for feedback from the group concerning the accuracy of the reflection. Another option is to ask one participant to reflect the feeling and the next participant to rephrase it in more natural terms.

Homework

Homework 1: A Midcourse Checkup

You have now learned something about all of the building blocks presented in this book. Although you have probably not mastered all of them, it is time for a brief review and checkup. Try to be as honest as possible. This will help you identify areas where more practice is needed. Review the feedback you have received during group exercises and your individual practice. Then take a look at the building blocks that follow and rate your current level of mastery for each skill.

1 = I understand the concept

2 = I can identify it and give examples

3 = I can do it occasionally

4 = I can do it regularly

_____ Eye contact

_____ Body position

_____ Attentive silence

_____ Voice tone

_____ Gestures and facial expressions

_____ Door openers and minimal encouragers

_____ Open and closed questions

_____ Paraphrasing

_____ Reflecting feelings

_____ Reflecting meaning

_____ Summarizing

Take a look at the pattern of your responses. If you are like most learners, your invitational skills are strong. You may also be doing fairly well with paraphrasing but you may well be at level 2 or 3 on the reflecting and advanced reflecting skills.

Homework 2: First Typescript

Now that you have read about and practiced the building blocks of the helping relationship, it is time to make a record of your present skill level by recording a longer session (20–30 minutes) on audio- or videotape and converting it to hard copy, or, as we will call it, a *typescript*.

Your goal as a helper in this typescript is to demonstrate your ability to move from cycles of questioning and paraphrasing to use of the higher skills of reflecting feelings and meanings. Rather than asking questions, fall back on paraphrasing, door openers, minimal encouragers, and even silence until you are able to make a reflection.

Step 1

With a partner from your training group, conduct and record a session based on a concern that her or she is willing to discuss. Alternately, your client may role-play the problem of a friend or acquaintance or fabricate a problem he or she might someday encounter in his or her own life.

Step 2

Choose the best 15 minutes of the tape and transcribe every word of both client and helper using the format of Table 6.1. It is important that the client's comments appear directly *below* your helping responses, so that the connection between the two can be examined. Be sure you have permission to record from the client. You can do this aloud on the tape and in writing.

Step 3

Listen to the tape or read the transcript and make comments, naming each of the skills that your response exemplifies. Sometimes, students describe their responses rather than categorizing them. It is important to identify the skills you are using to determine their frequency and appropriateness. Use only the names of the building blocks you have learned. The comments section is a place for you to reflect on your responses. Do not just note weaknesses; identify strengths as well. In the comments section, you may also wish to identify any other issues that come to mind as you review the transcript.

Table 6.1
Typescript Example

In your write-up, include a short description of the client and the nature of the issue to be discussed. Note that each helper and client response is numbered so that the instructor can refer to them.

Client and Helper Responses	The Skill You Used	Comments
H1: "What would you like to talk about today?"	Open question	Looking at this now, it seems a little trite. I think I will try something else next time.
C1: "Well, I have been having a problem with a nosy neighbor."		
H2: "Really? Tell me more."	Minimal encourager and door opener	Seems appropriate at this stage
C2: "Well, she comes over every day. I can't get anything done. I need to work on the computer. I need to do some work around the house. But she won't let me."		I notice that the client is blaming the neighbor. She is not owning the problem. Maybe next time I will get the client to focus more on that.
H3: "She doesn't have anything else to do?"	Closed question	Whoops, I missed the boat. I think it might have been better to reflect the client's frustration.

Homework 3: Alternative to the Typescript—Making a Video

Make a video as described in Homework 2. Instead of making a full transcript of the tape, watch the tape and classify each of your skills as you watch. The process of identifying skills can be a form of practice. Get feedback from fellow students and your instructor on your progress. Try not to be judgmental. One of the biggest mistakes at this point is to notice weaknesses. For example, many students see themselves on tape and don't like what they see. They see mistakes in body position or facial expression. Rather than reacting on a purely emotional basis, try to think about the following questions: "Did I help the client to go deeper into the problem? In the brief encounter, did we form the basis for a therapeutic relationship?" Build on your strengths before focusing too much on your weaknesses. Here are some questions:

- Was I able to get the client to open up?
- Are any of my gestures distracting to the client?
- Are my body position, facial expression, and voice tone inviting?
- Do I allow silence sometimes to urge the client to open up?
- Do I appear relaxed?
- Do I seem engaged with the client or am I too passive?
- How many paraphrases and reflections of feeling did I use?
- Did I rely too much on questions?
- Did I reflect soon enough?
- Did I overuse minimal encouragers rather than reflecting?
- How many reflections of meaning was I able to attempt?
- Are my words responsive to the client's last statement or to my own thoughts?
- What are my natural strengths as a helper?

References

Anderson, W. T. (1990). *Reality isn't what it used to be.* San Francisco: Harper.

Brammer, L. (1973). *The helping relationship: Process and skills.* Upper Saddle River, NJ: Prentice Hall.

Carkhuff, R. R. (1987). *The art of helping* (6th ed.). Amherst, MA: Human Resource Development Press.

Corey, G., Corey, M., & Callanan, P. (1988). *Issues and ethics in the helping professions.* Monterey, CA: Brooks/Cole.

Erdman, P. & Lampe, R. (1996). Adapting basic skills to counsel children. *Journal of Counseling and Development, 74,* 374-377.

Holmes, T. H., & Rahe, R. H. (1967). The social readjustment rating scale. *Journal of Psychosomatic Research, 11,* 213–218.

Ivey, A. E., Ivey, M. B., & Simek-Morgan, L. (1997). *Counseling and psychotherapy: A multicultural perspective.* Boston: Allyn & Bacon.

Lazarus, A. A. (1981). *The practice of multimodal therapy.* New York: McGraw-Hill.

Pedersen, P. B. (1987). Ten frequent assumptions of cultural bias in counseling. *Journal of Multicultural Counseling and Development, 14,* 16–24.

Rogers, C. R. (1957). The necessary and sufficient conditions of therapeutic personality change. *Journal of Consulting Psychology, 21,* 95–103.

Sue, D. W. (1981). *Counseling the culturally different: Theory and practice.* New York: Wiley.

Sue, D. W., & Sue, D. (1990). *Counseling the culturally different.* New York: Wiley.

Young, M. E., & Witmer, J. M. (1985). Values: Our internal guidance system. In J. M. Witmer (Ed.), *Pathways to personal growth* (pp. 275–289). Muncie, IN: Accelerated Development.

Assessment: Understanding the Client

7

> *A question not asked is a door not opened.*
> M. C. Goldberg, 1998, p. ix

Assessment is the general term that describes the activity of gathering information about a client and the client's problems. Helpers collect information in a variety of ways, beginning with the first contact as the helper observes the client's behavior and

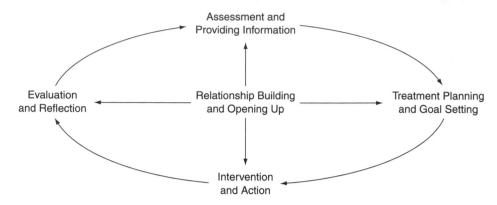

Figure 7.1
Stages of the Helping Process

listens to the story. Formal assessment methods include testing and filling out questionnaires and forms. Informal assessment encompasses all the other ways a helper learns about a client, including observing and listening. Formal assessment may occur at a specific time in the helping relationship, but informal assessment is an ongoing process. In this book, we recommend that the helper set aside time for assessment during the second stage of the helping process (Figure 7.1).

Because each client is unique, it is impossible to be precise about how much time to give to each stage of the helping process. Still, one rule of thumb is to spend one session primarily in relationship building, with the only assessment activities being the collection of basic demographics, observation of the client's behavior, and whatever else you can glean from the client's story. The second and possibly a third session are spent in more in-depth assessment before moving on to a goal-setting phase, which might include testing. Therefore, if a client is seen for 10 sessions, about 10% may be devoted to assessment.

In many places, it is common practice to have a formal period of assessment before the client and helper actually meet. In some agencies, the assessment may be done by an intake worker or a secretary before the client has any opportunity to talk about his or her problem. The decision to employ such an approach is based primarily on saving time and money, but it may also be a way of finding out if the client matches the services being offered. Beginning a relationship with formal assessment can be a mistake, even if it is conducted by the helper, because the initial moments of any human encounter are so important. Imagine how you would feel if you went for a doctor's appointment and were asked only to fill out forms, contribute blood samples, and answer questions, but you did not see the physician or receive any help for your problem.

Following are actual statements from two different client satisfaction forms at a community counseling clinic that relate the experiences of clients who underwent formal assessment in their first sessions:

> "I only came to two sessions. We had to fill out 21 sheets of paper before we could get started. It didn't seem worth it."
> "The helper didn't seem to care about my problem. He just kept writing on his papers."

The approach we recommend is to focus on the relationship first and ask questions later. When clients have been invited to tell their stories, they give much more information during the formal assessment period that follows. They leave the first session believing that they have made a start on solving problems, instead of feeling dissected by tests and probing questions.

Although formal assessment should probably be a scheduled part of every helping relationship, assessment continues through the duration of the relationship and overlaps with every other stage (Drummond, 2000; Whiston, 2000). For one thing, the helper learns more and more about the client, the environment, and the client's problem as the relationship deepens. Second, the helper needs different information later in the relationship. For example, assume that a child is referred to a school counselor for excessive school absences that seem to be linked to problems at home. The counselor spends time getting to know the client in the office (*relationship and opening up stage*) and later becomes familiar with the cumulative folder concerning the child's academic progress and behavior at school (*assessment and providing information stage*). Later, the child and counselor might set goals such as decreasing absences by 50% during the next grading period (*treatment planning and goal-setting stage*). To achieve the goal, the counselor contacts the parents for more information and, together, they identify a course of action to solve the problem. During this process, the counselor learns a great deal about the client's family and begins to understand which interventions will work and which will probably fail. Next, the school counselor suggests a plan involving parenting-skills training for the parents and a change in math teachers for the child (*intervention and action stage*). Once the plan has been established, the counselor regularly contacts the child, the teacher, and the parents to determine if the intervention is working (*evaluation and reflection stage*). During each stage, information has to be collected. Otherwise, the helper will set inappropriate goals, implement techniques that are rejected, or be unable to recognize success.

Testing as an Assessment Tool

Testing has gone through several stages of popularity and decline within the helping professions. Some of the ups and downs have been due to the enthusiasm and criticism associated with psychological testing. Psychologists embraced testing after World War II. Many other professionals also became enthralled with testing around this time. Later, in the 1960s, some realistic skepticism was directed at testing, as some of its abuses were uncovered. Many tests were found to be culturally biased (Anastasi, 1996). At that time, personality testing with instruments such as the Minnesota Personality Inventory and the Rorschach Test were used routinely with all kinds of clients. Now they are used more judiciously.

Carl Rogers' client-centered approach was at its height in the 1960s and 1970s; its adherents rejected testing as being antithetical to the goal of seeing the client as a unique person. Family therapy proponents have also been leery of instruments that focus on a single person rather than on the family system (Gladding, 1998). This lent impetus to the antitesting forces within the helping professions. Perhaps, today, we can look at testing with a more balanced perspective. We see testing as a tool, rather than as the only way of getting at the truth. Testing can certainly be valuable when diagnosis is difficult. Testing can alert you to dangerous behavior, substance abuse, and psychotic symptoms such as hallucinations and delusions. Testing can also give you insights into a client's functioning in areas you may not have inquired about, uncovering topics for discussion with the client (Hood & Johnson, 1997; Palmer & McMahon, 1997). At its worst, testing can be a waste of valuable time and reveal little beyond what could be found in a couple of sessions talking with the client. Testing can be inappropriate for those who are different culturally as their responses can be easily misconstrued (Paniagua, 1998).

Assessment Is a Critical Part of Helping

Sometimes you will hear that gathering a lot of historical information about a client is not worthwhile. Many theories today emphasize the present and the future rather than the past. It is true that some helpers do spend an inordinate amount of time on background information and administering tests; on the other hand, by failing to collect critical data, one takes the chance of making a serious mistake. You must know your customer thoroughly (Lukas, 1993).

Once I interviewed a 65-year-old man who had been a shoe salesman in Cleveland. He had led an interesting life before retiring about 2 years before we met. He reported no real difficulties and I couldn't seem to understand why he had consulted me. As a courtesy, I talked separately to his 28 year-old-son, who had waited patiently outside. The son told me his father had been a physician in Texas and 5 years ago developed a syndrome, which was thought to be Alzheimer's disease, a severe brain disorder with a deteriorating course. The client had simply filled in the gaps of his history with very convincing fiction. That incident taught me that it is best to get as much information about a client as possible *and* from a variety of sources. If I had tested the client's memory or talked to his son first, I might have saved some time. More important, I might have sent the client away without treatment.

Conducting superficial assessments, however, does not always lead to such spectacular embarrassment. It is very common, though, for helpers to accept the client's story without a critical thought. Even the most astute helper can make drastic mistakes. It is important to listen to what clients leave out and where they minimize or deny. Also, it is easy to forget to ask specific questions. Because someone is well groomed and comes from a prominent family does not mean that he or she should not be asked about drug abuse or suicidal thoughts. Our prejudices and worldview color our definition of pathology. Even the *DSM-IV,* the diagnostic bible, recognizes that misdiagnosis can occur when the helper is not familiar with a client's cultural background and interprets symptoms within his or her own cultural context (Paniagua, 1998).

Because of these common lapses in good assessment habits, helpers need to have a regular screening procedure. A systematic assessment assures us that we are helping the client with the most important issues, such as serious mental disorders, substance abuse, and danger to self or others (Sommers-Flanagan & Sommers-Flanagan, 1995). Perhaps you are thinking that you will never encounter serious problems like these in your future workplace. The reality is that nearly every helper comes into contact with these kinds of serious problems. Even school counselors deal with depressed parents and alcoholic co-workers.

Reasons to Spend Time in the Assessment Stage

Assessment Gives Crucial Information to Plan Useful and Realistic Goals

The main purpose of assessment is to gather information that will be useful in planning the goals that will guide the helper and client. Assessment must have both breadth and depth. As far as breadth is concerned, the helper must throw the net broadly enough to make sure nothing crucial escapes. Depth refers to focusing on specific issues such as suicide, the existence of mental disorders, and the crucial problems that catalyzed the client's decision to seek help.

Assessment Helps Clients Discover Events Related to the Problem

A woman came to a community clinic asking for help in dealing with problems at work. She recognized that her job was stressful, but she found that she was unusually irritable with her co-workers and wanted to work on that problem. After some reflection and homework by the client, we discovered that her angry outbursts all happened between 1:00 and 2:00 P.M. on days when she did not eat lunch. The client knew that she became grumpy when she was hungry, but had never connected this with her behavior on the job. A physician helped the client to deal with a problem of low blood sugar, and her extreme irritability diminished.

Assessment Helps Us Recognize the Uniqueness of Individuals

Unless we ask clients about family and cultural background issues, we make assumptions about them through our own cultural lens. People from a different cultural group may be judged as more pathological than someone who shares our own background. Attractiveness is another powerful social factor that may blind us to a client's problems, while unattractiveness may camouflage a person's strengths. A systematic assessment helps us be less manipulated by these strong social influences and more objective in recording everything about a client.

Assessment Uncovers the Potential for Violence

Some clients are prone to harm themselves or others. Assessment can identify individuals who are at risk for violence. Although it is not possible to always accurately predict violent behavior, a history of self-inflicted injury or harm to others can cue us to examine the client's situation more thoroughly and take precautions.

Assessment Reveals Critical Historical Data

Figure 7.2 shows a simple assessment device called a *timeline*. Rafael was asked to fill in the boxes with critical life events in sequential order. His choice of key interpersonal events gave a glimpse of his worldview and his major concerns.

Assessment Can Highlight Strengths, Not Just Weaknesses and Pathology

More and more helpers are using assessment that focuses on client strengths and competencies. Strength-based assessment instruments such as the Behavioral and Emotional Rating Schedule (Epstein, 1998; Epstein, Harniss, Pearson, & Ryser, in

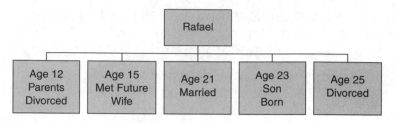

Figure 7.2
Timeline Assessment

press) have been developed in recent years in response to this need. Strength-based assessment is, in part, a reaction to medical models based on pathology. It is also being recognized that building on client strengths enhances client self-esteem and helps client and helper use time more effectively (Miller, Hubble, & Duncan, 1996). Another direction is to base assessment on a wellness philosophy that emphasizes evaluation of client physical, emotional, social, cognitive, occupational, and spiritual issues (Witmer & Sweeney, 1992). By focusing on what the client already knows and can do, we can plan strategies that capitalize on his or her native abilities and coping assets.

Assessment Helps Clients Become Aware of Important Problems

Frequently, painful issues are pushed out of awareness or remain unrecognized until brought to the surface through assessment procedures. A common example of this is substance abuse. When clients are asked to discuss the problems that alcohol has caused, the resulting list can be an eye-opener. Many alcohol treatment centers take thorough histories as a beginning step in breaking down the alcoholic's denial system.

Assessment Keeps You Focused on the Most Important Areas

If you are able to immediately rule out medical problems, assess substance abuse, discuss suicide and violence, and identify clients who are suffering from psychotic disorders, you will probably save yourself and the client valuable time. These issues outweigh most of the other concerns that a client may bring to the table. By doing a broad screening assessment to identify these "hot" issues, you can deal with these first before spending time treating less important areas.

Categorizing Clients and Their Problems

Although helpers realize that each person is unique, the irony is that in order to simplify our work, we like to categorize and label clients as having this personality or that mental disorder. We construct pigeonholes so that we have some way of deciding how to help people with similar problems. However, with this simplification, we lose some of the important information we need. Labeling a child ADD (attention deficit disordered) may describe something important about him or her, but, soon, every action of the child is seen in light of this classification. Although diagnostic systems can paint humanity in broad brush strokes, when it comes to an individual, so often, the person does not seem to fit neatly into any of the categories we devise and his or her unique strengths are lost behind a powerful label.

Recently, a magazine advertisement showed a photograph of people of many different nationalities wearing the company's T-shirts. The essence of the advertisement was that though people may look different and come from many cultures, from the company's perspective, there are only three types of people, Small, Medium, and Large. While the clothing firm was trying to portray the oneness of the human family, the ad made me realize that by trying to see everyone as the same, we are probably ignoring something important. There must be many people who fall between Small and Medium and are not comfortable in either size. Compared to differences in clothing, the helping process is even more personal and must be tailored to each client.

This T-shirt metaphor also applies to the area of assessment and diagnosis, especially in cases where a helper becomes enamoured with a specific tool. For example, if you use the Myers-Briggs Type Indicator (a commonly used test), there are only 16 types of people based on the configuration of preferences. Although 16 is quite a few, it is also not nearly enough to encompass all human differences. As the saying goes, "When the only tool you have is a hammer, everything looks like a nail." A familiar instrument can help you quickly summarize a person, but it will also limit your ability to describe an individual accurately, fairly, and in a culturally appropriate way. Instead of relying on a single test or intake form, it is suggested that you first listen carefully and gather information from any source that fills in the missing colors in the client's unique portrait. The more complete the picture, the better you will be able to design a treatment that really fits.

Organizing the Flood of Information: Making a Diagnosis

Professionals use paper-and-pencil tests, questionnaires, drawings, and similar instruments to gather data about clients and their problems. Besides formal testing, there are five other important sources of information to consider. Key information comes from things the helper *observes,* from *information provided by friends and family,* from *what the client supplies* (verbal descriptions, journals, recordings, and genograms), from *medical history,* and *from other agencies and the legal system.* Because there is so much information that can be collected, it may be confusing to know which sources to tap and how to manage the incoming data. As you learn to be a helper, you will take a course in evaluation and assessment or tests and measurements and probably diagnosis. These courses will provide you with a more complete background. However, it is still important that you recognize that all assessment tools are attempts to simplify the process by placing clients in categories based on a theoretical system.

Figure 7.3 shows the flood of information from the six sources of information entering a funnel that narrows as the data are examined and summarized into categories. Diagnosis is the simplifying process we use to organize the results of our examination. Diagnosis is identifying the overriding issues or problems that seem to encompass a large number of the client's complaints. Using this broad definition, all helpers engage in some form of diagnosis (Hohenshil, 1996).

Figure 7.3 also shows how the client's problems or diagnoses are placed on a treatment planning list, something like an in-basket to be sorted out during the goal-setting

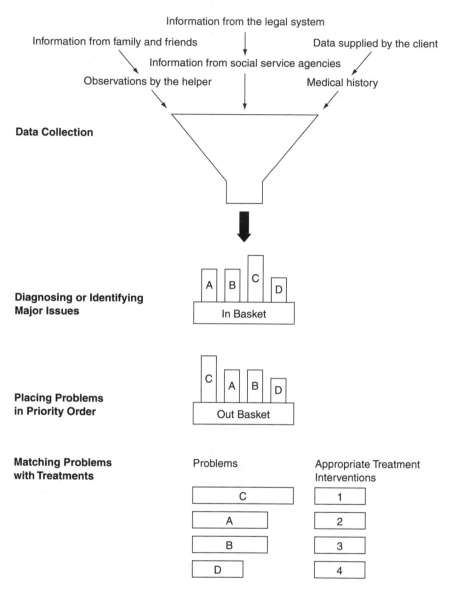

Figure 7.3
Process of Gathering, Sorting, and Matching Problems with Treatments In the Assessment Stage

stage of the helping process. For example, a typical client's in-box might contain marital problems, career confusion, and low self-esteem, which become the focus of the client-helper discussions. Once the client's problems are identified, it is the helper's job to consult with the client and place them in order of priority, noting those issues that will take precedence and those that will be placed on the back burner. The helper selects methods and techniques to treat each problem on the list. These methods might include referral to a physician, assertiveness training, group therapy, or any other method that the helper suggests. Typically, the treatment plan is constructed in conjunction with the client, who signs in agreement.

Beginning Assessment Methods

In this section, we will present four beginning methods of assessment: observation, questioning, constructing a genogram, and completing an intake form. With these four basic techniques, you can be confident that you have made a concerted effort to screen for major problems and determine if the help you have to offer fits the needs of the client.

Observation

Yogi Berra once said, "You can observe a lot just by watching." His statement underlines the fact that observation is something of a lost art. It also emphasizes that observation is not a passive process, but a conscious concerted effort.

Experienced helpers are able to detect patterns from a number of small clues that, on the surface, may seem inconsequential. For example, some helpers can catch signs of alcohol abuse from a client's appearance. Some time ago, a cardiac surgeon called the national offices of a television network because he had seen an interview with a national figure on a talk show. He encouraged the broadcasters to inform the speaker that he was in imminent danger of a heart attack. Although the surgeon had not examined the person, he had seen hundreds of cardiac patients over a 20-year period. Unfortunately, the information was not passed along and the individual died before seeking treatment. Through experience and training, observation can be just as crucial in the helping professions. Clients often carry the clues to their problems on their faces and in the way they walk and speak.

The Helper as Detective

The fictional detective Sherlock Holmes relied on inferences (which he called deductions) to solve mysteries. These inferences were based on his keen powers of observation. In *The Sign of the Four* (Doyle, 1929), Holmes discusses with his partner Watson the two different processes involved in his art; observation and deduction:

> Observation shows me that you have been to the Wigmore Street Post Office this morning but deduction tells me that when there you dispatched a telegram. . . . Observation tells me that you have a reddish mold adhering to your instep. Just opposite to the Wigmore Street Office they have taken up the pavement and thrown up bare earth which lies in such a way that it is difficult to avoid treading upon it . . . the earth there is of this particular reddish tint which is found, so far as I know, nowhere else in the neighborhood. So much for observation, the next is deduction. . . . Why of course I know that you had not written a letter since I sat opposite you all morning. What could you go into a post office for but to send a wire? Eliminate all other factors and what remains is the truth. (pp. 7–8)

Like Holmes, Sigmund Freud was aware of the importance of observation and a thinking process (deduction). Freud believed that evidence of unconscious motivation was available in the everyday activities of clients, including unconscious movements and slips of the tongue (parapraxes). For example, Freud described clients with marriage problems who twisted their wedding rings throughout the session. From *observing* unconscious acts, underlying problems could be *deduced.*

The helper can learn much about observation from Holmes and certainly from Freud, but, unfortunately, human behavior is too complex to take the next step and conclude that we can leap from our observations to accurate predictions about people based on only a few clues. In this age, helpers are a little less inclined to jump to conclusions without validating them against data from the client. In the case of the wedding ring, there are several possible reasons for ring-twisting behavior, including weight gain and anxiety. Therefore, helper hypotheses are guesses, not deductions. Instead of arriving at Holmes's single inescapable conclusion, the assessment process of observation involves documenting observations and forming a list of hypotheses, which, when linked to other information, may show a general pattern or theme. Instead of drawing swift conclusions, the helper confirms or disconfirms hypotheses more slowly through discussions with the client. By questioning and listening, a helper can determine if a client's disheveled appearance is due to depression, poverty, or apathy. Observation skills should be practiced, but conclusions should be drawn only when there is confirming evidence from the client and from other sources.

Avoiding Cultural Encapsulation

Our own cultural biases, assumptions, worldview, and experiences color what we observe. One of these biases is the human tendency to see and remember the things we are searching for. For example, if you are thinking about buying a new car, suddenly you may begin noticing more of them on the road than ever before (Goleman, 1985). Similarly, some helpers see pathology everywhere because their training has focused on seeing the half-empty glass rather than the half-full one.

Another example of the ways in which expectations can distort our observations comes from a landmark article entitled "On being sane in insane places," by Rosenhan (1973). In this study, individuals faked their way into a mental hospital by reporting auditory hallucinations. Once admitted and labeled psychotic, all of their subsequent behavior was seen as abnormal. For example, one man's diary writing was classified as "obsessive" by hospital personnel. As you can imagine, being trained to identify mental disorders can cause us to see them in everyone we meet. Helpers must be careful not to diagnose except when strict criteria are met. In addition, we must balance our training to see illness by also recognizing client strengths.

As the preceding discussion points out, observations are not objective. Our professional experience and training focus us on certain issues. In addition, our own family background and culture shape what we remember and pay attention to. We see clients through our own cultural lens and judge their behavior based on our standards. Freeing ourselves entirely from this conditioning is nearly impossible, but we can become more aware of our own cultural vision and become more open to other viewpoints, too.

The reflective process described in this book suggests that you think about and record your reactions to your learning. Keeping a diary and obtaining supervision can help avoid *cultural encapsulation,* the tendency to judge other people's behavior from our own narrow perspective.

Furthermore, helpers need to have first-hand contact with people from different backgrounds. Only by experiencing different cultures, can we even begin to understand client behavior within the context of their own culture. Every helper should consider finding ways to have experiences in another culture. Although it is enlightening to be a visitor to another culture, we can also learn about other cultures by being curious and becoming students of every culture we come into contact with. For example, on a recent trip to Europe, we encountered a large group of Japanese tourists taking hundreds of pictures of a Dutch windmill. My companions and I found this to be, on the one hand, amusing, and on the other, excessive and annoying. I began talking with the Japanese tour guide about this. She explained that living on an island means that travel is more restricted and off-island vacations are relatively rare for most people. In addition, she indicated that pictures are a way of sharing experiences with family and friends back home, who may expect and eagerly await a slideshow. When we heard these explanations, my colleagues and I were embarrassed by our cultural encapsulation, and we began to see the behavior in a completely different light. Since then, I have tried to take special care in recording and reflecting on my observations when a client is culturally different. In the following sections, remember that your impressions come through your own cultural lens. When you have the chance to record your observations with real clients, revisit this section and reflect on what you may be bringing to the picture you are painting.

What to Observe

Speech   Note all aspects of a client's speaking voice. Does the client's voice annoy or soothe? Is the client's tone slow and monotonous or excessively labile? Does the client have an accent of any kind? Is the client's speech hurried or forced? Does the client have a speech impediment of any kind? Does the client speak without listening?

Client's Clothing   Does the client wear expensive, stylish, well-coordinated, seductive, old, or outmoded clothing? Is there anything odd or unusual about it? Does the client reflect a particular style (artistic, conservative, etc.)? Is clothing appropriate to the weather (several layers on a hot day), and is it appropriate to the occasion? Does the client wear a little jewelry? A lot of jewelry? Does the client wear appropriate amounts of makeup? Does the client wear glasses or a hearing aid? Does the client's clothing suggest a different cultural background?

Grooming   Is the client clean? Does the client exhibit body odor and a general disregard for personal hygiene? Even if the client shows concern for cleanliness, is there a disorganized appearance to the hair and clothing, perhaps suggesting disorderliness, depression, or lack of social awareness? Do cultural differences in grooming account for the client's appearance? If the client is a child, what does grooming suggest about family environment?

Posture, Build, and Gait   What is the client's posture during the session? What is the position of the shoulders and head? Does the client sit in a rigid or a slouched position or with head in hands? Does the client's posture reflect the present emotional state, or is the client's posture indicative of a more long-term state of anxiety, tension, or depression?

Build refers to the body habitus. Is the client physically attractive? Is the client obese, muscular, or thin? Are there any unusual physical characteristics, such as excessive acne, physical disabilities, or prostheses?

Gait means the person's manner of walking. Does the client's manner of walking reflect an emotional state, such as depression or anxiety? Does the client's walk seem to indicate confidence or low self-esteem? Is the client tentative and cautious in finding a seat?

Facial Expressions   Facial expressions include movements of the eyes, lips, forehead, and mouth. Do the client's feelings show, or are the client's expressions, flat, devoid of any emotion? Shakespeare wrote that "the eyes are the windows of the soul." Does the client maintain direct eye contact or avoid it? Do the eyes fill with tears? Does the client smile or laugh during the session? Is the brow wrinkled? Could the client's facial expressions be due to cultural injunctions about eye contact or posture with one considered to be an authority?

Other Bodily Movements   A client may show anxiety by twisting tissue or by tapping restlessly with fingers, toes, or legs. One important way in which people express themselves is through their hand movements. Fritz Perls, the founder of Gestalt therapy, was fond of making clients aware of how bodily movements expressed their inner conflicts and impulses (Perls, 1959, p. 83).

General Appearance   In writing an assessment of the client, it is sometimes useful to note initial holistic impressions, which may become less noticeable as treatment progresses—for example, "The client appeared much older than his stated age," "The client appeared to be very precise and neat and seemed to carefully consider all of his statements before speaking," "I had the feeling that the client was a super salesman." Many of these holistic impressions are due to cultural differences. Are you judging the client based on your own upbringing?

Feelings of the Helper

Basing his observations on Harry Stack Sullivan's [1953] theories, Timothy Leary (1957) hypothesized that we react automatically and unconsciously to the communications of others. Our reaction, in turn, triggers the other person's next response. We tend to instinctively react in a positive, friendly manner to individuals whom we find attractive and friendly. Similarly, we instinctively respond negatively to individuals who are combative or aloof. They, in turn, become more abrasive and the cycle continues. These *interpersonal reflexes* (Shannon & Guerney, 1973) occur outside of awareness and are rarely discussed, but they can be very important in the helping relationship and in the client's social world.

If the helper finds himself or herself becoming annoyed with the client, is it possible that most of the client's social contacts have the same response? What would motivate the client to push people away? Is the client even aware of his or her effect on others? According to Ernst Beier (Beier & Young, 1998), the helper can learn to use his or her personal feelings as an assessment instrument. It requires detaching and not reacting to the client's overtures. Instead, think about how others in the client's world must feel about the client and record this information to add to the assessment.

Questioning

Asking too many questions was criticized earlier as being apt to strain the relationship between client and helper. In fact, the most common mistake for beginning helpers is relying on questions in the relationship-building stage, rather than taking the necessary time to understand the client and provide an atmosphere of openness and trust. On the other hand, introductory questions are extremely helpful in signaling the transition to the assessment phase once a relationship is established. Questioning is an important part of the assessment process because answers to direct and indirect questions are part and parcel of taking personal and sexual histories, structuring genograms, and allowing the client to elaborate on his or her construction of the problem. It is not that questions are inherently bad, it is just that they are used too often by beginning helpers and at the wrong time.

Questioning is an art (Goldberg, 1998). When used artfully, questions can be therapeutic devices to spur the client's thinking or stimulate action. Questions can also be used to gain valuable information and to focus the client on the agreed-upon goals. They serve an "orienting" function in that they tell the client what is important (Tomm, 1988). Following are some questions frequently asked by helpers early in the assessment stage in order to begin focusing on a client's concerns.

"How can I help you?"
"Where would you like to begin?"
"What prompted you to make today's appointment?"
"Has something happened in the last few days or weeks that persuaded you that help was needed?"
"What is it that you want to stop doing or do less of?"
"What is it that you want to begin to do or do more of?"
"What would your life be like if the problem were solved?"

Genograms

The genogram is a pictorial representation of the client's family tree. It quickly shows a family's history by depicting current and past relationships. In this chapter, we present a simple way of constructing a genogram. Figure 7.4 shows the symbols used in our approach to the genogram. Figure 7.5 is an example of a completed genogram for a client, Bob, and Figure 7.6 is a skeletal genogram you can use as you develop skills in using this method.

When a client comes from a large family or one with many siblings or stepsiblings, the genogram can assist the helper in identifying the individuals involved instead of continually quizzing the client. The genogram is therapeutic when a client's main concerns are family problems because the client gains insight into the issues by describing them to the helper as the genogram is constructed. Finally, the genogram is a tool to explore specific issues such as family influences on career choice (Dickson & Parmerlee, 1980; Okiishi, 1987), alcoholism, or abuse (Armsworth & Stronck, 1998; Young & Long, 1998).

Reasons to Consider Using the Genogram

1. To identify cultural and ethnic influences on the client
2. To represent the strengths and weaknesses in relationships between family members
3. To understand the present household composition and the relationships among the client's household, previous marriages, and past generations
4. To discover the presence of family disturbances that might be affecting the client, including alcoholism, abuse, divorces, suicides, sexual abuse, schisms and skews in marital relationships, mental illness in the family, and so on
5. To uncover sex-role and other family expectations on the client
6. To assess economic and emotional support resources for the client
7. To identify repeated patterns in the client's relationships
8. To determine the effects of birth order and sibling rivalry on the client

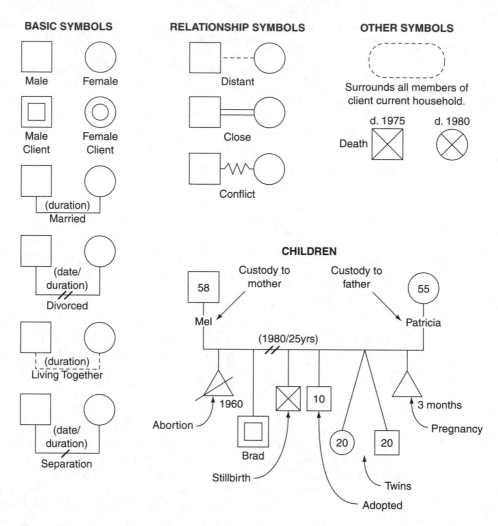

Figure 7.4
Genogram Symbols
Adapted from Figure 4.2, page 93, *Counseling Methods and Techniques: An Eclectic Approach* by Mark E. Young. Columbus, OH: Merrill/MacMillan, 1992.

9. To make the client and helper aware of family attitudes concerning health and illness
10. To identify extrafamilial sources of support
11. To trace family patterns of certain preferences, values, and behaviors, such as legal problems, sexual values, obesity, and job problems
12. To identify problem relationships
13. To document historical traumas, such as suicides, deaths, abuse, and losses of pregnancies

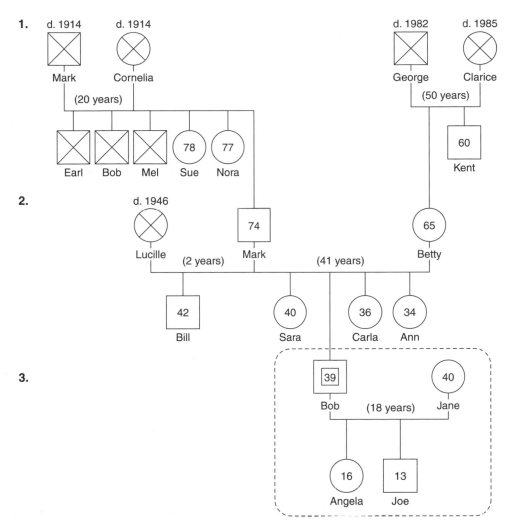

Figure 7.5
Sample Genogram

Stop and Reflect

Construct your own genogram using Figure 7.6. Copy the skeleton on a separate piece of paper and begin by filling in your grandparents' names and ages in the row entitled Generation 1. Note that men are squares and women are circles. Now fill in your parents' names in the boxes of the row labeled Generation 2 and then bring down a line for each sibling in your original nuclear family along the dotted line that connects your parents. When a person has been married more than once, his or her previous spouses are connected to that person horizontally.

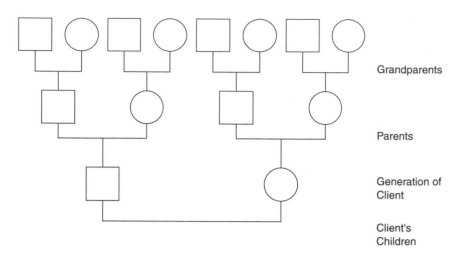

Figure 7.6
Skeletal Genogram

In the sample genogram in Figure 7.5, Bob is the third of five children. His box is dropped to show a fourth generation, his children, but because Bob is the client, we place him in Generation 3. Drop your own box, below that of your siblings, if you wish to show your own marriage or children. Indicate your present nuclear family by encircling it with dashes as shown in the example.

Check your drawing to make sure you have not missed any family members in the three generations. If parents or grandparents have been married more than once, place their other spouses to the side (see the example of Lucille and Mark in Figure 7.5). Place an X through anyone who is deceased. Place the ages of each person in his or her box or circle. Place the approximate years of marriage and make slashes to indicate divorces or separations. Place this information on the lines between spouses as shown in Figure 7.5.

Now review the genogram symbols in Figure 7.4. Add any additional symbols that you wish to include in your family genogram. Specifically, you may wish to depict relationships within your family as shown in the section entitled "Relationship Symbols."

When you have completed the genogram, answer the following questions:

1. What cultural or ethnic background characterizes each person in your family tree?
2. How do you think culture and history affect the values and rules around which your family functions?
3. Are differences in backgrounds ever the source of conflict in the family? Does cultural heritage beget closeness or conflict? If there are different cultural influences in your family, are you more a part of one specific side of the family or do you embrace more than one culture?

Completing a Brief Intake Form

One way of getting started in the assessment process is to systematically record your impressions about a client on some kind of standard form. A form is a good training device because it is a check to make sure you have not missed the big problems. In this chapter, we introduce you to a prototype form that you can use for reflection, case presentation, and treatment planning. The form asks you to jot down your evaluation of the client's: (A) *affective* or emotional issues and status; (B) *behavior* deficits, excesses, and strengths; and (C) thinking or *cognitions*. These three items will be referred to as A, B, and C for short. In addition, you are asked to accumulate data about the client's: (1) developmental level, (2) family history, (3) multicultural background, and (4) physical challenges and strengths.

Within this brief assessment questionnaire, several trigger questions are embedded within each area. These are questions that prompt the helper to reflect on the client's answers and seek assistance from a supervisor or consider referring the client to a more qualified practitioner. The trigger questions are:

1. Does the client meet criteria for a major emotional disorder such as anxiety or depression? Such a diagnosis might require referral or special treatment, including medication.
2. Does the client show any evidence of suicidal thinking, have a history of self-destructive behavior, or indicate thoughts or history of harming others? If so, a close assessment must be made by a qualified practitioner.
3. Does the client show any evidence of thought disorders, highly unusual thought processes, hallucinations, or delusions (bizarre fixed false beliefs)? If so, the client may require a medication evaluation and specific support groups.
4. Is the relationship between helper and client moving toward a healthy alliance? Have cultural differences been addressed? Does the client feel the helper is a trustworthy and credible resource for helping to achieve treatment goals?
5. Could any medical problems be causing or contributing to the client's statement of the problem?
6. Does the client need treatment for substance abuse?

Let us now take a brief look at each of the seven elements (ABC-1234) and why it is critical to collect these data on each client during a screening or intake interview.

A. Affective Assessment

Clients come for help because of overwhelming and confused emotions. They are seeking relief from anxiety, grief, depression, and anger. Whether these are disabling conditions or merely uncomfortable, the helper assesses the intensity, frequency, and duration of these negative emotions in order to plan effective treatment. It is similarly important to identify the client's positive affective states. If clients can identify the times when they feel satisfied and happy, they can attempt to recreate those states.

B. Behavioral Assessment

Many people are seeking assistance for *excessive* behaviors, ranging from smoking to sexual addiction. Others need help in learning new behaviors such as social skills or time management. Clients also have "positive addictions" or healthy habits that should be noted. If a client has a regular exercise regime, meditates, or is very organized, these behaviors can be identified and encouraged.

C. Cognitive Assessment

Cognition includes the client's thinking, images, and meanings (the client's worldview). For example, a client may be engaging in negative thinking and negative imagery about an upcoming event. By uncovering this in an assessment interview, the helper can help the client find specific constructive thoughts and images as an antidote. In this section of the intake form, the helper records intellectual deficits and strengths, any specific learning problems, or head injuries.

1. Developmental Issues

Helpers must have a basic knowledge of human development as major theorists such as Piaget, Erikson, Loevinger, and Kohlberg have described it. Then, assessment and helping techniques can be modified to deal with life-stage differences. In this section, we use the common age-related categories of children, adolescents, adults, and older people. The descriptions of these life stages are generalizations about groups of people. The discussion is meant to urge you to consider critical developmental issues. However, it is important to remember that each individual is unique. There are some octogenarians who are physically and intellectually younger than their chronological ages; some 7-year-olds demonstrate an unusual amount of intellectual and emotional maturity.

Children Take a look at the "Stop and Reflect" section in this chapter that discusses modifying your skills when helping children because of cognitive and power differences. Besides these suggestions, there are many specialized assessment and helping techniques that are effective with children (Sattler, 1997). School functioning is analogous to occupational functioning in adults and is a general indicator of adjustment. Contact a teacher for insight into a child's behavior toward adults and peers. To understand a child's family and his or her relationship with parents, interview parents, grandparents, and siblings.

Adolescents Adolescents are challenging but also intriguing and rewarding to work with. Issues of trust and betrayal, freedom, autonomy, dangerous behavior, and anger are just beneath the surface of their words. When assessing adolescent problems, it is particularly important to touch on drug and alcohol abuse, sexual behavior, and relationships with parents and siblings. Most adolescent deaths are not due to medical problems but to automobile accidents, suicide, homicide, and substance abuse. These areas must be carefully addressed in the assessment stage.

College Students College students are characterized by their focus on issues of self-esteem, separation from their family of origin, and their strong need to form close bonds with others. The helper who works with college students deals with alcohol and drug abuse, suicide attempts, eating disorders, intense love relationships and their dismal aftermath, problems with parents, pregnancy, and sexually transmitted diseases.

Older People   Understanding the problems of older people requires consideration of their unique histories. It is likely that your parents or grandparents lived through the Great Depression and World War II. These two events shaped their thinking and worldview. It instilled in them a cautious approach to life, especially where money is concerned. When choosing a career, for example, they might counsel, "Have something to fall back on!" In short, to know an older person, it may be important to get a sense of the time they grew up in because it affected their perspective on life and is the basis for their view of the future. Helpers who work with older people deal with issues of loss, deteriorating health, thinking about lost opportunities, and fears associated with loneliness. Helpers also assist older people who are trying to create new lives following the death of a spouse or when they need to let go of past experiences and disappointing family relationships.

2. Family History

Our family histories provide a deep insight into who we are. Our ideas of gender roles, parental roles, and what is normal and good all come from our original family group, or our *family of origin*. The visual nature of the genogram makes it an efficient way to understand a client's family history. In the absence of a genogram, you may simply want to question clients concerning important stressors in their family now and in the past.

A family history of depression, suicide, anxiety disorders, substance abuse, and sexual abuse is valuable information as it may shed light on the client's current concerns. Our ideas about normal family functioning, what it means to be a spouse and parent, are based on our family models. Taking the time to get a sense of the client's family will be rewarded by insights into the forces that shaped the client's worldview.

3. Multicultural/Gender Issues

Besides identifying a client's ethnicity, race, or class, it is important to understand the client's acculturation. A client's acculturation is the degree to which he or she personally identifies with a particular culture. For example, two children in a bicultural family may feel close to one parent's culture but not the other's. In addition, a girl whose parents are Russian Jews but who was born in the United States might conceivably have a minimal relationship to her culture and religion. Following are some additional questions that stimulate thinking about the degree of a client's cultural identity and its impact on the helping process:

- What is the client's cultural/ethnic identity?
- What is the client's religion or spiritual orientation?
- How closely does the client identify with his or her cultural or ethnic background?
- According to the client, how is seeking help from a helper viewed within his or her culture?
- How can the client's goals and problems be viewed in a way that is compatible with his or her cultural background?
- How does the client's upbringing regarding appropriate gender roles relate to the presenting problems?
- Is the client's culture a source of pride or shame?

4. Physical Challenges

For our purposes, physical challenges include medical diagnoses, physical disabilities and limitations, and drug and alcohol use and abuse. All of these may have physical, social, and psychological effects. Focus on the client's physical assets and abilities in this category, too.

Medical Diagnoses   A number of physical disorders have psychological effects. A helper can go wrong by trying to work on a symptom that turns out to be the result of a treatable medical condition (Pollak, Levy, & Breitholtz, 1999). For example, a brain tumor or other serious problem, rather than stress, may be the cause of a client's headaches. Symptoms of depression, anxiety, sexual disorders, irritability, weight gain or loss, headaches, and fatigue suggest that the client should receive a thorough medical checkup as part of the helping process. It is irresponsible and unethical to treat someone for these symptoms until medical causes have been ruled out. When in doubt, helpers should refer clients for medical evaluation. On the other side of the coin, be sure to note positive health and wellness behaviors such as good diet and physical exercise.

Physical Disabilities   The term *physical disabilities* suggests that there are normal and disabled people. Perhaps the word should be "physical differ-abilities," because abilities are probably better described on a continuum rather than within a disabled/abled dichotomy. It is not as important to know that a person is in a wheelchair as it is to know how he or she sees himself or herself in relation to other people and how the new way of getting around affects that person socially and professionally.

Not all disabilities are as obvious as a prosthesis or wheelchair. Heart conditions, multiple sclerosis, arthritis, diabetes, and a myriad of other problems have an effect on mood, behavior, and thinking. It is helpful to know the normal psychological effects of common diseases, and it is important to explore with a client the impact of the disease on his or her overall functioning.

Drug and Alcohol Use and Abuse   Alcohol and other drug use is difficult to assess because clients consciously and unconsciously minimize the amount they report. Prescription and nonprescription drug taking must also be discussed with clients because the mental, emotional, and behavioral effects can make other issues worse. For example, such medication can affect school or work functioning and family relationships. Once substance abuse is identified, many helpers try to treat this first because continued substance abuse undermines progress on other issues.

Because clients may not want to bring up substance abuse, one way to start a discussion and gain important information is by asking direct questions or by asking the client to fill out a questionnaire on substance use and history (see Evans, 1998). Figure 7.7 contains a list of additional questions that you might use to follow up on suspected substance abuse.

Summarizing Important Background Information

Figure 7.8 shows a blank copy of the ABC-1234 Intake Form. It can be used as a worksheet to summarize data collected about the client in the initial interview. Figure 7.9 shows a completed form on a fictitious client. Each section should contain problems and strengths. It is important to emphasize the client's abilities as well as disabilities, because strengths give the helper useful information about what methods and tech-

Figure 7.7
Some Key Interview Questions for Substance Abuse

"Do any of your friends and family think you have a substance abuse problem?"
"Have you ever been arrested for driving under the influence?"
"Have you ever been physically injured or had an accident while using?"
"Have you ever broken any bones as an adult? If so, how?"
"How much do you drink or use each day?"
"Have you ever had a blackout or amnesia while using?"
"Has your substance abuse changed any of your close relationships or affected your work?"
"Looking back at your family tree, which relatives have had a substance abuse problem?"
"Have you ever felt the need to cut back on your use of substances?"

niques might be most effective. For example, a client who is an excellent reader and enjoys books might profit from bibliotherapy. A client who has a strong religious background can be implored to use this strength in understanding and dealing with fear or depression.

The intake form begins with a statement by the client, indicating what issue(s) propelled him or her to seek help and what he or she hopes to achieve. It is useful to record this statement in the client's own words because the client's view of the problem is critical to treatment planning. Let us say, for example, that in the client's statement she indicates that she is mostly concerned with her adolescent son's marijuana abuse. Even if the helper focuses on what seem to be more critical problems, the client may not feel that she has received the treatment she has asked for.

Each section of the intake form contains a trigger question. This question, when answered positively, prompts a referral to specialized treatment or, at the minimum, identifies an issue that should be discussed with a supervisor. The trigger question is a reminder to look for serious issues that should be dealt with first or that might jeopardize the helping relationship.

Figure 7.8
ABC-1234 Intake Form Worksheet

Demographic Data

Name: _____

Age: _____

Date of Birth: _____

Street Address: _____

City: _____ State: _____ Zip: _____

Home Phone: _____

Work Phone: _____ Okay to call at work?   Yes/No

Level of Education: _____

continues

Figure 7.8—*continued*
ABC-1234 Intake Form Worksheet

Occupation: _____

Marital Status: _____

Children's Names and Ages: _____

Reason for Referral: _____

Referral Source: _____

Client's Statement of the Problem
Write down a paragraph in the client's own words that describes why he or she came for help.

A. Affective Assessment

What major and minor emotions are troubling the client? _____

Is the client sad? Angry? Fearful? Anxious? _____

Are these due to the helping interview or longer term states? _____

What emotional states does the client wish to reduce? _____

How does the client normally handle negative emotions? _____

What emotional strengths does the client have?_____

Trigger: Does the client require treatment for depression, mania, or severe anxiety?_____

B. Behavioral Assessment

What does the client want to do that he or she is not doing? _____

What behaviors does the client wish to reduce or eliminate? _____

What behaviors does the client need to increase? _____

What behaviors does the client want to learn? _____

What habits does he or she want to eliminate?_____

What positive behaviors does he or she want to strengthen?_____

Has the client ever engaged in violence toward self or others? _____

Identify the client's strengths and positive social and health behaviors. _____

Trigger: Does the client now require treatment for dangerous behavior toward self or

others? _____

C. Cognitive Assessment

Does the client show any signs of memory problems or other problems in thinking? _____

Does the client succeed in a typical classroom environment? _____

Does the client report *negative or positive* imagery about the problem? _____

What rational and irrational thoughts were detected in the client's statements? _____

Does the client show distorted thinking patterns such as overgeneralization, black-and-white thinking, etc. _____

How would you characterize the client's worldview and values? _____

What positive thinking patterns exist? _____

Trigger: Does the client show any evidence of thought disorders, highly unusual thought processes, hallucinations, or delusions (bizarre fixed false beliefs)? Does the client think about

hurting self or others? _____

1. Developmental Issues

How did the client handle major maturational milestones of childhood? _____

Compared to the client's peers, how is the client adjusting to normal developmental issues? _____

Describe the client's maturational level in terms of career development, intellectual, sexual, moral, and

social development. _____

Do any of the client's developmental issues relate to the statement of the problem? _____

2. Family History (Attach Genogram if Possible)

What does the genogram reveal about the client's family history as it relates to the statement of the

problem? _____

How many brothers and sisters does the client have? What is the client's birth order? _____

What problems in family relationships are revealed by the genogram or by questioning? _____

What family support does the client have? _____

Is the client on good terms with family members? _____

Has the client achieved a healthy interdependence with family compared to others of the client's

culture? _____

What traumatic events have affected the family? _____

What family changes have occurred recently? _____

What strengths has the client gained from his family background? _____

3. Multicultural/Gender Issues

What is the client's cultural/ethnic identity? _____

continues

Figure 7.8—*continued*
ABC-1234 Intake Form Worksheet

What is the client's religion or spiritual orientation?_____

How closely does the client identify with his or her cultural or ethnic background? _____

How culturally acceptable is it for the client to seek professional help? _____

Does the client's attitude regarding appropriate gender roles relate to the presenting problems? _____

Is the client able to identify the positive and healthy aspects of his or her culture and the part they might

play in solving problems? _____

Trigger: Does the client appear skeptical that the helping process and the helper are credible methods for achieving the stated goals? _____

4. Physical Challenges

Does the client report any medical issues or disabilities?_____

How does the client view himself or herself in relation to diseases or disabilities?_____

What is the extent of the client's current use of alcohol and drugs? Previous use? _____

What is the client's level of knowledge about substance abuse? _____

Does the client have a family history of substance abuse?_____

Does the client have a good diet and physical self-care habits such as exercise? _____

Trigger: Could any medical condition be causing or contributing to the client's statement of the

problem? _____

Trigger: Does the client need treatment for substance abuse? _____

Treatment Goals (Mutually Agreed Upon)   Treatment Plans
(Proposed Interventions)

1._____   1._____

2._____   2._____

3._____   3._____

Signatures_____ Date_____

Figure 7.9
ABC-1234 Intake Form Sample

Demographic Data

Name: Claudia O'Reilly

Age: 35

Date of Birth: 11/13/65

Street Address: 132 Shade St.

City: New Brunswick   State: OH   Zip: 45123

Home Phone: 614-555-2194

Work Phone: None   Okay to call at work?   Yes/No

Level of Education: H.S. diploma

Occupation: Homemaker

Marital Status: Married

Children's Names and Ages: Amber age 6, Heather age 4

Reason for Referral: Pastor felt she needed individual help to deal with feelings of depression.

Referral Source: Pastor, R. Brown Central Community Church

Client's Statement of the Problem

"My main problem is learning to accept my husband for the way he is. I get very depressed over the fact that he does not seem to want to spend time with me and the kids. He is not motivated at work. He smokes marijuana and drinks with his friends. Because I don't work, I have no say-so about the money. I go to church and to Alanon and that is my total social life. I would like to go out more with him and have a life."

A. Affective Assessment

Client reported lack of direction in her life. She feels ineffective in her work taking care of the children and her home. Client also indicated feelings of sadness over her marital problems. At times, she reported feelings of "frustration" with her husband that would best be described as anger and resentment. She did not meet *DSM-IV* criteria for a mental disorder associated with her feelings of depression.

On the positive side, the client reports that religious activities, including attending church and reading her Bible, have helped her during her worst "down" periods.

B. Behavioral Assessment

Client admits that she lacks assertiveness skills. She believes that she "sulks" at times as a way of getting her husband to respond. She wants to "go out more and have a life." By this, she means that she would like to return to school, eventually go to work, and have some free time outside of the house. The client has no history of harming self or others and does not appear to be a danger to herself or others. The client appears to be ready to return to school and has an interest in reading and learning.

C. Cognitive Assessment

The client shows no apparent problems with memory. She reports being an A and B student in high school. In fact, the client is aware of her above-average scholastic abilities, but sometimes berates

continues

Figure 7.9—*continued*
ABC-1234 Intake Form Sample

herself for not developing her mind earlier in life. In assessing the client's thinking about herself, she reports low self-esteem. She is perfectionistic in her thinking and often engages in black-and-white thinking. For example, she said that she was not a good housekeeper because her home is rarely spotless like her mother's. She had difficulty seeing that her expectations were rather high for someone with two young children. She believes that expressing her feelings and stating her preferences is "generally rude."

1. Developmental Issues
The client is approaching midlife and feels unfulfilled in her work as a wife and mother. She was married at 25, but says she lived a sheltered life before that, living at home with her mother. She wants to work outside the home and wishes to begin training of some kind.

The client and her husband have been married for 10 years. The marriage was apparently a happy one in the first 2 years, but there have been major problems and upheavals over the last 5 years. Although the marriage is now stable in that there is no talk of divorce, apparently both partners are dissatisfied with the way they interact.

The client sees herself as an excellent mother and takes pride in this fact. The client and her family are in transition because the youngest child is now entering preschool and will be gone most of the day. With two children in school, there are new pressures, including transportation. Because the children are in school, the client will also have some additional free time on her hands and conceivably might have enough time to take classes. She has received career testing at the community college and is interested in becoming a dental hygienist.

2. Family History
The client's parents were divorced 20 years ago. She has two older sisters, both of whom work in professional occupations. The client's mother is a retired bookkeeper and her father is still working as a building contractor. The client related that as she was growing up, both of her parents, but especially her mother, had high, even impossible standards for all the children. She feels that she has let them down by not achieving.

Today, Claudia and her mother are closer. Her mother helps with the children and Claudia can talk to her about most problems. Both of Claudia's sisters live out of state, but she receives some support via telephone.

The client is most disturbed by the lack of support she receives from her husband. Her opinion is that he does not wish to be a part of the family. The family has little money, and she is angry that he spends any amount on alcohol and drugs. He gives her money with which she pays the bills. She regards him as her "third child." About one year ago, she began attending Alanon. She claims that his drinking is not as much of a problem as it was a year ago, but that he smokes marijuana daily and this bothers her a great deal.

3. Multicultural/Gender Issues
The client's family members consider themselves to be "Southern." Her grandparents and even her father at one time worked as peanut farmers in Georgia, where the family originated. The client had a strict religious upbringing, a fundamentalist Protestant denomination. She has continued to be a member of this church and she takes her daughters every Sunday, although her husband does not attend. Her religion is definitely a support for her. Besides the time she spends at church, she also prays regularly and feels that her depression is reduced by both activities.

One of the cultural/gender issues surfaces when the client talks about "not being ladylike." She sometimes describes other people in this way and has indicated she has trouble standing up for herself because she does not want to "act like a man." In addition, the client has very traditional views about the roles of husband and wife that may clash with the mainstream of society and her own goals to have a more personally fulfilling life.

4. Physical Challenges

The client has suffered from periods of chronic fatigue. Her physician indicates that this is not solely the result of feeling depressed, but is associated with an endocrine dysfunction. She takes medication for the condition but occasionally has periods when she is unable to do much for two or three days.

The client has no regular exercise regime and eats a diet that is very high in fat, salt, and sugar. She claims that she has to cook what her husband likes and so she cannot really change her eating patterns. The client has never used drugs or alcohol.

Treatment Goals (Helper and Client Contract) Treatment Plans

1. Increase assertive behavior	1. Client will be referred to assertiveness training class.
2. Decrease depression, increase self-esteem	2. Individual sessions will decrease depression and increase self-esteem.
3. Improve marital relationship	3. Following treatment for items 1 and 2, client will be referred with husband to couples counseling.

Signatures_____ Date_____

Exercises for In and Out of Class

Group Exercise

In groups of three or four, one student acts as the helper, another is the client, and a third observes. The helper interviews a fellow student using the Intake Form. Before the interview, the client and observer identify and agree on a problem that the client is hoping to work on or that is fabricated for this exercise. The client should take a moment to look over the Intake Form and think about answers to key questions. The client should retain his or her real identity so that the other aspects of the intake are authentic, even if the problem itself is concocted. After the exercise, the client gives specific feedback to the helper on the following issues:

a. Was the helper able to intersperse questioning and listening? Or was the interview too businesslike?
b. Did the helper find the key problems? If not, why not?
c. What other suggestions do you have for the helper in terms of the quality of the interview?

Within your group, discuss the following questions:

- What is your reaction to the use of a standardized form such as this one?
- What important areas do you think are missing that you would have like to explore?
- How long did it take to complete the interview?
- Did the client react negatively to so many questions? If so, how might this be handled better?

Additional Exercise

Conduct a classroom discussion on gender issues in assessment. In small groups, discuss recent books such as *Men Are from Mars, Women Are from Venus*. Do these books help people understand the role of gender in the helping process or do they reinforce stereotypes? In your group, discuss the importance of including an assessment of gender-related issues in the assessment process. As you look at the Intake Form for Claudia (Figure 7.9), how important are these issues for her? If you were helping Claudia, would you bring up her perceptions about gender role? Why or why not?

Homework

Homework 1

Complete a genogram for yourself using the skeletal form in this chapter. Use the instructions in the "Stop and Reflect" section as a guide. Next to each person in your genogram, list his or her jobs or careers. If you do not know this information, do some research by asking other family members. Can you identify a family pattern to the selection of vocation? To go into a bit more depth, look up the Holland codes for each occupation in the *Dictionary of Holland Occupational Codes* (Gottfredson, Holland, & Ogawa, 1996) and see if you can see a family transmission of certain traits.

Homework 2

Search the Internet for resources for dealing with people who are HIV positive. What limitations do such people experience? What mythologies affect the way people look at them? What challenges would this present socially and professionally? Looking at the various Web sites, what must a helper know about current treatment, testing, and prevention? How would you feel about working with someone who tested positive for HIV? What issues might you expect them to bring to the helping session?

Journal Starters

1. Think back on assessment experiences in your own life. These may range from encounters with a high school guidance counselor to an intake interview at the college counseling center to a college board examination. What important decisions have you made based on testing or assessment results? What decisions have others made about you based on testing? Discuss any negative or positive experiences. How do these affect your views and feelings about testing clients?
2. This chapter suggests asking clients about religious and spiritual beliefs. How important are these issues to you? How often have you been able to discuss this part of your life with others? If you tend to hide this part of yourself, how do you think this affects others? How do you think others might react if they knew your religious or spiritual beliefs? If you were a client, how important would it be to discuss spirituality? If your spiritual or religious beliefs are not very well developed, how would you want a helper to approach this area?

For more journal ideas, as well as more practice with assessment, refer to Chapter 7 in *Exercises in the Art of Helping*.

References

Anastasi, A. (1996). *Psychological testing* (7th ed.). New York: Macmillan.

Armsworth, M. W., & Stronck, K. (1999). Intergenerational effects of incest on parenting: Skills, abilities, and attitudes. *Journal of Counseling and Development, 77,* 303–313.

Beier, E. G., & Young, D. M. (1998). *The silent language of psychotherapy* (3rd ed.). Hawthorne, NY: Aldine de Gruyter.

Dickson, G. L., & Parmerlee, J. R. (1980). The occupational family tree: A career counseling technique. *School Counselor, 28,* 131–134.

Doyle, A. C. (1929). *Conan Doyle's best books* (Vol. 2). New York: Collier.

Drummond, R. J. (2000). *Appraisal procedures for counselors and helping professionals* (4th ed.). Upper Saddle River, NJ: Merrill/Prentice Hall.

Epstein, M. H. (1998). Assessing the emotional and behavioral strengths of children. *Reclaiming Children and Youth, 6*(4), 250–252.

Epstein, M. H., Harniss, M. K., Pearson, N., & Ryser, G. (in press). The Behavioral and Emotional Rating Scale: Test-retest and inter-rater reliability. *Journal of Child and Family Studies.*

Evans, W. N. (1998). Assessment and diagnosis of substance abuse disorders (SUDS). *Journal of Counseling and Development, 76,* 332–336.

Gladding, S. T. (1998). *Family therapy: History, theory, and practice* (2nd ed.). Upper Saddle River, NJ: Merrill/Prentice Hall.

Goldberg, M. C. (1998). *The art of the question: A guide to short-term question-centered therapy.* New York: Wiley.

Goleman, D. (1985). *Vital lies, simple truths: The psychology of self-deception.* New York: Simon & Schuster.

Gottfredson, G. D., Holland, J. L., & Ogawa, D. K. (1996). *Dictionary of Holland occupational codes* (3rd ed.). Odessa, FL: Psychological Assessment Resources.

Hohenshil, T. H. (1996). Role of assessment and diagnosis in counseling. *Journal of Counseling and Development, 75,* 64–67.

Hood, A. B., & Johnson, R. W. (1997). *Assessment in counseling: A guide to the use of psychological assessment procedures* (2nd ed.). Alexandria VA: American Counseling Association.

Leary, T. (1957). *Interpersonal diagnosis of personality.* New York: Ronald.

Lukas, S. (1993). *Where to start and what to ask: An assessment handbook.* New York: Norton.

Miller, S. D., Hubble, M. A., & Duncan, B. L. (Eds.) (1996). *Handbook of solution focused brief therapy.* San Francisco: Jossey-Bass.

Okiishi, R. W. (1987). The genogram as a tool in career counseling. *Journal of Counseling & Development, 66,* 139–143.

Palmer, S., & McMahon, G. (Eds.) (1997). *Client assessment.* London: Sage.

Paniagua, F. A. (1998). *Assessing and treating culturally diverse clients: A practical guide* (2nd ed.). Thousand Oaks, CA: Sage.

Perls, F. S. (1959). *Gestalt therapy verbatim.* New York: Bantam Books.

Pollak, J., Levy, S., & Breitholtz, T. (1999). Screening for medical and neurodevelopmental disorders for the professional counselor. *Journal of Counseling & Development, 77,* 350–355.

Rosenhan, D. L. (1973). On being sane in insane places. *Science, 180,* 250–258.

Sattler, J. (1997). *Clinical and forensic interviewing of children and families.* San Francisco:

Sommers-Flanagan, J., & Sommers-Flanagan, R. (1995). Intake interviewing with suicidal patients: A systematic approach. *Professional Psychology, 30,* 1–7.

Sullivan, H. S. [1953] (1968). *The interpersonal theory of psychiatry.* New York: W.W. Norton. (Original work published 1953)

Shannon, J., & Guerney, B. G., Jr. (1973). Interpersonal effects of interpersonal behavior. *Journal of Personality and Social Psychology, 26,* 142–150.

Tomm, K. (1988). Interventive interviewing: Part III. Intending to ask lineal circular, strategic or reflexive questions? *Family Process, 27,* 1–15.

Whiston, S. C. (2000). *Principles and applications of assessment in counseling.* Belmont, CA: Wadsworth.

Witmer, J. M., & Sweeney, T. J. (1992). A holistic model for wellness and prevention over the life span. *Journal of Counseling and Development, 71,* 140–148.

Young, M. E., & Long, L. (1998). *Counseling and therapy for couples.* Pacific Grove, CA: Brooks/Cole.

Challenging Skills

8

> *My experience is what I agree to attend to. Only those items*
> *I notice shape my mind.*
>
> William James

In his book, *Vital Lies, Simple Truths,* Daniel Goleman (1985) relates the following story told by a woman at a dinner party:

> I am very close to my family. They were always very demonstrative and loving. When I disagreed with my mother, she threw whatever was nearest at hand at me. Once it happened to be a knife and I needed ten stitches in my leg. A few years later, my father tried to choke me when I began dating a boy he didn't like. They really are very concerned about me. (pp. 16–17)

175

Goleman claims this tale is a good example of how people deceive themselves. Because the client cannot face the fact that she was the victim of child abuse, she changes the story to its exact opposite, one of caring and concern. It is often the helper's unhappy duty to awaken the client to this defensive maneuver. Irvin Yalom goes so far as to compare this duty to that of an executioner (Yalom, 1990). The client has found a refuge and the helper's revelations kill off protective fantasies, potentially arousing resentment and discomfort.

Sometimes it becomes necessary for helpers to "dare" clients to examine the inconsistencies in their stories by *giving them feedback* and, at other times, by *confronting discrepancies.* Making clients aware of uncomfortable information moves them to act and change their circumstances. For most helpers, this step in the journey is a giant one. While the invitational and reflecting skills are supportive and convince a client to open up, these two challenging skills push the client to examine critically his or her choices, feelings and thoughts. When the helper uses challenging skills, he or she is giving the client an honest reaction or pointing out warring factions in the client's story. Invitational and reflecting skills do not necessarily encourage the client to follow through with plans and commitments but challenging skills do.

When challenging skills are used, the aura of safety and support, so carefully constructed by the helper, is at risk. There is a fundamental shift from relationship building to a focus on the goals set by the client and helper, conveying to the client that the helping relationship is not a friendship but a business partnership.

During the initial stages of the relationship, the helper strives to understand the client's unique worldview by getting the client to open up. As a client tells the story, the helper listens attentively using the nonjudgmental listening cycle. After several cycles, the helper begins to detect distortions, blind spots, and inconsistencies. He or she may then use feedback and challenging skills, not so much to straighten out the client as to teach the client the method of self-challenging. The essential aim of the challenging skills is to help clients operate with unclouded information about themselves. With heightened self-awareness, they are better able to make decisions and to operate free of illusions and "vital lies." This is consistent with the goal of helping: to empower clients by encouraging them to explore their own thoughts, feelings, and behaviors.

Clients need to be challenged when:

- They are operating on misinformation about the self. For example, a client may underestimate her intelligence, feeling that she is not capable of attending college when there is evidence to the contrary.
- They misinterpret the actions of others. This tendency is called *mind reading* and is a common problem among couples. A client may act on assumptions without confirming them, making statements such as the following: "I could tell by the way he acted, that he did not want to date me anymore."
- They are blaming others rather than examining themselves. For example, a client may blame the boss at work but refuse to look at his own responsibility for the poor relationship or his own work performance.
- Their behavior, thoughts, and feelings, and values are inconsistent. For example, a client talks about how much she values honesty but, at the same time, discusses how she hides her financial difficulties from her husband.

In this chapter, we will focus on two building blocks, or basic skills, used to challenge clients and help them deal more honestly with problems. The first of these is giving feedback, a skill that has wide application in group work, as well as with couples, individuals, and families. Second, we tackle the skill of confrontation, a powerful technique that must be used with great caution.

Giving Feedback

Why Is Feedback Important?

Disclosing oneself to others and receiving feedback from others are the twin processes of personal growth. The invitational, reflecting, and advanced reflecting skills that you have already learned are the primary methods helpers use to encourage client self-disclosure. The mere act of confiding in another person seems to have many health benefits (Pennebaker, 1990), and the ability to be "transparent" to others has been linked with mental health (Jourard, 1971). Learning to receive feedback is the other key to self-awareness and growth. Clients need accurate feedback in order to confront inconsistencies in their own attitudes and to know how they are affecting others.

Most problems that people face are "people problems." They come for help when they experience pain in their interpersonal worlds. Unfortunately, they often receive less-than-useful or conflicting messages about themselves from other people. Even family members and close friends may be afraid to give each other information about how they are affecting others. A friend or family member may say, "You look like a lunatic when you dance," or "Your driving makes me nervous!" during times of annoyance or stress. However, close friends and relatives are more likely to withhold feedback because they do not wish to jeopardize the relationship. Rosen and Tesser (1970) called this unwillingness to transmit bad news the "mum" effect."

The Johari Window

The *Johari window* (Luft, 1969) is a visual way of explaining that information about the self comes from two sources: things we observe about ourselves and feedback from those around us (Figure 8.1). The Johari window (named by Joe Luft and Harry Ingram, who invented it) helps to explain how we can gain greater self-awareness through the two tools of growth: self-disclosure and feedback. The window has four "panes":

I. Information Known Both to Others and to the Self (Public Area)
According to the model, the behavior of self-disclosure widens the public area (windowpane I) and shrinks the private area (windowpane III). A client who has a broader public area is able to disclose more deeply, will experience greater relief, creates better relationships, and supplies the helper with more complete information about problems. The relative size of this windowpane compared to the other three areas and the information disclosed vary depending on how open or transparent an individual is. Overdisclosure can be a problem when a person monopolizes conversations and drives people away.

II. Information Known to Others but Not to the Self (Blind Spot)
There is much about ourselves that we cannot know because we are not objective. As the poet Robert Burns said, "O wad some pow'r the giftie gie us to see ourselves

	Known to self	Not known to self
Known to others	I Public area	II Blind spot
Not known to others	III Hidden area	IV Unknown area

Figure 8.1
The Johari Window
Source: From Luft, J. (1969). *Of human interaction* (p. 13). Paolo Alto, CA: National Press. Reprinted by permission.

as ithers see us." One example of a blind spot is the fact that, even when we look in a mirror, we are not seeing an exact duplicate of ourself. Instead, we are really seeing the reverse image, similar to a slide backwards in the projector. We often do not know if we have bad breath, if we are annoying someone, if we appear judgmental, or if we have a whining tone to our voice. Conversely, we may miss our positive traits as well, unaware that others see us as attractive, kind, or a good listener. Feedback shrinks the blind spot (windowpane II).

III. Information Not Known to Others but Known to the Self (Hidden Area)

This is the area of secrets. People with large private areas usually are not known or liked by others. There is a saying in Alcoholics Anonymous that you are "only as sick as your darkest secret." This phrase suggests that through appropriate self-disclosure, many problems that have been lurking in our minds—our deepest secrets—tend to vanish in the light of a confiding relationship. When we keep secrets from others, we do not have to face our negative traits and bad habits. Most people keep secrets about their sexual activities, their drug or alcohol use, and the times when they have been dishonest or cowardly. Not everything must be emptied from this area, but many individuals seeking help have low quality interpersonal relationships because they have built strong walls around windowpane III, keeping their secrets safe and ironically depriving themselves of intimacy.

IV. Information Not Known to Others or the Self (Unknown Area)

The helping relationship reduces the size of the unknown area (windowpane IV). Clients have moments of insight or "aha!" experiences that occur when they consolidate information gained through both self disclosure and feedback. Invitational, reflecting, and challenging skills help clients gain more information about themselves and reduce this unknown area.

When we think about whether a helping session has been successful, we can evaluate it in two ways. We can look at whether the helper has demonstrated the invitational and reflecting skills as well as other building blocks. On the other hand, the Johari window gives us a glimpse of the big picture, a truer test of whether help has occurred. A session is successful if the client has disclosed important material to the helper and if he or she has reduced the blind spot by receiving feedback from the helper. Through disclosure and feedback the client comes away from the helping session having probed deeper into the problem. The invitational skills set the stage to entice the client to think and experience more deeply, while the helper's feedback provides additional information that is not filtering through the client's defenses. Recall again, William James's statement, "My experience is what I agree to attend to. Only those items I notice shape my mind." The helper can serve a valuable service of focusing the client's attention on unrecognized information.

How to Give Feedback

In the helping relationship, giving feedback means supplying information to a client about what you see, feel, or suspect about him or her. Feedback helps people grow because they are receiving constructive, specific information about themselves. When a professional helper gives feedback, the sole purpose is to help the client. Feedback from a professional—unlike that of family and friends—does not consider the needs of the helper or primarily concern itself with whether or not this will produce a strain on the relationship. Helpers only give feedback when clients ask for it or when the client needs information to progress. They give feedback for three purposes: (1) to indicate how the client's behavior affects the helper, (2) to evaluate a client's progress, and (3) to supply a client with information based on the helper's observation. When a helper says, "You say you want to be assertive but I experience your behavior as passive when you look away and avoid eye contact," the feedback indicates the effect of the behavior on the helper. The statement, "As I see it, you have now been successful in overcoming your anxiety by facing the situations you have been avoiding," is an evaluation of the client's progress. The helper is making an observation when he or she says, "I notice that you never seem to talk about your father."

Feedback may be rejected by clients because "the truth hurts." Clients use defense mechanisms to avoid accepting the information they receive. Therefore, helpers endeavor to present feedback so that it will be more palatable. In his classic book about raising children, *Parent Effectiveness Training* (1975), Thomas Gordon described the process of delivering feedback as "I messages." Most feedback statements delivered by helpers are I messages because using the word "I" conveys that the helper is expressing his or her own perspective. When a person starts a conversation by saying, "This is my viewpoint," we are more likely to listen nondefensively.

Here are some suggestions about how to give effective feedback in all sorts of situations. These are good rules for helpers and for trainees, who may be giving feedback to each other in group exercises.

1. Do not give people feedback on their personality traits. It is hard to see how one can change a description of one's character.

Poor Feedback (boss to subordinate): "You are a procrastinator."

Good Feedback: "For the past three months, your report has been late. That is unacceptable."

2. Be specific, concrete, and nonjudgmental.

Poor Feedback: "You're bugging me."

Good Feedback: "I find it annoying when you whistle during my favorite music."

3. Ask permission before giving feedback.

Helper: "You say that people at work are angry about your behavior. Would you like some feedback?"

Helper: "I would like to give you some feedback on something I have noticed. Is that all right?"

4. Sometimes, feedback about touchy subjects is accepted more easily if it is offered tentatively. You do not have to dilute the feedback; rather, find an acceptable route to get the client to think about what is being reported.

Poor Feedback: "Last time, we talked about your feelings that you deserted your father when he was ill. This time, you avoid the topic when I try to reopen it."

Good Feedback: "I got the impression last time that talking about your father was difficult for you and you seemed to steer away from that topic. Maybe it is because you think you deserted him when he was ill. Am I right about this?"

5. Give only one or two pieces of feedback at a time. When too much feedback is given, client defenses rear up like impenetrable walls and little gets through.

Poor Feedback: "I think you should improve your appearance at work. You look disheveled and you need to wear a tie. By the way, you left the copy machine on again last night and you forgot to call Marlene back."

Good Feedback: "I think you should improve your appearance at work. Your pants are wrinkled and you need to wear a tie."

6. Do not forget to give feedback that emphasizes the client's strengths. It is easy to assume that clients are aware of their strengths and to focus on their foibles. We tend to give more feedback that points out unknown weaknesses than unrecognized assets. More often, clients need to know what is going right, what is working, and what resources the client has to bring to the problem. Try focusing on the positive aspects first and bringing up the negative later.

Poor Feedback: "You asked someone out for a date but you did not work on the other part of the assignment, where you were to confront your friend on her behavior. Let's talk about that."

Good Feedback: "Based on what you've said today, I'm picking up that you have made real progress. Even though it was a little scary, you asked two people for a date and one of them said, 'yes.' "

7. Use a checking question to determine whether feedback was received and how it was accepted.

Helper: "A minute ago, I pointed out that you have spent the last few weeks talking only about your ex-husband. What is your reaction to that feedback?"

Stop and Reflect

There is a parallel in our own optic system that can demonstrate the existence of blind spots, at least from a physiological viewpoint. You may know that the optic nerve attaches to the back of the eyeball. Where it connects, there is a small gap in the picture your brain sees. Because we have two eyes, we correct for this tiny blind spot and never know that it exists. Take a look at the X and the large dot at the bottom of this page. Now, hold this book with your right hand and stretch it out to arm's length. Stare directly at the X on the left side of the page. Then, close your left eye and slowly move the book straight toward your face. At about 12 inches, the dot on the right side disappears.

The physical blind spot is only an analogy of the psychological phenomenon identified in the Johari window (windowpane II). Still, it alerts us to the fact that our knowledge about the world and ourselves is not complete. The rub is that since we are unaware of these things, how do we know what they are and how can we convince clients to listen to feedback? Consider the following questions:

- In this experiment, you learned about your blind spot through actual experience. Suppose I had merely told you about the blind spot? Which information is the most powerful in convincing you of its existence?
- How can we help clients have experiences of their psychological blind spots rather than merely talking to them?
- Suppose you gave the client some feedback that you were 98% sure was true and accurate and the client's response was to dismiss it completely. How do you think you might react? How could you get the client to consider it further without damaging the relationship?
- Suppose that a client feels rejected in her personal relationships. In her interactions with you and with other personnel, you notice that she talks constantly, rarely allowing anyone else to control the conversation. First, write down a nonjudgmental feedback statement exactly as you would deliver it:

_____

_____

_____

Next, identify one or two other situations where the client might get this kind of feedback. What assignments might you give the client to make her more aware of this tendency?

Confrontation

Confrontations are interventions that point out discrepancies in client beliefs, behaviors, words, or nonverbal messages. In addition, a good confrontation urges the client to resolve the inconsistencies. Confrontation creates emotional arousal and can lead clients to develop important insights and to change their behavior.

A *discrepancy* is an inconsistency, a mixed message, or a conflict among a client's thoughts, feelings, and behaviors. In fact, every problem a client presents contains discrepancies. For example:

A client says that she wants an equal sharing relationship, but dates only domineering men.
A client says that she loves her job, but complains about it constantly.
A client states that he wants to improve his marriage, but forgets to go to marriage counseling sessions.

Why Should Inconsistencies Be Confronted?

Ivey and Simek-Downing (1980) say that "the resolution or synthesis of incongruities may be said to be a central goal of all theoretical orientations" (p. 177). As a result of confrontation, client awareness of inconsistencies is stimulated, and the client moves to resolve them. In essence, it is an educational process that brings information to the client's attention that has been previously unknown, disregarded, or repressed.

Confrontation is a skill that is developed after the early helping building blocks are well established. As you gain more training and experience, you will realize increasingly that clients need to be challenged as well as supported. Recent research confirms that highly trained (doctoral) counselors use confrontation more often than students (Tracey, Hays, Malone, & Herman, 1988). At the same time, doctoral-level counselors demonstrated less dominance and verbosity than student helpers. It appears that experience and training teach helpers to use confrontation more frequently, to talk less, and to make confrontations in a gentler way.

Cognitive Dissonance and Confrontation: Why Confrontation Works

Do you remember the concept of cognitive dissonance from Psychology 101? Cognitive dissonance theory states that we are motivated to keep cognitions such as values, beliefs, and attitudes consistent (Festinger, 1957). When people experience inconsistencies in their thoughts, feelings, and behaviors, this creates tension and they are motivated to reduce the tension. We convince ourselves that the incongruity is unimportant or try changing one of the incompatible elements. For example, a client describes her good-paying but repetitive and boring job and says that she wants to go to college because she is not intellectually challenged in her present position. She deals with the tension caused by these conflicting thoughts by stating that intellectual challenge is not really important; it is better to be financially secure. We use such defense mechanisms to distort reality so that we can reduce anxiety. Many times, clients are using defense mechanisms to escape tension, rather than making choices based on thinking and planning. When helpers confront people with these discrepancies, anxiety often resurfaces.

Kiesler and Pallak (1976) reviewed dissonance studies and found a link between dissonance and physiological arousal (Cooper, Zanna, & Taves, 1978; Croyle & Cooper, 1983; Pittman, 1975; Zanna & Cooper, 1974). Attitude change occurs because clients are driven to reduce the arousal caused by the helper's discrepant messages. In short, when a helper confronts a client, the client becomes anxious when he or she realizes that there is a discrepancy in his or her story. The confrontation causes anxiety because the client must become aware of this split, which is normally kept out of awareness by his or her defenses. The client is then invited to change his or her ideas to ones that are more productive and reality based (Claiborn, 1982; Olsen & Claiborn, 1990).

Types of Discrepancies

There are five elements of a client's story that can come into conflict: the client's worldview or beliefs, the client's previous experiences, the client's verbal messages, the client's nonverbal messages, and the client's behavior. They can occur in many possible combinations, but the six most common forms are illustrated in the following dialogues:

Incongruity Between Verbal and Nonverbal Messages
Client: "It's been hell. This whole thing. It's almost funny [laughs]. You know. Sometimes he loves me, sometimes he hates me."

Helper: "Your laughing and smiling make me think the problem is not serious, and yet I can tell by what you've said that it has been very painful for you." (confrontation)

Incongruity Between Beliefs and Experiences
Client: "I do the best I can. But I'm not really good-looking. I've been dating the same two guys for about four months now. They say I'm pretty, but I don't believe it."

Helper: "You tell me that you believe you're not attractive and then you describe going on a lot of dates." (confrontation)

Incongruity Between Values and How the Client Behaves
Client: "My son is the most important thing in the world to me. But I just don't have time to see him every week. I need some recreation, too. If I want to get ahead at work, I have to put in the hours."

Helper: "If I understand you, you say that your relationship with your son means a lot to you, but somehow you've let other things get in the way." (confrontation)

Incongruity Between What the Client Says and How the Client Behaves
Client: "I've been going to Cocaine Anonymous as I said I would. But it's not really helping. Every time I see one of my old friends, I'm back into it again."

Helper: "I'm confused. You say that you want to give up cocaine, and yet you continue to see your old drug friends." (confrontation)

Incongruity Between Experiences and Plans

Client: "Sure, my girlfriend and I have been having a lot of problems lately. But if we moved in together, I think things would improve."

Helper: "Isn't one of the problems that whenever you spend any length of time together, you fight violently for days? How will living together and spending even more time together help the relationship?" (confrontation)

Incongruity Between Two Verbal Messages

Client: "My wife makes twice as much money as I do. It doesn't bother me. But I always feel that she looks down on me because of it. I should be making a lot more than I do. I often think about getting another job."

Helper: "Okay, on the one hand, you say that it doesn't bother you, and yet you also say that you feel inadequate in her eyes and talk about a career change!" (confrontation)

How to Confront

The helper's confrontational statement usually takes one of the following forms:

"You said _____, but your nonverbals said _____." (verbal vs. nonverbal)
"You believe _____, but you experience _____." (beliefs vs. experiences)
"You value _____, but you act _____." (values vs. actions)
"You said _____, but you acted _____." (verbal vs. actions)
"You plan to do _____, but your past experiences tell you _____." (plans vs. experiences)
"You said _____, but you also say _____." (verbal vs. verbal)

As you begin to identify discrepancies and present them to a client, you might find it helpful to memorize the following phrase, "On the one hand, _____; on the other hand, _____." Although you do not wish to overuse this statement with clients, this algorithm or template will help remind you to identify the conflicting aspects of a client's story.

Steps to Confrontation

Step 1   First, listen carefully and make sure the relationship is well established before confronting. Use the nonjudgmental listening cycle to fully understand the client's message and ask yourself if the timing is right or if a confrontation will prematurely place stress on the relationship. Have you earned the right to confront?

Step 2   Present the challenge in a way that the client will most likely accept it. The following example shows a helper using closed questioning and reflection of feeling to gently usher in confrontation and reduce the negative impact.

Jung Sook (Helper): "Can you tell me what you mean by the word 'independence?' " (closed question)

Olivier (Client): "Well, what I mean is that I am tired of having to report to my wife. I don't know what I'd do without her. But she is a pain in the neck most of the time."

Jung Sook: "You want to be independent, but you think you have to abide by your wife's wishes most of the time." (confrontation)

Olivier: "But she's a wonderful wife. I don't really mean it when I say those things, you know."

Jung Sook: "You think she's wonderful, and yet you find yourself angry with her a great deal of the time." (confrontation)

Olivier: "That's what bothers me, sometimes it's great, sometimes it's terrible."

Step 3   Observe the client's response to the confrontation. In this case, the client does not fully accept Jung Sook's first confrontation. She notes this and tries something different.

Step 4   Follow up the confrontation by rephrasing or retreating. When the client does not accept or rejects the confrontation outright, the helper should try another tack. Because clients often respond to confrontation either by denial or by superficial agreement, the helper must be ready to follow up with additional exploration, another confrontation, or clarification. Before abandoning the confrontation entirely, Jung Sook's second confrontation is accepted by the client because it is phrased in a way that the client can accept. Specifically, Jung Sook used the word, "wonderful" to gain the client's acceptance to the confrontation.

Evaluating Confrontation and Client Response

The Helper Confrontation Scale

One way to evaluate the potency of a confrontation is to score the helper's statement on a five-level scale that is similar to Carkhuff's levels of empathic response (Hammond, Hepworth, & Smith, 1977). We call this the *Helper Confrontation Scale* (HCS). Higher scores on the scale reflect a better ability by the helper to confront effectively.

At level 1, the helper overlooks or accepts the discrepancies, inconsistencies, or dysfunctional expressions of the client or uses a harsh, abrasive, or "put-down" confrontation. For example, a helper might say, "Your unwillingness to make this decision shows that you are a dependent person," or, "When are you going to realize that you are knocking your head against a brick wall?"

At level 2, the helper does not focus on discrepancies, but responds with silence or reflects without noting the inconsistency. This category also includes poorly timed confrontations such as a strong confrontation that is delivered in the first few interchanges between helper and client before a therapeutic relationship is established.

At level 3, the helper focuses attention on a discrepancy by questioning or by pointing out the inconsistency. At level 3, the timing is appropriate and the confrontation is not abusive. For example, the helper might point out, "After hearing your story, I understand your unhappiness with the college you have chosen, but, at the same time, it sounds like there are things you like about being there as well."

Level 4 involves a direct confrontation by the helper that includes a challenge to the client to modify the behavior or to resolve the inconsistency, while, at the same time, protecting the client's self-esteem. To guard the client's self-esteem, the helper uses a nonjudgmental tone and a tentative approach. For example, a helper might say, "What I am hearing is that, on the one hand, you love your mother, but, on the other, at age 30, you feel that you need a place of your own. This sounds like a really important issue for you to resolve and I would like to help."

Finally, level 5 includes all of the positive characteristics of the lower levels but is conveyed by the helper in a caring and helpful way along with enthusiasm for growth. For example, the helper might say, "You really care for Angela, but you are afraid of the consequences when the boss finds out that you are dating his ex-wife. This sounds like a problem that really deserves some quick attention and it could really help you because you desire to be more honest and straightforward about your feelings."

In essence, the scale points out that the best confrontations are well timed, direct, urge the client to act, and are delivered in a caring manner.

The Client Acceptance Scale

Another method of evaluating a confrontation is to look at how the client responds to it. Clients can react to a confrontation in three basic ways. Each represents a different level of acceptance of the confrontation, and each reaction gives the helper important feedback and direction. A client response on the *Client Acceptance Scale* (CAS) can be rated as a 1, 2, or 3, depending on the extent to which a client agrees on a discrepancy pointed out by the helper. A client who fails to agree with a confrontation is not necessarily "resistant." The confrontation may have been inaccurate or too discrepant with the client's experience. Very often, a client's response at levels 1 and 2 precedes full acceptance. The client has not yet identified the issue as a problem and may need some time to change viewpoints.

The three levels of acceptance are:

1. A client may deny that a discrepancy even exists. Examples of denial include attempts by the client to discredit the helper, to change the topic, to seek support elsewhere, or to falsely accept the confrontation. The helper must decide whether to pound away continually until the confrontation is accepted or to bring the topic up again at a later date. The more combative approach is likely to be detrimental to the relationship.
2. The client may choose to accept one part or aspect of the confrontation as being true, while finding another hard to swallow. Partial acceptance can lead to further dialogue on the issue. At such times, the helper is encouraged to explore and build on the areas of agreement.
3. The client appears to accept fully the confrontation and agrees to try to resolve the inconsistency that has been pointed out with new behavior.

    Previously, an example was given in which a helper confronted an individual (a) who stated that he wanted to give up cocaine and (b) who continued to associate with his old, drug-using friends. The continuation of their conversation is presented here to show how the helper can promote exploration, even when the client does not fully accept the confrontation. It also shows how a confrontation can lead to the setting of a new goal when the helper points out a discrepancy and then asks the client to resolve it.

Client: "I've been going to Cocaine Anonymous as I said I would. But it's not really helping. Every time I see one of my old friends, I'm back into it again."

Helper: "I'm confused. You say that you want to give up cocaine, and yet you continue to see your old drug friends." (Helper Confrontation Scale—3)

Client: "I do want to stop using. But what am I supposed to do? Stay by myself all the time?" (Client Acceptance Scale—2)

Helper: "So, what you really need is to be around people, socialize, have friends. How could you do this—stay away from cocaine and still have friends?" (helper moves on to setting goals)

Client: "You tell me."

Helper: "Hold it. I don't have all the answers to this. But you said you want to have friends and you want to stop using. Is this possible?"

Client: "It must be. People do it."

Helper: "Yes, but how do they do it?"

Client: "I don't know. I guess they have new friends that don't use. But it's hard to start all over again."

Helper: "I'm not an expert on this. But some people who have been off cocaine for a while must be familiar with this problem. It seems like it might be fairly common. Between now and when we next meet, would you be willing to think about this? Go to your next Anonymous meeting and ask one or two people about this, then let me know what they have to say."

Client: "All right. And I'll talk to my friend, Michelle. She's been sober for a year now."

Stop and Reflect

The following is a reflection by Cindy Yee about her upbringing and how her family and cultural values helped her become a nonjudgmental listener and also presented a challenge when she was forced to confront her clients.

Respect is a core value around which Chinese culture is based. "Respect your parents and do as they say." "Respect your teachers and don't question or challenge them." "Respect your family and don't discuss concerns or problems outside the family circle." "Respect your elders and don't talk back to them." These were the values and expectations instilled in me by my parents, especially my mother. She was born in China and believed most strongly in these rules.

When I first began working as a counselor, my job was to facilitate a group for court-ordered drunk drivers, one of the most angry and difficult client populations. You can imagine the challenges I had to face. For someone who is assertive, open, and willing to confront others, regardless of age or status, this would be a difficult job. For someone like me who was taught to listen, not interrupt, and agree with others, especially older people and those in higher positions, it was a daunting task.

Frequently, there were older clients in the group who tended to "ramble on" in their discussions. Interrupting them, in Chinese eyes, would have been very disrespectful. When doctors, lawyers, and teachers were in the group and expressed opinions contrary to my curriculum, it was nearly impossible for me, at first, to disagree with them. It has taken quite a while for me to overcome this reluctance to be what my culture would consider "disrespectful" and to develop the necessary skills as a counselor to be assertive in confronting others. This is still an area I am trying to improve. My cultural style of passive acceptance has helped me develop unconditional acceptance regardless of differences. This has helped me in developing rapport with clients and getting to the point in a relationship where they can accept confrontation. Chinese cultural values and beliefs have been both helpful and challenging to me as an emerging helper.

- Cindy Yee indicates that "respect" is one of the core values in Chinese culture. Thinking back on your own upbringing, what cultural or family values were stressed?
- What were your family's values about contradicting others, keeping the peace, and disclosing weaknesses? Was family business to be kept within the family? Do you think any of your own core values might have an effect on your willingness either to talk with clients about their deepest issues or to confront certain individuals?
- One of the most common difficulties for most of us is overcoming the "mum effect," that is, the social rule that says to keep feedback to yourself. As a helper, your contract with the client implies that you will give honest feedback despite your personal discomfort. Think about some specific situations that will create discomfort for you such as refusing an expensive gift from a client, informing a client that his or her personal hygiene is poor, dealing with tardiness, talking about sexual problems, discussing whether the client is having an affair, or asking if the client is being honest with you. Which do you think will be the most difficult for you? How might you increase your comfort with these topics?
- Would you find it more difficult to confront someone of a different ethnic or racial background, someone older or younger than you, someone who has a high-status profession, or someone of the same or opposite sex? How do you plan to overcome these limitations? Discuss with a small group some strategies for overcoming some of these roadblocks to feedback and confrontation.

Problems and Precautions

One writer called confrontation the "thermonuclear weapons" of helping. They are powerful and their force can help or harm. Confrontation may arouse the defenses of the client or damage self-esteem, rather than increasing awareness and motivating action. Therefore, confrontational interventions must be advanced carefully. Although the force of the confrontation should not be watered down with qualifiers, confrontation must be presented in a way that does not say, "Gotcha!" shaming the client. The target we are aiming for is to be able to deliver moderately confrontational statements with the client's best interests at heart.

Earlier, the notion of timing was mentioned. Timing means knowing when in the relationship and when in the course of therapy confrontation will do the most good.

Obviously, the time for confrontation is when the client-helper relationship is well established and the client trusts your motives. Knowing when confrontation will do the most good is a more tricky clinical judgment. It has been our experience that frequent and premature confrontations based on very little information tend to erode the credibility of the helper. Consider waiting to confront an issue until after it has been raised on several occasions and the chances of acceptance by the client are high.

Confrontation can have other negative effects on the therapeutic relationship. Confrontations, if made too forcefully, may seem to blame or humiliate the client and go against the goal of raising self-esteem. Inappropriate confrontations place the helper in a judgmental and superior position, arousing defenses rather than providing insight. Before confronting, the helper must be clear that the reason for the intervention is to increase client awareness, not just to unload a sense of frustration.

A general caveat is that any helper intervention that is in opposition to the client's social and cultural values may not only be disrespectful but also ineffective. Confrontation is an excellent example of a technique with important cultural implications. For example, Lazarus (1982) discusses how this technique can backfire with some Native American children in a school counseling setting. Others have recommended a gentle approach in using confrontation with African American and Asian American clients (Ivey, 1994).

Shock Confrontation

Confrontation is sometimes used as shock treatment. Several theoretical orientations use confrontational language to arouse emotions, rather than to point out discrepancies. For example, rational emotive behavior therapy's (REBT) founder, Albert Ellis, used loud voice tones or even curses to intensify confrontations. Some early group therapy methods (the Synanon approach) used personal attacks and abusive confrontation to create movement in dealing with deeply ingrained behavior patterns. Many alcohol and drug treatment facilities still favor these methods. Such confrontation is designed to provoke an emotional response, such as anger or sadness, in "hardened" clients. Following is an example of this shock treatment type of confrontation:

Client: "I'm always, you know, the last one, the fifth wheel. My parents favor my sister. At work, everyone ignores me. You only talk to me because I pay you. What's wrong with me? Why doesn't anybody like me?"

Helper: "Maybe it's because they don't want to be around a whiner!"

Prochaska (1984) describes an experience in which his co-helper confronted a husband about his domineering behavior toward his wife by saying, "You make me want to vomit!" The man returned to an individual session filled with consternation over this abuse. His anger triggered a great deal of discussion, introspection, and therapeutic movement because the client was able to see how he brought out these responses not only with the helper but with his wife.

The helper responses in both these examples could be called feedback. They are verbalizations of the helper's genuine reaction to the client (Prochaska, 1984), but they are also judgmental, comparing the client to some external standard. Although there may be times when such strong confrontation helps to motivate a client, there is evidence that, even with substance abusers, a consistent highly confrontational therapist style is not as effective as a moderately confrontational one (Miller, Benefield, & Tonigan, 1993). Shock confrontation cannot be recommended, especially to the beginning helper, because of its effects on the therapeutic alliance and on client self-esteem. The reason for discussing it here is that such methods are often portrayed in films, books, and dramatic demonstrations. They are appealing in their power and cleverness, but the client's welfare should be the primary consideration in their use.

Summary

Previously, you learned how to use the nonjudgmental listening cycle to create the proper conditions for a therapeutic relationship. In that relationship, the client feels accepted and explores the thoughts, feelings, and meanings that are implicit in his or her story. However, the story also has inconsistencies and conflicts or else the client would not be seeking help. All problems are due to opposing forces in the client's life. The helper must give the client feedback and use confrontational skills to help the client become aware of these discrepancies and also encourage the client to act to resolve them. Ironically, this places a strain on the therapeutic relationship because the client begins to realize that the helper is not going to stick to safe topics but will explore the touchy ones as well.

In this chapter, we presented the Johari window as a way of envisioning the big picture in the helping process. The client needs to gain information about the self as well as disclose. Although self-disclosure brings helper and client together, it has another beneficial effect. The client listens to his or her own words, gaining greater self-knowledge. Feedback is the other method for gaining knowledge of the self. This chapter presented some "dos and don'ts" for giving feedback.

Compared to feedback, confrontation is a serious challenge to the client's version of the story and pushes the client to act. Confrontation is an art because one must point out these discrepancies clearly, yet kindly. The Helper Confrontation Scale assists new helpers in evaluating the quality of their confrontations. On the other hand, the Client Acceptance Scale rates client reactions to confrontations to determine how much of an impact your confrontation is having and whether another tactic should be tried.

Group Exercises

Group Exercise 1:
Feedback—The Fishbowl

This exercise works best with groups of eight to ten people. Four or five people sit in chairs facing each other to form an inner circle. The same number of participants form an outer circle. Each member of the outer circle is paired with an inner-circle member. The outer-circle members sit behind the inner circle and across from the members they are paired with so they can observe them. See Figure 8.2. For 10–15 min-

Figure 8.2
Fishbowl Activity Diagram

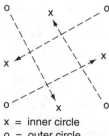

x = inner circle
o = outer circle
Arrows show partners

utes, the inner-circle members engage in a leaderless discussion on a topic such as "What are the most important personal characteristics of a helper?" or "What do you see yourself doing personally and professionally, 5 years from now?"

During the discussion, outer-circle members are instructed to carefully observe nonverbals and listen to the words of their partners in the inner group. At the end of the discussion, the groups break down into dyads of the inner-circle members and their outer-circle partners. Outer-circle members give feedback to inner-circle members using the following guidelines. When this is completed, inner-circle members should comment on the quality of the feedback they received. How accurate was it?

Feedback Guidelines

1. Do not give people feedback on their personality traits.
2. Be specific, concrete, and nonjudgmental.
3. Ask permission before giving feedback.
4. Sometimes, feedback about touchy subjects is accepted more easily if it is offered tentatively.
5. Give only one or two pieces of feedback at a time.
6. Give feedback that emphasizes the client's strengths, not just weaknesses.
7. Use a checking question to determine whether feedback was received and how it was accepted.

Time permitting, the exercise can be repeated with inner- and outer-circle members changing places. Following the feedback in dyads, a class discussion can be held in which members compare their experiences of giving and receiving feedback. Which role was more difficult, giver or receiver of feedback? Were you surprised by the accuracy of the feedback on your interpersonal style?

Group Exercise 2: Confrontation

Break into groups of three trainees who will assume the roles of helper, client, and observer. As the exercise continues, each member should have the opportunity to assume each role.

The Client's Role

Discuss a problem that is causing an internal conflict or moral dilemma. The problem might be the result of:

- Conflict about a job or whether to relocate
- Conflict about whether or not to be honest in a relationship, for example, whether to tell a friend she depends on you too much
- Conflict about something you have done that you do not feel good about, that you regret, or that you wish you could change.

The Observer's Role

Write down verbatim the helper's responses and evaluate the helper on his or her ability to use confrontation using the five-point Helper Confrontation Scale. Code the helper's responses using P for paraphrase, ROF for reflection of feelings, ROM for reflection of meaning, OQ for open question, CQ for closed question, CON for confrontation.

The Helper's Role

Review the list titled "Quick Tips: Confrontation" that follows this exercise. Use the nonjudgmental listening cycle to get the basics of the client's story. Do not spend too much time on setting up the relationship. Although this is critical in real helping situations, in this exercise, the main purpose is to practice identifying discrepancies and delivering them to a client. As soon as possible, identify discrepancies by pointing them out, then encourage the client to resolve the inconsistency.

Postexercise Discussion

The observer shares feedback with the helper, based on the Feedback Checklist and the five-point rating scale of effective confrontation. The client gives qualitative feedback concerning the effectiveness of the confrontation and the degree of discomfort caused by the confrontation. For example, were the confrontations presented as observations rather than accusations? Were they presented nonjudgmentally? Helper and observer can also attempt to recall the client's reaction to the confrontation based on the Client Acceptance Scale and by scoring them 1, 2, or 3.

Quick Tips: Confrontation

- Wait until you have heard the client's whole story before you identify discrepancies. What seems to be a discrepancy may be a minor point once you know more about the situation.
- If you are having trouble identifying discrepancies, remember that there would not be a problem if there were no discrepancy. Ask yourself, "What makes this a dilemma?" or, "What are the two sides to the client's problem that make this situation so bothersome? Use the memory aid, "On the one hand, ____; on the other hand, ____."
- Note the impact of your confrontation on the client. Does he or she deny, partially

accept, or fully accept your identification of the discrepancy? Follow up denial and partial acceptance with invitational and reflecting skills.
- After you identify a discrepancy, try using a checking question such as, "Am I on target ?" Often the client will correct you and clarify the discrepancy.

Group Exercise 3: Collaborating to Identify Effective Confrontations

In groups of four, one member (the client) describes a problem situation to the group (use the suggestions described in Group Exercise 1). After the client has spent a few minutes describing the situation, the remaining members each write down a confrontation and deliver it verbally to the client. The client responds to each confrontation in turn. As the client does so, the member uses the Client Acceptance Scale to evaluate the client's response. In a group discussion, the helpers and client discuss which responses rated highest on the Helper Confrontation Scale and how confrontations might be phrased to achieve better acceptance by the client. After this discussion, members trade roles and continue until each has had a turn as client.

Feedback Checklist: Confrontation

Observer Name_____ Helper Name_____

	Helper Statement	Coding*	HCS (1–5)	CAS (1–3)
1				
2				
3				
4				
5				
6				
7				
8				
9				
10				

*Do not include minimal encouragers.

Additional Exercises

Exercise 1

Break into groups of three or four. Come up with a client problem, then construct a role-play in which the client uses a defense mechanism to reduce anxiety. The helper's job is to point out the way the client is avoiding and encourage the client to reevaluate his or her choices.

Exercise 2

Following are five client situations. Try to identify the discrepancy in each, using the formula: "On the one hand, _____; on the other hand, _____." This will help you get a feel for identifying discrepancies.

In some of the following situations, the conflict is implied rather than actually stated. Imagine what conflicts you might be experiencing if you were in that situation. When you have written your answers, meet with a small group and discuss them. Looking both at the clients and the issues, which would be most difficult for you to actually confront?

a. An 18-year-old client describes how sad she is that she has to leave her parents and go off to college. She smiles as she talks about this.

b. The client is very religious and is very judgmental about nonbelievers. At age 22, he has only a few friends and has never had a longstanding romantic relationship. He comes for help because he has become "addicted" to 900-number telephone sex lines.

c. The client says that he loves his sister and that she is very important to him. During their last encounter, she "exploded" because he did not attend her wedding.

d. The client states that she has just been offered a job as a manager at a new company. They are very excited about having her because of her years of experience. She has worked at her current company on weekends and during the summer since she was 17. She says that she feels the owner relies on her, but her pay and responsibilities are unlikely to improve. She feels that she has made as much advancement as she can and would like a new challenge.

e. The client is a 17-year-old high school student in an alternative school. She has worked hard and improved her poor grades to B's and C's. She failed her High School Equivalency Examination by one point. She is discouraged and plans to drop out of school. She plans to continue working at her job, even though her boss has indicated she must have a high school diploma.

Homework

Homework 1

In a single page, identify an incongruity or discrepancy in your own life that you are willing to talk about. Alternately, you may write about, in a disguised fashion, a discrepancy you have noticed in another person. Write down the two sides of the dilemma. How deeply does this discrepancy affect your life (or theirs)? Do all problems contain discrepancies? Can you think of ways that you have used defense mechanisms or other methods of self-deception to decrease your discomfort? What action steps would be needed now to resolve the discrepancy?

Homework 2

Think about a particularly difficult piece of feedback you have received. It may have been about a weakness in your appearance, a job evaluation, or it may even have been feedback you received in this class. How did you respond emotionally to the feedback? Did it make you angry, hurt your feelings, or just make you feel incompetent? Did you try to protect yourself by denying or discounting the feedback? Did you learn anything constructive from the negative feedback?

Now think about a time when you received some positive feedback on a personal strength, for example, about a job well done or some aspect of your appearance or personality. What made the feedback positive?

Finally, have you ever had an experience where you received no feedback after expending considerable time and effort. For instance, have you ever turned in a lengthy project or paper and received no comments other than a grade? How did you react emotionally? What effect do you think a lack of feedback would have on a person's behavior in the long run?

Of the three kinds of feedback mentioned here—positive, negative and none—which helped you the most? How might you apply your reactions to your future dealings with clients? Summarize your reactions in two or three paragraphs.

Journal Starters

1. Identify three or four major problems you have had in your life. What conflicts were you experiencing internally? See if you can identify any patterns or themes to these conflicts. For example, do your conflicts seem to revolve around doing what you want to do versus doing what others want?
2. How comfortable are you with bringing up difficult issues with friends and family? Do you tend to be more tactful or more confrontational? When you go overboard, which end of the continuum do you approach? Where might this tendency have originated?

For more journal ideas, as well as more practice with challenging skills, refer to Chapter 8 in *Exercises in the Art of Helping.*

References

Claiborn, C. D. (1982). Interpretation and change in counseling. *Journal of Counseling Psychology, 29,* 439–453.

Cooper, J., Zanna, M., & Taves, P. A. (1978). Arousal as a necessary condition for attitude change following induced compliance. *Journal of Personality and Social Psychology, 36,* 1101–1106.

Croyle, R. T., & Cooper, J. (1983). Dissonance arousal: Physiological evidence. *Journal of Personality and Social Psychology, 45,* 782–789.

Festinger, L. (1957). *A theory of cognitive dissonance.* Stanford, CA: Stanford University Press.

Goleman, D. (1985). *Vital lies, simple truths.* New York: Simon & Schuster.

Gordon, T. (1975). *PET: Parent effectiveness training.* New York: Wyden.

Hammond, D. C., Hepworth, D. H., & Smith, V. G. (1977). *Improving therapeutic communication.* San Francisco: Jossey-Bass.

Ivey, A. E. (1994). *Intentional interviewing.* Pacific Grove, CA: Brooks/Cole.

Ivey, A. E., & Simek-Downing, L. (1980). *Counseling and psychotherapy: Skills, theories and practice.* Upper Saddle River, NJ: Prentice Hall.

Jourard, S. (1971). *The transparent self.* New York: Van Nostrand Rheinhold.

Kiesler, C. A., & Pallak, M. S. (1976). Arousal properties of dissonance manipulations. *Psychological Bulletin, 83,* 1014–1025.

Lazarus, A. A. (1982). Counseling the native American child: Acquisition of values. *Elementary School Guidance and Counseling, 17,* 83–88.

Luft, J. (1969). *Of human interaction.* Palo Alto, CA: National Press.

Miller, W. R., Benefield, R. G., & Tonigan, J. S. (1993). Enhancing motivation for change in problem drinking: A controlled comparison of two therapist styles. *Journal of Consulting and Clinical Psychology, 61,* 455–461.

Olsen, P., & Claiborn, C. D. (1990). Interpretation and arousal in the counseling process. *Journal of Counseling Psychology, 37,* 131–137.

Pennebaker, J. W. (1990). *Opening up: The healing power of confiding in others.* New York: William Morrow.

Pittman, T. S. (1975). Attribution of arousal as a mediator in dissonance reduction. *Journal of Experimental and Social Psychology, 11,* 53–63.

Prochaska, J. O. (1984). *Systems of psychotherapy.* Chicago: Dorsey Press.

Rosen, S., & Tesser, A. (1970). On the reluctance to communicate undesirable information: The MUM effect. *Sociometry, 33,* 253–263.

Tracey, T. J., Hays, K. A., Malone, J., & Herman, B. (1988). Changes in counselor response as a function of experience. *Journal of Counseling Psychology, 35,* 119–126.

Yalom, I. D. (1990). *Love's executioner and other tales of psychotherapy.* New York: Harper Collins.

Zanna, M. P., & Cooper, J. (1974). Dissonance and the pill: An attribution approach to studying the arousal properties of dissonance. *Journal of Personality and Social Psychology, 29,* 703–709.

Goal-Setting Skills

9

Until one is committed, there is hesitancy, the chance to draw back, always ineffectiveness. There is one elementary truth the ignorance of which kills countless ideas and splendid plans. That the moment one commits oneself, then Providence moves too. All sorts of things occur to help one that would never otherwise have occurred. A whole stream of events issues from the decision, raising in one's favor all manner of unforeseen incidents and meetings and material assistance which no man could have dreamt would come his way. Whatever you do, or dream you can, begin it. Boldness has genius, power and magic in it. Begin it now.

Goethe

I have always had Goethe's quote hanging in my office because it reminds me that my job is all about the power of beginnings. When I first started, I had grand plans for my clients. Frequently, I was disappointed when their goals and successes were different from the ones I had planned. I soon came to realize that significant and lasting

197

change came when the client was able to identify an important goal and stick with it. Even if that goal was, in my eyes, quite small, the act of identifying it and beginning to work on it seemed to bring about a great deal of relief and it seemed to bring about other healthy changes as well. Some research has focused on the fact that significant change takes place between the time a client makes an appointment and the first interview. Starting something has power and magic in it as Goethe says.

The second reason I like this quote is that it reminds me that commitment is required. To use an analogy, clients have often started a number of dry holes in their life, never sticking with something until progress is made. If you continue to dig deeply in the same place, you will eventually hit water, but you will waste much time by digging several holes at once. By setting goals and sticking to them, the helper mobilizes the magic of the beginning and also receives the benefit of persistence. Every helping session focuses on the client's goals and it serves as a reminder to think about the goals between sessions.

Where Do I Go from Here?

At this point in training, many students make the following statement, "I seem to be able to empathize with the client through the nonjudgmental listening cycle, but where do I go from here?" The helper feels that after a session or two, they have exhausted the client's story and explored the client's distress, but they do not feel that they have really helped. Goal setting helps to alleviate distress in the beginning helper just as it does in the client. When the client sets a direction, the helper now sees ways to help. Previously, we pointed out that beginning helpers tend to jump to goal setting long before they have really understood the client. There are many layers to the onion. The opening stages of the relationship require patience. Premature goal setting leads to establishing superficial goals.

Once the relationship is firmly established and the helper has heard the initial version of the client's story, helping progresses through five basic stages as described in Chapter 2 and shown in Figure 9.1. At the initial relationship-building stage, most

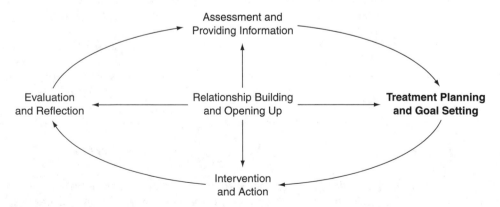

Figure 9.1
The Counseling Relationship: Goal Setting

of the helper's activities are based on the invitational, reflecting, and challenging skills, which invite the client to open up and examine himself or herself within the confiding relationship. Early in the relationship, the helper does not try to narrow the field of discussion, but dares the client to go deeper and disclose more. In the assessment stage, the helper gets in-depth information about the client, the client's problem, and the environment as the client reveals important background information. Without this knowledge, the treatment plan might turn out to be irrelevant or ineffective if the client is not motivated, is being influenced by others, or is in a nonsupportive environment. In addition, hidden areas of a client's life might not come to light without a thorough look into his or her background. These secrets such as substance abuse could undermine the therapeutic plans.

While invitational and reflecting skills encourage clients to open up and assessment provides crucial data, the skills at the goal-setting stage are methods for narrowing down the information into a few specific tasks and goals. Like a funnel, helping begins with wide-ranging discussions, but eventually narrows to focus on some particular areas. Goal setting is the stage when the helper begins to change the focus of counseling sessions from the introduction of new topics and assessment to the identification of the most crucial issues to be addressed in later sessions. In this chapter, you will be learning those helping skills that narrow the discussion and focus in on a smaller range of issues.

Besides the fact that goal setting allows the helper to focus on specific issues, goal setting has an extremely positive effect on the client because it separates the tangled mass of a problem into manageable units. Once a few goals have been identified, future sessions have a focus and the client begins to see the light at the end of the tunnel. Hope begins to dawn because the client now views the amorphous mass of trouble as a set of solvable problems. Figure 9.2 shows the client's problems as they first appear in the opening sessions and later after assessment and goal setting.

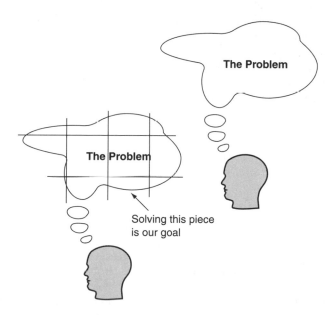

The Problem

The Problem

Solving this piece
is our goal

Figure 9.2
Breaking the Problem into
Parcels and Working on
One Part.

Through this process, the intangible cloud of problems has been broken into identifiable parts. Goal setting is based on the information we gain in the assessment stage,
but it culminates when we use goal-setting skills to separate the most crucial problems from those of lesser importance. In this chapter, we will look at two helping skills
that narrow the discussion and identify the key issues: (1) focusing on the client and
(2) boiling down the problem.

Who Owns the Problem? Focusing on the Client

Thomas Gordon (1975) suggested that helpers think about a key question as they begin the goal-setting stage of the helping process: Who owns the problem? The question can be most clearly answered by determining who is emotionally upset by the
problem. The emotional reaction not only provides the motivation to seek help, but
acts as a red flag for the helper by identifying the person most affected. For example, if both members of a couple are unhappy with the relationship, the couple will
"own" the relationship problem and may seek counseling together. On the other
hand, the man who complains about his employer's stinginess "owns" the problem
and must decide how to solve the problem by seeking another job, becoming more
assertive, or modifying his feelings and perceptions to better handle the situation. It
is unlikely that the employer "owns" the problem, since he or she is probably not upset by stinginess toward others.

One of the reasons this is such a critical question is that, early on in their practice, helpers can be easily sidetracked into helping a client change some other person: spouse, employer, or significant other. One of the clearest examples of this occurs in the case of an alcoholic's family. At first, the affected family members seek
professional help to try to control the drinking of the alcoholic member. Sometimes
they can actually force the alcoholic into treatment. Eventually, however, the helper
must confront other family members with the fact that they are troubled and need to
deal with their own emotional disturbance and develop their own goals. The family
members must come to realize the senselessness of trying to stop the alcoholic's
drinking and instead try to regain their own self-esteem and handle their own negative feelings, regardless of the alcoholic's behavior. The proper view of problem ownership is a central theme of Alcoholics Anonymous and is crystallized in its prayer,
"God grant me the courage to change the things I can change, serenity to accept the
things I cannot change, and the wisdom to know the difference." In short, before a
client can set a goal or solve a problem, he or she first must own it. The helper must
encourage the client to deal with his or her own issues first and not to focus on changing the values, feelings, and behaviors of others.

Stop and Reflect

A 65-year-old widow, Rhoda, complained that her 40-year-old son, Jorge, was irresponsible with money. She indicated that her two other children, Verna and Marta,
accused her of always rescuing Jorge financially when his drinking and gambling created a crisis. She was both resentful and worried about Jorge's spendthrift ways,
wanting suggestions about how to get her son to become more responsible. She was
also defensive about her need to protect her son whom she felt was incapable of con-

trolling himself. Verna and Marta were angry and shocked when they recently learned that Rhoda had left most of her money to Jorge in her will.

- If you were Rhoda's counselor, what would you identify as the main problem that Rhoda owns?
- What problems are owned by other members of the family?
- Assuming that you cannot help change any other family members, including Jorge, what do you think the main goals you and Rhoda might agree upon?
- If you saw the whole family together, what problem do you think everyone "owns" that might be the basis for family therapy?

How to Focus on the Client

Recently, a cartoon depicted a couple coming to their first counseling session. As they sit before the counselor, you can see the wife thinking, "Now, the counselor will find out how crazy he really is!" Meanwhile, the husband is thinking the same thing about her. One of the major issues we face in dealing with clients is getting them to deal with issues that they can control and trying to coax them to give up on the project of reforming others. The skill of focusing on the client is the skill of asking the client to take responsibility and ownership of his or her problems, rather than trying to convert everyone else. Nearly all major theoretical orientations agree that effective helping involves getting clients to change themselves. The skill of focusing on the client is the elementary method for shifting the focus away from others and the environment and onto the issues that the client owns. Following is an example of a helper who has taken the bait and has begun to listen to Bradley's story—a story that seems to point out that Bradley's life would be better if only others or the world would change:

Bradley: "With the economic slowdown and my bills, I can't change jobs right now, no matter how angry I get with my boss."

Helper: "Your boss makes the job miserable but you can't leave because of money. You don't have many options right now." (Here, the helper is paraphrasing with a focus on others and the environment.)

Bradley: "Yeah, my boss is a jerk, and all around me I see other people getting ahead because either they have connections or maybe they have a boss who helps them."

Helper: "You feel angry because your boss is unfair." (Here, the helper is reflecting feelings with a focus on others and the environment.)

Bradley: "Yeah, sometimes I get pretty steamed when he gets on his high horse."

Helper: "What does the boss do that makes you angry?" (Here, the helper asks a closed question, with a focus on others as the cause of Bradley's anger.)

Bradley: "He is always on me, criticizing my work. He never has a good word to say."

This dialogue may seem exaggerated but, in fact, it is typical of what can occur when the helper keeps the focus on external issues such as the boss and the economy. When the client responses center on others or the environment, he or she becomes dispirited and disempowered and does not gain any personal awareness of emotions or engage in thoughtful self-examination. In effect, when the helper asks the client to focus on others or the environment, the helper is agreeing that other people or external events are the cause of the client's problems.

On the other hand, focusing on the client is empowering and prevents the client from blaming other people and external circumstances, a time-draining sidetrack. Focusing on the client does not encourage passive acceptance of the behavior of others or the vicissitudes of life; rather, it challenges the client to become responsible for his or her own happiness. Although there are certainly times when it is helpful to analyze others and try and change the environment, we recommend that at this stage of the helping process, the helper keep the focus primarily on the client, and stay away from interventions that would direct the focus elsewhere.

Let us take another look at the example of Bradley, this time keeping the focus on the client. Note that keeping the focus on the client is a general skill that can apply to all kinds of different responses from reflection of feeling to questions:

Bradley: "With the economic slowdown and my bills, I can't change jobs right now, no matter how angry I get with my boss."

Helper: "It is a difficult situation you find yourself in, caught among a stressful situation at work, financial pressure, and fewer job opportunities." (Here, the helper is paraphrasing with a focus on the client.)

Bradley: "It is difficult. But one thing I would like to work on is getting rid of some of my bills so that I have more freedom."

Helper: "You feel trapped in your job right now, and you're experiencing stress from financial problems, too." (Here, the helper is reflecting feelings with a focus on the client.)

Bradley: "I don't feel like I have one place in my life where things are calm and going right. I feel like everything is out of control."

Helper: "It's always been important for you to feel that you have a handle on things. Now, without that, you can't seem to find many peaceful moments." (Here, the helper is reflecting meaning with a focus on the client.)

Bradley: "It's hard to feel in control when everyone else is putting pressure on you. I go from one pressure cooker to the next."

Helper: "In what part of your life do you experience the most pressure?" (Here, the helper asks a closed question with a focus on the client. The purpose is goal setting.)

Bradley: "I have a big car payment, student loans, and a lot of credit card bills."

Can you see that with these interventions the helper is keeping the focus on the client as the one who needs to make decisions and deal with the pressure? The helper acknowledges that external forces are at work and that they affect the client's decisions, but by keeping the focus on the client, the helper indicates that the client can be the one who does something about the situation. The examples reflect our experience that focusing on the client rather than on other people and circumstances leads in a more productive and positive direction, with more client self-examination and empowerment. Focus on problems owned by the client—rather than being railroaded into attempts to change others. Focusing on the client should be reflected in all of the responses a helper makes, but it is especially important in the goal-setting stage.

Why Must We Set Goals?

Steve de Shazer says that one of the most important questions a helper can ask is, "How will we know when therapy is done?" (de Shazer, 1990). This question can be answered in several ways. Some helpers use a time-limited approach, where the client attends counseling only for a certain amount of time or a certain number of sessions. Helping is finished when the time is up, typically between 6 and 20 sessions (Grayson, 1979). Ben Johnson pointed out that the threat of execution tends to focus the mind. Setting a date for termination motivates helper and client to work quickly to solve problems.

Another commonly accepted method is for either the helper or the client to declare unilaterally that helping is completed. Clients are frequently terminated despite their protests if the helper feels that the client has obtained the maximum benefit from helping or if the helper feels that the problems have been solved. Even more commonly, the client independently terminates.

The problem with the time-limited approach is that we terminate the relationship regardless of success or failure. On the other hand, allowing one person to discontinue makes the ending more of a whimper than a bang. The best measure of whether the work is done is to determine if the treatment goals have been reached. If we have formulated goals at the beginning of the helping relationship, client and helper will have a shared vision throughout the relationship and will know when it is time to end. It is the time when both agree that the goals have substantially been achieved.

What Are the Characteristics of Constructive Goals?

In this section, we will present a rationale for selecting goals that are specific, simple, important, realistic, and reflective of the presence of something rather than the absence of something. Each of the following sections covers one of these topics and each contains a set of questions or statements the helper can use to refine the goal with a client.

Goals Should Be Specific

One of the first problems that a helper faces in goal setting is dealing with the client whose goals are vague and elusive. Goals that are difficult to pinpoint or express are those that are either not in the client's conscious awareness or are too broad (Rule, 1982). A vague goal is exemplified in this type of client statement: "I don't really know what's wrong; it's just that I am uneasy with everything," or, "I haven't been feeling right for about a year." A specific, clear, and easily restated goal sounds more like this: "I want to be able to be more assertive with my friends and co-workers."

When clients have clear goals, they make better progress (Borelli & Mermelstein, 1994; Hart, 1978). Specific goals make the direction of the helping process more understandable. Clients begin to feel that they have a handle on how to begin making changes. The client who is clear about goals will be able to work on them in and out of session.

It is not only clients that have trouble setting goals. For one reason or another, some helpers prefer to focus on the process of helping, letting the client deal with issues as they arise, rather than establishing landmarks of progress. In this book, we take the position that helping has changed radically in the last decade. Nearly all therapy is brief and focusing on specific issues helps make the best use of therapeutic time. Besides these general advantages, at least five other favorable outcomes accrue from negotiating specific goal statements:

1. When based on specific individual goals for the client, the counseling process is more likely to be aimed at the client's needs rather than derived from the helper's theoretical orientation alone. A client who has the goal of overcoming shyness in work situations will perceive this as more relevant than "becoming self-actualized."
2. When goals are clearly understood by client and helper, the helper can determine if he or she possesses the requisite skills to continue with the counseling or if a referral is needed. Sometimes it is only during the goal setting process that the helper realizes that the client needs some specialized assistance such as sex therapy, couples counseling, or even substance abuse treatment.
3. Many clients have problems imagining or envisioning success. Thinking about and imagining specific positive outcomes has the effect of focusing the client's resources and energies and increasing hope. For this reason, goals that are stated positively such as the acquisition of skills are considered to be more useful than goals that are only focused on eliminating a negative behavior.
4. Identifying specific goals provides a rational basis for selecting treatment strategies that agencies, third-party providers, and supervisors can understand. Specific goals reassure others that the outcomes of helping will result in measurable changes.
5. Specific goals enable helpers to determine how successful helping has been for the client. Goal statements allow the client to gauge their progress as helping progresses. At termination, the helper can realistically evaluate the client's achievements.

Interventions to Help a Client Make a Goal More Specific

"I understand that you want to be 'happy,' but if you were happy, what would you be doing that you are not doing now?"

"When you say things are not going well, specifically what things are you talking about?"

"You say you want things to be better in your relationship with your husband, specifically what would you like to be better?"

"You have said that you want higher self-esteem. How would you like to see yourself exactly?"

"Once you said that you live in the past. Where would you like to live?"

Goals Should Be Stated Positively

Frequently, you will hear clients say, "I want to get over my depression," or stop drinking, stop binging on food, stop feeling anxious in social situations, stop arguing with my wife, and so on. When goals are stated as negatives, they have less power to influence and motivate us. For example, I have heard it said that the goal of Alcoholics Anonymous is not "stopping drinking." AA's goal is to help people lead happy lives without alcohol. If you think about it, if we focus all of our attention on "not drinking," we are still focusing on drinking! Instead, setting a goal to lead a happy life without alcohol allows us to consider what things we would like to have in our lives, what people we would like to interact with, and many other possible futures.

One way of explaining this is to say that the helper should try to turn problems into goals. It seems like a small difference, but it would be much better to develop a list of goals than a list of problems. Although we must be willing to understand what problems brought a client for help, we must eventually focus on where we want to go. We spend too much time mapping the prison and too little time planning our freedom. When a clear vision of success is formulated, it is easier to see the steps needed to attain it (O'Hanlon & Weiner-Davis, 1989).

Questions to Help a Client Turn a Problem into a Goal

"If a miracle occurred while you were asleep and during the night your problem just vanished, what would be some of the things you would first notice that let you know that the problem had disappeared?" (the miracle question; O'Hanlon & Weiner-Davis, 1989).

"You say that you and your husband argue constantly. If you were not arguing, what would you like to be doing?"

"If the problem were solved, what would you be feeling, doing, or thinking that you are not now?"

"If you were not procrastinating, what kinds of things would you be doing to get your work in on time?"

"Suppose I gave you a job with all the money, benefits, and resources you required. Think about this for a moment and design your own job. Where would it be? With whom would you be working and what would you be doing?" (Beck & Hoppock, 1998).

Goals Should Be Simple

A rule of thumb in developing a goal is that it should be extremely simple, so simple that "an eight year old could understand it" (Steiner, 1976). Developing simple goals that have a high probability of success is especially important when the client is demoralized. Whenever small goals are achieved, the client will be encouraged to continue with more difficult or more time-consuming projects (Dyer & Vriend, 1977; Egan, 1994). As Milton Erickson once said, "Therapy is often a matter of tipping the first domino" (Rossi, 1980, Vol. 4, p. 454).

Many agencies require that helpers set quantifiable behavioral goals. Behavioral goals are concrete, measurable, and observable. They indicate the client's current behavior (baseline) and the target or goal behaviors that represent success. Here is an example of how you can develop a behavioral goal:

Client's Stated Goal (Client's Description of the Goal)

The client would like to increase comfort and decrease anxiety in social situations. The client's job entails several social functions each week, and they are necessary for his employment.

Target Behaviors (Described in Frequency, Duration, and Intensity)

The client would like to be able to attend a social gathering, hold two or more conversations (frequency), at least one of these with a woman, stay for a period of more than one hour (duration), and maintain a subjective distress level (SUDS) of 3 or 4. (The SUDS level is the client's feelings of discomfort in the situation and is measured on a 10-point scale of intensity, with 10 being the most uncomfortable and 1 being mildly uncomfortable.)

Baseline (Current Level of Target Behaviors)

The client states that he can currently remain at a party for only about 15 minutes before he leaves. He can hold a brief conversation with a male co-worker, but has not recently talked to a woman in this setting. He currently experiences a SUDS level of 8 or 9 during social conversations with any woman.

Behavioral goals have advantages in that they specify exactly what must be achieved in the helping process. Many helpers will be required to set behavioral goals at their place of work because agencies use the numbers to quantify success. Other agencies look at goal attainment in other ways, including client feedback forms and helper and client assessments of success. Even when helping goals are not quantifiable, they can still be simple and concrete (Goodyear & Bradley, 1986). For example, the helper might not want to accept the following goal: "I want to improve my relationship with my mother." The helper might be willing, though, to accept the following revision: "Well, I would like to be able to politely stop her when she starts trying to give me advice." Whether goals are described behaviorally or not, simple goals make it easier for both helper and client to identify when helping is on the right track.

Questions to Help Simplify a Goal

Client's Goal: "To decrease stress in my life."

Helper's questions: "What activities would help you reduce stress?"
   "How often would you like to engage in stress reducing activities?"
   "How many times per week would you like to meditate?"

Goals Should Be Important to the Client

Clients will be successful when they are pursuing goals that are important to them (Barbrack & Maher, 1984; Evans, 1984; Goodyear & Bradley, 1986; Hart, 1978; Miller & Rollnick, 1999). It seems obvious that clients will work harder when they are focusing on a goal that really matters to them. However, many people are referred by friends, families, courts, and student judiciary boards to solve problems that the client has little or no interest in solving. In cases where the court orders treatment for a particular problem, neither client nor helper has participated in the goal-setting process, and they may not feel personally involved or motivated to achieve the aims, the likelihood of success is low. This third-party problem is evident in the example of a client who has been referred by a probation officer following an incestuous relationship. The probation officer wants the client treated for sexual dysfunction to ensure that this kind of thing does not happen again. The client is divorced now and has had no contact with his teenage daughter, the incest victim. At this point, the client's concerns center on forming new relationships and dealing with family members' rejection. He is not willing to rehash the incestuous relationship and is resentful of the helper's intrusions. This kind of situation is quite common (Ritchie, 1986). In fact, clients pressured to attend by a third party may comprise as much as one-third of all new clients referred for counseling (Haley, 1989). Helpers must therefore be clear about whose goals will be the focus with each client. Sometimes they are forced to accept the goals of third parties, but goal setting involving both client and helper provides the best opportunity for success.

Students often raise the question, "What if the client's goals are morally unacceptable to the helper?" Although helpers are generally nonjudgmental and accepting of differences, there are times when a helper cannot help a client to set and achieve a goal because of personal religious convictions or ethics. For example, many helpers will refuse to take sides in custody cases when they have seen a couple for marriage counseling. Some helpers may not choose to help clients achieve goals related to sexuality, such as accepting homosexuality or conducting extramarital affairs. Professional helpers inform clients early in the counseling process about issues they will not address, so that the relationship does not develop too far before a referral is needed.

Sample Questions to Gauge a Goal's Importance

"How likely are you to follow through with this goal?"

"How important is this goal to you?"

"If we accomplished this goal, what difference would it make in your life?"

"How are you likely to talk yourself out of trying to accomplish this goal?"

"Is this your goal, or is it something other people want you to accomplish?"

Goals Should Be Realistic

The helper's expertise is important in defining goals when a client has unrealistic aims. Sometimes the client has insufficient information about the self. At other times, the client wants to accomplish two incompatible aims. For example, a client recently said, "I want to be better paid at my job, but I don't want to work harder and give up my free time." One method of dealing with unrealistic goals is to confront the client or invite him or her to explore the goal and collect information to see if the goal is really possible. Often, a helper discloses his or her own concerns about the likelihood that the goal can really be accomplished. Consider the following client statements and possible helper responses:

Example 1

Client: "I don't like science or math and I am not very good at them. My aptitudes in those areas are not very good, according to the national exams. I want to be a doctor, though, because I need to have a good salary and I want to be respected as a professional."

Helper: "It sounds like you want the status and the money that being a physician might bring, but you are not sure you have the ability or the interest needed for the training. Perhaps we need to look at both of these things a little closer."

Example 2

Client: "I want to get my girlfriend back. She's living with someone else right now and she won't even return my calls. She hates me because I was dating other people behind her back while we were going out. I still have a problem with being faithful to one person, but I know if I got her back, we could make it work."

Helper: "I'm not sure that reuniting with your ex-girlfriend is a realistic goal. For one thing, you say you're having trouble being with only one person and, second, she is showing no interest in getting back together."

Example 3

Client: "I want to stay married and enjoy the safety and security of the married relationship. Myra and I have a problem with communication and that is something we can work on. But there is someone else that I am seeing right now. The excitement and romance is something that is missing in my marriage. I can't hurt Myra or the kids by letting it come out in the open. So I have decided to keep it a secret. When Myra and I come in for marriage counseling, I don't want to bring up this other relationship."

Helper: "I would like to help, but I am not sure you can improve your marital relationship while you are carrying on a secret affair."

When a client is operating with faulty information or is engaging in self-deception, as in the preceding cases, the helper uses challenging skills and helps the client gain self-knowledge or information about the problem that will help him or her set better goals. For example, in the case of the student who wants to be a physician, the helper might help the client gain experience and knowledge of medicine in several ways, including volunteering in a hospital, looking at the courses medical schools offer, and asking physicians directly about how important it is to enjoy and do well in math and science.

Stop and Reflect

There is a saying among career and life planning counselors that if you don't know where you are going, you will arrive somewhere else. The meaning is that if we do not set goals for our lives, other factors besides our own plans will intervene. A well-known football coach, Lou Holtz, has said, "Write down everything you hope to achieve in life, then make sure you do something every day to realize one of your dreams. You are going to encounter adversity but you will also . . . take big, satisfying bites out of life" (1998). Holtz set several hundred personal goals over 20 years ago. Recently, he indicated that he had completed over three-fourths of them. Think about the following areas of your own life and write down a goal under each heading that you would like to accomplish in the next 5–10 years:

1. A job I would like to have:

   _____

   _____

2. A project I would like to be involved in:

   _____

   _____

3. The kind of friendship or intimate relationship I would like to develop:

_____

_____

4. An area of learning I would like to master or a formal degree program I would like to complete:

_____

_____

5. A hobby or interest I would like to develop:

_____

_____

Next, evaluate each of the goals that you have identified according to the following criteria:

   a. Is the goal specific?
   b. Is the goal stated in positive terms?
   c. Is the goal simple enough for an 8-year-old to understand?
   d. How motivated are you to accomplish the goal?
   e. Is the goal realistic considering your abilities?

   • Choose one of the goals that appears to meet some or all of the preceding criteria and rewrite it in a simple, specific sentence or two. List the steps you must go through to accomplish this goal.
   • As you look at the steps that you have identified, does the goal seem more manageable or more difficult now that it has been broken down into parts?
   • Discuss this exercise with a friend who knows you well. Ask him or her to evaluate the goal as to how realistic it is and how clearly it is stated. What are your conclusions?

The Technique of Boiling Down the Problem

Usually, clients do not arrive with clearly defined questions and problems; more often, they present tangles of feelings, people, and events that can easily sidetrack both client and helper. Achieving clarity of purpose is a major task of helping. At some point, the helper must choose areas to develop and others to set aside for the moment. Just sorting the work into "piles" or cutting the job into "pieces" reduces client anxiety and offers fresh hope. Most of us are aware of the experience of motivation and relief that accompanies making a "to-do list" when we feel overwhelmed.

As we said earlier, goal-setting skills are "narrowing skills." One therapist used to say to clients, "Well, we've chased a lot of rabbits out of the bush, now let's track down a few of them." This metaphor worked well to signal that a more specific focus was needed. Boiling down the problem follows this metaphor. First, the client is encouraged to open up and then specific issues are identified and evaluated. The steps in boiling down the problem are as follows:

Step 1: Summarizing

The helper uses summaries, advanced reflecting skills, and paraphrasing to determine agreement on the overall content of the counseling session to that point.

Helper: "So, let me pull this together a little. You're living at home and feel embarrassed because you think that you should be out on your own. The man you have been dating for a year has called it quits and in the middle of all this upset, your teenage sister is causing turmoil in the home. Meanwhile, your mother's illness worries you. You're feeling overwhelmed since everything has happened at once."

Tricia: "That's about it. I'm living at home. My life is going nowhere and right now everyone needs me to be strong."

Step 2: Asking Closed Questions

Next, the helper uses one or more closed questions to ask the client to evaluate which problems are the most critical, thereby narrowing down the number of issues to be addressed.

Helper: "I realize that all of these issues, your mother's health, your sister's problems, getting over your boyfriend, and becoming financially able to have your own place, are all important issues to you. Of these, which do you think are the most critical and are ones that we can deal with in these sessions?"

Tricia: "There is nothing I can do about my mother's illness and, unfortunately, there is not much I can do about my sister, either. But I want to get on my feet financially and emotionally. I need help in thinking about where I am going in my career so I can earn enough to live on, and I've got to think about how I am going to make it through the next few months without my boyfriend. I need to focus on myself for a little while."

Step 3: Selecting the Problem

In this activity, the helper uses a mental checklist to evaluate client goals and advocates for those that are:

- Specific
- Simple and easily restated
- Mutually agreed upon by helper and client
- Realistic

Helper: "So, it sounds like one of the emergency issues is to help you find some ways to take care of yourself emotionally so that you can cope with your loss. At the same time, you want to look at the future a little bit, too. You want to explore some career ideas."

Tricia: "I know I can get some help with the career thing. You've already offered to do the tests and talk about that. The main thing is how I can deal with my angry and depressed feelings all the time. I am bored and angry and alone. I feel like a baby."

Step 4: Changing the Problem to a Goal

In this step, the helper encourages the client to think about success. What will the problem look like when it is solved? This step helps us make sure that the goal is stated positively, one of the criteria for constructive goals.

Helper: "You have told me that you are in a lot of distress about losing your boyfriend and we have discussed that topic pretty thoroughly. As you think about the future, I wonder if you can envision your life when this is no longer a problem? What would you be doing then that you are not doing now? What would you be feeling and thinking?"

Tricia: "I would be going out with my friends and enjoying life again. I wouldn't be thinking about him all the time, sitting there waiting for him to call. I would be able to concentrate at work."

Helper: "So, these are the goals that you would like to work toward."

Tricia: "Sure!"

Step 5: Reaching a Final Goal Statement

Here, the helper summarizes the mutually agreed upon goals. In addition, the helper may ask the client to state them aloud or write them down, so that the agreement is clear. At this point, clients often need encouragement and a message from the helper that the goals are reachable.

Helper: "Let's see if I can restate them: You would like to go out with friends and enjoy life again, instead of spending so much time thinking about your exboyfriend. Is that about right?"

Tricia: "Yes, but it is not that easy."

Helper: "I agree, it won't be easy. Are we on the right track though? Are these your goals?"

Tricia: "Yes."

Helper: "Would you mind restating the goals as we talked about them so that I am sure we are both operating with the same understanding?"

Tricia: "Okay, I am going to find a way to have fun again and spend time with friends again."

Helper: "Like you said, it won't be easy but I am confident that you can make this happen. Let's talk about how you can go about this."

Summary

The first stage of the helping process can be summarized as "opening," the second as "assessing." The next stage, goal setting, described in this chapter, might be called "narrowing": Once the client's important issues have been identified and a working relationship is under way, it is time to select and target the important issues. One of the key questions in "narrowing" is, "Who owns the problem?" Helpers develop the skill of *focusing on the client* to keep the client directed toward the issues that are causing pain. This compels the client to deal with issues he or she can really make an impact upon.

This chapter advocates that the helper develop goals collaboratively with the client, melding the helper's expertise with the concerns and needs of the client. Constructive goals are therefore mutually agreed upon; they are also specific, positively stated, simple, and those that the client is motivated to achieve. The skill of boiling down the problem uses summarizing and questioning to help clients clearly define and negotiate specific achievable goals.

Group Exercise

The purpose of this exercise is to practice the process of boiling down the goal of the counseling relationship to a workable agreement between helper and client. To accomplish this in a short period of time, the helper and client should spend only a little time of the interview (perhaps 5 minutes) on the invitational and reflecting skills, to enable the helper to understand the basics of the problem. The helper should jump into a discussion of what the client would like to accomplish as soon as possible.

One or two observers can be used in this exercise. One observer can write down the helper's interventions that help the client develop a goal. The other can note the final goal and facilitate discussion about how closely the goal matches the ideal characteristics.

Part I: Instructions to the Observer Record what you feel are the key statements by the helper that help the client boil down the goal to a workable contract. In the space provided, write down your understanding of what the client's final goal statement looks like.

1. _____
   _____

2. _____
   _____

3. _____
   _____

4. _____
   _____

5. _____
   _____

Part II: Instructions to the Observer In the space provided, write down your understanding of the goal finally arrived at by client and helper.

_____

_____

_____

_____

_____

Read this to the client and helper to determine if your articulation of the goal is accurate. Then give the helper feedback on how closely the goal matches the following characteristics. Is the goal, as written:

- Specific?
- Positively stated? (the presence of something versus the absence of something)
- Simple?
- One that the client is motivated to achieve?
- Realistic?

Additional Exercise

In the helper-client interview, one of the mistakes beginners make is to ask too many closed questions that focus on others and the environment. Examine the client situations listed here and formulate one question or paraphrase that focuses on the client and another that would take the client off track.

High School Student: "I don't know where I am going with my life. My grades are good enough to get into college and my parents want me to go. But I am more interested in music. My music teacher thinks I should go that route. What do you think?"

Client Focus: _____

_____

_____

Other Focus: _____

_____

_____

Student Who Doesn't Do Homework: "In study hall, it's too distracting. There are these three guys who sit next to me and all they do is talk. The teacher doesn't even try to stop them. I never have time to do it at home. My parents have a lot of chores for me."

Client Focus: _____

_____

_____

Other Focus: _____

_____

_____

Parent of a Teenager: "He smokes pot continually. I am caught between him and his father. I found some pot under his bed. He says that he is not smoking now and I am afraid to tell his father. He will blow up. What am I going to do about his drug problem?"

Client Focus: _____

_____

_____

Other Focus: _____

_____

_____

Client Who Has Accepted a Job Out of State: "My family is upset with me. They can't see that this is my best chance for success. They want me around to come over for Sunday dinner. I want that, too, but it is so hard to balance these things."

Client Focus: _____

_____

_____

Other Focus: _____

_____

_____

Homework

Homework 1

One aspect of boiling down the problem that takes practice is changing a problem into a goal. Create two short dialogues between client and helper whereby the client is helped through the five steps of boiling down the problem. Following each dialogue, identify the problem as stated by the client and the goal as reformulated by the helper.

Homework 2

Talk with two friends about their short- and long-term goals. See if you can get each friend to identify five goals in each of these categories. In a single page, describe your experiences. Be sure to include the reactions of your friends.

Journal Starters

1. Make a list of goals you would like to achieve in the next 5 years. Now, look at each one and indicate what you think might keep you from accomplishing it. Do you notice any personal unwillingness to think about this issue? Does it raise any anxiety? Discuss your reaction.
2. Imagine that you are a very old person talking to your relatives about your life. What were the major things you enjoyed in your life? Don't just recount your accomplishments, but focus on those times when you were the happiest. It has been suggested that successful people are those who "follow their bliss." What things have you discovered that you really like to do? How can you incorporate them more into your present life? How can you use them to motivate yourself? What use can you make of this when you are trying to help another person?

For more journal ideas, as well as more practice with goal setting, refer to Chapter 9 in *Exercises in the Art of Helping*.

References

Barbrack, C. R., & Maher, C. A. (1984). Effects of involving conduct problem adolescents into the setting of counseling goals. *Child and Family Behavior Therapy, 6,* 33–43.

Beck, E. S., & Hoppock, R. (1998). Vocational fantasy: An empowering technique. In H. G. Rosenthal (Ed.), *Favorite counseling and therapy techniques* (pp. 34–36). Washington, DC: Accelerated Development.

Borelli, B., & Mermelstein, R. (1994). Goal setting and behavior change in a smoking cessation program. *Cognitive Therapy and Research, 18,* 69–83.

Bruce, P. (1984). Continuum of counseling goals: A framework for differentiating counseling strategies. *Personnel and Guidance Journal, 62,* 259–263.

Cormier, W., & Cormier, L. S. (1991). *Interviewing strategies for helpers: Fundamental skills and cognitive behavioral interventions.* Pacific Grove, CA: Brooks/Cole.

de Shazer, S. (1990, May). Brief therapy. Symposium conducted at Stetson University, DeLand, FL.

Dyer, W. W., & Vriend, J. (1977). A goal-setting checklist for counselors. *Personnel and Guidance Journal, 55,* 469–471.

Egan, G. (1994). *The skilled helper* (5th ed.). Pacific Grove, CA: Brooks/Cole.

Evans, M. H. (1984). Increasing patient involvement with therapy goals. *Journal of Clinical Psychology, 40,* 728–733.

Goodyear, R. K., & Bradley, F. O. (1986). The helping process as contractual. In W. P. Anderson (Ed.),

Innovative counseling: A handbook of readings (pp. 59–62). Alexandria, VA: American Association for Counseling and Development.

Gordon, T. (1975). *PET: Parent effectiveness training.* New York: Wyden.

Grayson, H. (1979). *Short term approaches to psychotherapy.* New York: Human Sciences Press.

Haley, J. (1989, May). Strategic family therapy. Symposium conducted at Stetson University, DeLand, FL.

Hart, R. (1978). Therapeutic effectiveness of setting and monitoring goals. *Journal of Consulting and Clinical Psychology, 60,* 24–28.

Holtz, L. (1998). *Winning every day.* NY: Harper business.

Miller, W. R., & Rollnick, S. (1999). *Motivational interviewing: Preparing people to change addictive behavior.* New York: Guilford.

Nicoll, W. (1997). Personal communication.

O'Hanlon, W. H., & Weiner-Davis, M. (1989). *In search of solutions: A new direction in psychotherapy.* New York: Norton.

Ritchie, M. H. (1986). Counseling the involuntary client. *Journal of Counseling and Development, 64,* 516–518.

Rossi, E. (1980). *Collected papers of Milton Erickson on hypnosis* (Vols. 1–4). New York: Irvington.

Rule, W. R. (1982). Pursuing the horizon: Striving for elusive goals. *Personnel and Guidance Journal, 61,* 195–197.

Steiner, C. (1976, April). Radical psychiatry. Symposium conducted at the University of Dayton, Dayton, OH.

Solution Skills

10

In this chapter, we will introduce four new skills: giving advice, giving information, alternate interpretation, and brainstorming. These building blocks are called *solution skills* because they are all methods that helpers use to invite clients to find solutions to their problems.

The solution skills represent the final set of building blocks. Although you will learn more advanced techniques in later chapters, the building blocks can help you successfully navigate the opening stages of the helping process from relationship building to assessment to goal setting. With the addition of solution skills, you will be able to begin mobilizing the change process by involving the client in problem-solving and experimenting with new behavior.

Solution skills can be used inappropriately. By their very nature, they place the helper in a superior position, which can change the client-helper relationship. Also, the helper could breed dependency in the client by overuse of these skills. Properly applied, however, solution skills can stimulate clients to work toward resolving their

217

own problems, getting in touch with creative ideas, and examining their self-limiting assumptions. Most important, when clients begin to focus on solutions, they are living in the future rather than ruminating over the past.

Giving Advice, Information, and Directives

Giving Advice

When a helper makes a statement that attempts to solve a client's problem for him or her, the helper is giving advice. Like salt, advice giving is beneficial but only in the right amount. Advice giving can be beneficial in emergency situations when a client is engaging in unsafe behavior, such as practicing unsafe sex, considering an affair, or using drugs, or when a client is being exposed to physical violence.

Because beginning helpers like to give advice too liberally, many teachers tend to ban it outright in the initial stages, and, as a consequence, textbooks often have little to say about it. However, because advice giving is rarely addressed, students tend not to be aware of its drawbacks, and may find it an easy habit to fall back on. When college students come for counseling, they typically expect advice, and they freely dispense advice to their friends in an attempt to help. They feel that it is effective mainly because they view it as tangible assistance. In fact, advice giving is a veritable minefield. It lures us into thinking that we are actively helping a client. However, there are good reasons for leaving this skill out of your practice sessions for the present. If you have a tendency to give advice, we urge that you consider "retiring" that skill at this point and that you develop other alternatives.

Why Are Professional Helpers Reluctant to Give Advice?

In the *Peanuts* cartoons, Lucy sits at the psychiatrist's booth with a sign that says, "Advice: 5 cents." Generally, this is how the media portray the helping professions. Someone pays and someone gives a good dose of advice. If helping were merely giving advice, we could set up such a booth at the local grocery store. However, as one writer notes, "Clients can get all the advice they want from acquaintances, friends, and family members. They hardly need to pay a therapist to tell them what to do" (Kleinke, 1994, p. 9). To give exactly the same advice as everyone else in the client's world makes the helper seem impotent.

Another reason that professional helpers avoid giving advice is that while others may listen politely, they simply do not act upon it. Real helping is an art that involves getting people to solve their own problems and that is much more difficult than supplying solutions by giving advice. Sometimes advice does stimulate a client's thinking about the problem, but more often, it is simply disregarded (Mallett, Spokane, & Vance, 1978). Eric Berne identified a "game" that illustrates this point. It involves a frequent set of transactions between client and helper called, " 'Why don't you . . .' Yes, but . . . ,' " or WDYYB. When the helper gives advice, he or she begins, "Why don't you . . .," and the client responds, giving reasons why the advice will not work, "Yes, but. . . ." Most of us are familiar with this "game" from work and social situations. The advice giver feels confused and frustrated when good suggestions are rejected. Even when clients ask for advice, they frequently refuse it. What we need to remember is that while a client may appear to be asking for advice, he or she is really looking for opportunities to think aloud, to be understood, and to explore the options.

Another crucial drawback to advice giving is that if the client follows the helper's advice, the helper is responsible for the resultant change. If the helper gets the glory for having supplied good advice, how has this empowered the client to solve future life problems? There is an aphorism that states, "Give me a fish and I will eat today; teach me how to fish and I will eat forever." The long-term goal of helping is not to supply a quick fix but to help the client, even when the helper is no longer in the picture. Sometimes, advice may be needed to solve emergent problems, but when clients resolve their own difficulties they gain confidence and skills. Thomas Gordon (1975) considers lecturing and preaching to be one of the "dirty dozen" of bad communication practices because it communicates to a client that he or she is incapable of solving the problem.

Lecturing and preaching are disguised advice giving (Patterson & Eisenberg, 1983). For example, during the goal-setting phase, a client identifies excessive anger as one of the areas she wishes to work on. Frequently, beginning helpers launch into a sermonette on expressing anger and self-acceptance. The effect on the relationship is that the helper moves into the role of expert and begins to speak in generalities, rather than focusing on the client's unique situation.

Another persuasive argument against giving advice is that the consequences of giving the wrong advice can be severe, both to the client's life and to the client's faith in the therapeutic relationship. A final reason to avoid advice giving is that it may violate the values of an individual's family, culture, or religion. Such advice will probably be rejected and it may also harm the therapeutic relationship. Consider these examples of inappropriate advice:

"I advise you to get an abortion."
"I suggest you learn to be more assertive with your mother."
"If you don't like all the arguing, why don't you get a divorce?"

When Is It Appropriate and Inappropriate to Give Advice?

A helper who gives advice must have the following knowledge or experience:

- Special knowledge and training in the specific issue the client is facing
- First-hand experience or experience helping many people deal with the particular issue
- Knowledge that his or her own experiences are not the same as the client's experience
- Ability to give advice in a way that outlines the risks as well as the opportunities that following a certain course of action entails
- Thorough understanding of the client's history, including the client's ethnic, religious, and cultural background

Appropriate advice is concrete and invites reaction and discussion. It is presented as one alternative along with other solutions generated by the client. It suggests that the client should alter the instructions to fit the circumstances. Advice about what to expect from certain courses of action may be quite helpful. Advice is also appropriate when the client is in some physical danger and a helper's directive can reduce the risk. Here are some examples of advice that might be appropriate:

"Your statement that you are drinking too much has me concerned, especially since you drive home in that condition. If you continue to drink, you can expect to be in an accident or in court. I want you to go to an alcohol treatment center for an assessment interview. Would you be willing to do that?" This advice is given to inform the client about the likely outcomes of drinking and also identifies potential physical danger.

"You know, my wife and I always try to spend 15 minutes at the end of every day, playing cards or backgammon. It has been a way of building in a moment of contact in our hectic lives. Do you think something like that might work for you?" This advice invites discussion and asks the client to tailor the advice to fit his or her particular situation.

"You've outlined several possibilities, let me add one more. Have you considered directly confronting your co-worker about her unsafe behavior on the job? What effect do you think that might have?" This advice asks the client to think and to discuss the alternative suggested by the helper.

On the other hand, here are some situations in which advice is inappropriate and could be harmful to the therapeutic relationship:

- When the client seems to be dependent on others to make decisions and needs to learn to choose his or her own course of action. He or she might ask, for example:
  "Do you think I need a new haircut?"
  "Do you think I should go home this weekend as my parents ask or do what my boyfriend wants?"
- When the client has not heeded advice previously.
- When the client is asking for assurance on issues with unpredictable outcomes, such as:
  "Should we have a baby?"
  "Should I get married?"
  "Should I move to Saudi Arabia?"
- When the purpose of obtaining advice is to influence another person:
  "My husband believes in spanking our child, but I don't. What do you think?"
  "My mother thinks I am too old to date. Do you agree?"
- When the client has information available and is capable of solving the problem without advice.
- When the advice conflicts with a client's basic values, upbringing, or culture. The helper is giving inappropriate advice, for example, when he or she says: "You may come from an Indian culture, but you live in America now. You have to do what you want and your parents will have to understand."

Clearly, the times when advice giving is useful are quite limited. Advice giving is appropriate only at carefully considered moments rather than as standard procedure. If advice giving is something you rely on in your natural helping style, try this experiment: Avoid advice giving altogether until you have learned to conduct an entire session using invitational and reflecting skills. There is an analogy in boxing training in which a left-handed puncher is taught to operate only with the right arm. By letting go of an old way of responding, a new set of skills has the chance to take hold and become stronger. Similarly, if you can let go of your tendency to sermonize and give advice, you will have the chance to develop the subtler skills of helping the client find his or her own solutions.

Stop and Reflect

Think back for a moment on pieces of advice you have received from teachers, guidance counselors, friends, parents, grandparents, or other family members. It might have been about the purchase of a car or house, about which college to attend, or what to do in a relationship. Identify one piece of good advice and one that was not very helpful, then consider the following questions:

- What was it about each piece of advice that made it helpful or not helpful?
- When considering the helpful advice, did the person giving it have particular expertise in that area?
- What other characteristics did the person giving the advice have that encouraged you to accept it?
- If you cannot recall any advice given by friends, teachers, counselors, parents, or family members, what conclusions might you draw from this?
- When you have a problem, do you want advice, or is it more important to have someone listen?
- Have you ever given advice to a friend that was really heeded? How did it turn out?
- What can you conclude about the role of advice in helping you to make decisions in your own life? Will your conclusions have a bearing on your willingness to give advice as a helper?

Discuss your answers with a small group of classmates.

Giving Information

Information giving is the supplying of data or facts to help a client reach his or her goal. Information giving might include providing ideas about how to gain access to social services or community resources. It can include correcting erroneous ideas about topics such as sexuality, drugs, parenting, and stereotypes about different ethnic groups. A helper uses information giving sparingly because too much information will overload the client and will likely be ignored. Information giving can also subtly change the relationship between client and helper. It can become a lecture that clients may disregard. Here is an example of an appropriate use of giving information:

> "Based on what you have told me, your financial problems are significant and you could use some professional help. I would like to refer you to the Consumer Credit Counseling Service. They can help you make the decision about whether bankruptcy is a good answer for you. Would you be willing to go?"

Recently, one of my supervisors referred one of her clients to Alcoholics Anonymous after helping him identify his alcohol problem. She was elated after the session because, "It really felt like I did something for a change instead of just listening." I tried to point out that it was the relationship that she had so painstakingly constructed that provided the atmosphere where the client could face his problem. If she had referred him for treatment at their first session, he would never have accepted the referral. It took time and trust to bring him to that realization. Like advice giving,

giving information feels like we are really accomplishing something. But the proof is in the pudding. Like advice giving, most information we give clients does not sink in. Although the helper feels effective, it is important to find out if the client has really been helped.

Helping and Creativity

According to Holland's typology of personalities and career environments (Holland & Gottfredson, 1976), helpers frequently show three personality traits: investigative, social, and artistic. Clearly, a helper must have investigative interests to untangle the client's issues in the same way that a detective or scientist tries to solve a puzzle. Helpers also have strong interpersonal interests, represented by the social trait; they want to help people. The artistic aspect of helping is perhaps less obvious but, as the title of this book suggests, there is a side to helping that cannot be quantified and is purely artistic. Artists use different media to express themselves and create beauty. The helping arts are not focused on self-expression by the artist but on the helper's desire to create something beautiful out of human disarray: harmony, peace, wholeness, and fulfillment. This holistic sense cannot be achieved merely through application of a scientific process any more than it is possible to use a formula to reproduce a Picasso.

Helpers are often creative people. They are open to considering options when a problem arises and they try to help clients devise novel ways of thinking and problem solving. Indeed, they may at times use artistic media—drama, poetry, painting, sculpture, and music—to help clients express themselves (Gladding, 1998). Helpers also encourage their clients to think creatively when they have problems. A major difficulty in problem solving is that we tend to see things through the lens of our outmoded ideas, social conventions, and our personal history. As Emerson noted, consistency can be a hobgoblin, leading us into foolish repetitions when what we need is to break out of our old ways of thinking.

Perhaps you have heard of the nine-dot problem. Take a look at the nine dots in Figure 10.1. The problem is to take a pencil and draw four straight lines that connect

Figure 10.1
The Nine-Dot Problem

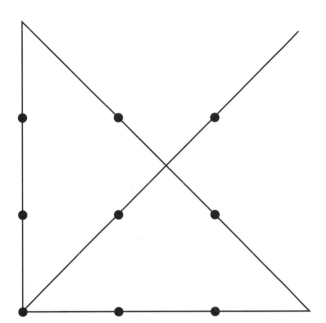

Figure 10.2
Solution to the Nine-Dot
Problem

all of the dots without lifting your pencil from the page. The answer to this puzzle appears in Figure 10.2 but try to solve it yourself.

Whether you have seen this puzzle before or not, it illustrates an important aspect of human thinking. We tend to rely on previous experience. In the nine-dot problem, we have usually been told to "color in the lines." We see a box shape represented by the points and conclude that we must stay within the shape rather than expand into the page beyond. This same kind of thinking affects us when we encounter a problem in life. As the nine-dot problem suggests, we see rules when none exists. Perhaps you have heard the story of the man who takes his son to the emergency room and the doctor exclaims, "I can't operate on this child, he's my son!" We do not automatically recognize that the doctor must be the child's mother. Because of our training and the pervasive influence of the media, we unconsciously fall back on our usual way of thinking.

During crisis states, when we become even more conservative and less creative, a sort of tunnel vision occurs that convinces us that we have very few options. For example, people with suicidal thoughts have concluded that killing themselves is the only option available. It is also well known that battered women see few options to their abusive relationships because their experience tells them that the situation has no exit. The concept of learned helplessness has been advanced to explain why people fail to look for alternatives following experiences of failure. When people seem to find that nothing works to solve their dilemmas, they stop trying, even when circumstances change. The job of a helper is to be an "expander" (not a "shrink") who tries to help clients enlarge their viewpoint, open up their thinking, and engage their creativity.

What Is Brainstorming?

Brainstorming originally was developed by Madison Avenue advertising firms to increase the creativity of staff members responsible for commercials. To brainstorm, a group of people sit around a table and generate ideas. The conditions and ground rules, however, are a little different from those of an average meeting: The atmosphere is relaxed and even playful. Cooperation rather than competition is encouraged. Everyone in the group is called upon to participate and no one is allowed to dominate. All ideas are recorded, but the focus remains on a specific problem that the group wants to solve. Beyond these general conditions for brainstorming, there are some specific rules that differentiate it from other problem-solving activities:

1. No ideas generated by brainstorming are evaluated. They are simply brought before the group and recorded. Evaluation involves a critical function of mind rather than a creative one. Creativity flows best in a nonjudgmental atmosphere.
2. Freewheeling is encouraged. Practical considerations are not brought up during a brainstorming session. In fact, the wilder the ideas, the better, so that the limits of creativity can be reached. A playful attitude by the facilitator can increase freewheeling.
3. The quantity of ideas is more important than the quality. The more ideas the better. A large pool of ideas is needed as a source of good solutions. Seemingly unimportant ideas actually can spark thoughts from other members of the group.
4. Hitchhiking is encouraged. Hitchhiking, or "piggybacking," is building on the ideas of other people. By combining ideas, a concept grows and develops.

Research has suggested that sometimes when two or more people brainstorm together, they do not generate as many new ideas as the people would constructing their lists separately (Diehl & Stroebe, 1991; Mullen, Johnson, & Salas, 1991). The reason sometimes given is "production blocking." Production blocking means that people are sometimes too polite in a group situation to spontaneously blurt out their ideas while others are talking. Brainstorming requires that each person be allowed to express his or her ideas without having to wait for others to stop speaking (Johnson & Johnson, 1997). This same situation often occurs in a therapeutic relationship. The client is reluctant in that setting to really think in a spontaneous and freewheeling way because of the weight that he or she places on the helper's ideas. Sometimes it is more effective for each person in a brainstorming session to write down his or her ideas, or for one person to generate ideas and the other to record them. This allows for more freewheeling than the start-and-stop approach that a conversation entails.

How to Brainstorm

Brainstorming between a helper and a client involves the same basic activities that groups use, with slight modifications. The helper acts as a facilitator and participant, but a major aim is to help the client develop skills of creative thinking, which can be generalized to other situations.

In the helping relationship, brainstorming should not be an activity that keeps a client talking about options rather than taking action. Brainstorming is a solution skill. At the end of a brainstorming session, both helper and client should have a clear idea about the next steps to take to solve the problem. Brainstorming takes a client through three basic steps:

1. Challenging the client's assumptions and identifying the problem
2. Generating ideas
3. Evaluating and agreeing upon potential solutions

Brainstorming with a client does not differ much from the steps in group brainstorming except that, at the outset, more attention is devoted to identifying and challenging assumptions. The client thinks about the assumptions he or she has about the problem and tries to shake free of them. Otherwise, preexisting ideas will color the next idea-generating step, leading the client to substitute previous solutions rather than to think creatively.

One tactic for dealing with assumptions is to reverse them. For example, while designing an innovative program for training school counselors, participants listed all their assumptions about school counselors. One of them was, "School counselors work during school hours." This assumption was reversed and written down on the blackboard, "School counselors do not work during school hours." Ideas based on this new concept were then generated. Participants began thinking about how school counselors should be available to parents after school and in the evenings. This led them to include family counseling training as part of the curriculum. A nearby public school system is now incorporating this idea in its new school. The plans for next year allow flexible working hours for school counselors so that they can meet with parents several evenings per week.

Another story illustrates how assumptions about problems can be challenged and how, in turn, creative thinking leads to better solutions. David and Gloria have been married for 5 years. David's job requires that he move to another state for a 2-year period to work on an exciting project. David cannot refuse the assignment or he risks losing his job. The couple came for help because they have come to an impasse in their decision-making process. David wants Gloria to quit her job as a part-time graphic designer and move with him. Gloria wants to stay where she is and she wants David to stay, too, even if he gets demoted or loses his job. Neither wants to live alone for the 2-year period. Acting as a facilitator, the helper took them through the three basic steps of brainstorming to help them arrive at a solution.

Step 1: Challenging Assumptions and Asking the Right Question

The first step is to ask the right question. This can be determined by asking what is to be achieved in the end. What is the goal? The reason this step is so crucial is that often clients are examining previous solutions rather than the current problem. A good example of how this happens comes from the food industry. For several years, the question was often asked in this way, "How can we make a better can opener?" This formulation generated a number of new can openers, both manual and electric; however, a can opener is a previous solution, not the real problem. Someone ultimately was able to ask the question in a different way: "How do we open a can?" When the problem was stated in this way, a whole new set of creative opening features developed. Helpers assist clients in identifying the key issues by asking closed questions such as:

"What do you want to achieve by solving this problem?"
"What is it you are afraid of losing?"
"What is the most important thing you want to accomplish?"

Similarly, David and Gloria might argue over who is going to move, but what is the real question? With the assistance of the helper, the couple realized that the question that really needed to be asked was, "How will we be able to spend enough time together and feel close to each other if David goes out of state for 2 years?" Previously, the couple had assumed:

"Someone is going to have to move."
"Someone is going to be unhappy."
"Someone is going to lose his or her job."

Once the problem assumptions had been put aside and the real problem identified, the couple was ready to start generating ideas.

Step 2: Generating Ideas

In a freewheeling and cooperative atmosphere, David and Gloria took a couple of minutes to identify creative answers to the question: "How can we remain close if David takes the job for 2 years?" Since quantity is wanted, the helper insisted that they generate at least 10 ideas. They came up with the following list:

1. We will e-mail every day.
2. We will call every day.
3. We will meet halfway every weekend.
4. David will come home once a month and Gloria will travel to see David once a month.
5. We can send telegrams.
6. We will spend our vacations and holidays with each other for the next 2 years, not with other family members.
7. We will install a videophone or videoconferencing software on the computer.
8. We will send recordings to each other.
9. Gloria will take some of her work with her to David's place and stay for a week at a time.
10. David will ask the company for time off to come home.
11. We can take pictures of things that happen and share them with each other.
12. We could both take a class to fill our time and discuss it with each other.
13. We can send smoke signals.
14. We can meet halfway in Mexico.

As the ideas got crazier, they began to hitchhike on each others' ideas. When Gloria said, "We could take a class," David suggested that they take a Spanish class and share their learning when they meet in Mexico.

Step 3: Evaluating and Selecting a Solution

The final step of brainstorming is evaluating and selecting a solution. David and Gloria went through the list at this point and discussed each possibility. They settled on four or five suggestions to implement that best fit the goal of keeping their relationship vital while they lived separately. Although the case of David and Gloria may seem too good to be true, many clients and helpers have learned to use brainstorming in just this way. When a client and helper devise a creative solution to a knotty problem, the therapeutic relationship is enhanced and the client's confidence and sense of hope is increased.

The Skill of Alternate Interpretation

The skill of brainstorming encourages clients and helpers to collaborate and create new solutions. When we challenge our assumptions in the first steps of brainstorming, we begin to recognize that there are many different ways to frame a problem and that the way we conceptualize it has important implications for the eventual solution. *Alternate interpretation* is another method to help clients recognize that problem situations can be seen in many different lights. The method of alternate interpretation does not attempt to reach into the past to find the correct interpretation or meaning of an event. Rather, its sole purpose is to convince the client that there are several possible alternatives to a negative first impression or catastrophic appraisal. For instance, many people continue into adulthood to misinterpret events that happened when they were children. This method of alternate interpretation tends to loosen the hold of outmoded ideas and to convince clients that there are many possible ways of looking at a problem, some of them helpful and some of them self-defeating.

How to Teach a Client to Use Alternate Interpretation

The decision to use alternate interpretation usually comes within a session when a client describes an event that has occurred and then begins to catastrophize about it. The helper stops the process and asks the client to stop imagining the worst case scenario and examine the premises that led to the conclusion that a catastrophe has occurred or is imminent. Consider the case of Jane, who has been working at a new job for only a short while. She was recently fired from another position and is feeling very insecure about her new situation:

Jane: "On Monday, my boss mentioned that I had not finished last week's reports. My boss is criticizing me. Things are starting all over again. I know I'll lose this job now."

Step 1   Using the skill of alternate interpretation, the helper proceeds as follows: The helper listens to the client's problem and then previews and explains the concept of alternate interpretation.

Helper: "I recognize that you are concerned about losing your new job, but I wonder if I could stop you for a moment and ask you to try something."

Jane: "Okay."

Helper: "This technique is called alternate interpretation. The way it works is that we take the situation and try to identify some different conclusions than the one that you have drawn. As I understand it, your boss stopped you and mentioned you had not done last week's reports, right?"

Jane: "Right."

Helper: "And your conclusion was that the same thing is happening that occurred at your old job and that you will probably be fired, right?"

Jane: "It sounds kind of silly when you say it that way."

Helper: "Well, what I would like to do is get you to try and generate some other interpretations of the facts. For example, perhaps your boss needed that information for some reason and was more interested in the content of the reports than in firing you."

Jane: "All right, I see."

Step 2   The helper asks the client to make a list of three or four other interpretations that fit the facts at least as well as the catastrophic conclusion of the client.

Helper: "I am wondering if you would try and think for a moment about some other ways of interpreting the same situation."

Jane: "Well, in the past, I have not received this kind of criticism. It is unfamiliar. Perhaps she is trying to help me improve and become a better employee."

Helper: "That's good. What else?"

Jane: "Um, I guess I could realize that I have just received feedback that will help my performance. Maybe it will actually help me keep the job."

Helper: "Very good. Can you think of any other way to interpret this situation."

Jane: "Like I said, this is the first time that my work has been criticized. My boss probably doesn't place that much importance on a single instance like this. She's probably forgotten about it. I am just nervous because of my past history."

Step 3   The helper assigns a homework task of developing three or four alternate explanations to the first interpretation of any disturbing event that occurs between sessions. The only requirement for the alternatives is that they have as much likelihood of being true as the first impression.

Stop and Reflect

1. Think about the following scenario and consider how you might help the client develop alternate interpretations of the same situation.

    "My best friend Pam isn't talking to me. We were out together on Friday night. Well, I met someone that I knew from work and wanted to spend more time with. He and I left the coffee shop. It was crowded, I didn't see Pam, so I didn't say good-bye. When I saw her at church, she waved but didn't stay to talk. I know she hates me now. We have been so close for 2 years and now it's over."

2. Now, take a moment to consider an event in your own life where your first impression was incorrect. Might the skill of alternate interpretation have been helpful in your situation? As you think about it, list two or three other possible interpretations you might have made had you been able to be more objective.

3. What client problems do you think might respond best to the technique of alternate interpretation? Compare your ideas with those of your classmates.

Summary

Up to this point, we have looked mainly at skills for developing the therapeutic relationship, exploring client problems, and setting goals. In this chapter, we talked about five building blocks that help move clients toward solutions: giving advice, giving information, giving directives, alternate interpretation, and brainstorming. Advice giving is the most controversial skill presented and the one that can potentially create the most harm to the therapeutic relationship. It is discussed be-cause helpers need to understand the appropriate and inappropriate uses of advice rather than ignoring it completely.

The major focus of this chapter was on the skills of brainstorming and alternate interpretation. Both skills are aimed at getting clients to free themselves from their first interpretations of events or the mental constraints that keep them from developing creative solutions to their difficulties.

Group Exercise

Students work in groups of three or four. One student becomes the client, another the helper, and the others act as observers. The client discusses a dilemma with a helper. The dilemma should be a situation in which the client is forced to make a difficult choice between two alternatives. It may be a current dilemma or it may be one that the client faced in the past. Suggestions of possible topics for the client to discuss include:

- Whether or not to commit to a relationship
- Whether or not to end a relationship
- Whether to move or stay in the same place
- Whether or not to begin an academic degree program

Before beginning the brainstorming process, the helper uses the nonjudgmental listening cycle for several minutes to understand a little more about the client's problem. Next, the helper moves with the client through the three steps of brainstorming:

1. The helper challenges the client to review his or her assumptions about the problem and to identify the real issue.
2. The helper and client brainstorm solutions.
3. The helper and client agree on a solution.

Following the brainstorming session, the client and observer(s) give the helper general feedback on:

1. The handling of the nonjudgmental listening cycle.
2. The helper's success in getting the client to think creatively.
3. The final solution. Was it realistic and appropriate for this client?

Quick Tips: Brainstorming

- Use closed questions to help the client pinpoint the real problem.
- Create a playful and cooperative atmosphere in the session by modeling free-wheeling. Come up with a few unusual ideas yourself to encourage the client's creativity.
- The helper should take the role of facilitator and write down all of the ideas that are generated.
- Add humor when possible and exaggerate to encourage a sense of play.
- Make sure that the final creative solution between helper and client meets the "reality criterion": It must effectively address the problem.

Additional Exercises

Exercise 1

This activity can be used as a whole-class activity or for groups of at least six or eight students. One student acts as the client and describes a real problem to the group. The client is asked to identify a problem that is not too personal so that he or she does not feel uncomfortable discussing it in some detail. The helper (student or teacher) uses the nonjudgmental listening cycle to understand the issue. When the story has been fully articulated to the helper, the group thinks about the client's story and each person writes down a piece of advice.

In the second part of the exercise, the helper collects the written advice and reads each student's advice to the client. After hearing the advice, the client discusses with the class which advice he or she is most likely to follow and why.

In the third part of the exercise, the helper uses a brainstorming approach to get the client to think about the issue and to come up with his or her own plan. Finally, the client is asked to review both the advice-giving and brainstorming sessions and indicate what course of action he or she is most likely to take. The class or group discusses the results.

Exercise 2

This exercise is suitable for a large class or for groups of six to eight students. It is designed to help students learn to identify assumptions and generate ideas.

Begin by generating ideas about how to improve the blackboard. The task is to produce as many ideas as possible in 2 minutes. These are recorded on the board so that everyone can see. For the first part of the activity, remember that it is important to let go of the mind's evaluative function and allow creativity to flow. Do not think about how practical the ideas are at first. Give equal time to wild ideas.

Next, list on the board the assumptions you have about blackboards—for example, they are black, you write on them, and so on. Next to each assumption write a reversal of the assumption—for example, blackboards are not black, you do not write on them, and so on. Then brainstorm any ideas about improving the blackboard that seem to come out of these reversals. Add any new ideas to the list. Now, see whether you can force-fit any two ideas on the list together, or hitchhike, to devise any new creative ideas. If so, add them to the list.

As the final step in the process, evaluate each idea, and select the best. Can any of the good ideas be combined to create a new product? The final design should meet the reality criterion: Is the product really an improvement? How likely would it be to sell?

Homework

Homework 1

Consider the case of Arnold, a 30-year-old man who had recently broken up with a woman he had been dating for a short time. The client described the problem like this: "I can't seem to make a relationship last. I thought this one was it! There must be something wrong with me. I think that women can see how incapable I am at maintaining a relationship." Identify three or four alternate interpretations for Arthur's first impression. Next, identify two alternate interpretations for each of these client statements.

- "My marriage is on the rocks. We're not in love anymore."
- "Everybody else has a direction for their lives by the time they're my age. What's wrong with me?"
- "I can't stand this anxiety anymore. I want it to go away."

- "My life is not going anywhere. I am in graduate school and I am working, but when does it get to be fun?"

Homework 2

It has been said that creativity is an important trait of helpers. According to Witmer (1985), creative individuals are said to possess the following characteristics:

Curiosity
Openness to new experience
Independence
Sense of humor and playfulness (spontaneity)
Persistence
Flexibility
Originality
Ability to accept that opposing points of view may both be right

Do you see yourself as a creative individual? Is this something you would like to develop? Write a paragraph or two about why you think creativity might be useful in helping others. Indicate specifically how you might employ creativity in homework assignments for clients.

Journal Starters

1. Some helpers use a technique in which the client sits in the counselor's chair and gives himself or herself advice. This is a way of tapping into that wise person in each of us. Think for a moment about your relationships, your family, money, children, or your career. Imagine yourself as this older, wiser self and write down your advice. When you have finished writing, react to the activity by sharing your evaluation of the advice.
2. Begin your journal entry by writing a poem about your life. It doesn't have to rhyme. The poem should be a picture of your life at this moment in time. Use metaphors to indicate how much effort you are putting forth, how you are dealing with problems and setbacks, and how you see your future goals. Reflect on your poem and decide whether this activity gave you any insight on your present situation. How important is it for you to have a creative outlet in your life? Can you see any value in assigning this activity to a client?

References

Diehl, M., & Stroebe, W. (1991). Productivity loss in idea-generating groups: Tracking down the blocking effect. *Journal of Personality and Social Psychology, 61,* 392–403.

Gladding, S. T. (1998). *Counseling as an art: The creative arts in counseling* (2nd ed.). Alexandria, VA: American Counseling Association.

Gordon, T. (1975). PET: *Parent effectiveness training.* New York: Wyden.

Holland, J. L., & Gottfredson, G. D. (1976). Using a typology of persons and environments to explain careers: Some extensions and clarifications. *Counseling Psychologist, 6,* 20–29.

Johnson, D. W., & Johnson, F. P. (1997). *Joining together.* (6th ed.). Boston: Allyn & Bacon.

Kleinke, C. L. (1994). *Common principles of psychotherapy.* Pacific Grove, CA: Brooks/Cole.

Mallett, S. D., Spokane, A. R., & Vance, F. L. (1978). Effects of vocationally relevant information on the expressed and measured interests of freshman males. *Journal of Counseling Psychology, 25,* 10–15.

McMullin, R. (1986). *Handbook of cognitive ther-apy techniques.* New York: Norton.

Mullen, B., Johnson, C., & Salas, E. (1991). Produc-tivity loss in brainstorming groups: A meta-ana-lytic integration. *Basic and Applied Social Psy-chology, 12,* 3–25.

Patterson, L. E., & Eisenberg, S. (1983). *The coun-seling process* (3rd ed.). Boston: Houghton Mif-flin.

Witmer, J. M. (1985). *Pathways to personal growth.* Muncie, IN: Accelerated Development.

Enhancing Efficacy and Self-Esteem

11

This section of the book is dedicated to implementing techniques. The techniques one chooses are based on the aims identified in the goal-setting stage of the help- ing process (see Figure 11.1). In these chapters, we will suggest some very basic techniques that can be used to address common client goals.

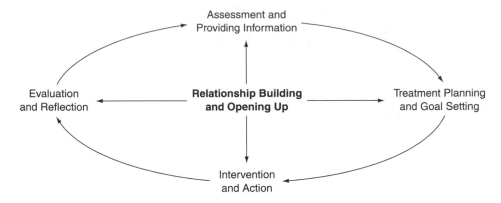

Figure 11.1
Stages of the Therapeutic Relationship: Relationship Building

In this and the next four chapters of the book, we will address each of the six curative factors first identified in Chapter 2 (see Figure 11.2). As we discussed in Chapter 2, a curative factor is a common or underlying factor that explains why many different therapy systems seem to be effective; they are all evoking the healing potential in one or more of these curative elements. We use the concept of curative factors because it provides a way of organizing the techniques you will be learning and because it will help you to understand the purpose of the techniques you are choosing. The whole range of helping skills and techniques can be organized under one of these six factors. For convenience sake, we refer to each of the factors by a letter. Together, they form the acronym REPLAN, which is a way of remembering them when we think about constructing a treatment plan.

R = A Strong Helper-Client Relationship

The therapeutic alliance was discussed in Chapter 3. You have learned invitational and reflecting skills that improve and deepen the therapeutic relationship while inviting the client to explore the inner world. It involves both skills and attitudes of the helper and the client's willingness and ability to enter the relationship. Not only must the helper provide a therapeutic atmosphere, but he or she must also take into account client differences in background, family, religion, and culture that can influence the client's reaction to the helper and to the helping relationship. In addition, the helper must deal with transference and countertransference issues when they interfere with achieving the client's goals.

E = Enhancing Efficacy and Self-Esteem

In this chapter, we will look at techniques that improve a client's confidence in his or her abilities and also deal with a person's underlying lack of self-worth. Nearly all helpers agree that improved self-esteem is a desired goal but changing longheld beliefs is a challenge.

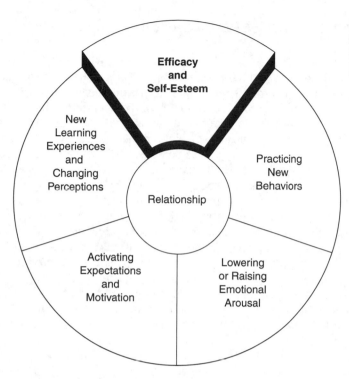

Figure 11.2
Curative Factors in the
REPLAN System:
Efficacy and Self-Esteem

P = Practicing New Behaviors

In Chapter 12, we will look at ways of helping clients practice a new behavior once it has been learned. For example, clients may learn communication techniques to improve the couple relationship, but they need to practice both within sessions and between sessions so that the new skills are firmly established. Practice techniques are available to strengthen fragile learning.

L = Lowering and Raising Emotional Arousal

Chapter 13 presents techniques that helpers use to quiet strong emotions and methods that are used to arouse client emotions. Quieting techniques involve such things as relaxation training, whereas arousing techniques include asking clients to become more aware of suppressed feelings.

A = Activating Client Expectations, Hope, and Motivation

Chapter 14 introduces ways that a helper can help motivate a discouraged client, including the use of encouragement and dealing with so-called resistance. This chapter also discusses ways of identifying the techniques that match the client's level of motivation.

N = New Learning Experiences

The number of techniques in this category far surpasses all the other groupings. Helpers stimulate new learning by provoking insight, direct teaching of social skills, cognitive restructuring, and many other methods. These will be discussed in Chapter 15.

Treatment Planning and the REPLAN System

Let us now briefly look at how the concept of curative factors not only helps us categorize the wide variety of helping techniques, but can also aid us in setting up a general treatment plan. *Treatment planning* means developing a list of strategies or techniques to address a corresponding list of problems that have been identified in the goal setting stage. Most people are familiar with the diagnostic treatment planning method. It is the medical methodology that begins by assessing the client and arriving at a diagnosis. The diagnosis becomes the basis for determining what treatment the client will receive. If you have major depression, for example, you receive a certain treatment; if you have obsessive-compulsive disorder, you receive another. Other systems of treatment planning reject the diagnostic model because it does not adequately take into account individual differences.

Alternately, many clinicians construct treatment plans based on the theory to which they subscribe. The techniques one eventually chooses come from the Gestalt, Adlerian, psychodynamic, or behavioral armory. As we indicated earlier in the book, there is good reason to think that an eclectic or integrative approach to treatment planning is useful, particularly early in training. Before one is entrenched in a particular viewpoint, one can utilize the techniques of different theories.

REPLAN is the goal-oriented, treatment planning model using the six curative factors: outlined previously. The REPLAN system does not conflict with making a *DSM-IV* diagnosis or theoretically oriented models, but it does assert that nearly all clients with the same diagnosis need different treatments. Therefore, treatment strategies must be tailored to the client's goals and the unique characteristics of the client rather than to a specific diagnosis.

The REPLAN system is distinguishable from other forms of treatment planning because it focuses on a relatively few number of client goals, using strategies associated with one or two curative factors. This makes it a brief treatment model. This approach has the benefit of focusing clients on a few goals at a time, rather than planning an elaborate treatment regimen that may collapse over time as the client's situation changes. The approach is not incompatible with long-term therapy, but it approaches client problems as distinct goals that must be regularly evaluated and replanned. Replanning occurs frequently during the helping process since client goals shift as some problems are resolved and new insights on old problems emerge.

The two basic steps in REPLAN treatment planning are:

1. Formulate mutually agreed-upon treatment goals, as a result of assessment, that are understandable to both client and helper. These goals are then boiled down to a workable, solvable form and placed in priority order.
2. Use the curative factors (relationship, enhancing efficacy and self-esteem, practicing new behaviors, lowering and raising emotional arousal, activating expectations and increasing hope, and providing new learning experiences) to generate a list of possible treatment strategies or techniques to achieve the goals.

The helper generates a list of potential techniques by asking himself or herself two questions: "What curative factors are most likely to help the client reach the goals?" and, "What strategies, methods, or techniques will be most effective and acceptable to the client?"

To illustrate how this works in practice, let us look at the case example of Matthew, 25-year-old single white male, a chemist, who is shy and wishes to meet and date women but has not been successful. Matthew's main problem is anxiety in social situations. Together he and the helper, Nadia, identify the following positive goal: to be able to go out with a woman and have fun.

To initiate the REPLAN method, Nadia asks herself which curative factors would be most helpful for Matthew in achieving his goal. Based on her knowledge of Matthew's situation, it seems clear that practicing new behaviors and new learning experiences would be the most useful place to begin.

Now that Nadia has identified the major curative factors, she asks herself a second question, "What specific methods under these therapeutic factors would be most effective with Matthew?" She then selects strategies to evoke the therapeutic factors. Following is part of the treatment plan that she developed for Matthew with a set of strategies or steps to help him learn social skills and then practice new behaviors. The practice section is expanded so that you can see the specific steps that Matthew and Nadia designed.

Curative Factor	Strategy
New learning experiences	1. Learn basic communication theory, listening, and self-disclosure.
Lowering emotional arousal	1. Learn a basic relaxation technique to reduce anxiety before entering social situations.
Practicing new behaviors	1. Practice self-disclosure and listening skills with helper and a friend.
	Objectives
	a. Role-play asking someone out for coffee.
	b. Ask any friend out for coffee.
	c. Ask female friend out for coffee.

In summary, the notion of curative factors is a way of identifying what the client needs and selecting a general approach to the client's problems. The use of curative factors is a heuristic or method for stimulating thinking about possible techniques to employ. Then, the helper narrows down the list of potential techniques based on the client's needs. The rationale for this kind of approach is that it encourages the helper to weigh a wider variety of planned interventions than a theoretically oriented or a diagnostically oriented treatment planning model.

The Therapeutic Factor of Enhancing Efficacy and Self-Esteem

There is wide agreement that a positive self-concept is a keystone of mental health and that raising self-esteem is a fundamental task of helping (Bednar & Peterson, 1995; Carlock, 1998; Kurpius, Rockwood, & Corbett, 1989; Walz, 1990). Humanistic theorists have identified the helper's task as increasing "Can-ness." For example, Carl Rogers focused on reducing the gap between one's perceived self and one's ideal self. Adler felt that a clear sign of mental health was "faith in oneself." Likewise, low self-esteem has long been identified as a cause or contributing factor in many psychological diagnoses and symptoms, especially anxiety (Rosenberg, 1962), depression (Beck, Rush, Shaw, & Emery, 1979; Burns, 1999; Wilson & Krane, 1980), stress, dependency, pathological

guilt, borderline personality (Ingham, Kreitman, Miller, & Sasidharan, 1986), and substance abuse (Brehm & Back, 1968).

Still, self-esteem has been attacked as too vague, overpopularized, and a cure-all
for problems ranging from addictions to misbehavior (Kaplan, 1995; Street & Issacs,
1998). One way of clarifying the concept is to recognize that self-esteem has two aspects: efficacy (competence) and self-worth (Branden, 1969, 1971; Witmer, 1985).
Both increasing a client's efficacy and self-approval or self-worth are common targets
for the helping relationship.

Efficacy is an expectation that one can perform a specific task (Bandura, 1982,
1997). For example, when an experienced driver sits behind the wheel of a car, he or
she feels a sense of confidence or expectation that driving a car is a manageable task.
Efficacy is tied to specific activities, though it may generalize to similar situations. It
is also subject to modification by experience. Having an auto accident could undermine one's sense of efficacy as a driver. Many clients are afraid to try new activities
because of past failures or because they do not expect to do well at anything. In addition, individuals with low self-esteem often do not pay sufficient attention to successes and improvements, tending to focus on their losses and failures. They may
possess needed skills but do not recognize their abilities and strengths. The helper,
by focusing on strengths and competencies, enhances the possibilities for success
and improved self-esteem (Thompson, 1991).

In contrast to efficacy, *self-worth* is a global feeling that one has the right to exist, that one is basically good and is worthy to live. In short, it is self-approval. It is
the sum total of one's attitudes about the self: the fundamental belief that one is
"okay" or "not okay" (Berne, 1972). It is possible to feel competent or efficacious at
a number of tasks and still experience low self-worth. As helpers, we often meet intelligent, attractive, skilled individuals whose major problems are deeply held negative beliefs about themselves, despite their obvious skills and abilities.

Stop and Reflect

Ten Things I Can't Do

Self-esteem can be improved by increasing client self-efficacy. Efficacy is increased
when clients recognize their current abilities or learn new skills. The chances that a
client will attempt a new activity are increased if he or she engages in warmup activities, including thinking about, talking about, and visualizing the new behavior. To
become more familiar with this process, try the following:

1. Make a list of 10 things you cannot do at the present time but would like to be
   able to do. For example, your list might include:

   "I would like to learn to swim."
   "I would like to ask someone out on a date."
   "I would like to be able to use a spreadsheet on the computer."
   "I would like to be able to learn ballroom dancing."
   For this exercise, do not include personal qualities that you would like to de-
   velop or global statements about self-worth such as "I would like to be more
   patient," or "I would like to be a better person."

2. Once you have developed a list of 10 items, place the letter *T* next to each
   item if you have talked to a friend or family member about engaging in this ac-

tivity. Place the letter *V* if you have *ever* visualized or daydreamed about your-self performing this task. Place the letter *M* for "models" if you have seen other people perform this task *on several occasions.* Place the letter *A* next to each task that you have attempted to perform in the last year.

3. It is thought that a person is more likely to engage in a new behavior if he or she gets ready by talking about it, visualizing it, and watching others. Con-versely, when we have not readied ourselves through these activities, we are farther away from actually attempting the behavior. Look at your list and de-cide if your answers confirm this "readiness hypothesis." Identify one or two behaviors that have the fewest letters next to them. Which letters are miss-ing? The missing letters should indicate which activities you can initiate if you wish to increase your readiness.

4. Do you think you might experience any change in your self-esteem if you were able to engage in all of the activities on your list?

5. Compare your answers to this exercise and your reactions with others in your training group.

Sources of Low Self-Esteem

Drivers

Messages received during childhood sometimes become internalized images or phrases about the self. In transactional analysis (Berne, 1972), a theory of psy-chotherapy, the individual's life plan or "script" is thought to be transmitted from the parents along with accompanying injunctions, such as "You'll never amount to any-thing," "Don't trust anyone," and so on. The script could be called a worldview that the family passes on, but transactional analysis proposes that families actually hand down specific phrases that affect self-esteem. Some of these injunctions or themes become preeminent and rule a person's life. These ruling injunctions are called *driv-ers* because they broadly motivate or drive behavior (Kahler, 1977). The person at-tempts to maintain self-esteem by attempting to live up to the standards of parents and others because they are playing these tapes when they think about success. Un-fortunately, these internalized sentences may not be relevant to the present, or healthy, or even possible to uphold.

An obvious example of an impossible driver is "Be perfect." A client reported that she never plays the guitar anymore even though she enjoys it because she cannot afford lessons, nor can she stand to make mistakes. She was raised with the injunction that "Anything worth doing is worth doing right." In reality, some things, like playing the gui-tar, are worth doing sloppily if one enjoys them. Perfectionism keeps people from trying new things and from enjoying activities that they perform less than flawlessly.

Table 11.1 shows physical, psychological, and behavioral manifestations of some common drivers. The author of the table suggests that drivers give rise to physical manifestations, internal discounts or beliefs, specific word uses and tones, as well as gestures, postures, and facial expressions. The internal discounts or beliefs are the silent sentences a person says over and over that maintain low self-esteem. A helper can recognize the manifestations of a driver in a client by the behaviors associated with it.

Table 11.1
Drivers: Sources of Negative Self-Image

| Drivers | Compliance (Inner Feelings) | | | Important Behavior | | | | |
	Physical	Psychological: Internal Discount	Words	Tones	Gestures	Posture	Facial Expressions
Be perfect	Tense	"You should do better."	"Of course." "Obviously." "Efficacious." "Clearly." "I think."	Clipped, righteous	Counting on fingers, cocked wrist, scratching head	Erect, rigid	Stern
Try hard	Tight stomach, tense shoulders	"You've got to try harder."	"It's hard." "I can't." "I'll try." "I don't know."	Impatient	Clenched, moving fists	Sitting backward, elbows on legs	Slight frown, perplexed look
Please me	Tight stomach	"You're not good enough."	"You know." "Could you." "Can you." "Kinda."	High whine	Hands outstretched	Head nodding	Raised eyebrows, looks away
Hurry up	Antsy	"You'll never get it done."	"We've got to hustle."	Up and down	Squirms, taps fingers	Moving quickly	Frowning, eyes shifty
Be strong	Numb, rigid	"You can't let them know you're weak."	"No comment." "I don't care."	Hard monotone	Hands, rigid, arms folded	Rigid, one leg over	Plastic, hard, cold

Source: "Driver Chart" In "The Miniscript" by Taibi Hahler from *Transactional Analysis After Eric Berne.* Copyright © 1977 by Graham Barnes. Reprinted by permission of Harper Collins Publishers.

Irrational Beliefs

Irrational beliefs are self-destructive ideas about ourselves that lead to low self-esteem (Daly & Burton, 1983). They cause us to suffer emotionally, but are so firmly entrenched that they are difficult to challenge and expunge. Albert Ellis (1973) ascribes low self-esteem to a set of "nutty beliefs" about ourselves and the world. It is not our experiences that keep us in a state of low self-esteem, but our ideas that hold us there. For example, Ellis asserts that it is not a black cat that makes us afraid but the belief that a black cat causes bad luck. Similarly, if we rid ourselves of irrational beliefs and develop more realistic ones, we relieve ourselves of emotional turmoil. Although we each probably have something unique about our belief systems, Ellis found that most people's irrational ideas fall into some broad categories and he has identified seven of the most common. These include:

1. The idea that it is a dire necessity for an adult human to be loved or approved of by virtually every significant other person in his or her life
2. The idea that one should be thoroughly competent, adequate, and achieving in all possible respects to consider oneself worthwhile
3. The idea that certain people are bad, wicked, or villainous and that they should be severely blamed or punished for their villainy
4. The idea that it is awful and catastrophic when things are not the way one would like them to be
5. The idea that human unhappiness is externally caused and that people have little or no ability to control their terrors and disturbances
6. The idea that it is easier to avoid life's difficulties and self-responsibilities than to face them
7. The idea that one's past history is an all-important determinant of one's present behavior and that, because something once strongly affected one's life, it should definitely continue to do so (Ellis, 1973, p. 37)

Body Image

Psychological literature tells us that attractiveness is a valuable social asset (Adams, 1977) and that feeling unattractive is often equated with low self-esteem (Greenspan, 1983). Those with high self-worth generally feel good about their bodies. Those who do not like their bodies tend to be negative about themselves as a whole. An individual may have a negative *body image* because of a physical disability, a difference, or a lack of attractiveness by media standards. Although low self-esteem associated with body image may have been mainly the province of women in the past, men's magazines now reflect that society has chosen some male ideals as well. Now men are expected to have "washboard abs" and other perfect features that provide a negative comparison for the average person.

Helpers must also become aware of their evaluations of individuals who are unattractive. Helpers like attractive clients and feel less hopeful about those that are overweight and unattractive. We are all products of our culture and cultural ideas about mental health. Frequently, beginning helpers are unforgiving of clients who do not want to lose weight or who dress unattractively.

A client with a distorted body image might be a symptom of more serious psychological syndromes, especially eating disorders, resulting in the evaluation that one is fat or unattractive despite evidence to the contrary (Baird & Sights, 1986). The belief that one must be perfect is probably behind this powerful dissatisfaction that propels starvation, causes self-induced vomiting in extreme cases, and engenders low self-esteem, anger, and distress even in those without major emotional problems (Thompson & Thompson, 1986).

To deal with the perfectionism associated with body image, helpers have adopted strategies such as:

1. Asking the client to describe the perfect body and then to compare his or her own body to this description. The client is confronted with the fact that the self-description is not far from the ideal.
2. Helping the client to focus on aspects or positive qualities of the self that do not require a perfect physical appearance.
3. Having the client describe childhood experiences that involved the importance of appearance, from early memories to parental statements, and asking the client to be specific and to identify those individuals from whom this learning took place. If clients realize that their tendency to emphasize physical attractiveness actually comes from early influences of significant others, it may lead them to reevaluate and ask themselves if appearance is really that important. These ideas are often so basic to the client's worldview that they do not easily disappear.

Stop and Reflect

One way to increase self-esteem is to ask clients to pay more attention to their strengths and abilities. Because helping is a profession where results are not often immediate, even helpers need to pause and reflect on their accomplishments from time to time. Take this moment to reflect on your own personal assets.

A Self-Esteem Personal Inventory

1. Write down eight personal characteristics that you are proud of. For example, you may be creative, organized, humorous, goal oriented, and so on.
2. List eight things that you do well.
3. Write down a few compliments about yourself that you hear from friends and family. What are the good things people say about you?
4. List three occasions when you feel that you have truly helped another person.
5. List the top three accomplishments of your life so far.
6. Write down three things that you like about your body.
   - When you have completed this exercise, conduct a brief scan of your emotional state. Do you notice any difference in the way you feel?
   - Were there any answers you felt reluctant to write down? Were you apprehensive about "bragging"? What are the rules in your own family or culture governing when it is all right to give yourself a compliment?
   - If you were given this assignment as a client, how do you think you might react to it?
   - Which question was the most difficult to answer? Why? If you had been asked to list your negative qualities, would it have been easier or more difficult?

Table 11.2
Some Common Defense Mechanisms and Their Functions

Defense Mechanism	Function in Maintaining Self-Esteem
Avoidance/withdrawal	Escaping responsibility (no attempt, no failure)
Denial	Refusing to admit to problems
Fantasy	Imagining self as powerful and achieving
Substance abuse	Creating grandiose and powerful self-image
Rationalization	Denying failure by giving excuses
Projection	Denying negative traits and feelings in the self and ascribing them to others
Compensation	Denying inferiority by achieving in other areas

Defense Mechanisms: Guardians of Self-Esteem

Defense mechanisms are psychological techniques designed to reduce anxiety and protect self-esteem (see Table 11.2). Excessive use of defense mechanisms is considered unhealthy since, by definition, they avoid or distort reality rather than help us cope with it. Defense mechanisms may not be all bad, though. Denial, for instance, has been found to be quite useful in the beginning stages of coping with death and calamities such as hurricanes and floods (Grayson, 1986; Lazarus & Folkman, 1984; Lazarus & Golden, 1981). Defense mechanisms may serve to pace or to slow down the experience of anxiety so that individuals are not forced to face more arousal than they can cope with (Epstein, 1983).

Helping Clients Recognize Defense Mechanisms

When a client is using defense mechanisms, he or she is distorting rather than coping with life. A client who does not deal with the death of a spouse, the loss of a job, or the consequences of a divorce is unable to move on and handle life's new challenges. The major method for confronting clients with defensive reactions is a blend of reflecting meaning and confrontation (i.e., making a suggestion about the reason for the client's behavior and, at the same time, challenging the unproductive nature of the behavior). Two helper responses that reflect meaning and confront defensive maneuvers are given here:

Helper's Response to Compensation: "Because your sister was so good in school, you decided to excel in sports. (reflection of meaning) Now I'm wondering if your belief that you are no good at academics is entirely accurate or something you just didn't develop." (confrontation)

Helper's Response to Avoidance/Withdrawal: "It sounds to me as if you have decided to give up on the relationship because you have been hurt before. (reflection of meaning) Even though you don't know what might come of it, you'd rather stop now and avoid the potential pain. Is that right?" (confrontation)

In summary, client defensive responses are designed to preserve self-esteem, but they typically trade growth for safety. The helper must not always insist on growth, but should bring defensiveness into awareness and let the client decide how to proceed.

Setting viable goals and examining defended areas is necessary, as the examples illustrate. Defenses serve a purpose, though: to maintain and support self-esteem. They should not be callously exposed to ridicule, but deliberately and respectfully explored.

Other Self-Protective Strategies

Self-handicapping is a strategy involving attributing all failures to one's handicap, such as "I am an alcoholic" or "I have test anxiety," and attributing all successes to the self. Believing that one has a disability, one can avoid labeling himself or herself as stupid or lazy (Smith, Snyder, & Handelman, 1981; Tucker, Vuchinich, & Sobell, 1981). Those using self-handicapping strategies should be encouraged to become aware of strengths, and confronted when the helper feels the label is being used to avoid changing.

Learned helplessness refers to an attitude of acceptance, demoralization, and unwillingness to try in what appear to be unalterable circumstances, because of a person's previous experiences, even if change may now be possible (Seligman, 1975). For example, victims of domestic violence often feel that their situation is hopeless because attempts to change the circumstances have been thwarted for so long. They reach a point where they no longer believe that another kind of life is possible. Helping such individuals may be frustrating for the helper who has not experienced such hopeless circumstances. Out of their own frustration, helpers may try to confront such clients too early. Patience, support, empathy, and exposure to others who have made significant changes are the most important factors in changing people's views of themselves as helpless.

In a similar vein, seeing oneself as a victim is usually the result either of a lifetime of neglect or abuse or of sudden, catastrophic events. This view of the self helps the person survive, but it also keeps the person stuck. Helping those who have suffered tragedies is a long-term project. Beyond initial crisis intervention, the stages of the victim's experience, including feelings of anxiety, depression, and rage, must be taken step by step. For some events, such as the death of a child or sexual assault, no time limit can be assigned to the mourning and recovery period. Certainly a point comes, however, when the client must release the role of victim in order to grow. Instead of blaming others or engaging in self-recrimination, he or she must begin to consider the future. It does not mean that he or she forgets about the event, but instead begins to see himself or herself as a survivor and to take responsibility for making personal changes.

Methods for Developing Self-Esteem

In this section, we will learn two key methods for increasing client self-esteem: countering and assertiveness training. Countering is a cognitive therapy method for decreasing the internal, negative voices that depress performance and focus on failure. Assertiveness training, on the other hand, is a set of techniques to help one feel more efficacious and confident in the social arena. Both avenues hold promise for individuals with low self-esteem. One reduces internal criticism, whereas the other enhances interpersonal functioning. It is the helper's job to identify when these are appropriate, depending on the client's needs.

Silencing the Internal Critic: The Technique of Countering

Before one can experience self-worth, it is often necessary to silence the internal critic, the "voice in the head" that reproaches and finds fault. This critic is probably created early in life through the learning of irrational beliefs and drivers (McKay & Fanning, 1987). These irrational beliefs and drivers persist later in life as silent sentences that the individual repeats in the mind and sometimes even aloud. Characteristically, these thoughts tend to occur automatically. For example, before giving a speech, the following thought might occur: "I am going to get up and make a fool of myself." The negative thought leads to negative emotions of anger, depression, and lowered expectations of the self. Thus, before self-esteem can be built, it is often necessary to reduce the power of the internal critic and to modify these self-statements (Dowd, 1985).

How to Counter

Countering is a term coined by McMullin (2000) to describe the production of a self-statement that is incompatible with the critical thought. Countering consists of identifying the discouraging or self-downing statements a person says to himself or herself, and replacing them with equally powerful affirmations. The countering method has several steps:

Step 1: Do a Brief Assessment

Once helper and client have agreed that negative self-talk is a problem, it is critical to determine the frequency of the negative self-statements and their effects on the client. For this purpose, ask the client to engage in self-assessment or self-monitoring activities to determine the frequency and types of self-downing behavior. Typically, the client carries an index card in a pocket, wallet, or purse and notes each time a self-criticism occurs. The client writes down the exact words of each self-criticism and the associated negative emotions. The client brings the card back to the next session and discusses the thoughts he or she has noticed. The self-criticism card serves two functions: It gives client and helper more data about the problem, and it helps the client make the connection between negative self-statements and the feeling states they produce. The client can begin to see that instead of providing valid criticisms, the internal monologue is producing negative emotions.

Step 2: Identify the Negative Thought Patterns and Core Beliefs

Once the client has completed at least a week's worth of self-monitoring, the major negative thought patterns and core beliefs about the self may be identified from the compiled results of the self-monitoring task. Together, helper and client look at the self-monitoring material and choose a few negative patterns to focus on. Often three or four general ideas about oneself come to the surface—for example:

"I am not disciplined and never get anything accomplished."
"I am disorganized."
"I'll never be able to reach my goals."

Step 3: Identify Effective Counters

The counter can be a phrase, a sentence, or a single word such as "Nonsense." The counter is a way of talking back to oneself and disputing the self-criticism. The best counters are those that are not too disturbing to the client's values and philosophy and that are the most powerful in neutralizing the client's negative thoughts.

Together, client and helper brainstorm a number of possible counters, and the client selects several with which to experiment. An example of a self-criticism and the list of counters generated by client and helper follows:

Self-Criticism	Counters
"I am stupid."	1. "I have always performed well in school; there's no evidence for this."
	2. "Feeling stupid doesn't mean I am stupid."
	3. "That's something my Dad always told me. But it's not true!"
	4. "Not true!"

Step 4: Test Counters and Modify Them

The final stage in the process of eliminating self-criticism is to evaluate the effectiveness of the counters that the individual has practiced since the last helping session. The client will likely need more than one week to experience much success in neutralizing negative thoughts. Negative thoughts are automatic, and it takes time before clients can learn to "catch themselves" thinking negatively.

One method for evaluating the effectiveness of a counter ahead of time is for the helper to practice the countering technique with the client during a session. First, the client selects a statement from a list of self-criticisms and reads it aloud to the helper. After making the self-criticism, the client rates his or her emotional reaction to the criticism on a 100-point SUDS (subjective units of discomfort scale). On the SUDS, 100 equals high emotional distress and 0 equals no emotional distress. Next, the client reads a counter from the list that was brainstormed earlier and again rates his or her feelings of distress. In the following example, the client learns that this self-criticism is very disturbing (80) and that the counter is very effective because it reduces the strength of the emotional reaction to about 20.

Self-Criticism	Counter
"I am stupid."	"I have always performed well in school; there's no evidence for this."
SUDS after self-criticism—80	SUDS after counter—20

Step 5: Practice and Report

Once the client has identified some effective counters for one or two negative thoughts, the client is asked to practice and report at the next session. At follow-up sessions, the helper and the client gauge progress and continually seek more effective counters. The client is asked to notice if negative thoughts are now less frequent.

Problems and Precautions when Teaching the Countering Technique

Ineffective counters should be discarded, and the client should be prepared for the fact that some counters are more potent than others. The client can be asked to modify the counter slightly in any way that might refine it or make it more effective. The helper should also suggest any personal words or phrases that might produce more self-confidence. For example, one client found that introducing each counter with "Clearly . . ." gave the counter more power for her.

Counters should be realistic. They should not be simply positive thinking or "affirmations," but should actually dispute the negative ideas. A statement such as "Every day in every way, I'm getting better and better" is a pep talk without real substance; it is not tied to any particular self-criticism. Some negative self-statements are quite persistent, and it may take months to eliminate insidious automatic thoughts.

McMullin (2000) suggests that the counter should be in the same mode as the thought it is disputing. Negative visual images should be countered with positive visual images. Angry thoughts should be countered with compassionate ones, and "passive thoughts with assertive ones" (p. 5). Also, shorter counters tend to be more effective than longer ones.

A Variation on Countering: Thought Stopping

Sometimes clients are troubled by unwanted thoughts and images that create anxiety and depression and damage self-esteem. Unwanted thoughts and images may be memories of failure or concern about upcoming events. We are all familiar with lying in bed at night thinking about all the upcoming responsibilities. Once such thoughts get started, they snowball, creating more and more anxiety unless we have the skills to suppress our thinking when it gets out of control.

Compared to the developing of counters, *thought stopping* can be considered more of an emergency measure to halt the flow of negative messages. The helper teaches the client the technique in the office and the client practices it whenever a severely disturbing thought arises. Three steps in the thought-stopping technique have been identified (Davis, Eshelman, & McKay, 1980; Lazarus, 1971; Witmer, 1985):

1. Stating the thought
2. Creating a startling interruption
3. Substituting a new thought

Once the troubling thought has been identified, the client is asked to label and state it either mentally or aloud—for example, "I have to get an A on this paper!" This repetition brings the thought into clearer focus.

The client then creates a startling response strong enough to interrupt the negative thinking pattern. One practical method when practicing thought stopping privately is to yell "Stop!" as loud as possible. In public, it is best to use "the tongue of thought" and say "Stop!" mentally. Some helpers suggest wearing a rubber band around the wrist, snapping it along with a mental "Stop!" to produce the startle effect.

The final step is to insert a positive thought to replace the irrational, self-downing thought. This can be either a spontaneous or a planned counter that the client produces to counteract the negative thought. In this case, the substituted thought might be something such as, "I'm not going to worry about the grade. I'll do the best that I can."

Assertiveness Training

Assertiveness training is a term that became popular in the 1970s (Alberti & Emmons, 1974; Rathus, 1975; Smith, 1975). *Assertiveness* refers to a broad set of social skills used to enhance self-esteem and deal effectively with emotions (Goleman,

1995). It has been used successfully with a wide variety of client concerns, including marriage problems, depression, sexual dysfunction, aggressive behavior, substance abuse, and dependency, as well as raising low-self-esteem (Enns, 1996; Gambrill, 1985; Tanner & Holliman, 1988).

Recently, the term *assertiveness training* has been replaced with *social-skills training*. This change reflects a recognition that assertion is not as simple as standing up for one's rights or saying "No." Rather, it includes other positive interpersonal skills such as self-disclosure. Today, when we speak about assertiveness training, we are talking about educational programs that include specific combinations of a number of social skills, depending on the needs of the person or group. This training may include:

> Giving and receiving compliments
> Greeting others and initiating conversation
> Refusing requests and saying "No"
> Disclosing oneself to others and developing intimacy
> Asking for information
> Asserting beliefs, preferences, requests, and rights (Witmer, 1985)

Ineffective social behavior can be classified as either submissive (nonassertive) or aggressive (Alberti, 1977). Assertiveness is usually described as falling in the middle of a continuum between these two poles. Although it may be useful educationally to explain assertiveness as a compromise between submission and dominance, and as a counterbalancing of one's own needs and those of others, it has been found that assertiveness is also very situation specific. A woman who is a very assertive director of a large business may be very nonassertive with her parents. Therefore, clients in assertiveness training should be exposed to some general principles, but they should also have the opportunity to work within specific situations where they have difficulty. Assertiveness training for individuals and groups includes some common components, which we will discuss next.

Assertive Verbal Behaviors

One of the most basic assertive behaviors you can teach clients is to use the word "I" instead of "you." When we use "I" at the beginning of a statement such as "I am bothered by your smoking," we take responsibility for the statement and, at the same time, avoid a "you statement" that might place blame or make the other person defensive. Other examples of "I statements" include:

> "I disagree with you" rather than "You are wrong."
> "I get angry when . . . " rather than "You make me angry."
> "May I have one of those programs?" rather than "You forgot me."

Help your clients understand also that different levels of assertion are needed for different situations. At the first level, a polite request is attempted: "I'm having trouble hearing the movie; would you mind speaking more quietly?" Notice that the request describes the situation in nonjudgmental terms and specifies what is wanted of the other person. If the assertive request does not have the desired effect, it may be necessary to increase the power of the request. This is done by adding feelings to the polite request, as in the following statement: "I feel very uncomfortable when you tell racist jokes, and I wish you wouldn't." In extreme situations, it may be necessary to indicate the consequences if the behavior continues—for example, "I find this situation with my stereo very frustrating because I have had to bring it back for repairs on three occasions, and I would like you to refund my money. If you don't, I will talk to the manager about this."

A quick way of remembering the components of a verbal assertive response is the DERC system. *D* stands for describing in a nonjudgmental way. *E* stands for expressing your feelings or the way in which the other person's behavior is affecting you. *R* is making a request, and *C* is specifying the consequences if the person does not change the behavior. In the preceding example of the stereo, all four of these components are exemplified. The use of the final step, specifying consequences, is one that should be used mainly as a last resort, since indicating the action you will take will arouse defenses and might be seen only as a bluff. Most assertive responses should describe the situation nonjudgmentally, express feelings or the effects of the situation, and end with a request.

Assertive Nonverbal Behaviors

Remind clients that many body postures reflect assertiveness or nonassertiveness.

Eye Contact   Maintaining direct eye contact is an effective way of expressing sincerity. Looking away or looking down, in this culture, suggests a lack of confidence or deference to the other as the authority.

Body Posture   An assertive body posture involves squarely facing the other person, sitting or standing appropriately close, and perhaps leaning forward slightly with head erect. A side-tilted head is a questioning rather than an assertive position.

Touch   Touch can be used in making a request from a close acquaintance, since it gains the attention of the listener and affirms the relationship. When denying a request, a touch can lessen the feelings of rejection.

Gestures   Gestures add emphasis to the message and can be descriptive and visually communicative. A few strong gestures that accentuate the message can be useful. On the other hand, extensive gesturing can be viewed as indication of confusion and discomfort, and thus nonassertive.

Facial Expression, Voice Tone, Inflection, and Volume   The verbal message and the facial expression should match in an assertive response. Usually, a well-modulated conversational tone accompanies assertion. Speaking softly will water down an assertive message, and a loud dominating tone of voice may seem aggressive, activating the other person's defenses.

Responding Assertively to Criticism: Helpful and Unhelpful Reactions

Knowing Your Rights

Smith (1975) states that one way to educate clients about assertiveness is to hold a discussion about "assertive rights." A discussion of this sort may encourage a client to realize that one can be polite and yet be fully justified in standing up for oneself.

The following list includes some of Smith's ideas and some additional ones:

1. You have the right to change your mind.
2. You have the right to try something and make mistakes.

3. You have the right to say, "I don't know."
4. You have the right to make a request.
5. You have the right to refuse a request.
6. You have the right to refuse destructive feedback.
7. You have the right to be illogical when making decisions.

Viewing Criticism as Valuable

As a helper, encourage your clients to see criticism as valuable and not just something to tolerate. Help them learn to take a detached attitude and to find the constructive aspects of criticism, even if it is uttered in a most offensive way. In order to do this, clients must be taught to distinguish between destructive and constructive criticism. Destructive criticism tends to be global, using such words as "always" and "never." Global statements are hard to profit from because exceptions easily leap into mind. Destructive criticism also encompasses situations where a person tries to make us feel guilty, to manipulate us through outbursts of anger, to engage in lengthy monologues, or to resort to name calling. Finally, destructive criticism may take the form of bringing up irreconcilable issues from the past, rather than focusing on what can be changed in the present. Teach your clients to recognize these destructive forms of criticism, which can be harmful to the self-concept if accepted at face value.

More often than not, criticism contains a germ of truth that an individual may examine and benefit from. According to Egan (1990), constructive criticism:

1. Includes noticing positive as well as negative aspects of a performance
2. Is brief and specific
3. Does not require the other person to change instantly, but acknowledges that change takes time
4. Involves an openness to the other person's viewpoint and is stated tentatively to acknowledge this
5. Includes a commitment to negotiate and take positive action to solve the problem

Although clients cannot expect that they will receive constructive criticism at all times, they can learn to ask for this type of feedback. In the following example, Alicia receives some destructive feedback but handles it well by asking questions, listening nondefensively, making sure her opinion is heard, and obtaining a constructive suggestion:

Boss: "Your attitude has got to change."

Alicia: "Tell me what you mean."

Boss: "You've got a bad attitude."

Alicia: "Okay, can you give me an example so I can think about how to change this situation?"

Boss: "Well, yesterday, when I gave you that big order to input into the computer, you sighed. You don't seem to like your job."

Alicia: "You're right, I did sigh, but I don't think that reflects my usual attitude."

Boss: "It is just that this job is really important to me and I wish everybody on the team would feel that way."

Alicia: "I understand how you feel, but I also want you to realize that I am excited about this project and I am happy on the job. Your comment was helpful, though; I don't want to appear to have a bad attitude."

Stop and Reflect

Table 11.3 contains the Rathus Assertiveness Schedule (RAS) (Rathus, 1973). The RAS is a well-known self-report inventory designed to measure assertiveness or "social boldness." It is designed to give clients feedback on their frankness. Complete the inventory for yourself and consider the questions that follow.

How to Score the RAS
Add the answers to all of the questions. For questions that have an asterisk next to them, change the valence; that is, change all negatives to positives and all positives to negatives.

Norms
The RAS was tested with undergraduates from about 17–27 years of age. The average score was about .3, with a standard deviation of approximately 29. High scores, say over 40, suggest the possible need for assertiveness training, but the best use of the instrument may be to gauge the change that takes place in assertiveness training. A client can look at scores before and after training to see the changes.

- After looking at your own scores on the RAS, examine some of the individual items. Do they suggest any specific behaviors that you have difficulty with?
- What situations or behaviors does the inventory seem to neglect?
- Has this inventory changed your ideas about your view of yourself as an assertive person?
- In a small group, discuss the possible uses of an inventory such as this in assertiveness training.

How to Teach a Client to Be More Assertive

The goal of teaching a client to be more assertive—like any therapeutic goal—must be carefully established on the basis of a good working relationship with the client. Assertiveness training is best done in a classroom setting because participants can obtain support from a group and see others practicing assertiveness. When such groups are not available, assertiveness training can be taught one to one in an office setting.

Step 1: Preparing and Educating the Client
Begin by familiarizing the client with the theory behind assertiveness training, which also helps to gain his or her trust and assistance in learning the method. This preparation is based on the client's level of knowledge and the specific goal he or she is trying to accomplish. Information presented earlier in this chapter on assertive behaviors and responding to criticism may be a useful starting point. Preparation can be accomplished by the helper in the office or by homework or reading assignments.

Table 11.3

Rathus Assertiveness Schedule

Directions: Indicate how characteristic or descriptive each of the following statements is of you by using the code given below.

+3 very characteristic of me, extremely descriptive[a]
+2 rather characteristic of me, quite descriptive
+1 somewhat characteristic of me, slightly descriptive
−1 somewhat uncharacteristic of me, slightly nondescriptive
−2 rather uncharacteristic of me, quite nondescriptive
−3 very uncharacteristic of me, extremely nondescriptive

_____ 1. Most people seem to be more aggressive and assertive than I am.*

_____ 2. I have hesitated to make or accept dates because of "shyness."*

_____ 3. When the food served at a restaurant is not done to my satisfaction, I complain about it to the waiter or waitress.

_____ 4. I am careful to avoid hurting other people's feelings, even when I feel that I have been injured.*

_____ 5. If a salesman has gone to considerable trouble to show me merchandise that is not quite suitable, I have a difficult time in saying "No."*

_____ 6. When I am asked to do something, I insist upon knowing why.

_____ 7. There are times when I look for a good, vigorous argument.

_____ 8. I strive to get ahead as well as most people in my position.

_____ 9. To be honest, people often take advantage of me.*

_____ 10. I enjoy starting conversations with new acquaintances and strangers.

_____ 11. I often don't know what to say to attractive persons of the opposite sex.*

_____ 12. I will hesitate to make phone calls to business establishments and institutions.*

_____ 13. I would rather apply for a job or for admission to a college by writing letters than by going through with personal interviews.*

_____ 14. I find it embarrassing to return merchandise.*

_____ 15. If a close and respected relative were annoying me, I would smother my feelings rather than express my annoyance.*

_____ 16. I have avoided asking questions for fear of sounding stupid.*

_____ 17. During an argument I am sometimes afraid that I will get so upset that I will shake all over.*

_____ 18. If a famed and respected lecturer makes a statement that I think is incorrect, I will have the audience hear my point of view as well.

_____ 19. I avoid arguing over prices with clerks and salesmen.*

_____ 20. When I have done something important or worthwhile, I manage to let others know about it.

_____ 21. I am open and frank about my feelings.

_____ 22. If someone has been spreading false and bad stories about me, I see him (her) as soon as possible to "have a talk" about it.

_____ 23. I often have a hard time saying "No."*

_____ 24. I tend to bottle up my emotions rather than make a scene.*

_____ 25. I complain about poor service in a restaurant and elsewhere.

_____ 26. When I am given a compliment, I sometimes just don't know what to say.*

_____ 27. If a couple near me in a theater or at a lecture were conversing loudly, I would ask them to be quiet or to take their conversation elsewhere.

_____ 28. Anyone attempting to push ahead of me in line is in for a good battle.

_____ 29. I am quick to express an opinion.

_____ 30. There are times when I just can't say anything.*

[a]Total score obtained by adding numerical responses to each item, after changing the sings of reversed items.
*Reversed item.

Source: From Rathus, S. A. (1998). A 30-item schedule for assessing assertive behavior. *Behavior Therapy, 4,* 399–400. Reproduced with the permission of the Association for Advancement of Behavior Therapy.

Step 2: Identifying Target Behaviors

Once the client has a grasp of the theory, move on to specific areas of concern with the client, agreeing upon the specific assertive behaviors that would help the client feel a greater sense of confidence in a particular situation. Have the client list these behaviors in hierarchical order, based on his or her evaluation about how easy or difficult each behavior would be to perform. The general principle is that clients move from mastery of easy behaviors to more difficult ones. In the following example, a helper and client identify steps to confronting her boss.

Nadine, a graphic artist, wanted to be more assertive at work. The helper, Pat, asked her to identify a specific situation that, if changed, would help her feel more confident and assertive. Nadine indicated that she would like to be able to respond more assertively to her boss's criticism, which she sees as unjustified. He normally walked by her office every morning, looked over her shoulder, then made negative comments about her work. Nadine usually said nothing, but just listened until the boss was finished. This left her feeling upset and self-critical for at least an hour.

Nadine and Pat explored and listed the kinds of assertive things she would like to do when the boss came by for an inspection. Nadine ordered them from easiest to most difficult as follows:

1. Ask the boss to go into greater detail, then consider later whether any of the boss's criticisms constituted valuable feedback.
2. Remind the boss that the idea he is criticizing is not hers.
3. Remind the boss that the design he is criticizing was approved by him.
4. Disagree with the boss's criticism but agree to change the product.
5. Disagree with the boss's criticism and politely argue for her own viewpoint.

Step 3: Present a Model of Assertive Behavior

If the client is working in a group situation, he or she will undoubtedly have the opportunity to see role-playing situations in which a person demonstrates assertive behavior. This can go a long way in easing the client's fears that assertiveness is destructive. In an individual counseling setting, you, the helper, will need to demonstrate assertive behavior for the client. For example, in working with Nadine, Pat asked Nadine to select a response on the list that she was ready to practice. Nadine selected item 1, and Pat initiated a role-play situation in which Nadine was asked to play the part of the boss and Pat explored the boss's criticism to see what constructive elements there might be. Nadine felt that Pat's behavior was not aggressive and she said she thought she was ready to try this herself.

Step 4: Rehearsal and Feedback

Once the client has seen a positive model, he or she must rehearse assertive behavior in a role-playing situation, receiving feedback from the helper or other trainees in an assertiveness training class.

At this stage, Pat arranged her office to fit Nadine's description of her workplace. Then she and Nadine role-played the morning ritual in which the boss came in and began criticizing Nadine's work. This time, Pat played the role of the boss and Nadine, in her own way, practiced listening nondefensively, searching for the constructive elements (item 1 on her list). Pat then gave her feedback on her performance, mentioning both positive behaviors and ways to improve.

Step 5: Give a Homework Assignment to Be Assertive

Homework assignments are real life practice sessions. Normally, the client and the helper choose an assertive behavior from the client's own list, beginning with the easiest one and progressing until all behaviors have been displayed.

Pat and Nadine agreed that the next time the boss came by, she would begin to respond assertively by asking him to go into greater detail concerning his criticisms, then politely reminding him that she did not select the design. Pat suggested that the real situation might not go as smoothly as the practice session. She and Nadine talked about the possibility that the boss might not cooperate with her assertive behavior and might even leave the room. They agreed that Nadine was not to concern herself with his behavior, but was simply to begin trying out her assertive skills.

Problems and Precautions of Assertiveness Training

Sometimes clients complain that although they may look assertive (display the appropriate nonverbals), they do not feel assertive and are scared or angry during their practice of assertive behaviors. Explain that, initially, one simply tends to go through the motions before actually feeling the results. Alcoholics Anonymous has the following maxim: "Fake it 'til you make it." The saying implies that acquiring a behavior sometimes precedes positive feelings, and that one must persevere.

Occasionally, clients will feel that assertiveness training is inconsistent with their values. Religious clients, in particular, may feel they should be more selfless. Other clients may wrongly believe that the aim of assertiveness training is to turn them into very aggressive persons who are only "looking out for number one." Helpers need to be sensitive to such concerns. Assertiveness can be presented as a social skill designed to ensure that both members in a relationship find satisfaction rather than dominating each other. The education phase of the method is also crucial in eliminating misconceptions that can lessen the client's willingness to participate.

Gambrill (1985) reports that assertive people are not always viewed as positively as are submissive people. This might mean that assertiveness, if only aimed at getting one's needs met or at standing up for one's rights, may have longer term negative effects. The squeaky wheel may get the grease, as the saying goes, but nobody likes to hear the squeaking. However, assertiveness training, as it is now practiced, is more likely to emphasize the use of tentativeness, politeness, and a more humble attitude, especially when dealing with long-term relationships. Reporting a recalcitrant store clerk to the store manager may help a client stand up for his or her rights. On the other hand, applying too much force with family and friends or bosses may be counterproductive, disrupting these relationships and creating adverse consequences.

Other Methods for Assertiveness Training

Broken-Record Technique

This technique is one of the most widely taught assertive tricks. It is especially useful when trying to get a point across to another person who is trying to change the topic instead of responding to your request. The method involves repeating one's feelings, needs, or major points over and over. It is not an attempt to bully the other person into submission; rather, it is an attempt to get the other person to at least acknowledge that a request has been made. For example, consider this exchange between employee and boss:

Employee: "I think this has been a banner year for me. I have broken the company sales record and I would like a raise."

Boss: "This has not been a good year for the company as a whole. The president says we have to keep raises at 3 percent."

Employee: "I understand, but my case is different. I think I deserve a raise."

Boss: "I would like to give everybody a raise in my department."

Employee: "It would be great if everyone got a raise, but I think I have done better than the average employee and I would like a raise. Can you understand that?"

Boss: "Yes, I hear what you are saying."

Fogging

Fogging is letting criticism go in one ear and out the other. Fogging has been very effective for some clients, especially when dealing with family members or others who want to give unsolicited advice or criticism. The client actively listens to the advice giver but is taught to internally dispute the criticism or merely ignore the suggestion. For example, a client was told to silently say the following phrase when criticism from her sister began, "What she is saying is nonsense, I can just ignore it and stay calm."

Summary

Self-esteem has two components: self-worth and efficacy. Enhancing both is critical for boosting self-esteem. Client's with better self-esteem are more likely to succeed in accomplishing other goals. Clients can learn to enhance efficacy by attempting new behaviors and by paying attention to their present strengths and skills. Low self-worth is a general attitude that the self is "not okay," worthless, or ineffective. Low self-worth is responsible for a number of serious psychological conditions, negative emotions, a demoralized attitude toward life. We have explored causes of low self-worth and identified injunctions learned early in life, including drivers, irrational ideas, and negative body image.

In the second half of the chapter, we have looked at two methods for enhancing self-esteem. The first technique, called countering, is aimed at reducing negative self-talk or internal dialogue. The second technique, assertiveness training, helps to decrease criticism from others and enables people to feel more efficacious in social situations. These two techniques are fundamental to working with clients who present with problems of low self-esteem. They are nonetheless dependent on the helper's building an effective therapeutic relationship using the therapeutic building blocks of invitational, reflecting, advanced reflecting skills, and challenging skills. Unless the helper utilizes the building blocks, clients will not be able to explore deeply held beliefs about themselves, question them, and consider new ways of behaving.

Group Exercises

Group Exercise 1: Identifying Irrational Beliefs

Part I

First, form groups of four with each student, in turn, taking on the roles of client, helper, and observers. The client discusses one of the following topics with the helper:

- A time when the client was very angry at someone
- A time when the client was very angry at himself or herself
- A time when someone disappointed the client
- Something the client has a difficult time forgiving

The helper's job is to listen, using all of the skills in the nonjudgmental listening sequence, for 5–10 minutes. He or she is not to make an effort to challenge the client's beliefs, but simply to draw them out.

Observer 1 writes down all of the helper's interventions verbatim. Observer 2 reviews the list of Ellis's seven irrational beliefs described earlier in the chapter. Then, during the session, observer 2 listens carefully to the client's statements and records the gist of those that seem to indicate an underlying irrational belief.

Part II: Debriefing

1. Take a couple of minutes to allow client, helper, and observers to share their thoughts about this exercise.
2. Then, observer 1 gives the helper the list of interventions and feedback about his or her performance on the nonjudgmental listening sequence. The helper can keep the list of interventions and review them later. At this point, the list of interventions should include several paraphrases, reflections of feeling, and perhaps a reflection of meaning or two, depending on the depth of the client's story. If questions predominate, the helper should return to

previous chapters for review, and schedule additional practice sessions with classmates.
3. Observer 2 indicates any irrational ideas that he or she identified in the client's statements. As a group, the helper and the two observers can identify some counters that might be used by the client as an antidote to these beliefs. The client either confirms or disagrees with the observer's ideas and then indicates which he or she feels might be the most effective.

Group Exercise 2: Assertiveness Training

Form groups of three. Members take turns sharing "a time in my life when I was not as assertive as I wanted to be." In this situation, you may have been either too passive or too aggressive. Students take turns as helper, client, and observer. The helper should follow the general steps for assertiveness training given in this chapter. In the preparing and educating phase, be sure to help the client understand the components of an assertive response according to the DERC system. The observer fills out the Feedback Checklist for the helper, giving examples of the various steps.

Feedback Checklist: Assertiveness Training
Observer Name _____   Helper Name _____

Preparing
1. Specifically, how did the helper educate and prepare the client for assertiveness training?
2. Was the preparation relevant to the client's problem?

Specifying the Target Behaviors
3. Did the helper lead the client to focus on a specific situation?

Presenting a Model
4. Did the helper model an appropriate behavior for the client or give examples of statements that might be assertive alternatives to nonassertive client statements? If so, indicate in a few words how the helper did this.

Rehearsal

5. Did the client rehearse a specific behavior that he or she wants to work on?
   a. Did the helper give the client feedback on the rehearsal?
   b. Was this feedback specific and understandable to the client?
   c. How closely did the client's assertive statements mirror the DERC system described earlier in the chapter?

Homework

6. Did the helper suggest homework for the client to practice one of the assertive behaviors?
   a. In your estimation, how likely is the client to actually practice the assertive behavior?
   b. Do you think the helper should have suggested an easier or more difficult behavior to practice?

Quick Tips: Assertiveness Training

- When preparing a client, there is no need to do a complete overview of the field of assertiveness; instead, focus on some ideas that will help the client with a particular problem.
- Preview the technique. Tell the client the steps that you are going to go through.
- Emphasize that assertiveness is a skill not a personality trait. Anyone can learn to be more assertive.
- Show enthusiasm, but indicate that changing to more assertive behavior will be hard work and will feel unnatural at first.
- Feel free to shift gears during the training and return to the nonjudgmental listening cycle if the client needs to talk about the issues, but eventually return to the training sequence.
- Make a hierarchy of the client's assertive behaviors and try to take small steps rather than attack the big issues right away.

Additional Exercises

Exercise 1: Confronting Defense Mechanisms

Form groups of four or five. Review the section on defense mechanisms and the sections on learned helplessness, victimization, and self-handicapping. As a group, devise a role-play in which the client uses defensive mechanisms in a self-defeating way or shows other self-protective strategies. Present your role-play to the class. The student who plays the helper in this exercise should utilize invitational and reflecting skills initially, but should move very quickly to challenging skills. In the class discussion, make a list of discrepancies in the client's story.

Exercise 2

In small groups, conduct a discussion on the dangers of assertiveness training. From your experience, do you think that, during initial training, clients should be warned that they might tend to go overboard and become aggressive when they practice? How important is it for an assertive statement to be polite? Does politeness water down the force of an assertive statement?

Exercise 3

Look at the example in the section on the broken-record technique, in which an employee and a boss are engaged in negotiations over a raise. Was the employee's verbal behavior assertive as judged by the DERC system? If not, how might it be improved? See if you can identify some alternate employee responses that would be too polite or nonassertive and some that represent the other end of the scale—too aggressive.

Homework

Homework 1: Personal Experiments

Think about something that you don't do very well, or think about a part of your body that you do not feel is very attractive. Get opinions from eight friends or family members. How accurate is your self-concept? If they do not agree, why do you cling to this belief? In what ways have you distorted your view of the self? Write a half-page reaction to this exercise.

Homework 2: Assertiveness Script Writing

One way that clients can rehearse assertiveness is to write out "scripts" or imaginary conversations with someone with whom they would like to be assertive. Think about a situation in your own life and write out what you would like to say. Write the other person's likely responses, even if you believe the person will not grant your request or appreciate your feelings. Remember that your initial goal is to respond in the way you would like, in a caring but firm way. Next, make a second version of your script, improving your statements to make them clearer. Give a copy of your script to a classmate for feedback on the effectiveness of your assertive responses.

Journal Starters

1. Sometimes helpers ask clients to consider incidents in their lives in which low self-esteem might have originated. For example, was the client affected by excessive criticism or perfectionistic expectations? Some authors have even said that self-concept is "the reflected appraisals of others." On the other hand, Eleanor Roosevelt believed that no one can make you feel bad about yourself without your permission. Think about your own life experiences and decide which view is closest to your opinion on the subject? Are both true for you?

2. In the Group Exercises in this chapter, you were asked to think about a time when you were not as assertive as you wished you had been. Reflect on that incident for a moment. What historical, cultural, and family issues are bound up with the concept of assertiveness? Is the concept of assertiveness congruent with your cultural or family background? If not, what is the most acceptable way that it might be presented to someone like you? In other words, if you went to a helper, what would be needed before you would be able to feel good about learning to be more assertive?

References

Adams, G. R. (1977). Physical attractiveness research: Toward a developmental social psychology of beauty. *Human Development, 20,* 217–239.

Alberti, R. E. (Ed.). (1977). *Assertiveness: Innovations, applications, issues.* San Luis Obispo, CA: Impact.

Alberti, R. E., & Emmons, M. L. (1974). *Your perfect right: A guide to assertive behavior.* San Luis Obispo, CA: Impact.

Baird, P., & Sights, J. R. (1986). Low self-esteem as a treatment issue in the psychology of anorexia and bulimia. *Journal of Counseling and Development, 64,* 449–451.

Bandura, A. (1982). Self-efficacy mechanism in human agency. *American Psychologist, 37,* 122–147.

Bandura, A. (1997). *Self-efficacy: The exercise of control.* New York: Freeman.

Beck, A. T., Rush, A. J., Shaw, B. F., & Emery, G. (1979). *Cognitive therapy of depression.* New York: Guilford.

Bednar, R. L., & Peterson, S. R. (1995). *Self-esteem: Paradoxes and innovations in clinical theory and practice.* Washington, DC: American Psychological Association.

Berne, E. (1972). *What do you say after you say hello?* New York: Grove Press.

Branden, N. (1969). *The psychology of self esteem.* Los Angeles: Nash.

Branden, N. (1971). *The disowned self.* New York: Bantam.

Brehm, M., & Back, W. (1968). Self image and attitude towards drugs. *Journal of Personality, 36,* 299–314.

Burns, D. D. (1999). *Ten days to self-esteem.* New York: Quill.

Carlock, C. J. (1998). *Enhancing self-esteem* (3rd ed.). Muncie, IN: Accelerated Development.

Daly, M. J., & Burton, R. L. (1983). Self-esteem and irrational beliefs: An exploratory investigation with implications for counseling. *Journal of Counseling Psychology, 30,* 361–366.

Davis, M., Eshelman, E. R., & McKay, M. (1980). *The relaxation and stress reduction workbook.* Richmond, CA: New Harbinger.

Dowd, E. T. (1985). Self statement modification. In A. S. Bellack & M. Hersen (Eds.), *Dictionary of behavior therapy techniques* (p. 200). New York: Pergamon.

Egan, G. (1990). *The skilled helper* (4th ed.). Pacific Grove, CA: Brooks/Cole.

Ellis, A. (1973). *Humanistic psychotherapy.* New York: McGraw-Hill.

Enns, C. Z. (1996). Self-esteem groups: A synthesis of consciousness-raising and assertiveness training. *Journal of Counseling and Development, 71,* 7–13.

Epstein, S. (1983). Natural healing processes of the mind: Gradual stress inoculation as an inherent coping mechanism. In D. Meichenbaum & M. S. Jaremko (Eds.), *Stress reduction and prevention* (pp. 39–65). New York: Plenum.

Gambrill, E. (1985). Assertiveness training. In A. S. Bellack & M. Hersen (Eds.), *Dictionary of behavior therapy techniques* (pp. 7–9). New York: Pergamon.

Goleman, D. (1995). *Emotional intelligence: Why it can matter more than IQ.* New York: Bantam.

Grayson, P. A. (1986). Disavowing the past: A maneuver to protect self-esteem. *Individual Psychology: Adlerian Theory, Research and Practice, 42,* 330–338.

Greenspan, M. (1983). *A new approach to women and therapy.* New York: McGraw-Hill.

Ingham, J. G., Kreitman, N. B., Miller, P. M., & Sasidharan, S. P. (1986). Self-esteem, vulnerability and psychiatric disorder in the community. *British Journal of Psychiatry, 148,* 373–385.

Kahler, T. (1977). The miniscript. In G. Barnes (Ed.), *Transactional analysis after Eric Berne* (pp. 220–241). New York: Harpers College Press.

Kaplan, L. (1995). Self-esteem is not our national wonder drug. *School Counselor, 42,* 341–345.

Kurpius, D., Rockwood, G. F., & Corbett, M. O. (1989). Attributional styles and self-esteem: Implications for counseling. *Counseling and Human Development, 21*(8), 1–12.

Lazarus, A. A. (1971). *Behavior therapy and beyond.* New York: McGraw-Hill.

Lazarus, R. S., & Folkman, S. (1984). *Stress, appraisal, and coping.* New York: Springer.

Lazarus, R. S., & Golden, G. (1981). The function of denial in stress, coping and aging. In E. McGarraugh & S. Kiessler (Eds.), *Biology, behavior and aging.* New York: Academic Press.

McKay, M., & Fanning, P. (1987). *Self-esteem.* Oakland, CA: New Harbinger.

McMullin, R. E. (2000). *The new handbook of cognitive therapy techniques.* New York: Norton.

Rathus, S. A. (1973). A 30-item schedule for assessing assertive behavior. *Behavior Therapy, 4,* 398–406.

Rathus, S. A. (1975). Principles and practices of assertiveness training: An eclectic overview. *Counseling Psychologist, 5,* 9–20.

Rosenberg, M. (1962). The association between self-esteem and anxiety. *Journal of Psychiatric Research, 1,* 135–152.

Seligman, M. E. P. (1975). *Helplessness: On depression, development, and death.* New York: Freeman.

Smith, M. J. (1975). *When I say no, I feel guilty.* New York: Bantam.

Smith, T. W., Snyder, C. R., & Handelman, M. M. (1981). On the self-serving function of an academic wooden leg: Test anxiety as a self-handicapping strategy. *Journal of Personality and Social Psychology, 42,* 314–321.

Street, S., & Issacs, M. (1998). Self-esteem: Justifying its existence. *Professional School Counseling, 1,* 46–50.

Tanner, V. L., & Holliman, W. B. (1988). Effectiveness of assertiveness training in modifying aggressive behaviors in young children. *Psychological Reports, 62,* 39–46.

Thompson, J. K., & Thompson, C. M. (1986). Body size distortion and self-esteem in asymptomatic, normal weight males and females. *International Journal of Eating Disorders, 5,* 1061–1068.

Thompson, S. C. (1991). Intervening to enhance perceptions of control. In C. R. Snyder & D. R. Forsyth (Eds.), *Handbook of social and clinical psychology* (pp. 607–623). New York: Simon & Schuster.

Tucker, J. A., Vuchinich, R. E., & Sobell, M. B. (1981). Alcohol consumption as a self-handicapping strategy. *Journal of Abnormal Psychology, 90,* 220–230.

Walz, G. (1990). *Counseling for self esteem.* Alexandria, VA: American Association for Counseling and Development.

Wilson, A., & Krane, R. (1980). Change in self esteem and its effect on symptoms of depression. *Cognitive Therapy and Research, 4,* 419–421.

Witmer, J. M. (1985). *Pathways to personal growth: Developing a sense of worth and competence.* Muncie, IN: Accelerated Development.

Yalom, I. R. (1995). *The theory and practice of group psychotherapy* (4th ed.). New York: Basic Books.

Practicing New Behaviors

12

Anyone who has ever learned to play a musical instrument or gained proficiency in a sport knows the value and the drudgery of practice. Practice is also an integral part of any educational curriculum. Besides the fact that practice helps to perfect a skill, it is also the key to success in making a change permanent. What is tentative at first, through practice, becomes second nature.

Helping can be conceived of as a learning process, too. The "psychoeducational" approach to helping is exemplified by all sorts of skill-based therapies, which you will learn more about in Chapter 15 (Guerney, Stollack, & Guerney, 1971; Schutz, 1981; Young & Rosen, 1985). Clients often need to learn such behaviors as better parenting, communication skills, facing fearful situations, or developing effective thinking skills. As an educator, the helper cannot be content for the client to eliminate a problem behavior or merely gain insight into the fact that he or she is operating in a self-defeating manner. Clients must overcome the force of old habits by establishing a new pattern of behaviors through practice and rehearsal.

Figure 12.1
Curative Factors in the REPLAN System: Practicing New Behaviors

The best instruction for any skill includes the following sequence: (1) Some theory is explained that provides a rationale for learning the new skill; (2) the learner is exposed to a model who correctly demonstrates the skill; and (3) in-class practice and homework assignments require that the learner demonstrate the behavior in the real world. For example, if you were learning to play the guitar, the instructor might explain the fingering using a chart or graph. Then the instructor would probably demonstrate how the piece is to be played, or you might listen to a recording of the selection. You would then attempt the music with the instructor present and later you would be sent home to practice. The process of acquiring a new behavior or a new thinking pattern takes place in much the same way. Helpers use each of these steps when teaching a new skill: explanation of theory, modeling, and in-session practice and homework.

In this chapter, we will focus on three specific methods used to aid clients in practicing new skills: imaginal rehearsal, role-playing, and homework. These three techniques exist on a continuum, with imaginal rehearsal being an exclusively mental practice, role-playing being even closer to real life, and homework or independent practice as the final step. The helper must select the level of practice that the client needs, based on the client's readiness. Clients who cannot see themselves attempting a new behavior will benefit from imagining a successful performance first. Then they can move to the next level of practice, role-playing, with the helper present. Finally, they are ready to try out a new behavior in a natural situation as a homework assignment.

Imagery in Helping

Imagery has become more popular in recent years after a long period of neglect in the helping professions; it is now used for a variety of purposes (Gladding, 1986; Shorr, 1994). Imagery techniques have been used to help clients plan for the future, enhance career development, gain control over undesirable behavior, treat physical illness, improve memory, reduce stress, treat physical illness, and increase creativity and problem solving in everyday living (Pope, 1982; Sheikh, 1983). Imagery has been used successfully with adults and children (Witmer & Young, 1985, 1987). A few examples of client problems currently treated with imagery show its range. These include bulimia (Gunnison & Renick, 1985), career indecision (Sarnoff & Remer, 1982; Skovholt, Morgan, & Negron-Cunningham, 1989), posttraumatic stress disorder (Grigsby, 1987), smoking (Wynd, 1992), and parenting decision making (Skovholt & Thoen, 1987).

Imagery for Skill Development

Have you ever seen Olympic divers on the three-meter board go through the preparation for a dive? Typically, they close their eyes and imagine the twists and turns they must make. Sometimes they even display minor muscle movements that mimic the dive they are imagining. Imagery, when practiced regularly, has been found to enhance performance in a variety of situations from sports to social skills (Fezler, 1989). Mental, or imaginal, rehearsal has sometimes been termed *covert rehearsal* (Bellack, 1986; Kazdin, 1978). The term *covert* in this context means hidden or invisible, as contrasted with the term *in vivo,* which means behaviorally or in real life. Imaginal rehearsal allows a client to practice a skill when live practice is not feasible (Cautela & Bennet, 1981). Live practice may not be possible because the client's emotional state is such that confronting the real life situation would be too stressful or the opportunity for practice in a real situation is not available on a regular basis. Imaginal rehearsal can be accomplished in minutes, may be repeated several times in a therapeutic session, and can be assigned as homework, too.

Stop and Reflect

Take a few minutes, close your eyes, and imagine the following scenes, one by one:

Group A
   1. A bowl of fruit that has just been taken out of the refrigerator and placed on a table; moisture is condensing on the surface
   2. The place where you live, starting with the front door and moving through all of the rooms

Group B
   1. The sound of an engine starting
   2. The cry of seagulls or the sounds birds make in the morning

Group C
   1. The smell of food frying
   2. The smell of a rose

Group D
1. The feel of a warm shower
2. A pin prick on your finger

Group E
1. The taste of a lemon being squeezed into your mouth
2. The taste of dark chocolate

- People differ in their ability to imagine. Some of us cannot imagine or sustain an image in our minds. This is not a handicap, but an individual difference. Clients who have little ability to imagine will not benefit much from imaginal rehearsal. Out of the preceding scenarios, how many were you able to imagine clearly?
- Each group represents a different sense modality: sight, hearing, smell, touch, and taste. Go back and rate each image on a 10-point scale, indicating how vivid it was for you. A 1 indicates very fuzzy imagery and a 10 indicates very clear and vivid imagery. Do you find any differences among the groups in terms of what you can imagine? If you were a client, which sensory modality could a helper use most effectively with you?

How to Conduct Imaginal Rehearsal

Step 1: Assess the Client's Potential for Imagery Work and Identify the Target Behaviors

Because not all clients can produce vivid, controllable imagery, begin by testing the client's ability to form and sustain vivid images like the ones in the "Stop and Reflect" section. Clients who have great difficulty in this regard will probably benefit more from another kind of rehearsal.

Once imagery has been selected as a technique to address a client's goals, the first task of the client and the helper is to cooperatively transform the client's goal into a list of skills (target behaviors) that are required to perform the desired task successfully. For example, Danielle would like to be able to ask someone out for a date, but she lacks confidence since she is recently divorced and has not dated for several years. She and the helper, Ben, break the skill into the following components:

1. Dialing the phone
2. Greeting Tom (a co-worker she has become interested in)
3. Describing the outdoor jazz concert
4. Asking Tom to join her at the concert
5. Politely ending the call

Those who are adept at social skills might find this list simplistic and rather clinical. It may come as a surprise to know that helpers are commonly asked by clients to help them acquire elementary social skills such as making small talk, telling friends how they feel about them, or asking for a raise. Having a script like Danielle's can significantly reduce anxiety for someone who is trying an unfamiliar activity. It prepares him or her for various consequences and instills confidence.

Step 2: Prepare the Client for Imagery

Imaginal rehearsal is ideally performed in a quiet environment, away from glaring lights, with eyes closed. The helper may reassure the client that the technique is not hypnosis but an active rehearsal process. The purpose is explained as a method of learning to avoid or to eliminate negative images of failure and to develop positive, successful ones. In our example, Ben explains to Danielle that she is not simply trying to get a date. The real goal is to develop the social skills that will make her more comfortable and effective in similar situations in the future.

Step 3: Give Directives to the Client—Imagine Each of the Target Behaviors

The client is reminded of the first target behavior on the list and is instructed to visualize performing it in a specific situation in which it is likely to occur. The helper asks the client to visualize each successive aspect of the behavior, moving ahead only when the client can vividly imagine that step. During this process, it is important to carry on a dialogue with the client to make certain that the client has a clear understanding of each step and can accurately and vividly imagine it. This is a stop-and-go procedure, during which the helper is testing to make sure the client can imagine completing each individual skill in a competent manner.

Step 4: Give Directives to the Client—Imagine a Successful Sequence

Once each step has been visualized, the client is then guided through the entire sequence by the helper, this time without stopping. The description is done in the present tense as if the helper were telling a story. For example, Ben says to Danielle, "It is late afternoon on Saturday and you decide to call Tom. You go to your bedroom with a glass of water in case your mouth gets dry. You look up Tom's number and dial it. When he answers, you say, 'Hi Tom, this is Danielle, how are you? When he responds, you tell him a little bit about the jazz concert next Friday night. You tell him it is outdoors and you thought it might be fun. You say you are wondering if he is free to come along."

At this point, Ben asks Danielle to rehearse two different endings. In the first scenario, Ben suggests she imagine the following: "Tom apologizes and says he can't come. You say, 'Oh, too bad, maybe another time. I'll see you at work next week, okay?' " In the second scenario, Ben instructs her to imagine that Tom says "Yes." In that case, she is to arrange a time and place for their meeting.

Step 5: Give Directives to the Client—Imagine Reinforcement

At the end of the first complete visualization, the client receives a covert reinforcement or imagined reward. In this example, for both scenarios, Ben instructs Danielle to imagine herself sitting on the bed after hanging up, congratulating herself for having made the call, and feeling good about having practiced a difficult new skill.

Problems and Precautions with Imaginal Rehearsal

1. Imagery tends to evoke a much fuller experience of remembered events than simply talking about them. Some clients may be overwhelmed by these feelings and may require support from the helper if the imagery involves painful

events from the past. This is a cue for the helper to ask the client to open his or her eyes. The helper then shifts gears and returns to the nonjudgmental listening cycle. Although the focus of the imagery technique is on positive future performance, memories of past failures occasionally intrude. Through practice, the client will be able to keep attention focused on the successful scenario.

2. Clients differ in their capacity to produce imagery. The ability of individuals to produce vivid images can be tested and improved by methods described by Lazarus (1984). In our experience, about 10% of clients in group settings report an inability to sustain mental imagery long enough for helping purposes. Some clients feel inadequate because of this, and it is important to explain that the technique is not essential for helping to take place. Other rehearsal methods are available.

3. Some clients resist imagery because of anxiety, embarrassment, or fear of losing control. They may feel that they are being hypnotized and object to it. Sometimes lack of vividness or the inability to imagine may be the result of a client's fear of losing control. Clients can be reassured that learning to develop imagery will actually lead to greater mental control. If negative imagery can be controlled, anxiety about improbable imagined events can be eliminated.

4. Imagery techniques are not appropriate for individuals reporting hallucinations or delusions.

5. Some children may overuse fantasy and story telling as an escape. They may wish to use magical images rather than acquiring social tools to deal with problems.

Role-Playing

Role-playing is a technique commonly used by helpers in social-skills training and for helping clients face situations they are avoiding (Kipper, 1986). It involves practicing a behavior in a contrived situation with the helper playing an auxiliary or observer role. It may also take place in a group setting with other participants who can give valuable feedback and act as auxiliaries. Role-playing is frequently confused with a Gestalt therapy technique called "the empty chair." The empty chair is a role-playing method, originated by Moreno, in which an individual holds a dialogue between two warring parts of the self. Role-playing is not limited to an internal dialogue. Instead, an individual can create conversations with other people as he or she perceives them, constructing scenarios that approximate the actual setting.

Role-playing was introduced by the creative genius, J. L. Moreno, a Viennese psychiatrist who formulated the psychodramatic method. Moreno has been called the "father of group therapy" because he was one of its first practitioners and because he developed a number of important group techniques. However, Moreno was a very controversial figure. He had a revolutionary bent, sometimes expressed in virulent attacks against psychoanalysis and other forms of therapy. It is probably for this reason that his contribution to the helping professions is largely unacknowledged. On one occasion, following a lecture by Freud, Moreno is said to have responded, "Well, Dr. Freud, I start where you leave off. You meet people in the artificial setting of your office. I meet them on the street and in their home, in their natural surroundings. You analyze their dreams. I try to give them the courage to dream again . . ." (Moreno, 1964, pp. 5–6). Moreno's response reflects his belief that helping should involve learning in as naturalistic a setting as possible. Part of what Moreno objected to in traditional therapies was the separation of a client's problems from the natural environment, just as a religious sculpture or painting cannot be fully appreciated in a museum but must be seen in a church or temple. Since it is not always possible to see individuals in their natural contexts, the psychodramatic method proposes to recreate an individual's joys and sorrows on the psychodramatic stage (Starr, 1977). Moreno's famous dictum was, "Show me, don't tell me!" He felt that most "talk therapies" relied on the client's descriptions of problems. Since we cannot reach into the subjective experience of the person through words, we should transfer the mind onto the stage where the person's total behavior, including thoughts, feelings, and intuitions, are observable and changeable. Those who want to learn more about psychodrama should consult Adam Blatner's book, *Acting-In: Practical Applications of Psychodramatic Methods* (1998).

Elements of Role-Playing

The technique of role-playing is a limited form of psychodrama and usually involves an encounter between two individuals or two or more different parts of the self (monodrama). Role-playing can be performed by a single individual (the protagonist) who plays all of the roles in the drama, or with the help of other individuals called auxiliaries.

Three Phases of Psychodramatic Role-Playing

Psychodramatic role-playing has always been conceived of as having three phases: warmup, action, and sharing (Yablonsky, 1976). Each of the three phases of psychodynamic role-playing is described next.

Warmup

The warmup is any activity that helps the client get in touch emotionally with the experience he or she is trying to express. The warmup decreases stage fright and allows the protagonist to develop readiness and involvement in the process. Most of us have warmups, or rituals, we use to prepare us for action. For example, the runner does stretching exercises and the actor rehearses lines. In role-playing, proper warmup is crucial to the success of the technique. Warmup might include asking the protagonist to discuss the situation or introducing a physical activity, such as pacing back and forth.

The helper may also use *role reversal* to allow the client to experience the other person's viewpoint. In role reversal, the helper instructs the client to pretend to be the other person and respond as he or she might. For example, the client changes places and sits on the empty chair that previously represented his mother. He responds as his mother might respond in a similar circumstance. Role reversal is one of the most effective ways of getting the client involved in the role-play. Besides, role reversal makes the situation more real. The client is able to anticipate the responses of a significant other and strategies can be devised to cope with them.

The phrase "moving from the periphery to the center" is connected to the notion of a warmup. It is a rule of thumb or a reminder to the helper to begin with tangential events before moving to more significant or central issues. For example, if the role-play involves returning home to see a dying grandfather, the helper would not begin with the deathbed confrontation, but would move the client through several less potent scenes. In this case, these scenes might include driving to the house while reminiscing about the relationship or replaying previous encounters between the two. This method also gives the helper more information about the client and the client's relationships and life circumstances. With sufficient warmup, the client overcomes stage fright and is more in tune with the actual role-play when it takes place.

Action

After the warmup, the helper asks the client to take on his or her own role and enact the situation. Scene setting is the preliminary step of this action phase. It involves asking the protagonist to set up the stage to resemble the actual setting where the incident took place or where the behavior will possibly occur in the future. The client is given free rein to use available props and to orient the stage in whatever way feels comfortable. The helper assists the client in defining the stage, designating the time of day and date, describing the situation verbally, using props, and identifying important people to be portrayed.

Sharing and Analysis

In group therapy, the sharing phase of role-playing allows the individual to reenter the group situation, that is, to get out of the spotlight. The other group members use this opportunity to relate personal experiences evoked by the client's role-play. This technique reinvolves the audience and helps the client feel less alone and exposed. At some later time, a feedback or analysis session is held, during which members give feedback to the client and the role-play is discussed. In an individual session, the helper normally gives the client feedback immediately after each role-play.

How to Conduct Role-Playing

Role-playing is one of the most effective ways of practicing a new behavior. The immediate observation and feedback allow for actual practice, not simply talking about problems. At a deeper level, role-playing and role reversal can help the individual to become more fully aware of feelings and to explore the phenomenological worlds of the significant people in his or her life.

The method described here is a generic role-playing technique for practicing new behavior. To make the method easier to understand, a hypothetical example unfolds throughout the explanation. The client, Martin, is anxious because he has to give a presentation to his board of directors concerning progress on his yearly goals. The helper, Andrea, suggests that they role-play the situation to rehearse his talk.

Step 1: Warmup

In the warmup, Andrea previews and explains the purpose and the elements of role-playing. Using the principle of proceeding from the periphery to the center, Andrea begins the warmup by asking Martin to discuss aspects of his job that he will be presenting, details of the workplace, and other tangential topics. The most important aspect of this step is for Andrea to get Martin to describe the target behaviors very specifically. In this case, he wants to:

1. Maintain eye contact with his audience.
2. Speak from notes in a loud, clear voice.

3. Smile when questions are asked.
4. End the session by thanking the audience.

Step 2: Scene Setting

After Martin has discussed the situation, he appears more relaxed. Andrea then invites him to describe his own office (peripheral) and later the board meeting room (central). Andrea then lets Martin set the scene, rearranging Andrea's office furnishings to approximate the setup of the boardroom. Andrea encourages Martin to point out various features such as the color of the walls and the furniture to establish the scene.

Step 3: Selecting Roles and Role Reversal

In this step, the client identifies important people in the scene and briefly describes them. In a group setting, other members of the group would be assigned to these roles. In an individual session, empty chairs represent these significant persons. For example, Andrea asks Martin to reverse roles and pretend to be his boss to get a sense of his demeanor and attitude. She also asks him to point out the chairs of some of the other board members and briefly describe them.

Step 4: Enactment

At this point, the helper asks the client to briefly portray the target behaviors as described during the warmup. In Martin's case, the scene begins in his office and culminates with his entrance into the "boardroom." Andrea acts as a coach during the first run-through, prompting Martin to display each identified behavior. The helper is dissatisfied with Martin's portrayal of the final behavior, thanking the audience. Andrea stops the action and takes on Martin's role to model an effective closing statement. Following the modeling, Andrea asks Martin to try the closing a second time in his own way using whatever parts of Andrea's closing he liked.

Step 5: Sharing and Feedback

In this step, the helper shares feedback with the client. The feedback should be specific, simple, observable, and understandable to the client. It should mainly reinforce positive aspects of the behavior. In our example, Andrea tells Martin, "Your voice was very strong and clear. I think you got your points across very well. I would like to see even more eye contact with the board members during the next run-through."

Step 6: Reenactment

Reenactment is a repetition of the target behavior from entrance to exit. The sequence is repeated until the client is confident that each of the behaviors in the target list has been mastered.

Step 7: Homework and Follow-Up

At the next session, the client is asked to report practice results. Martin has practiced the behavior by giving the presentation to some family members, and he describes this to Andrea. Further role-playing practice may be given during the session, if necessary. When the helper feels that the client has consistently demonstrated the target behaviors, the helper urges the client to attempt the behaviors in a real situation.

Problems and Precautions with Role-Playing

1. The most frequently encountered difficulty with the role-playing technique is stage fright. Resistance to the technique is ordinarily the result of insufficient warmup, inadequate preparation time, the client's lack of confidence, or inadequate reassurance by the helper.
2. Because of the power of the technique, both the helper and the client may be unprepared for the strength of the emotion that is sometimes evoked. This is unlikely when using role-playing for practicing a new behavior. Beginning helpers should not attempt to reenact traumatic scenes from the past.
3. Because most helpers are focused on the client's thoughts and feelings, we sometimes have trouble thinking in dramatic terms. In the usual session, the client is encouraged to describe an encounter with another person by saying, "I am angry because she neglected me." In a role-playing session, the client would be instructed, "Show me how you expressed your anger to her." By creating a dramatic situation, the helper learns a great deal about the quality and context of the behavior, rather than just the client's description of it.

Homework

Homework has been identified as a crucial tool in effective helping (Beck, Rush, Shaw, & Emery, 1979; Ellis, 1962; Shelton & Ackerman, 1974). Homework refers to any tasks or assignments given to clients to be completed between sessions (Last, 1985). Some tasks are used for assessment purposes; others are used to increase client awareness of the behavior (Martin & Worthington, 1982); still other homework assignments are designed as independent practice sessions.

In this section, the main emphasis will be on homework that is used to practice new behaviors. These new behaviors are normally learned during the therapeutic session and may be modeled or rehearsed in the office before they are assigned as homework. Review of homework provides a starting point for each new session with a review of progress made and problems encountered in the assignment.

Reasons for Using Homework

A major advantage of using homework assignments is that it provides follow-up or treatment continuance between sessions. When one realizes that a client spends 1 hour out of 112 waking hours per week in counseling, it is easy to see how helping can be diluted by other activities. Homework assignments, especially if they require some daily work, can enhance treatment considerably (Shelton & Ackerman, 1974; Shelton & Levy, 1981). Second, homework assignments turn insights and awareness into tangible behaviors and prevent helping from being only a place to unload one's feelings. Transfer of training or generalization of learning is facilitated by applying descriptions and models of behavior to real-life situations as soon as possible. Homework practice also begins the shift of control from the helper to the client. If the client attributes progress to his or her own effort in outside assignments, greater efficacy and self-esteem will result.

Examples of Homework Assignments

Bibliotherapy

Bibliotherapy means assigning readings to clients to help them achieve their goals. The plethora of self-help books now on the market is evidence of a growing awareness that psychological literature can bring about change; however, much of the offerings in trade books is oversimplified, based on opinion or a few anecdotes. Before recommending a book to a client, the helper should have read the book and should carefully think about whether the book will be acceptable to the client's present frame of reference and assist with the client's goals. At each session, the helper should discuss the client's reading and go over important points, perhaps even asking a few relevant questions as to how the assignment fits the client's current dilemma.

Although it is not possible to provide an exhaustive list of good bibliographic materials here, resources for selecting books and manuals are available (cf. Glasgow & Rosen, 1978). A very good stress management workbook-and-tape set, *Kicking Your Stress Habits* (Tubesing, 1981), is available. Many clients with marital problems have benefited from Michele Weiner-Davis's (1992) *Divorce-Busting,* while David Burns's (1999) *Feeling Good* contains an excellent cognitive approach to depression that the average person can easily grasp. A number of other books, such as Arnold Lazarus's (1982) *Personal Enrichment through Imagery,* are now available on audiotape and can be listened to while driving or relaxing.

Besides informing the client, bibliotherapy can provide covert practice by exposing the client to a fictional or historical model of a desired behavior. Clients may identify with case studies or with fictional characters who face similar problems. The "Big Book" of Alcoholics Anonymous contains a number of true accounts of individuals who have successfully overcome drinking problems.

Aides

One way to increase the efficacy of homework practice is to enlist the help of a client's friend, spouse, or family member as an aide who provides either feedback or support for completing assignments. Generally, an aide comes to sessions with the client. The helper specifically identifies the aide's role as either support or feedback. Let us say that the client is attempting to become more assertive. The aide would be given specific verbal and nonverbal behaviors to observe and would report observations to the client. Alternately, the aide might simply be enlisted to provide support or to accompany the client while he or she completes assignments. The client who is attempting to exercise regularly may use an aide as a regular walking partner. The aide would help the client increase regularity and provide encouragement from session to session. The major pitfall of using aides is that they must be supervised by the helper. Sometimes aides are too helpful and wish to take excessive responsibility for the client. If this behavior cannot be modified, the client should proceed alone.

Journaling and Record Keeping

Journaling is a daily writing assignment given to the client by the helper. Ordinarily, the client brings these journals to the next session for the helper's reaction. Journals usually serve one of two purposes. Sometimes journals are assigned as an open-ended writing assignment to help the client do more in-depth examination of his or her thoughts, feelings, and behaviors.

Alternately, the helper may use journaling to record practice sessions. These might include keeping track of countering skills (cognitive), recording the amount of emotional discomfort (affective), or noting the number of times a new behavior was actually practiced (behavioral).

Consider the following case study of Joe, a 29-year-old administrator for an insurance company who has come for help to deal with problems associated with "stress." He has borderline high blood pressure, is often tense and angry after work, and, as a result, sometimes becomes rude to his fiancée, alienating her. He plays racquetball competitively, and last week he purposefully broke an expensive racquet after a bad shot. He wishes to control his anger and feel less "stressed" at work.

During the assessment, the counselor identified negative self-statements as a major cause of the client's stress and felt that, in general, the most useful path for Joe was to increase self-esteem. Joe agreed, but also felt he needed better organizational skills. The initial plan was negotiated as a two-pronged attack: to decrease self-criticism and to develop better time management and organizational skills. Joe enrolled in a 3-day time management workshop sponsored by his company and, at the same time, began keeping a journal, as shown in Table 12.1. Figure 12.2 is a graph of Joe's SUDS levels and negative self-statements over the first 10 days. SUDS is an acronym for subjective units of discomfort scale. In this case, 0 represents no discomfort and 100 represents extreme distress. Using a homework card, Joe found that he was producing anger by his self-statements, which were first aimed at himself and sometimes directed at innocent bystanders. Joe agreed to continue to monitor his self-statements for two more weeks and noticed a marked diminishing of his self-criticism. In Joe's case, there seemed to be a correspondence between his self-criticism and his emotional discomfort. Although the major purpose of keeping this journal was to encourage practice, the client also developed insight into the way he maintained his anger.

Table 12.1
Self-Criticism Homework Card for Joe

No.	Time	Self-Statement	Feeling	SUDS
1.	8:15	I'll never get all this work done.	Discouraged	85
2.	9:00	I didn't do a good job on that report.	Disgust	50
3.	10:00	I'll never be good at this job. I'm just average and that's all.	Self-pity	60
4.	10:35	I'm daydreaming again. Why am I so lazy?	Anger	35
5.	12:00	I offended the secretary again. Why can't I just keep my mouth shut?	Anger	45
6.	1:00	I feel fat after eating so much. I'm turning into a blimp.	Disgust	35
7.	2:40	Another day almost done, and I've completed nothing.	Anger	40
8.	3:30	My desk is a mess. What a slob!	Discouraged	50
9.	5:15	Even my car is full of trash. I wish I were more organized.	Anger	25

SUDS = subjective units of distress

0 100

No emotional distress   Extreme emotional distress

Emotions = fear, anger, sadness, guilt, interest-excitement/(boredom), joy, disgust, surprise

Summary

9 = negative self-statements; average SUDS = 47 (approx.)

Most prevalent emotion = self-anger/disgust

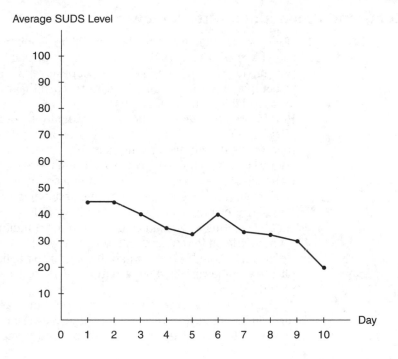

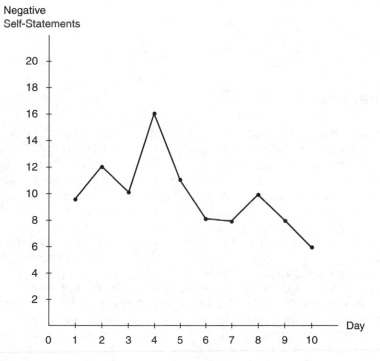

Figure 12.2
Graph of Daily SUDS Levels and Critical Self-Statements for Joe

Problems and Precautions with Homework

1. Homework assignments that have a high probability of success should be chosen (Dyer & Vriend, 1977). This is true especially early in the helping relationship in order to keep the client's hope alive. Also, by promoting small, easily completed goals, the client begins to learn that most change is gradual, not an overnight phenomenon.
2. Homework strategies should be individually tailored for each client (Haley, 1978, 1989). Too often, the helper uses a standard homework assignment that, to the discouraged client, may feel impersonal. By stretching one's creativity, some assignments can incorporate more than one of the client's goals. If the client likes to read, recommending self-help books as homework might work well. If the client enjoys writing, assign a journal.
3. Regularity of practice is important. It would be better, for example, if the client performs an imaginal rehearsal for 10 minutes, once per day, rather than practicing for an hour, one time per week.
4. Homework should be simple and fit easily into the lifestyle of the client. Complicated homework involving extensive record keeping may not be completed.
5. As the client progresses, homework should increase in difficulty or discomfort. Clients usually have a feel for when they are ready for more challenging tasks and for tasks that are presently beyond them.

Summary

Practice is used to put insights into action and to help clients successfully try out new behaviors in a protected environment. Three levels of practice were described in this chapter: imaginal rehearsal, role-playing, and homework, or *in vivo* practice. Each has its appropriate use, but imaginal and role-playing practice may be considered initial steps that lead to eventual *in vivo* practice.

Imagery as a helping method has become popular in recent years as a means of self-exploration, but it can also be used to rehearse desired behaviors. Imagery can provide a first practice of a new behavior in a nonthreatening way.

Role-playing is a practice technique that involves recreating the context of a desired behavior right in the helper's office. Major contributions to this technique have come from psychodrama and the behaviorists (Lazarus, 1985). This technique allows the helper to obtain firsthand knowledge about the client's behavioral style, while the client benefits from rehearsal and feedback.

Homework assignments are given to clients to prolong treatment between sessions as well as to establish the new behavior as a habit. Assignments should be individually tailored to the client and may involve journaling activities, lay helpers as aides, and bibliotherapy. Helpers who regularly utilize practice in the office or as homework are more likely to increase the transfer of training to real-life situations.

Group Exercises

Group Exercise 1: Role-Playing

Role-playing as a rehearsal technique some-times focuses on situations in the past that clients would like to resolve. By attempting to bring them to closure in a role-play situation, the client is rehearsing for a later time when the issue can be addressed in real life.

The exercise begins with the client who identifies an individual in the past or present with whom he or she has "unfinished business." Unfinished business refers to a relationship or an issue that he or she was unable to adequately resolve in the past, but would like to bring to bring to a positive conclusion. It is recommended that participants chose minor situations such as:

> "My friend did not invite me to her wedding."
> "My boyfriend criticized me in front of his mother but I did not mention it."
> "A teacher treated me unfairly and I was never able to explain."
> "I was attracted to someone in the past but I never told her."

For this exercise, students form groups of four with roles of helper, client, observer 1, and observer 2. Observer 1 gives the client feedback and observer 2 gives the helper feedback on his or her ability to demonstrate the skill of role-playing.

Briefly, this exercise has the following phases:

1. The roles of helper, client, observer 1, and observer 2 are assigned.
2. The client thinks of a situation involving unfinished business.
3. The helper directs the client through the first five steps of role-playing.
4. Observer 1 and the helper give the client feedback; the client reenacts the role-play if more practice seems advisable.
5. Observer 2 gives the helper feedback and discusses the exercise.

Step 1: Warmup

As a warmup, the helper invites the client to explain the situation and uses the nonjudgmental listening cycle to get a clear understanding of the situation.

Step 2: Scene Setting

The helper asks the client to briefly describe where and when a meeting with the affected individual might take place. The client sits in one chair and an empty chair is left for the person with whom the client has unfinished business.

Step 3: Selecting Roles and Role Reversal

In this exercise, the client will play both himself or herself and the other person with whom the client has unfinished business. To begin, the helper asks the client to "reverse roles" and sit in the empty chair while completely taking on the identity of the other person. The helper asks this significant other to describe himself or herself and to give a little bit of background about the situation from that person's perspective.

Step 4: Enactment

Once the client has presented the other person, the helper asks him or her to return to the original chair and resume his or her natural identity. Now, the client expresses some of the thoughts and feelings that he or she has wanted to get out into the open. The helper facilitates the client to express this in any way the client wishes. The client speaks these to the empty chair as if the other person were actually present.

Once the client has had the opportunity to express his or her thoughts and feelings, the client "reverses roles" again and becomes the other person, responding to the charges leveled against him or her. The enactment ends when the client returns to his or her natural role and original seat and responds to the other person's reaction.

Step 5: Sharing and Feedback

In this step, the helper and observer 1 give the client feedback on how well the client was able to finish the unfinished business. For example, was the client able to express everything he or she intended in an assertive and straightforward way? Was the client overly aggressive or too tentative and passive?

Step 6: Reenactment

Reenactment follows sharing and feedback if the client needs to make improvements. In reenactment, the client stays in the client chair and has another opportunity to clearly and assertively make complaints and requests. Following this, the helper and observer 1 give the client feedback.

Step 7: Homework and Follow-Up

Group members discuss what possible homework and follow-up procedures they might employ had this been a real client problem.

The final phase of this group exercise is for observer 2 to give feedback to the helper on how well he or she was able to assist the client in practicing the new behavior. Observer 2 should have notes on each of the steps of role-playing and give specific feedback. Both client and observer 1 may also have feedback to share.

Quick Tips: Role-Playing

- Help the client overcome stage fright and initial discomfort by using a warmup process such as a discussion of the situation before the role-play begins.
- Getting the client to physically move around, arrange chairs, and set the scene help to warm up the client.
- If clients resist the role-play technique, you may have to abandon it until trust is better developed. On the other hand, your confidence in the procedure will encourage them and reassurance that "you'll get into it" may help them to get over their initial reluctance.

- If clients experience emotional arousal as a result of the role-play, the helper may find it necessary to implement the nonjudgmental listening cycle rather than continuing with the role-play.

Group Exercise 2

Consider the following case studies:

a. Carol is a 37-year-old married woman with one child. She and her counselor agree to work on her extreme reluctance to leave home even for a few hours to go to the grocery store. She experiences fear and panic attacks in public situations. She has not been shopping in 2 years and has lost respect for herself as a contributing member of her family. Following two sessions of history taking and a medical evaluation (the client incorrectly believes she has a heart condition), the counselor and client, following a complete assessment, agree that she needs assistance in dealing with low self-esteem and that she needs to practice going out in public. The client has a number of dysfunctional beliefs, including "I am weak," that seem to contribute to her inability to attempt new behaviors.

b. Maureen is a 20-year-old only college student whose parents appear to be on the verge of divorce. She comes to the college counseling center complaining that she is always in the middle and that each parent calls to tell her about the other's failings. In her attempts to placate both sides, Maureen has become anxious and depressed and has trouble studying. She experiences periods of crying and expresses sympathy for both parents. Maureen initially frames her problem as "how to help my parents cope with their divorce." In the second session, Maureen agrees that what she wants is to maintain a relationship with both parents, be supportive of both, and not to listen to their complaints about each other.

What does each client need to practice? Which issues would you address first? What level of rehearsal seems best suited to each of these client's problems? In a small group, brainstorm two or three creative homework assignments for each client. Role-play one of these situations, with one student playing the client and the other, the helper, making a homework assignment.

Homework

Homework 1: Diary

Select a personal growth goal for yourself that involves practicing a new behavior. For example:

"I would like to play my guitar every day."

"I would like to cook regular meals to combat my tendency to snack throughout the day."

"I would like to take time every day to improve my relationship with people at work."

- At the end of each day, for one week, write down the number of times you engaged in the behavior, or indicate if you did not practice during the day. Write down any ideas you have about why you did or did not practice the behavior during the day.
- At the end of a week, summarize your conclusions in a half-page reaction. Do you think that self-monitoring by keeping a journal was helpful to you? What kinds of clients might benefit from this approach? What kinds of problems are best suited to keeping a diary such as this?

Homework 2

Select a building-block skill from this book that you would like to improve.

a. Write down the name of the skill:_____

_____

b. Does the skill need to be broken down into small components? If so, list them here:

_____

_____

c. Spend 5 minutes imagining yourself successfully demonstrating each part of the skill.
d. Ask a fellow student who is proficient in the skill to model it for you.
e. Ask a student partner to act as an observer and practice the skill with a third student, who will serve as the client.
f. Get feedback and rehearse again, incorporating the suggestions you received.
g. With help from your training group, select several situations in real life where you might practice this skill.
h. Make an appointment with a fellow student to call him or her and report on your progress in a week.

Journal Starters

1. The curative factor, Practicing New Behaviors, implies that the helper should encourage the client to act. For example, it is suggested that a client act assertively even if he or she does not think or feel assertive. It is assumed that practice leads to change even if the change did not start within. What is your reaction to these ideas? What have been the most significant catalysts for change in your own life? Can you identify any times in your

own life when you have tried to face fears, or used action to produce a change?

2. Imagine yourself working as a helper five years from now. Where are you working? What are your coworkers like? Imagine yourself as very effective in your job and try and imagine in as much detail as you possibly can. Now, reflect on this future image. How realistic are these images? What feelings did the exercise evoke? Are these images merely fantasies or is there anything about this future scenario that could help to guide you towards a work situation that might really fit your needs?

References

Beck, A. T., Rush, A. J., Shaw, B. F., & Emery, G. (1979). Integration of homework into therapy. In A. T. Beck, A. J. Rush, B. F. Shaw, & G. Emery (Eds.), *Cognitive therapy of depression* (pp. 272–294). New York: Guilford.

Bellack, A. S. (1986). Covert rehearsal. In A. S. Bellack & M. Hersen (Eds.), *Dictionary of behavior therapy techniques.* New York: Pergamon.

Blatner, A. (1996). *Acting-in: Practical applications of psychodramatic methods.* New York: Springer.

Burns, D. D. (1980). *Feeling good: The new mood therapy.* New York: Avon.

Cautela, J. R., & Bennet, A. K. (1981). Covert conditioning. In R. Corsini (Ed.), *Handbook of innovative psychotherapies.* New York: Wiley.

Dyer, W., & Vriend, J. (1977). *Counseling techniques that work.* New York: Funk & Wagnalls.

Ellis, A. (1962). *Reason and emotion in psychotherapy.* New York: Lyle Stuart.

Fezler, W. F. (1989). *Creative imagery: How to visualize in all five senses.* New York: Simon & Schuster.

Gladding, S. T. (1986). Imagery and metaphor in counseling: A humanistic course. *Journal of Humanistic Education and Development, 25,* 38–47.

Glasgow, R. E., & Rosen, G. M. (1978). Behavioral bibliotherapy: A review of self-help behavior therapy manuals. *Psychological Bulletin, 85,* 1–23.

Grigsby, J. P. (1987). The use of imagery in the treatment of posttraumatic stress disorder. *Journal of Nervous and Mental Disease, 175,* 55–59.

Guerney, B., Stollack, G., & Guerney, L. (1971). The practicing psychologist as educator: An alternative to the medical practitioner's model. *Professional Psychology, 11,* 276–282.

Gunnison, H., & Renick, T. F. (1985). Bulimia: Using fantasy-imagery and relaxation techniques. *Journal of Counseling and Development, 64,* 79–80.

Haley, J. (1978). Ideas which handicap therapists. In M. Berger (Ed.), *Beyond the double blind: Communication and family systems, theories, techniques with schizophrenics* (pp. 24–36). New York: Brunner/Mazel.

Haley, J. (1989, April). Strategic family therapy. Symposium conducted at Stetson University, DeLand, FL.

Kazdin, A. E. (1978). Covert modeling: The therapeutic application of imagined rehearsal. In J. L. Singer & K. S. Pope (Eds.), *The power of human imagination.* New York: Plenum.

Kipper, D. A. (1986). *Psychotherapy through clinical role-playing.* New York: Brunner/Mazel.

Last, C. G. (1985). Homework. In A. S. Bellack & M. Hersen (Eds.), *Dictionary of behavior therapy techniques* (pp. 140–141). New York: Pergamon.

Lazarus, A. A. (1982). *Personal enrichment through imagery* (Cassette Recording). New York: BMA Audio Cassettes/Guilford.

Lazarus, A. A. (1984). *In the mind's eye: The power of imagery for personal enrichment.* New York: Guilford.

Lazarus, A. A. (1985). Behavior rehearsal. In A. S. Bellack & M. Hersen (Eds.), *Dictionary of behavior therapy techniques* (p. 22). New York: Pergamon.

Martin, G. A., & Worthington, E. L. (1982). Behavioral homework. In M. Hersen, R. Eisler, & P. M. Miller (Eds.), *Progress in behavior modification* (Vol. 13, pp. 197–226). New York: Academic Press.

Moreno, J. L. (1964). *Psychodrama* (Vol. 1, 3rd ed.). New York: Beacon House.

Pope, K. S. (1982). A primer on therapeutic imagery techniques. In P. A. Kellar & L. G. Ritt (Eds.), *Innovations in clinical practice: A sourcebook*

(Vol. 1, pp. 67–77). Sarasota, FL: Professional Resource Exchange.

Sarnoff, D., & Remer, P. A. (1982). The effects of guided imagery on the generation of career alternatives. *Journal of Vocational Behavior, 21,* 299–308.

Schutz, W. (1981). Holistic education. In I. R. Corsini (Ed.), *Handbook of innovative psychotherapies* (pp. 378–388). New York: Wiley.

Sheikh, A. (Ed.). (1983). *Imagery: Current theory, research and application.* New York: Wiley.

Shelton, J. L., & Ackerman, J. M. (1974). *Homework in counseling and psychotherapy.* Springfield, IL: Thomas.

Shelton, J. L., & Levy, R. L. (1981). *Behavioral assignments and treatment compliance.* Champaign, IL: Research Press.

Shorr, J. E. (1994). *Psychotherapy through imagery.* Santa Barbara, CA: Fithian Press.

Skovholt, T. M., Morgan, J. I., & Negron-Cunningham, H. (1989). Mental imagery in career counseling and life planning: A review of research and intervention methods. *Journal of Counseling and Development, 67,* 287–292.

Skovholt, T., & Thoen, G. A. (1987). Mental imagery in parenthood decision making. *Journal of Counseling and Development, 65,* 315–316.

Starr, A. (1977). *Psychodrama: Rehearsal for living.* Chicago: Nelson Hall.

Tubesing, D. (1981). *Kicking your stress habits.* Duluth, MN: Whole Person Press.

Weiner-Davis, M. (1992). *Divorce busting.* New York: Summit Books.

Witmer, J. M., & Young, M. E. (1985). The silent partner: Uses of imagery in counseling. *Journal of Counseling and Development, 64,* 187–190.

Witmer, J. M., & Young, M. E. (1987). Imagery in counseling. *Elementary School Guidance and Counseling, 22,* 5–16.

Wynd, C. A. (1992). Personal power imagery and relaxation techniques used in smoking cessation programs. *American Journal of Health Promotion, 6,* 184–189.

Yablonsky, L. (1976). *Psychodrama: Resolving emotional problems through role-playing.* New York: Basic Books.

Young, M. E., & Rosen, L. S. (1985). The retreat: An educational growth group. *Journal for Specialists in Group Work, 10,* 157–163.

Lowering and Raising Emotional Arousal 13

The fourth curative factor in the REPLAN system is lowering and raising emotional arousal (see Figure 13.1). In this chapter, we discuss ways of helping clients deal with overpowering feelings of anger, stress, and fear, primarily through methods of relaxation and mental quieting. In addition, we will look at methods that arouse emotions to act as catalysts for change and encourage clients to express deep feelings within the therapeutic relationship.

These two methodologies, quieting and arousing, are at each end of a continuum and the decision to excite or calm the client is determined by his or her unique circumstances. Many clients benefit from relaxation training, meditation, and other quieting techniques. "Hurry sickness," or high levels of stress, are common symptoms in this increasingly hectic world. On the other hand, methods that encourage clients to experience and then express deeply held feelings are helpful for clients who have not dealt with painful or traumatic events, who are underexpressive, or who are using defense mechanisms rather than dealing with important emotional problems.

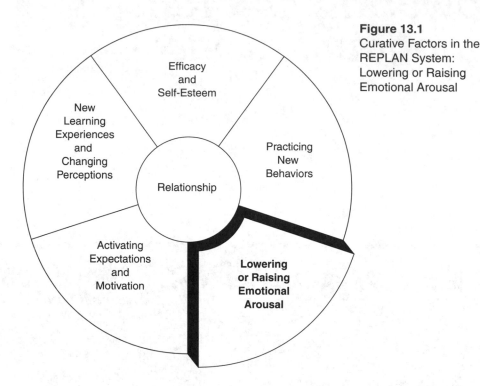

Figure 13.1
Curative Factors in the REPLAN System: Lowering or Raising Emotional Arousal

Although quieting methods are safe and quickly lead to positive experiences by clients, arousing emotions in clients is risky without a long period of training and close supervision. Most of these methods, such as the "empty-chair" technique of Gestalt therapy and several psychodramatic methods, are too advanced for the scope of this book; this does not mean, however, that the beginning helper must shy away from exploring unexpressed emotions. For one thing, you have already learned methods for reflecting emotions and personal meanings. Exploring deeper emotions and beliefs often leads to an experience of strong emotions. In this chapter, you will learn the technique of increasing emotional awareness to prevent the client from ignoring emotionally charged issues. You will also learn to help clients reduce emotions when emotions become overwhelming or interfere with the enjoyment of life.

Reducing Emotional Arousal

While a little anxiety may actually enhance performance at times, and anger may motivate us to act assertively, these emotions can easily run out of control, causing distress and interfering with relationships and job performance. Modern life, with more crowding, more work pressure, and more choices, has led to greater stress levels in just about everyone. The emotional arousal associated with anger and fear (fight or flight) may have been useful in more primitive times. Today, however, these emotions can be destructive as they are experienced by more and more people sitting behind a desk. What once may have increased the chances for survival now threatens our health, because the physiological by-products of stress cannot be easily dissipated in a sedentary lifestyle. Today's helper is frequently called upon to help clients learn to reduce the causes of stress by acquiring time management skills; developing a capacity for self-care, including exercise and good nutrition; and gaining a more healthy outlook on life. In addition, helpers assist clients to lower stress by reducing emotional arousal through quieting techniques.

Some of the better known methods for reducing emotional arousal are systematic desensitization for phobic anxiety (Wolpe, 1958), progressive relaxation (Jacobson, 1938), coping-skills training (Tubesing, 1981), guided imagery (Overholser, 1991), confession/ventilation (Menninger, 1958), emotional support (Gilliland, James, & Bowman, 1989), stress inoculation (Novaco, 1977, 1983), biofeedback training (Fair, 1989), and meditation (Bogart, 1991; Carrington, 1978; Shapiro, 1994; Shapiro and Walsh, 1984; Singh, 1996, 1999). These techniques are often combined and offered in a psychoeducational format as stress reduction or coping skills training courses. In a group setting, participants can also benefit from the support of fellow participants, which also helps to reduce stress.

The most fundamental method for helping clients reduce arousal is muscle relaxation. Muscle relaxation training brings about relief from troubling symptoms of anxiety immediately and lets clients experience the positive sensations associated with lowered muscle tension. This technique is explained in detail here, since it is part of most stress reduction courses and forms the basis of systematic desensitization and biofeedback training.

Relaxation Training

Edmund Jacobson's progressive relaxation technique (1938) was, for many years, the favored method for teaching clients deep muscle relaxation. Muscle relaxation had been found to reduce emotional arousal in fearful clients. Jacobson's method, if faithfully followed, enables the client to identify and relax every major muscle group in the body. The traditional training process may actually take several months in weekly sessions, although abbreviated versions have been used successfully (Gatchel & Baum, 1983; McKay, Davis, & Fanning, 1981). Following is a simpler and quicker format developed by Witmer (1985), which can be learned in three or four sessions, each lasting about 20 minutes. Every session is identical and provides a complete tensing and then relaxing of all the major muscle groups (see Table 13.1).

It has been known for some time that relaxation alone is not as effective as a treatment program that includes mental or cognitive control of anxious thoughts (Hazaleus & Deffenbacher, 1986). For some people, slowing down and relaxing focuses them on their worries even more. A typical case of a person who benefited from relaxation training was Terrence, a 45-year-old owner of a small factory, who was referred for help by his family doctor. The physician had found high levels of back and neck tension, which were causing headaches. Terrence had started out working at a small machine shop and had eventually purchased it with a partner. The shop had grown into a thriving business and many of the personnel and production problems fell on Terrence. In the initial session, the counselor interviewed Terrence and determined that the client would benefit from lowering emotional arousal to decrease back and neck tension. Terrence began to learn the technique of deep muscle relaxation; at the same time, the counselor encouraged him to build in regular exercise,

Table 13.1
Instructions to the Client for Tensing and Relaxing Muscle Groups

Major Muscle Group and Area of Tension	Tensing and Relaxing Instructions
1. Hands and Arms	
Hand: The back of your hand, fingers, and the wrist	Tense the muscles in the right hand and lower right arm by making a tight fist. Hold for at least five seconds. Feel the tension. Now relax. Notice the difference between the tensing and relaxing. Repeat the same procedure. Now do the same thing with your left hand. Finish by tensing and relaxing both hands together.
Lower Arm: The forearm and the wrist	Hold both arms out in front of you with palms up, bend the hands down. Feel the tension in the hand, wrist, and forearm. Then relax. Repeat the same procedure. Now extend your arms out in front of you but with palms down. Bend your hands up. Feel the tension. Relax. Repeat the same procedure. Now let both arms hang loosely at your side.
Upper Arm: The bicep muscles	Start with your right arm. Bend the elbow, touch your shoulder with your fingers, and tense the bicep just like you want to show off your muscles. Feel the tension, then relax and notice the contrast. Repeat the same procedure. Now do the same thing with your left arm. Finish by tensing, then relaxing both arms together. Now let both arms hang loosely at your side.
2. Head, Face, and Throat	
Forehead and Scalp: The entire forehead and scalp area	Wrinkle your forehead by raising your eyebrows as high as you can. Feel the tension in the forehead and scalp area. Now relax, notice the difference between tension and relaxation. Repeat the procedure. Next frown by pulling your eyebrows down as far as you can. Feel the tension, then relax. Repeat the same procedure. Let go of all tension, then relax. Repeat the same procedure. Let go of all tension in the forehead and scalp area. Feel the smoothness of the muscles.
Eyes and Nose: The eyelids and muscles around the eyes, nose, and upper cheeks	Squeeze your eyes shut and at the same time wrinkle up your nose. Feel the tension, then relax. Repeat the procedure. Next roll your eyes left and right, up and down or rotate them in both directions. Finish by opening your eyes as widely as you can, then relaxing them. Now feel the relaxation of muscles around your eyes.
Mouth and Jaw: The area around the mouth and the lower face	Bite your teeth together and pull the corners of your mouth back. Feel the tension, then let go. Now press your lips tightly together and extend them as though you are sucking a straw. Feel the tension and relax. Next open your mouth widely, then relax. Now pull your mouth to the left side of your face, then to the right. Repeat any of the above exercises until this part of your face is deeply relaxed.
Throat and Jaw: Muscles inside the mouth and throat	Push your tongue against the roof of your mouth. Feel the tension, then relax. Clench your jaw tightly, then relax.

Table 13.1
Instructions to the Client for Tensing and Relaxing Muscle Groups—*Continued*

Major Muscle Group and Area of Tension	Tensing and Relaxing Instructions
Entire Head and Facial Area	Try a final tensing and relaxing by making a face. Scrunch up your face so your eyes squint, your nose is wrinkled up and your mouth is pulled back. Now your face feels smooth and relaxed as you let go of any tension left over.
3. Neck and Shoulders *Neck:* The muscles in the back of the neck, at the base of the scalp, and across the shoulders	Drop your chin down against your chest. Press down hard enough so you feel tension under your chin and at the back of your neck. Now lift your head and press it backward. Roll your head to the right, then forward to your chest, then to the left and back to where you started. Go slowly and gently. Repeat this at least twice in the same direction. Next, do the same exercise in the other direction. Relax with your head in a normal position, stretching it in whatever way you need for working out remaining tension spots.
4. Chest, Shoulders, and Upper Back *Muscles in the Chest, Shoulders, and Upper Back Area*	Take a deep breath, hold it and at the same time pull the shoulders back, trying to make the shoulder blades touch. Feel the tension around your ribs, shoulders, and the upper back. Exhale slowly and feel the relaxation as your return to a natural position. Now pull your shoulders as far forward as you can, then as far up, as far back, and as far down as you can, making a kind of circular motion. Repeat this at least twice. Feel the tension and relaxation. Next go in the opposite direction in your rotation of the shoulders. Sense the looseness and relaxed feeling in this part of you body.
5. Lower Back, Stomach, and Hips *Lower Back:* The muscles across the lower back area	Begin by taking a deep breath and sitting up straight. Pull the shoulders back and arch your back so your stomach sticks out. Exhale and let all the air and tension flow out. Repeat this procedure. Next bend forward arching your back the other way with your head down to your knees and your hands touching the floor. Feel the muscles stretching. Return to a normal sitting position and feel the relaxation. Repeat the procedure.
Stomach and Hips: The muscles in the abdominal area and hips	Take a deep breath and hold it as you make your stomach muscles hard. Just tighten them up as though you were going to hit yourself in the stomach. You should feel a good deal of tightness in the stomach area. Breathe out and feel the relaxation as you do let go of this tension. Repeat the procedure. Next breathe out as far as you can, feeling the tension in your stomach area as you hold your breath. Now let go and allow yourself to breathe naturally, noticing the difference between tension and relaxation.

Reproduced with permission from Accelerated Development.

better nutrition, and regular days off from work. Along with the relaxation training, Terrence needed a change in outlook (see Chapter 15 on new learning experiences) because of his unwillingness to take care of himself and a self-critical attitude that drove him to neglect physical warning signs. Relaxation training helped reduce the client's headaches, but it took some time before Terrence was able to reduce his constant self-downing. Terrence's helper assisted him with countering techniques and thought stopping to reduce his mental stress. Eventually, Terrence's wife was able to get him to take regular vacations, and Terrence agreed to hire a human resource consultant to deal with stressful personnel issues. Together, the two curative factors, lowering emotional arousal and new learning, created a reduction of bodily tension, a shift in attitude, and a lifestyle that supported the change.

The Technique of Deep Muscle Relaxation

Step 1: Preparation

Ask the client to find the most comfortable position with eyes closed. This may be sitting or lying down, but in either case, there should be support for the head. The legs and arms should not be crossed. The procedure is best practiced without the distractions of noise or glaring lights. Instruct the client to speak as little as possible and to avoid moving except as necessary to achieve a more comfortable position. The client may be instructed to raise one finger to indicate when an instruction has been understood or completed.

Step 2: Tighten and Relax

Ask the client to progressively tighten and then relax each muscle group, using the instructions in Table 13.1. Encourage the client to hold each tensed muscle about 6 or 7 seconds until the experience of tightness is fully felt. If the posture is held too long, cramps and spasms may result. While a muscle group is tensed, ask the client to focus attention on that area, simultaneously relaxing other parts of the body and holding the breath.

Step 3: Relax Fully and Breathe

Following the tensing of a muscle group, instruct the client to exhale and relax fully and completely. This relaxation is to be accompanied by slow, deep, diaphragmatic breathing and should last 20 seconds or so. The tension and relaxation of the same muscle group is then repeated before moving on.

Diaphragmatic breathing consists of inhaling and exhaling below the ribs rather than in the upper chest. It is the relaxed breathing demonstrated by sleeping babies and practiced by singers. Help clients learn diaphragmatic breathing by placing one hand on the chest and the other on the diaphragm/stomach area. Diaphragmatic breathing occurs when the stomach hand goes up and down but the chest hand remains relatively immobile.

Step 4: The Body Scan

The most important phase of the lesson is the body review, or *body scan*. This phase is critical because the client is asked to return to specific, discrete areas of tension during the relaxation procedure and to relax them. This allows the helper to individualize the relaxation so that the client can spend time on the areas that he or she tends to tighten. Tell the client that a body scan can be used any time during the day to check bodily tension.

Step 5: Assign Practice

The first administration of the relaxation technique should be recorded on audio-cassette for the client, or a standardized commercially available version of the technique should be provided. Ask the client to practice the relaxation technique twice daily, usually once upon arising and once in bed before falling asleep. Have the client note which of the six bodily areas show the greatest sources of tension during the day and ask the client to report this information at the next session.

Meditation

Meditation may be one of the most effective means for decreasing anxiety, panic, and persistent anger (Brooks & Scarano, 1985; Kabat-Zinn et al., 1992; Smith, 1975). Moreover, meditation is not merely a method for reducing tension, it actually produces positive states of alertness, improved concentration, fearlessness, optimism, joy, and feelings of well-being (Chandler, Holden, & Kolander, 1992; Singh, 1999).

An immediate benefit of meditation is that it stops the constant chattering of the mind and eliminates the mental images that produce anxiety. For example, have you ever tried to sleep and found plans for the next day going around in your head? Meditation is a means of putting such thoughts to rest for a while. Unlike relaxation techniques, meditation has the effect of producing mental quietude not just physical rest and is therefore, for some, a good alternative to tranquilizers.

Like relaxation, meditation must be practiced on a regular basis for at least 15 minutes per day for several weeks, before real benefits can be realized (Benson, 1984). Like any skill, a teacher is helpful at all stages of training (Singh, 1996). To keep the mind occupied, meditation practitioners have found that a "mental device" (Benson, 1984), or *mantra,* is an effective way of reducing the stressful thoughts coming from the mind. A mantra gives the mind something to occupy itself while you are concentrating. A word or phrase is repeated slowly and at intervals, mentally, not aloud but with the "tongue of thought" (Singh, 1996). For those who are spiritually inclined, any name of God can be used. Others have found it effective to repeat a word such as "one" or "calm." Learning to quiet the mind is a challenge, but the benefits make the investment of time worth the effort. If you are interested in learning more about meditation, read Rajinder Singh's book entitled *Inner and Outer Peace through Meditation.* It contains complete and simple instructions for nondenominational spiritual meditation and exercises for getting started. For those who are not attracted to a spiritual meditation procedure, Patricia Carrington's *The Book of Meditation* (1998) may be of interest.

Raising Emotional Arousal

The patient only gets free from the hysterical symptom by reproducing the pathogenic impressions that caused it and by giving utterance to them with the expression of affect and thus the therapeutic task consists solely in inducing him to do so.
Breuer and Freud, 1895/1955, p. 283

The earliest records of cathartic methods are found in ancient Greek drama. The word *katharsis* indicates a purging or purification experienced after the expression of emotions. The effectiveness of traditional uses of cathartic methods is documented in the history of religious rituals, confession of sins, mesmerism, drug-induced emotional states, and rituals of mourning. Today, helpers use cathartic techniques to encourage clients to open up verbally and emotionally. The basis for the modern approach comes from the very beginnings of psychoanalysis (Bemak & Young; 1998, Young & Bemak, 1996).

The quotation that opens this section is from the classic book *Studies on Hysteria*. It was in this publication that Breuer and Freud (1895/1955) presented their discovery that reliving past traumas by provoking emotional reactions and getting clients to express their feelings had healing power. Freud's idea was that relief from emotional suffering can be obtained by releasing pools of stored emotions that are held in the unconscious. When freed, these stored emotions dissipate like water running down a drain. In all fairness to Freud, he modified his ideas about emotions later in his life, but this idea of releasing stockpiled emotions became popular and took root in many other therapeutic systems. Since Freud's time, the terms catharsis, abreaction, emotional insight, corrective emotional experience, releasing blocked emotion, and experiencing have been used to describe the release of emotions in the helping relationship (Nichols & Efran, 1985; Nichols & Zax, 1977).

Not all helping professionals believe that the effectiveness of cathartic techniques is explained by Freud's "hydraulic" metaphor, but they still embrace arousal and expression of emotions as a major technique. This group includes practitioners of Gestalt therapy (Perls, 1977; Prochaska & Norcross, 1994), psychodrama (Moreno, 1958), and a number of group approaches, including encounter and marathon groups. Emotional arousal has been activated through hypnosis and drugs (Wolberg, 1977), psychodramatic methods (Moreno, 1958), guided imagery (Witmer & Young, 1985), reflective listening in client-centered therapy, confrontation, deprecating and devaluating feedback in Synanon groups, free association in psychoanalysis, the empty-chair technique of Gestalt therapy (Polster & Polster, 1973), focusing (Gendlin, 1969), flooding, implosive therapy (Stampfl & Levis, 1967), bioenergetics (Lowen, 1967), primal therapy (Janov, 1970), reevaluation counseling (Jackins, 1962), provocative therapy (Farelly & Brandsma, 1974), and many others.

Arousal and Expression

The term *catharsis* is the most commonly used term in the context of arousal and expression, but it has become a catchall that actually encompasses two separate activities: (1) stimulating emotional arousal of the client and (2) encouraging emotional expression by the client (Young & Bemak, 1996). Arousing techniques frustrate, shock, anger, or evoke some other state of emotional arousal for the purpose of motivating change. Expressive techniques, on the other hand, help clients fully experience their feelings and allow them to communicate these emotions to the helper. Clients report "cathartic events" as extremely significant; however, several studies indicate that emotional arousal should be accompanied by a cognitive change or perspective shift to achieve maximum effectiveness. Furthermore, there is some indication that individuals who are underexpressive will benefit most from highly arousing and expressive techniques (Young & Bemak, 1996).

It is extremely important to be aware right from the start that methods that arouse emotions can be traumatic and potentially harmful to clients. Arousing techniques, in their simplest and most benign form, can push clients to talk about troubling experiences and feelings rather than avoiding them. At the most harmful level, helpers applying these techniques can force clients to face powerful emotions that make the client feel out of control. Because some arousing techniques can produce such harmful reactions, in this chapter we will discuss methods that encourage clients to focus on their emotions but do not pressure them to do so. The more confrontational and cathartic methods are very advanced skills to be used only by experienced practitioners within strict ethical guidelines and in conjunction with close supervision (Young and Bemak, 1996). We mention them here because, sooner or later, every helper will see these methods on films or at conference workshops. Like a knife that cuts both ways, it is important to keep in mind that while these methods can produce powerful reactions, the risks are substantial.

Besides the risks associated with arousing and expressive techniques, there is what Goleman (1995) calls the "ventilation fallacy." Because expressing anger feels so good immediately, we are seduced into thinking that we have dispelled it. In fact, the opposite may be true (see Tavris, 1989). Expressing anger tends to arouse a person more, making him or her more likely to feel anger later.

Why Do Arousal and Expression of Emotion Stimulate Change?

1. They promote greater self-understanding. Earlier in this book, we mentioned the work of Pennebaker (1990, 1995), who asked college students to write about traumatic events in their lives. These students experienced better mental and physical health compared to control subjects. When the students were asked about why they found the exercise helpful, they did not think that positive changes were simply due to the release of pentup emotions. In fact, participants did not feel better after the writing experience. Eighty percent of them explained the benefits as due to greater self-understanding, as opposed to getting negative emotions "off their chests." The following are some examples of client statements (Pennebaker, 1990, pp. 48–49):

"It helped me think about what I felt during those times."

"I never realized how it affected me before."

"I had to think and resolve past experiences. . . . One result of the experiment is peace of mind, and a method to relieve emotional experiences. To have to write emotions and feelings helped me to understand how I felt and why."

2. Powerful emotional experiences convince clients that help is needed and that significant feelings have been denied or repressed. Emotions have been called "hot cognitions" (Greenberg & Safran, 1988). In other words, the emotional aspects of a problem are the most pronounced to the client. Therefore, dealing directly with the emotions is persuasive since it brings about an immediate sense that core issues are being dealt with. It is a confirmation, by direct knowledge, of the power of the helping relationship when a client experiences emotional relief, and is more persuasive than an intellectual insight. When helpers use listening techniques or ask clients to focus on emotional pain, the client becomes aware that there are strong emotions lurking beneath the surface. This gives the client hope that the

helping relationship is working on a deeper level (Greenberg & Safran, 1988; Greenberg, Rice, & Ailed, 1993).

An example of the power of a direct emotional experience occurred when we were seeing a physician and his wife, a nurse, who came for help to deal with their 25-year-old son, who was a drug addict and who lied to and stole from his parents. At first, the father was skeptical about how counseling would help and he was only minimally involved. In the third session, as he discussed the effects of the son's behavior on their lives, he suddenly became aware of a deep and troubling experience. He hated his own son. He broke into tears and was inconsolable for nearly an hour. He later reported that he knew he was angry at his child, but had never come face to face with his own feelings of failure and rage at the situation. This incident, among other things, helped to convince him that counseling was a potent tool and that he had deeper feelings than he was willing to admit intellectually. He became more involved in counseling, and he and his wife were able to begin dealing with their son more cooperatively.

3. Expressing deeply felt emotions to the helper cements the helping relationship. When clients express their feelings of anger, attraction, or dependency in front of another person, they fear rejection and feel guilty for even having such emotions. When the client's feelings are accepted by the helper, the client feels a greater sense of trust and a willingness to tackle deeper issues. As Yalom (1975) said, "Catharsis is part of an interpersonal process; no one ever claimed enduring benefit from ventilating feelings in an empty closet (p. 84)."

4. Arousal melts down old attitudes. Kurt Lewin (1947) talked about therapeutic change being an "unfreezing and refreezing" process, meaning that the client's worldview can be catalyzed by emotional arousal. During periods of intense emotion, client attitudes are most susceptible to modification by the helper (Frank & Frank, 1991). When emotional arousal subsides, the insights gained "refreeze" or solidify into a new and stable viewpoint. McMullin (1986) calls this phenomenon the "melted wax theory." Emotional arousal can be used to provide the heat needed to melt down old beliefs so that they may be reformed.

Techniques That Stimulate Emotional Arousal and Expression

One does not destroy an emotion by refusing to feel it or acknowledge it; one merely disowns a part of one's self.

Nathaniel Branden, 1971, p. 28

Stimulus Techniques

Several methods for emotional arousal/expression can be grouped together as *stimulus techniques*. Helpers supply clients with media such as music, films, or books that relate to their personal problems. The ability of the client to identify with the protagonist of the story enhances the emotional arousal and subsequent expression. For example, a helper might suggest the movie *The Great Santini* to a client from a military family. Later, helper and client discuss the film in terms of what feelings and thoughts were aroused.

Creative Arts

A second set of techniques is associated with the use of the creative arts in counseling (Gladding, 1998). Helpers encourage clients to express themselves through artistic media. Arts as emotional catalysts differ from stimulus methods in that clients are not passive, but actively create an artistic work that reflects an inner state. These works may include dance and movement, music performance, expressive writing of poetry, journaling, painting, drawing, sculpting, making collages, sandtray work, and dramatic use of puppets and dolls. For example, a client who has trouble understanding his feelings about a past relationship could be asked to paint a picture or write a poem about the experience to be shared during the next session.

Stop and Reflect

Journal writing is an activity that can be used in the helping relationship for the expression and release of emotions. Writing down our inner thoughts is a different activity from merely thinking about them or talking about them. In writing, we have the opportunity to really examine thoughts in detail, to think about them, and to challenge them. We may record dreams, daily feelings, reflections on self-concept, or spiritual progress, or we may write about particularly troubling or significant periods of change in our lives. All of these activities may help us become more deeply aware of emotional issues behind these events.

In this activity, called a "period log" (Gladding, 1998), you are asked to indicate a particular interval of your life during which you experienced a number of changes or personal growth and to reflect on your experiences at that time. Once you have identified a particular time period, begin writing and do not stop to edit your thoughts. Since you need not show this work to anyone, turn off the internal censor and try and write whatever comes up or emerges without editing your thoughts or feelings. This is a free-association, or stream-of-consciousness, method that psychodynamic therapists have found to be effective for uncovering underlying issues. Some practice is required before one can really let go and let thoughts and feelings flow. One way of doing this is to place your pen on a blank sheet of paper with a headline indicating the particular time period and write without picking up the pen for about 5 minutes. Start with the words, "I felt. . . ," and continue writing for the allotted time. When you have finished, answer the following questions.

- What were the major feelings you experienced during this period in your life? Did you reexperience any of them while writing?
- Did you find it hard to write in a stream-of-consciousness style?
- How did you block yourself from letting the ideas flow out?
- Do you think clients censor their true feelings about issues or a particular period in their lives?
- Did you encounter any personal reluctance to look at this period in your life?
- Do you see any value in reviewing the past or would it be best to let these issues lie?
- What does your writing indicate about how comfortable you are now with this important period in your life?

- What other artistic media would you personally be most likely to use if it were suggested by a helper?
- How could you determine which methods would be best for a specific client?

Psychodrama

In our earlier discussion on role-playing, we discussed the basic elements of psychodrama (see also Blatner, 1998). Some of the most intensely emotional methods are those elicited in psychodrama. Psychodrama was conceived by Moreno (1958) as a method of emotional expression similar to dance and visual art; it is the re-creation of an individual's joys and sorrows on a therapy stage. Typically, in a group, the protagonist is asked to recreate a scene from the past and to explore his or her thoughts and emotions in as much depth as possible. Considerable experience and training are required before a helper can responsibly use psychodramatic methods for arousing emotions (Bemak & Young, 1998).

The Technique of Increasing Emotional Awareness

As we mentioned at the beginning of this chapter, many of the techniques for arousing client emotions and encouraging them to express them are quite advanced and can be harmful if misused. Increasing emotional awareness, however, is a technique that directly flows from your work on the nonjudgmental listening cycle in Chapters 5 and 6. There, you learned to reflect feelings and to relate these to deeper meanings in a client's life. These methods focus the client on emotions that they are defensively avoiding. The technique of increasing emotional awareness is, in essence, asking the client's permission to stay with these emotions, even if they are painful, in order to fully explore the problem and to help the client communicate these feelings within the therapeutic relationship. The technique of increasing emotional awareness rests on the building blocks of reflecting feelings, reflecting meaning, and summarizing.

The steps for increasing a client's emotional awareness can be summarized as follows:

Step 1   Observe and note the client's attempts to move away from the emotion. The client's avoidance of emotion may take various forms, including changing the subject, blocking of speech, stuttering, fidgeting, and other nonverbal changes such as facial sagging or tightening or the presence of tears hidden by downcast eyes. The helper brings awareness to nonverbal expression of emotions, such as voice tone, gestures, eye movement, bodily tension, or movement. For example, the helper may simply encourage the client to pay attention to a particular area by saying, "Are you aware that you are clenching your jaw?"

Client: "Well, um, I love them to death. They're great kids. But . . ."

Helper: "You keep mentioning your positive feelings for the kids, but I can tell by your voice that you get really angry sometimes as well."

Step 2   Stop the client's movement away from the emotion and direct the client to focus on the emotional content. The helper interrupts the conversation and asks the client to express how he or she feels about the problem right now.

Client: "I do. I get really angry at them. Sometimes I feel like hitting them. But that's okay, I know I won't. I'm not a child beater, you know. Besides, school is about to begin again and they'll be out of my hair soon."

Helper: "Let's go back to your feelings of anger toward the kids for a moment. Can you help me understand a little more about how you feel?"

Step 3   Invite the client to become aware of the emotion. The helper asks the client to focus on the emotion underlying the story the client is telling, to explore the meaning of that emotion, and to express it as fully as possible. As the client responds, other emotions often come to the surface as well. For example, the helper might observe that the client has brushed by or glossed over the feeling aspects of a problem and ask, "What are you experiencing now?" "What are you aware of right now?" "How does that statement feel to you?"

Helper: "For a moment, just try and stay with the emotion you feel when you are really frustrated with the kids. What is that like?"

Client: "I'm angry. Why can't we have a happy family? Why is there so much fighting? I've done everything I can."

Helper: "You feel guilty because there is so much fighting."

Step 4   In a summary, challenge the client to follow through and act on the discoveries made through awareness of the emotion. When it seems that the client is in touch with underlying feelings, the helper attempts to focus on what the client wants to do next. The motive power of the emotion has been released and needs a direction. Helpers encourage this action tendency by challenging clients to develop plans and goals with the following kinds of interventions: "What do you need?" "What do you want?" "Where do you go from here?"

Helper: "From what I've gathered in this session, despite your best efforts, your teenage kids argue a lot, creating a difficult climate in the home. In the past, this has made you angry, and you feel guilty because you see it as your job to create a happy family. Is this about right?"

Client: "Yes, that's mainly it. What I really need to do is stay out of their fights and remove myself from that situation rather than feeling guilty. They are not going to hurt each other physically and my involvement does not seem to stop their fighting. I just get upset."

Helper: "Your plan to stay out of their disagreements sounds like a good one. I think that would be a good homework assignment for next week. Would you be willing to try your new approach and report back to me then?"

Stop and Reflect

Eugene Gendlin has developed a technique called *focusing.* It is a way of becoming more aware of troubling issues in one's life. Central to this method is the idea of a "felt sense." A felt sense is a physical sensation or a bodily awareness that can help us get to the heart of a problem (Gendlin, 1978). Try Gendlin's technique yourself in the following adaptation and then answer the questions.

Step 1: Preparation.

Find a quiet time and place and sit quietly and comfortably. Close your eyes if you wish. You may read the instructions yourself or ask a friend to read them to you.

Step 2: Clearing a Space

Ask yourself, "How do I feel?" "What is keeping me from feeling good?" "What is bothering me right now?" Then stop and quietly listen. A number of problems might start to arise, some important and others trivial. Let them all emerge. Don't let your mind focus too long on any one problem. Let go. Take on an air of detachment as these problems surface. Let them pile up and then observe them as if at a distance.

Step 3: Feeling for the Problem

As you survey your problems, ask yourself which problem *feels* the most pressing right now. Can you sense one that is heavier than the others? Ask yourself how the problem feels. Get a sense of the whole thing, but do not analyze it with your mind. Use your bodily sensations to get a grasp of what the entire issue feels like. It may take some time and concentration to experience this feeling that encompasses the entire issue. Don't try to solve the problem or dissect it; just let it be and experience your feelings about it.

Step 4: Finding the Crux

In this step, focus on the problem and see if you can find one aspect of it that feels the worst—the crux of it. Instead of searching for an answer, just wait quietly and see if something emerges. The response may be only a special feeling or sensation such as tension or fear. Don't attach any words to your experience; just let the feeling come forth.

Step 5: Labeling

Allow words and pictures to flow from the feeling you are experiencing. Keep your concentration on the crux of the problem and see what words or images you experience.

Step 6: Checking Back with the Feeling

Place the words you have come up with next to your feeling or bodily sensations about the problem. Do they match? Make sure they fit precisely. If they are correct, you will have a physical experience of completeness or a "confirming sensation." Get in touch with your feeling about the problem again to make sure the words you have found really fit for you. Spend a moment or two in silence as you experience this. When you are finished, open your eyes. You may wish to record your experience in a journal.

- What insights did you have about the problem that came to the surface in this exercise?
- Did you tend to visualize your problems? If so, what form did they take?
- Were you surprised by the problems that came to the surface?
- How did you feel about getting in touch with this issue? Was it uncomfortable, or was it a pleasant experience?
- Which clients might have difficulty with a technique like this? Which clients might respond well?
- Gendlin suggests that you can also get in touch with positive feeling and experiences through focusing. Try this exercise again and this time ask yourself, "Why do I love _____?" in step 2 and move through the cycle.

Summary

Some clients come for help because they are experiencing excessive emotional arousal; they are suffering from intense fear or anger. Relaxation techniques are simple but effective ways of beginning to help such clients. Teaching deep muscle relaxation is not a very complicated procedure. It involves training the client individually or in a group to tense and relax the major muscle groups of the body. The client is assigned practice sessions as homework; the main task of the helper is to encourage practice and to help the client stick with the technique until he or she begins to benefit from it. Like relaxation, meditation can be effective in producing physical relaxation, but it also has the benefit of promoting quietude and other positive mental states. Meditation can be incorporated into a holistic approach to wellness; it can be practiced successfully by those who are spiritually inclined and those who are not.

Increasing emotional arousal and expression is another time-honored method in the helping professions. It is not written about frequently because of the potential negative results that may occur if a client becomes highly aroused. With clients who are underexpressive or not in touch with the emotional side of their problems, stimulating arousal and expression may be very useful. The viewpoint expressed in this chapter is that experiencing and expressing emotions is not sufficient to produce real change. When clients become more aware of deeply held emotions, they must place their experience in a new cognitive framework and act on their insights. Some of the methods used to produce cathartic experiences can be dangerous if practiced by inexperienced helpers. Still, even a beginner can learn to help clients face the emotional content of their problems by using the technique of increasing emotional awareness. This technique involves asking clients to focus on emotions and inviting them to fully experience and act responsibly on their feelings.

Group Exercises

Group Exercise 1: Relaxation Training

For this exercise, the training group divides into dyads. Each person has a turn as either client or helper. Each dyad finds as quiet a spot as possible to practice the training. The helper takes the client through an abbreviated version of deep muscle relaxation given in Table 13.1. In this shorter variant, steps 2 and 5 are eliminated and the helper reads the instructions for steps 1, 3, 4, 6, and 7 only. For time considerations, each muscle group is to be tightened and relaxed only once rather than twice, as one would do in normal practice.

Following the relaxation sequence, take 5 minutes to discuss the effectiveness of the procedure. The client should answer the following questions.

- Using a 100-point scale (0, most relaxed you've ever been; 100, very tense), how deeply were you able to relax in this exercise?
- Were the helper's instructions presented in a calm and methodical way?
- Did the helper allow sufficient time for relaxation before proceeding to a new muscle group?
- What might the helper have done to deepen your relaxation?

Following this feedback, client and helper switch roles and repeat the exercise.

Quick Tips: Relaxation Training

- Ask the client to move around slightly and find the most comfortable seating position before you begin the relaxation instructions.

- Keep your voice tone modulated and soothing.
- Watch the client for signs of tension or discomfort. When the procedure is complete, do a body scan by returning to those areas where the client has difficulty relaxing, and ask the client to tense and relax those areas again.
- Make sure that you suggest deep diaphragmatic breathing as a transition between tensing and relaxing muscle groups.

Group Exercise 2: Relaxing with Imagery

Since you have already learned something about imagery in Chapter 12, you can now apply that technique to relaxation training. Form groups of four, with three clients and one helper. The helper asks the clients to find a comfortable position and then reads the instructions for the body review in Table 13.1. This quick tense and relaxation of the body provides a beginning point for the exercise, but participants should be instructed to notice any area where tension lingers and to attend to that area by tensing and then relaxing it. If time permits, participants may practice diaphragmatic breathing to finish the first part of the exercise. Each member is to mentally note on a 100-point scale how tense he or she feels at the end of the

relaxation (100 represents extreme tension; and 0 represents the most relaxed he or she has ever felt).

In the second phase of the exercise, the helper reads the following material to the group: "Imagine that you are lying on a beach in a very comfortable lounge chair. It is a bright and sparkling day. You can hear the sounds of waves brushing the shoreline as you relax. In the distance, you can also hear the cries of seagulls. The sun is beating down and it feels almost like a weight as your body becomes relaxed and heavy. Stay with this scene and imagine it in as much detail as you possibly can, letting your relaxation deepen."

For 3 minutes, participants continue to imagine this scene. End by saying, "This concludes the exercise. When you feel ready, slowly bring yourself back and open your eyes." Finally, the helper leads a discussion with the following questions:

- Comparing your level of relaxation from beginning to end, would you rate your relaxation as deeper following the imagery exercise?
- Can you think of some other, more relaxing scene than the beach?
- What elements of the relaxation image were the most relaxing? Did any part of the image increase your tension rather than relax you?

Homework

Homework 1

Listen to a piece of classical music for about 15–20 minutes, for example, orchestral pieces by Beethoven, Wagner, Mozart, or Bach. Close your eyes and relax. As you listen, note any feelings that you are experiencing. If you can, draw a picture associated with the music. Do you notice an overall emotional theme in the music? How could music be effective in helping clients get in touch with emotions? For more information, see Gladding's (1998) book entitled *Coun-*

seling as an Art: The Creative Arts in Counseling. For contrast, listen to another, more relaxing kind of music or environmental sounds, ocean waves, and the like. How might listening to relaxing music and sounds be a helpful activity for clients who want to learn relaxation?

Homework 2

Make two separate collages using photos, drawings, and words from newspapers, magazines, and other print media. The first collage should represent a time in your life when you were experiencing troubling or conflicting emotions. Prepare a second collage that represents your feelings and experiences during one of the best times of your life. Identify these feelings in writing beneath each picture. As you look back at each period of your life, does it reawaken any of these feelings in you? Which of these periods do you think about the most in your daily life? How might a collage such as this be useful for a client who is trying to deal with conflicting emotions from the past? How would you develop a conversation with a client using the collage as a stimulus?

Homework 3

The skill of relaxation requires the therapeutic factor of practice to make it a part of one's life. Find a way of building relaxation practice into your daily life. Consider the following suggestions and then implement one in your own daily life. Report on your attempts in a paragraph or two.

- Every time you stop at a traffic light, do deep diaphragmatic breathing to lower your tension.
- Use small colored dots, available in office supply stores, to remind you to do a body scan. Place these dots on your computer screen, watch, or appointment book. Whenever you see one, tense and relax those muscles that seem the most tense.
- Before going to sleep each night, do a complete body scan and note the areas where the most tension resides. Keep a diary for a week and see if the same areas tend to hold much of your tension.
- Meditate for 10–15 minutes each morning. What effects does it have on your level of tension and your mental attitude?

Journal Starters

1. Maslow (1968) discusses the concept of *peak experiences*—times of optimal functioning when you feel more integrated, in charge of your life, spontaneous, and less aware of space and time. Many of these experiences seem to take place in nature and often when you are alone. Have you ever experienced anything like this? If so, reflect on these "natural highs." What emotions were you feeling? What insights did you gain, if any, from these times? To what extent do they seem to mirror religious or meditative experience?

2. Reflect on a time in your life when you have been overcome with emotion. How did you cope with these feelings? Did you seek social support, express your feelings, deny them, try to solve the problem causing the situation? As you review one or two of these incidents, what would you say is your basic coping style? How do you handle emotional problems automatically? What improvements or new techniques might help you cope better in the future?

References

Bemak, F., & Young, M. E. (1998). Catharsis in group psychotherapy. *International Journal of Action Methods, 50,* 166–184.

Benson, H. (1984). *Beyond the relaxation response.* New York: Berkley.

Blatner, A. (1998). *Acting-in: Practical applications of psychodramatic methods.* New York: Springer.

Bogart, G. (1991). The use of meditation in psychotherapy: A review of the literature. *American Journal of Psychotherapy, 45,* 383–412.

Branden, N. (1971). *The disowned self.* New York: Bantam.

Breuer, J., & Freud, S. (1895/1955). *Studies on hysteria.* In J. Strachey (Ed.), *The complete works of Sigmund Freud,* Standard Edition (Vol. 2). London: Hogarth.

Brooks, J. S., & Scarano, T. (1985). Transcendental Meditation in the treatment of post-Vietnam adjustment. *Journal of Counseling & Development, 64,* 212–215.

Carrington, P. (1998). *The book of meditation: The complete guide to modern meditation.* Boston: Element Books.

Chandler, C. K., Holden, J. M., & Kolander, C. A. (1992). Counseling for spiritual wellness: theory and practice. *Journal of Counseling & Development, 71,* 168–175.

Fair, P. L. (1989). Biofeedback-assisted relaxation strategies in psychotherapy. In J. V. Basmajian (Ed.), *Biofeedback: Principles and practice for clinicians* (3rd ed., pp. 187–196). Baltimore: Williams & Wilkins.

Farelly, F., & Brandsma, J. (1974). *Provocative therapy,* Cupertino, CA: Meat.

Frank, J. D., & Frank, J. B. (1991). *Persuasion and healing: A comparative study of psychotherapy.* (3rd ed.). Baltimore: Johns Hopkins University Press.

Gatchel, R. J., & Baum, A. (1983). *An introduction to health psychology.* Reading, MA: Addison-Wesley.

Gendlin, E. T. (1969). Focusing. *Psychotherapy: Theory, Research and Practice, 6,* 4–15.

Gendlin, E. T. (1978). *Focusing.* New York: Everest House.

Gilliland, B. E., James, R. K., & Bowman, J. T. (1989). *Theories and strategies in counseling and psychotherapy.* Upper Saddle River, NJ: Prentice Hall.

Gladding, S. T. (1998). *Counseling as an art: The creative arts in counseling* (2nd ed.). Alexandria, VA: American Counseling Association.

Goleman, D. (1995). *Emotional intelligence: Why it can matter more than IQ.* New York: Bantam.

Greenberg, L. S., Rice, L. N., & Ailed, R. (1993). *Facilitating emotional change.* New York: Guilford.

Greenberg, L. S., & Safran, J. D. (1988). *Emotion in psychotherapy.* New York: Guilford.

Hazaleus, S. L., & Deffenbacher, J. L. (1986). Relaxation and cognitive treatments of anger. *Journal of Consulting and Clinical Psychology, 54,* 222–226.

Jackins, H. (1962). *Elementary counselor's manual.* Seattle: Rational Island.

Jacobson, E. (1938). *Progressive relaxation.* Chicago: University of Chicago Press.

Janov, A. (1970). *The primal scream.* New York: Dell.

Kabat-Zinn, J., Massion, A. O., Kristeller, J., Peterson, L., Fletcher, K. E., Pbert, L., Lenderking, W. R., & Santorelli, S. F. (1992). Effectiveness of a meditation-based stress reduction program in the treatment of anxiety disorders. *American Journal of Psychiatry, 149,* 936–943.

Lewin, K. (1947). Frontiers in group dynamics, *Human Relations, 1,* 5–14.

Lowen, A. (1967). *The betrayal of the body.* New York: Collier.

Maslow, A. H. (1968). *Toward a psychology of being.* Princeton, NJ: Von Nostrand.

McKay, M., Davis, M., & Fanning, P. (1981). *Thoughts and feelings: The art of cognitive stress intervention.* Richmond, CA: New Harbinger.

McMullin, R. (1986). *Handbook of cognitive therapy techniques.* New York: Norton.

Menninger, K. (1958). *Theory of psychoanalytic technique.* New York: Harper & Row.

Moreno, J. L. (1958). *Psychodrama* (Vol. 2). New York: Beacon House.

Nichols, M. P., & Efran, J. S. (1985). Catharsis in psychotherapy: A new perspective. *Psychotherapy, 22,* 46–58.

Nichols, M. P., & Zax, M. (1977). *Catharsis in psychotherapy.* New York: Gardener Press.

Novaco, R. W. (1977). Stress inoculation: A cognitive therapy for anger and its application to a case of depression. *Journal of Consulting and Clinical Psychology, 45,* 600–608.

Novaco, R. W. (1983). Stress inoculation therapy for anger control. In P. A. Keeler & L. G. Rift (Eds.), *Innovations in clinical practice: A source book* (Vol. 2, pp. 181–201). Sarasota, FL: Professional Resource Exchange.

Overholser, J. C. (1991). The use of guided imagery in psychotherapy: Modules for use with passive relaxation training. *Journal of Contemporary Psychotherapy, 21,* 159–172.

Pennebaker, J. W. (Ed.) (1995). *Emotion, disclosure and health.* Washington, DC: American Psychological Association.

Pennebaker. (1990). *Opening up: The healing power of expressing emotions.* New York: Guilford.

Perls, F. S. (1977). *The gestalt approach: An eye witness to therapy.* Palo Alto, CA: Science and Behavior Books.

Polster, E., & Polster, M. (1973). *Gestalt therapy integrated.* New York: Brunner/Mazel.

Prochaska, J., & Norcross, J. C. (1994). *Systems of psychotherapy: A transtheoretical analysis* (3rd ed.). Pacific Grove, CA: Brooks/Cole.

Shafii, M. (1974). Meditation and marijuana. *American Journal of Psychiatry, 131,* 60–63.

Shafii, M. (1975). Meditation and the prevention of alcohol abuse. *American Journal of Psychiatry, 132,* 942–945.

Shapiro, D., & Walsh, R. (Eds.). (1984). *Meditation: Classic and contemporary perspectives.* New York: Aldine.

Shapiro, D. H. (1994). Examining the content and context of meditation: A challenge for psychology in the areas of stress management, psychotherapy and religion/values. *Journal of Humanistic Psychology, 34,* 101–135.

Singh, R. (1996). *Inner and outer peace through meditation.* Boston: Element.

Singh, R. (1999). *Empowering your soul through meditation.* Boston: Element.

Smith, J. C. (1975). Meditation as psychotherapy: A review of the literature. *Psychological Bulletin, 82,* 558–564.

Stampfl, T. G., & Levis, D. J. (1967). Essentials of implosive therapy: A learning-theory-based psychodynamic behavioral therapy. *Journal of Abnormal Psychology, 72,* 496–503.

Tavris, C. (1989). *Anger: The misunderstood emotion.* New York: Touchstone.

Tubesing, D. (1981). *Kicking your stress habits.* Duluth, MN: Whole Person Press.

Witmer, J. M. (1985). *Pathways to personal growth: Developing a sense of worth and competence.* Muncie, IN: Accelerated Development.

Witmer, J. M., & Young, M. E. (1985). The silent partner: Uses of imagery in counseling. *Journal of Counseling and Development, 64,* 187–189.

Wolberg, L. B. (1977). *The technique of psychotherapy.* New York: Grune & Stratton.

Wolpe, J. (1958). *Psychotherapy by reciprocal inhibition.* Stanford, CA: Stanford University Press.

Yalom, I. (1975). *Theory and practice of group psychotherapy.* New York: Basic Books.

Young, M. E., & Bemak, F. (1996). Emotional arousal and expression in mental health counseling. *Journal of Mental Health Counseling, 25,* 1–16.

Activating Client Expectations, Hope, and Motivation

14

Ripeness is all.
Shakespeare

In this chapter, we will take a closer look at the curative factor involved in instilling hope, increasing expectations, and overcoming client resistance to change. Figure 14.1 shows this factor highlighted among the six curative factors. Before learning the techniques for increasing hope and expectations, it is important first to understand

Figure 14.1
Curative Factors in the REPLAN System: Activating Expectations and Motivation

the problem that they attempt to address, the discouragement, lack of confidence, and demoralization that most clients are experiencing when they come for help. Beginning helpers are often surprised when a client fails to follow through with plans or seems unwilling to try. Remember that seeking professional help is often a last resort. The client has already tried several ways to solve the problem before coming to the helper, even seeking help from family and friends. Therefore, before clients can attack the problems they are facing, they must first overcome the conviction that their situation is hopeless.

The Demoralization Hypothesis

According to Jerome Frank (Frank & Frank, 1991), those who seek counseling are demoralized. *Demoralization* is described by Frank as a "state of mind characterized by one or more of the following: subjective incompetence, loss of self-esteem, alienation, hopelessness (feeling that no one can help), or helplessness (feeling that other people could help but will not)" (p. 56). Demoralization is known by many different names in various theories, but the concept was best developed by Adler (1954). Seligman (1975) experimentally discovered an aspect of demoralization called *learned helplessness*, a state of demoralization analogous to depression. It was discovered in animal research and later in humans. Seligman found that persons exposed to unsolvable problems became so discouraged that their later performance on solvable problems was negatively affected.

Frank believes that anxiety, depression, and loss of self-esteem (the most common presenting symptoms) are due primarily to demoralization. Frank also proposes that symptoms and mental demoralization interact. In other words, client problems and symptoms are worsened by the sense of discouragement and isolation. For example, a physical problem may be seen as a minor annoyance by one person, whereas the demoralized individual sees it as another sign of the hopelessness of his or her situation.

Many clients improve radically early in the helping process. Even those on waiting lists show improvement! This has been attributed to the *placebo effect,* a medical analogy that has been unfortunately applied to the psychological realm. The placebo effect implies that the helper is fooling the client with an imaginary treatment. In actuality, the placebo effect, or expectancy effect, is tapping well-established factors in social influence, especially the attractiveness and trustworthiness of the helper, and high expectations for treatment (Frank, Nash, Stone, & Imber, 1963; Patterson, 1973). It is the expectation itself that is healing. Faith is powerful medicine (Siegel, 1986).

Encouragement

A close analysis of the word *encouragement,* shows that it means "to cause to have heart" (Witmer, 1985). Encouragement is closely aligned with Alfred Adler's theory of individual psychology. Encouragement, in the Adlerian sense, is the major method by which the helper assists the client in overcoming demoralization or discouragement. It is a set of techniques that the helper uses throughout the helping process to coax the client away from discouraging beliefs.

In a national survey conducted by the author (Young & Feiler, 1993), encouragement was the second most frequently used counseling technique. It was utilized by 90% of the mental health counselors and counselor educators surveyed. We cannot be certain from these data that all respondents were operating under the same definition of encouragement; however, the survey is supportive of the notion that encouragement is an essential therapeutic ingredient for most helpers.

Encouragement versus Praise

Earlier, we indicated that praise can be a roadblock in the helping process. This idea goes against the grain for many beginning helpers, especially those who work with children. We sincerely want to uplift the client's spirits and we want them to pay attention to their positive attributes and there are times when praise is useful. However, praise definitely puts the helper in the role of a judging parent and the client in the role of the child. Most adults do not need a cheerleader; instead, they need to develop faith in themselves. This is where encouragement comes in. Through encouragement, the helper focuses on respectfully pushing the client to develop a more positive view of life.

To get a clearer idea about encouragement, look at Table 14.1, which compares the concepts of reinforcement from the behavioral tradition and the Adlerian concept of encouragement. The table shows that praise (positive reinforcement) and encouragement each have important but distinct uses. In general, encouragement is designed to

Table 14.1

Comparison of Encouragement and Praise/Reinforcement

Dimension	Encouragement	Reinforcement
Purpose	To motivate, inspire, hearten, instill confidence	To maintain or strengthen a specific behavior
Nature	Focuses on inner direction and internal control; emphasizes personal appreciation and effort more than outcome	Focuses on outer direction and external control; tends to emphasize material appreciation; emphasizes outcome
Population	All ages and groups	Seems most appropriate for children, situations with limited self-control and development, and conditions of specific problem behavior
Thoughts/Feelings/ Actions	A balance of thinking, feeling, and actions with feeling underlying the responses; i.e., satisfaction, enjoyment, challenge	Attending primarily to an action (behavioral) response that is observable
Creativeness	Spontaneity and variation in how encourager responds; encouragee has freedom to respond in spontaneous and creative ways; however, it may be difficult to understand the expectations of the encourager	Reinforcer responds to very specific behavior in a specific way; reinforcee is expected to respond in a specific and prescribed way; little doubt about the expectations of the reinforcer; helpful in establishing goals
Autonomy	Promotes independence, less likelihood of dependency on a specific person or thing; more likely to generalize to other life situations	Tends to develop a strong association, perhaps dependence, between a specific reinforcer and a behavior; less likely to generalize to other life situations

Source: Witmer, J. M. (1985). *Pathways to personal growth.* Muncie, IN: Accelerated Development. Reprinted with permission.

inspire, to foster hope, to stimulate, and to support (Pitsounis & Dixon, 1988), whereas praise is designed to increase the likelihood that a specific behavior will be repeated. Encouragement focuses on developing autonomy, self-reliance, cooperation rather than competition (it avoids comparisons), and an internal locus of control (Hitz & Driscoll, 1988). Praise is a reward that strengthens a behavior when it occurs. In summary, praise has several drawbacks in the helping relationship, since it only recognizes success not intentions and it places the helper in a position of superiority.

Who Benefits Most from Encouragement?

According to Losoncy (1977), persons who are dependent, depressed, cut off from social support systems, or suffering from low self-esteem respond to encouragement. Encouragement also helps clients who show an excessive need for attention, for power, for control of situations and people, and for revenge. It is useful as well with clients who avoid participation and responsibility, who are perfectionistic, or who tend to be close-minded.

Types of Encouraging Responses

In a review of the literature, we identified, in the writings of Dinkmeyer and Losoncy (1980, 1995), Losoncy (1977), Sweeney (1998), and Witmer (1985), 14 types of effective encouraging behaviors:

1. Acknowledging the client's efforts and improvement
2. Concentrating on the client's present capacities, possibilities, and conditions rather than on past failures
3. Focusing on the client's strengths
4. Showing faith in the client's competency and capabilities
5. Showing an interest in the progress and welfare of the client
6. Focusing on those things that interest or excite the client
7. Asking the client to evaluate his or her own performance rather than comparing it to another standard
8. Showing respect for the client and the client's individuality and uniqueness
9. Becoming involved with the client through honest self-disclosure
10. Offering assistance as an equal partner in the counseling process
11. Using humor
12. Providing accurate feedback on deeds rather than on personality
13. Confronting discouraging beliefs
14. Lending enthusiasm and asking for commitment toward goals

Summarizing these 14 interventions may oversimplify the Adlerian concept, but it may also give some general direction to helpers and improve the understanding of the method. I have divided these interventions into three major helper activities: focusing on the positive and the changeable, emphasizing equality and individuality, and pushing with enthusiasm.

Focusing on the Positive and the Changeable

Optimism is the tendency to view the world as a benign, friendly source of support. Not everyone has this point of view, but optimism can be learned (Seligman, 1991). The work of Simonton and Mathews-Simonton (1978) with cancer patients has pointed to the potential health benefits of optimism. More recently, the work of Bernard Siegel (1986) has interested millions in the power of optimistic attitudes in dealing with medical crises. An optimistic point of view is also associated with good mental health and freedom from stress (Witmer, 1985). On the other hand, research indicates that pessimism correlates with depression, lowered achievement, and health problems (Seligman, 1991).

In the preceding list, interventions 1 through 4 are grouped together into the encouraging helper behavior of focusing on the positive and the changeable. All foster development of an optimistic attitude by helping to shift the client's attention from the deficits to the strengths in his or her life. Such encouragement entails noticing the client's success as well as showing faith in the client's ability to succeed. Focusing on the positive and the changeable also includes redirecting the client's discussions from the past to the present. Interventions of this nature are apparent in the following client-helper dialogue:

Client: "I feel like I've totally messed up my future."

Helper: "Tell me what you really enjoy doing."

Client: "What? . . . Oh, well, I really enjoy working in the garden." (The client goes on to describe the feelings he enjoys and the helper encourages him.)

Helper: "How do you feel now?"

Client: "Better. But I always feel better when I think about good things like that."

Helper: "Yes, so do I. I prefer to feel good."

Client (laughing): "So do I. But it isn't always easy."

Encouragement should not be seen as trying to get the client to ignore difficult issues; instead, it asks the client to develop a balanced view that includes the positives. In addition, it helps to focus the client on the parts of the problem that can be changed, rather than ruminating over the unchangeable. Here is an example:

Client: "We went to the picnic and it was a total disaster just like I said it would be. Her mom started criticizing us again, so my wife and I ended up spending most of the time playing with the kids and talking to each other."

Helper: "It sounds like there were some uncomfortable moments, but it also sounds like you did something positive to deal with her mother's criticism."

Client: "What?"

Helper: "Well, instead of getting involved in the argument, you got away from it and spent some time with each other and with some of the kids. It sounds like you hit on a good strategy. Do you agree?"

Communicating Equality and Respect for the Individuality of the Client

The essence of interventions 5 through 10 on the list of encouraging responses is to communicate to the client that the helper and client are on equal footing and that each is unique. By self-disclosing, the helper takes away some of the artificiality of the helper role and connects with the client in a more genuine way. Finally, the helper teaches the client to challenge the idea that the worth of a person is judged by external standards. The client must come to evaluate performance against internal standards and to appreciate his or her personal strengths and unique approach to life as in the following client-helper exchange:

Client: "I finally got off drugs, got a job and an apartment. My life is back on track, but it's still not good enough."

Helper: "What do you mean?"

Client: "My mom won't let up about how I disappointed her, how I was supposed to finish college 2 years ago. Even though I'm back in school in the fall, all she can say is, 'Two years too late.' "

Helper: "What about you—how do you look at it? Are you proud of what you've accomplished in the last 8 months?"

Client: "Well, don't you think I've done a lot?"

Helper: "You tell me."

Client: "I have. I have come a long way. It was hard, too."

Pushing with Enthusiasm

Interventions 11 through 14 demonstrate that encouragement is not merely support; it does not mean accepting the status quo. There is an element of confrontation and a sincere effort to produce movement in the client. Discouragement is actually a defensive maneuver that seeks to maintain the *status quo* through inaction. Encouragement pushes the client by giving feedback, confronting the private logic of the client, asking for a commitment, and using humor to turn the client around (Mosak, 1987). The following example continues the client-helper dialogue from the previous section. Notice the confrontation and the helper pushing the client to make a commitment:

Helper: "So, although you know you've overcome a lot, sometimes you still use your mother's yardstick on your life rather than your own. Would you agree?"

Client: "That's when I get depressed. I'm not sure I can ever please her, but that's not going to stop my recovery."

Helper: "So how are you going to stop doing that?"

Client: "Well, first of all, I will try to let it go in one ear and out the other. But really, I think I'll just spend less time over there."

Helper: "That sounds like a good start. Let's consider that as a plan for this week and when we get back together, you'll let me know, right?

Client: "Right."

How to Encourage

Following are general guidelines that can assist the helper in dealing with discouragement. The steps to take in encouraging a client are shown in conjunction with a case example that includes client statements and helper responses. This example shows that the technique of encouragement consists of giving the client directives to pay attention to his or her own strengths and to focus on what can be changed. Notice that the nonjudgmental listening cycle forms the foundation for the encouraging remarks of the helper.

Step 1   The helper uses the nonjudgmental listening cycle to gain rapport and understand the problem. Encouraging responses will not be appropriate if the helper does not fully understand the client's problem. The nonjudgmental listening cycle is encouraging in and of itself because it promotes a relationship based on equality and respect, one of the hallmarks of encouragement.

Herb was a furniture salesman out of a job. He was very pessimistic about getting hired again after being out of work for 4 months. Although he had initially been rather active, recently he had spent more time driving around in his car than actually looking for a position. His wife accompanied him to the first session, but refused to return to later appointments. During the first session, she strongly expressed her worry, anger, and frustration. According to Herb, he had lost all ambition, he was embarrassed, and he feared he would never be able to locate a new job.

Helper: "So tell me what it is like to be out of a job."

Herb: "It is hell! Everyone blames me. I get depressed and resentful, but mostly I am angry."

Helper: "You're mad at yourself for being in this situation."

Herb: "Exactly. What kind of a man am I? My father never lost a job. Neither did my father-in-law."

Helper: "You mention your father and father-in-law. You seem to be saying that working is an important part of being a man."

Herb: "Of course, I am supposed to be the provider. Now my wife is taking care of me."

In this part of the dialogue, the helper begins with an open question, reflects feelings, and finally reflects meaning. These responses convince the client that the helper understands the situation at a fairly deep level.

Step 2 The helper offers to be an ally.

Helper: "Herb, my feeling is that what you really need right now is a coach. You seem to have job-seeking skills, a good work history, and a positive attitude about your chosen profession. You've shown a lot of success in sales previously. Perhaps together we can help you find your enthusiasm again."

Herb: "I guess you're right that I have had success in the past, but I am at a dead end now. Sometimes I think it is hopeless."

Helper: "My thought is that we begin to look at this thing from a different angle. Perhaps if we put our heads together, we might be able to find a solution."

Step 3 The helper focuses on the positive and notes client attempts, however small, to accomplish the goal.

Client: "I still get up at 6:30 A.M. like I did when I was working. I get dressed and start out all right. First, I read the paper and start to make a call or two. That's when I start getting down. I end up driving around town, killing time until dinner, making my wife think that I am out looking for a job. Why am I doing this?"

Helper: "Well, one of the things I notice is that the rhythm is still there. You are set to get back into a work routine, and you seem to like that. Even though you are not making the contacts, you are practicing, rehearsing for that day when you are back to work. That is a good sign and something we can build on."

Step 4 The helper offers feedback or confrontation and asks for commitment.

Helper: "I've got some feedback for you if you want it."

Herb: "Okay."

Helper: "It seems like one of the problems is that you are not being honest with yourself or your wife about what you do all day. I would like you to keep track of your activities a little better. I think this would help you feel better about yourself and it might help the relationship, too."

Herb: "It is hard to do when I get nothing back."

Helper: "I agree, it is difficult. But I am only asking that you begin to keep a log of what you're doing toward finding a job each day, and we will see if we can increase that or make some changes in the direction of your search."

Herb: "All right. I can do that."

Step 5   The helper shows continued enthusiasm for the client's goals and interest in the client's feelings and progress.

Herb (one week later): "Since the last time we talked, I didn't do what we decided. I didn't make two calls a day looking for a job. I guess I averaged about one call per day. The first day I did three, then one, then one again, and I took the weekend off. I got no response."

Helper: "I am very glad to hear about this. That kind of progress is what we've been looking for. It seems that getting off dead center is the hardest part, and you've gotten through that. Besides, by being honest about it, you've now included me in what's going on. Now what is needed is keeping up your efforts. Right?"

Client: "I guess so. I'm afraid that this won't work, that it will be just like last time and fizzle out."

Helper: "Yes, it can be scary, but let's try to focus on the present if we can, rather than look back. I have been hoping that you'd make this beginning and then hang in there until something breaks. Let's continue with this plan. I'll call you about Wednesday to see how things are going. Again, I feel good about these first steps."

Summary

The technique of encouragement is an antidote to the demoralization that a client feels when he or she first seeks help. Encouragement also helps the client examine and challenge pessimistic attitudes about life that will surface again during times of crisis. If successful, Herb will leave the helping relationship with the ability to focus on the positive and the changeable and will be able to encourage himself.

Stop and Reflect

The Precursors Assessment Form (Figure 14.2) comes from the work of Fred Hanna (1996) and Martin Ritchie (Hanna & Ritchie, 1995). The form lists seven precursors or client characteristics that predict and enhance therapeutic change. The form can be used by clinicians to identify missing elements in the client's involvement and motivation as well as motivational strengths. When the client seems unmotivated, the clinician can rate the client on each of these seven precursors and attempt to enhance the areas that are lacking. For example, a helper might find that a client scores well on the first six variables, but has little social support for change. This could be the missing element in the client's ability to act.

Now, identify a specific personal issue you are working on. Write it down in a sentence or with a single cue word.

Rate your readiness and motivation for change using the Precursors Assessment Form. Make a check next to each of the seven precursors, indicating your

PRECURSORS ASSESSMENT FORM					
Precursor & Its Markers	None (0)	Trace (1)	Small (2)	Adequate (3)	Abundant (4)
1. Sense of Necessity expresses desire for change feels a sense of urgency					
2. Ready for Anxiety openness to experience likely to take risks					
3. Awareness able to identify problems identifies thoughts, feelings					
4. Confronting the Problem courageously faces problems sustained attention to issues					
5. Effort eagerly does homework high energy; active cooperation					
6. Hope positive outlook; open to future; high coping; therapeutic humor					
7. Social Support wide network of friends, family strong therapeutic relationship					

Total Score =

Scoring Guide*

0-6:   Change is unlikely: Educate client on change; Focus approach on all precursors.
7-14:   Change limited and slow: Educate client and focus on precursors with lowest ratings.
15-21: Change is steady and noticeable: Use the lowest rated precursors to stay on track.
22-28: Highly motivated to inspired client: Change occurs easily: Standard approaches work well.

*Scoring is intended only as a general guide to a complex process: Some precursors may be more potent.

Figure 14.2
Precursors Assessment Form
Source: Hanna, F. J. (1996). Precursors of change: Pivotal points of involvement and resistance in psychotherapy. *Journal of Psychotherapy Integration, 6,* 227–264. Reproduced with permission of Kluwer Academic/Plenum Publishers.

level of motivation from 0 (none) to 4 (abundant). Now get a grand total by adding up your scores for all seven precursors. Check your score against the scoring guide and answer the following questions:

1. Based on your score, how likely are you to change in the direction you hope?
2. Which precursors have the lowest scores? Identify two and indicate what you might do to increase or enhance these elements of change.

What Is Resistance?

Traditional Definitions

Resistance is the term used to describe a client's opposition to change. Freud (1900/1952) first identified resistance as a defensive reaction against anxiety when unacceptable thoughts, feelings, and impulses are driven into conscious awareness through the uncovering process of the therapeutic relationship. In other words, clients seek change but react defensively when uncomfortable feelings are dredged up. Clients are said to be "resistant" when they do not cooperate with the help they are offered or continue in self-destructive behaviors despite suggestions to change.

Marty was a 53-year-old woman who suffered from periods of depression and poor interpersonal relationships. She was placed in group therapy, since many of her issues involved her tendency to become very judgmental of others and then retreat from people who disappointed her. During the first five sessions of the group, Marty dominated the conversation and told long involved stories about people she knew. The stories never seemed to reach any conclusion and disclosed little about her. Eventually, group members confronted her with the fact that she was avoiding interacting with them by persisting in her monologues. Some clients, like Marty, show their resistance to change quite clearly. For others, change just seems to stall just when success is within reach.

Resistance remains a hot topic in the helping professions because it is connected with the notion of the reluctant client (Dowd & Milne, 1986; Harris & Watkins, 1987). The reluctant client is one who does not wish to come for help in the first place, but who has been forced or pressured to do so. It is estimated that 50–75% of clients could be described as reluctant (Dyer & Vriend, 1977; Haley, 1989; Ritchie, 1986). Reluctant clients are not technically "resistant," but rather they are unmotivated. Ordinarily, they are coerced by the courts or by the corrections system, are brought for help by a spouse or a family member, or are being disciplined by a school or college. There has been a great interest in techniques for engaging reluctant clients, probably because they represent such a large proportion of clients (Amatea, 1988; Larke, 1985; Larrabee, 1982).

Do Clients Want to Change?

Clients do want to change, but change is upsetting and disorienting to all of us. We all suffer from ambivalence about change. Consequently, resistance has been described as present in every therapeutic situation (Brammer, Shostrom, & Abrego, 1989). When progress is stymied, resistance on the part of the client is often identified. Redl (1966) goes so far as to name client resistance as the cause of most therapeutic failures. Similarly, Hart (1986) says, "Therapy is difficult because clients are resistant to change and defensive about revealing their urges" (p. 211).

This tendency to place the entire blame on the client is found in other therapies besides psychodynamics quoted previously. Perls (1971), the founder of Gestalt therapy, saw resistance as an attempt on the part of the client to decline responsibility for change. He felt that clients were consistently avoiding their problems and that this was apparent in the way they interacted with the helper (Brammer et al., 1989). Rational emotive therapy practitioners have thought of resistance as either laziness or fear (Mahoney, 1988a), and transactional analysts have accused clients of playing games.

Family therapists, in contrast, have traditionally seen resistance as attempts by the family to maintain a homeostatic balance. Jackson (1968) pointed out that most families come to the helping process because something has "upset the apple cart," and they are looking for a return to peace and security. Since they are seeking stability rather than disruption, they may be unwilling to risk very much. For example, once a man named Robin came for help to deal with a career decision he had to make. During the initial interview, the helper made a detailed inquiry of the client's family life and found that Robin had two children from a former marriage. Although the kids lived only an hour away, he spent about two days a year with them and rarely phoned. When asked about this, Robin became tearful, expressing his guilt and his sense of being torn between the two families he had created. Robin never returned for his second session, during which he and the helper had planned to find a way to bring his children more toward the center of his life. Resistance in family therapy often takes the form of prematurely dropping out as in the case of Robin. At other times, clients react with anger when they are pushed to try new behaviors. Families who resist change have even been described as "barracudas" (Bergman, 1985), presumably because they can be aggressive when asked to change.

Another viewpoint is that resistance is communication from the client to the helper. The client is indirectly telling the helper about his or her defenses and coping patterns. It may be signaling that helping is proceeding too rapidly for comfort or that the helping process is slowing down and may be headed for termination (Brammer et al., 1989). It could be said that the client is communicating that he or she has found a way to minimize anxiety and maintain some sort of stability and the helping relationship is endangering that homeostasis (Singer, 1970).

A new idea has been advanced by some cognitive therapists, who point out that resistance is a natural reaction when one's schemata, or mental constructs about the world, are challenged (Dowd & Seibel, 1990; Mahoney, 1988b). The client naturally clings to habitual ways of thinking about life, no matter how dysfunctional. When the helper begins to disrupt long-held and cherished beliefs about the world, the client tries to protect his or her core beliefs from sweeping changes that may bring chaos. Cognitive therapists believe that helpers should help clients proceed gradually in their worldviews so as to limit the amount of resistant behavior.

Finally, a new viewpoint about resistance is developing in the strategic therapy and solution-focused schools (de Shazer, 1985, 1988; Haley, 1976; Lawson, 1986; Otani, 1989). One way of expressing their ideas is to simply say that, for them, resistance does not exist. To emphasize this, one group of practitioners actually held a funeral for the concept of resistance. Among these writers, a client's failure to comply with directives is seen and interpreted as an attempt to improve on or to individualize assignments. Rather than being seen as uncooperative behavior, failure to follow helper directives is perceived as the client's best attempt to change (O'Hanlon & Weiner-Davis, 1989). When a client does not comply with suggestions or agreed-upon plans, the helper interprets this behavior as a signal that assignments are missing the mark and need to be modified or eliminated.

What Does Resistance Look Like?

Resistance may be active or passive. For example, a client may refuse to engage in a role-playing exercise or may simply "forget" to do homework assignments. Much has been written about resistance and its many forms have been documented. Following is a list of common manifestations reported by various writers (Blanck, 1976; Brammer et al., 1989; Lerner & Lerner, 1983; Otani, 1989; Sack, 1988; Wolberg, 1954):

1. The client criticizes the helper or the counseling process.
2. The client comes late to sessions, fails to keep appointments, or forgets to pay fees.
3. The client is silent or talks only minimally.
4. The client intellectualizes and philosophizes.
5. The client terminates prematurely or reports a sudden improvement that is actually a protection against further change.
6. The client uses excessive humor, silliness, or facetiousness.
7. The client persistently says, "I don't know."
8. The client does not wish to terminate and wants to extend session length.
9. The client delves into the helper's personal life or asks for personal favors.
10. The client presents irrelevant material designed to intrigue the helper.
11. The client develops insights but does not apply them, dissociating the helping process from everyday life.
12. The client engages in small talk or is preoccupied with the past.
13. The client makes last-minute disclosures.

What Causes Resistance?

Although different theorists explain resistance in varying ways, a number of common causes have been suggested (Bugental & Bugental, 1986; McMullin, 1986; Ritchie, 1986). The explanations are sometimes divided into client, helper, and environmental sources (Cormier & Cormier, 1991). Here, we define resistance as any client or helper behavior and any environmental force that interferes with a client's progress toward the goals of helping, whether intentional or not.

Client Sources of Resistance

Sometimes clients lack the skills to comply with the helper's suggestions. For example, clients may not possess certain social skills needed to develop better relationships at work or may lack the ability to follow homework assignments due to lack of skill in self-expression rather than an oppositional attitude.

A second area of resistance involves client fears. Clients fear the helping process because they find self-disclosure with a stranger uncomfortable. They fear the intensity of emotions that might be unleashed. They fear exposure and lack trust and are afraid that the helping process will cause disequilibrium and distress. They may fear change most of all because it represents the unknown (Bugental & Bugental, 1986). Fearful clients slow down the helping process by disclosing little and often drop out because they fear exhuming painful emotions.

Another major source of resistance is involuntary status, the feeling of being coerced into the helping process by some third party: employer, spouse, or court (Driscoll, 1984). Today, every helper will have reluctant clients and must spend considerable time in the first sessions overcoming the resistance that comes with having little choice. Some people are rebels and have a difficult time with being forced to receive help. Others resist bureaucracy, seeing the helper as an extension of government control.

Clients can be labeled resistant when they experience a conflict between their own values and those of the helper or the community. Some religious groups feel that the helping process attempts to shift their values toward those of an unhealthy society. Others feel that exposing problems to a professional is shameful to their families. Still others reject the helping process because of cultural injunctions against being dependent on strangers or revealing family secrets. A great deal of time and trust is needed to overcome these cultural barriers to helping.

Dislike of the helper can also be a reason for a slowing of progress. The client may not like the helper because of the helper's gender, religion, appearance, class, race, or cultural background, or for very personal reasons. The helper's personal style and even the school of therapy to which the helper belongs can be aversive to the client (Stream, 1985). Sometimes the chemistry is just wrong and progress stops because the relationship has a competitive feeling.

Resistance can be a reflection of the client's readiness and motivation. McMullin (1986) reminds us that not all clients who walk in the door are really seeking to change. Clients sometimes consult a professional because they want to change someone else or because they are lonely and want the companionship of an intelligent and sensitive friend. Other clients may just enjoy the temporary relief that accompanies unloading their feelings and frustrations. Still others are sampling the helping process as some people go for a massage.

Helper Sources of Resistance

When a client does not seem to be changing, helpers become frustrated. Ironically, helper frustration often leads to a further slowdown in progress. Unfortunately, when a helper acts frustrated or angry, the client may feel that he or she is being punished or may infer that the situation is hopeless (Martin, 1983). The root of the helper's frustration is often due to the fact that the helper wants more for the client than the client wants for himself or herself (Cormier & Hackney, 1987). When helpers become frustrated, they may react by putting less effort and energy into the session or by becoming aloof. A client's failure to make progress makes the helper feel impotent and discouraged. Alternately, a helper's frustration may tempt him or her to criticize or blame the client for the lack of progress or may prompt the helper to make an inappropriate referral just to get rid of the client.

Environmental Sources of Resistance

Engaging a professional helper can be expensive. It is common for clients to drop out simply because they cannot afford to continue. This is one example of an environmental hurdle or environmental resistance. One of the most important sources of environmental resistance, ironically, comes from family and friends. A client who wants to lose weight or become more assertive may find family members actively opposing his or her efforts. If we accept the concept that a family system attempts to maintain equilibrium, a member who tries to upset the rules and roles of a family may meet stiff opposition.

How to Deal with Resistance

Preventing Resistance

Before discussing the subject of dealing with a resistant client, let us think about some ways to prevent resistance before it negatively affects progress. Resistance frequently surfaces when the helper suggests that the client try out a new behavior or assigns extensive homework. The best inoculation for resistance is taking the time to establish a strong therapeutic relationship before attempting to implement techniques that require a great deal of client commitment. If open communication exists, clients are more likely to be honest and will be better able to share their reasons for noncompliance.

Also, try to recognize that all clients are ambivalent about change and keep this in mind when the client does not appear to be cooperating. Anticipate client resistance and consider it to be a normal and expected developmental step. One way to do this is to predict resistance and develop plans to deal with it when it arises. For example, when it appears that a client is fearful or reluctant to change, before giving a homework assignment, ask the client to brainstorm all of the excuses he or she might give for not completing assignments or for accomplishing goals.

Finally, Meichenbaum and Turk (1987) suggest that the helper have more empathy for the resistant client. These researchers studied noncompliance with medical treatment and were astonished to find that as much as 50% of the medication prescribed by doctors is never taken. Their major finding is that we must see noncompliance from the client's point of view. They believe that many of the methods they used to increase client adherence to medical treatment can also apply to the helping setting. Here are nine of their suggestions:

1. Expect noncompliance and do not react negatively.
2. Consider the homework assignments and treatment plan from the client's point of view. Would you be willing to undergo this kind of treatment yourself?
3. Develop a collaborative relationship and negotiate the goals with the client.
4. Be client-oriented.
5. Customize treatment.
6. Enlist family support.
7. Provide the client with a system of continuity and accessibility to the helper.
8. Make use of community resources (such as support groups).
9. Don't give up.

Readiness for Change

Identifying Levels of Motivation

Earlier, in the "Stop and Reflect" section, you saw seven variables, or precursors, identified by Hanna and Ritchie (1995) that predict and enhance change. Some of these variables involved seeking social support and the willingness to take risks and experience attending anxiety. These writers also addressed the key issue of motivation or involvement of the client in the therapeutic process by naming a sense of necessity, willingness to confront problems, effort, and hope as factors that precede and heighten the client's ability to change.

Clients vary in their motivation for change. Some are merely considering change, while others are ready to act. Two different groups of writers have begun to classify clients based on their levels of motivation, so that specific treatments can be matched with the client's state of readiness. One view is promoted by the eclectic thinkers Norcross, Prochaska, and DiClemente (Prochaska & DeClemente, 1983,

Table 14.2
Stages of Motivation and Change

Prochaska and DiClemente	de Shazer	Possible Interventions
Precontemplation	Visitor	Awareness exercises
		Education
		Feedback
		Relationship enhancement
		Observations/confrontation
Contemplation	Complainant	Encouraging commitment
		Noting rewards and drawbacks
		Promoting ownership/responsibility
Action	Customer	Action strategies
		Rehearsal/practice
		Tasks, ordeals, and homework
Maintenance		Follow-up contacts
		Support groups
		Self-control strategies
		Relapse prevention

1986; Prochaska & Norcross, 1994; Prochaska, Norcross, & DiClemente, 1994). An-other comes from the Brief Family Therapy Training Center (de Shazer, 1988). Both groups see the client's level of readiness for the helping process as an important aspect of planning treatment.

The eclectic model of Prochaska and DiClemente (1983, 1986) proposes that clients move through four stages in the process of change. Each stage represents a period of time and a set of tasks needed for movement to the next stage. This model is particularly applicable to the addictions field, since it mirrors the process that individuals undergo in the decision to receive treatment and in their relapse or recovery (Marlatt, 1988). The model also indicates that a helper can select the most effective interventions depending on the client's level of motivation (see Table 14.2).

Clients who are unaware of a problem are in the stage of *precontemplation*. At this point, they are not even considering a change and are surprised when friends and family suggest that they have a problem. Courts and significant others refer many such people for help each year. The best treatments for clients at this level are primarily educational. The helper avoids moralizing and instead invites the client to think more and more about the problem.

When a person becomes aware that a problem might exist, he or she has entered the stage of *contemplation*. A client at this stage may admit that a problem exists, but he or she denies that it is a serious problem or that professional help is needed. Many who suffer from alcoholism cannot cross the threshold of the Alcoholics Anonymous 12-step program because the first step begins with the admission that one's life has become unmanageable because of alcohol. People may remain in this "I'll quit tomorrow" stage for years until they experience enough pain to motivate further movement.

Action, or determination, is the phase of treatment in which the individual is ready to change behavior patterns or begins to seek outside help. The balance may shift suddenly toward the action phase or it may be a gradual process. Normally, the decision to take action is made when the client experiences so much discomfort that "something has to change." Clients at this stage benefit from directives, treatment programs, and homework assignments that involve experimenting with different behaviors.

Once a client seeks help and receives treatment, the *maintenance* stage begins. When the problem has come under control, the client attempts to change his or her lifestyle to accommodate the changes made. This is a crucial period in the process of change and one that is often neglected in treatment programs. The maintenance stage may lead to stable change or relapse, depending on how well the helper is able to extend treatment through follow-up and the degree to which the client can develop personal and environmental supports for new behaviors. Clients at the maintenance stage need continuing support from peers and family and need to practice self-care and self-control strategies.

de Shazer's Model

Another way of looking at levels of motivation is in a model suggested by Steve de Shazer (1989). His model divides clients into three categories: visitors, complainants, and customers. At the lowest level of motivating, *visitors* are individuals who seemingly have no complaints. They may be forced or coerced into the helping process by some third party who does have a complaint. Visitors can be helped by giving them information, suggesting educational programs, and getting them to think about their problems. The helper may be able to help the client recognize that a problem exists or at least prepare the client to get help later by helping the client become aware of available resources when help is needed.

Complainants are those clients who are uncomfortable and are seeking solutions. They clearly wish to consider a change of some kind, but they may not be ready to do much about it. On the other hand, clients who are ready, willing, and able to take action are labeled *customers*. Helpers frequently become frustrated because they confuse complainants with customers. With complainants, the helper's job is to try and tip the balance and make the client aware of the need to change. Complainants will not follow through with action-oriented directives or homework, so it is best to avoid these. Only customers should be given homework or other behavioral tasks. Table 14.2 shows a comparison of the viewpoints of de Shazer and of Prochaska and DiClemente, highlighting their similarities and some possible interventions associated with each level of motivation. A helper can refer to this chart to think about possible interventions when it appears that the client is not ready to change. Thinking about motivation in its various levels can stimulate us to devise appropriate interventions and accept the client's current state of readiness without getting frustrated.

Tipping the Balance

Tipping the balance is a name for helper activities that motivate clients to change by focusing them on the rewards of change or emphasizing the negative aspects of the current situation. Tipping the balance works when clients are stuck. The situations or problems that bring clients for help can be thought of as a temporary balance of driving and restraining forces (Lewin, 1951). Take, for example, the situation of Latrice, a young accountant who is considering a move from Ohio to Seattle. Latrice has a problem and is stymied because she must consider both the forces pushing her to move and others urging her to stay. She might list the pros and cons of moving. The problem with this method is that a good decision should not be based on whether there are more pros or more cons. Reasons for staying or leaving carry different weights. Being close to family might be more important, for example, than a salary increase.

Like two sides of a scale, movement only occurs when one side outweighs the other. For example, being satisfied and remaining in Ohio is a condition of homeostasis or balance. It can be modified by diminishing the ties that hold her to Ohio or by increasing her incentives to move on. A person may stay put because of loyalty, high pay, supportive friends, and so on, but he or she may move either when a better offer comes along (driving force) or when a restraining force, such as fringe benefits or opportunities for advancement, is reduced. By the same token, a client who wishes to lose weight could decrease the pleasure of eating (restraining force) by eating quickly. Conversely, the desire to feel more attractive (driving force) can be increased by incentives, such as buying clothes in a smaller size or by obtaining positive feedback on attractiveness from supportive friends. Helpers assist clients in tipping the balance toward change when it appears that the client is in the doldrums, caught between opposing forces.

One set of methods for tipping the balance involves rewarding change and taking away rewards for behaviors that are maintaining the status quo. It is important to ascertain which aspects of the client's environment promote maintenance of the status quo and then to remove them. The family of a patient in chronic pain, for example, might be asked to discontinue expressions of sympathy and to stop doing things for the client that he or she can do independently. Using methods of self-control (Kanfer, 1986), clients can also learn to increase the positive consequences associated with their own behavior and to build in rewards for change. In short, the client's resistance to change is sometimes due to the fact that the rewards for giving up a behavior are not as powerful as the reasons for retaining it. Helpers encourage clients to use powerful rewards to tip the balance. For example, a client who wishes to lose 25 pounds may be more motivated to lose weight if the client promises himself or herself a trip to Europe rather than merely a new outfit.

Contingency Contracting: A Method for Tipping the Balance

Negotiating contracts for change has become widespread in schools and counseling centers (Kanfer, 1980). Contingency contracts are agreements between individuals who desire behavior change and those whose behavior needs changing, such as between parents and their children. Individuals can make formal contracts with themselves, their spouses, or others. All contracts specify the positive consequences of adhering to the contract and the negative consequences of noncompliance. They also specify contingencies or "if-then" statements, such as "If you take out the trash without being told, then I will give you your allowance regularly." Such contracts have been effective with academic problems, social skills, bad habits, marital problems, and delinquent behaviors (Dowd & Olson, 1985).

Based on Dowd and Olson's recommendations (1985), the following guidelines for effective contracts are suggested:

1. All aspects of the contract should be understood and agreed to by both partners.

2. The contract should be in written form with a solemn signing indicating commitment to the agreement.
3. The contract should stress rewarding accomplishments rather than merely reinforcing obedience.
4. The contract should be considered the first of a series of steps if the behavior to be changed is complex.
5. The contract is not a legal document and can be renegotiated at any time by any of the signers.
6. The behaviors to be achieved should be clearly and objectively defined. They should be relatively short-range goals.
7. If possible, behavioral goals should be quantified and specified (who, what, where, when, and how often), so that it is clear when the contract is being adhered to.
8. The contract should not contain goals either of the parties is incapable of living up to. Success should be simple to understand and achieve.
9. The rewards and privileges for displaying each behavior should be specified.
10. The reward for each behavior should be commensurate with the behavior needed to earn it.
11. The reward should be timed to be delivered as soon after the behavior is displayed as possible.
12. The contract should specify small penalties for each person's failure to abide by the contract.
13. Bonuses should be given if goals are exceeded or if they are accomplished more quickly than expected.

Stop and Reflect

Often, a problem is not merely a hurdle that must be jumped or a puzzle to be solved. It may be something like a tug-of-war where each side is equally strong and there is no movement. A problem can be seen as a temporary state in which forces that propel or drive change are balanced by forces that restrain or motivate against change. To understand this better, answer the following questions and then complete Figure 14.3. Look over Figure 14.4, an example of a completed worksheet.

1. Describe a problem or decision you have to make that is important to you. Describe it as simply and specifically as possible.
2. Who is involved? What other people influence this problem or will be affected if you change?
3. If it were in your power to change one part of the problem, what would you change?
4. List up to six forces that are restraining you from changing (see the example in Figure 14.4) and place a number from 1 to 5 next to each, indicating the strength of that force as shown:
   1 = the force is unimportant
   2 = the force has a little impact
   3 = moderate importance
   4 = an important factor
   5 = major factor

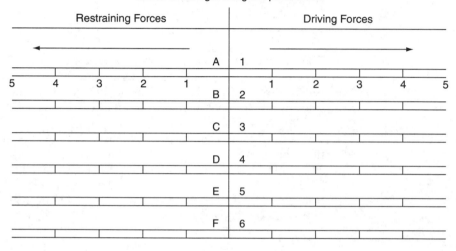

Figure 14.3
Driving and Restraining Forces Worksheet

5. List up to six forces that are driving you to change. Place a number from 1 to 5 indicating the strength of each of these forces that are pushing you to change, using the scale described in item 4.

6. Chart your answers in Figure 14.3 similar to the example in Figure 14.4.

7. When you have completed the exercise, consider the following questions individually or share them with some classmates.

   a. Review your answer to item 2. Did you include your feelings of obligation to others as factors?

   b. Does your answer to item 3 give you any ideas about what would really motivate you to change?

   c. Look at the items in your list of restraining forces. Can any of these items be reduced? For example, in Latrice's case, she enjoys her garden and hates to leave it. In Seattle, she would live in an apartment. Could Latrice decrease this restraining force by looking into community garden efforts or window-box gardening to decrease the power of this restraining force? Again, consider your list of restraining forces. Which could be reduced?

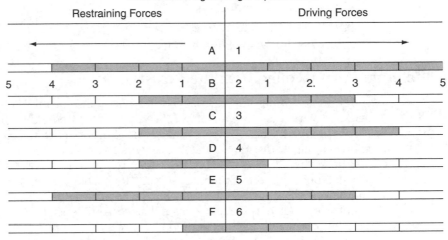

List restraining and driving forces that affect the problem:

Closer to family in Ohio	A.	1.	Better pay in Seattle
Good fringe benefits in Ohio	B.	2.	More social life in Seattle
Job Security in Ohio	C.	3.	I'll be independent
Better housing in Ohio	D.	4.	More scenic beauty
Good friends in Ohio	E.	5.	Better chance for advancement
Calmer pace of life	F.	6.	More cultural opportunities

Show the strength of restraining forces to the left and driving forces to the right using a 5-point scale:

Figure 14.4
A Completed Driving and Restraining Forces Worksheet

d. Now take a look at your list of driving forces. Can any of these be strengthened? For example, Latrice might increase the force of "more social opportunities," which she labeled as a 3, by taking one or two trips to Seattle, getting to know her co-workers better, or even investigating a dating service. Now take a look at your list. How might you strengthen any of your driving forces to propel change?

Confronting Resistance Directly

The language of war has been used to describe the friction in the helper-client relationship when resistance crops up. Helpers have traditionally explained to clients that they are resisting improvement because they are afraid to change. This is called *interpretation of resistance.* The helper continually confronts clients with their unwillingness to take their medicine. As Sifenos says, "Pounding patients with a truth produces good results" (Davanloo, 1978, p. 241). A gentler version is to confront the client's resistant behavior directly and then to ask the client to explore why he or she might be reluctant to change as in this dialogue between helper and client:

Jonathan (Client): "I didn't do that assignment we talked about last week. To tell you the truth, I was so busy that I forgot about it. I also didn't do any writing."

Kristi (Helper): "Interesting. On the one hand, you come to therapy to get over the writer's block and yet you don't do the things that might help you overcome it. Can you explain this to me?" (confronting)

Jonathan: "Well, I do want to get over it, but I just don't have the motivation."

Kristi: "I think this idea of motivation is more of an excuse for not doing the assignment. How much motivation would it have taken to do the homework assignment?" (confronting)

Jonathan: "Not much, I guess."

Kristi: "Let's talk some more about your reluctance to change. Can you think of any reasons why you might not want to write again?" (inviting exploration)

The Technique of Traveling with the Resistance

Adler, Rogers, Sullivan, and Maslow all assert that a hostile, competitive view of resistance with the rhetoric of warfare is counterproductive (Lauver, Holiman, & Kazama, 1982). These helpers and a host of others have developed methods in response to client resistance that "travel with the resistance." *Traveling with the resistance* refers to helper behaviors that attempt to normalize and accept the oppositional behavior (cf. Brammer et al., 1990; Dyer & Vriend, 1977; Egan, 1990; Guidano, 1988; Walker & Aycock, 1986). When the helper accepts and normalizes the client's resistance, the client does not become defensive and the therapeutic relationship is not damaged. In addition, this reaction helps the client to become more aware of his or her resistant behavior. The following suggestions are all ways of accepting the client's resistance and finding a new way of achieving compliance without using strong confrontation:

1. Remind the client that resistance is a normal part of the helping process and that avoidance is an important coping mechanism.
2. Describe the client's resistant response as a positive step forward rather than as a failure. The helper may even ascribe noble intentions to the client's deviations from therapeutic goals (Palazzoli, Boscolo, Cecchin, and Prata, 1978).
3. Use group counseling procedures to provide peer encouragement and support for change.
4. Invite the cooperation and participation of the client in the setting of goals.
5. Tap the client's social support systems, including family, friends, and significant others, to help encourage or maintain change.
6. Get a foot in the door (Roloff & Miller, 1980). This technique involves asking the client to complete a very minor homework assignment and then following it with a request for a more significant change.
7. Ask the client to change for one week only, as an experiment.
8. Decrease the frequency and length of sessions when conflict arises. Slow down the pace of the helping process. There is nothing sacred about weekly counseling sessions. When resistance surfaces, consider reducing sessions to once per month.

How to Travel with the Resistance

The technique of traveling with resistant behavior rests on the assumption that when a client does not follow directives or homework assignments, the helper should shift gears and look for a new angle. Traveling with the resistance involves three steps: (1) using the nonjudgmental listening cycle to convey understanding, (2) communicating acceptance of the client's unwillingness to change, and (3) devising a new strategy based on the client's level of motivation. This technique is demonstrated in Kristi's response to Jonathan, a professional writer with writer's block. In a previous example, Kristi confronted Jonathan and encouraged him to explore the reasons for his resistance. Here let us examine how she might instead travel with the resistance. In this case, Jonathan returns to the second session, not having done the homework assigned by the helper, Kristi. As a beginning exercise, Kristi had asked him to sit at his desk and write anything for 15 minutes per day.

Step 1   Use the nonjudgmental listening cycle to convey understanding. The helper spends a few minutes trying to understand and reflect the client's feelings and the underlying meanings behind the client's noncompliance.

Jonathan: "I didn't do that assignment we talked about last week. To tell you the truth, I was so busy that I forgot about it. I also didn't do any writing."

Kristi: "You sound sort of disappointed in yourself."

Jonathan: "I am. I am just avoiding it. Like that desk was deadly or something. Why can't I get started?"

Kristi: "You're angry at yourself for avoiding your writing. It sounds like you're almost afraid to begin."

Jonathan: "I get really nervous when I sit down at the desk."

Step 2   Communicate acceptance of the client's resistant behavior. The helper surprises the client by accepting the client's resistant behavior and normalizing it.

Jonathan: "For some reason, I just blocked that homework out of my mind."

Kristi: "If you get really anxious when you sit down, I can understand why you did not want to complete this homework assignment. Still, I think this assignment was very helpful because I understand the problem much better."

Step 3   Determine the client's level of motivation and develop a new strategy that matches it. The helper shifts gears at this point and develops a different assignment that the client is more likely to complete. It may be useful to refer to the levels of motivation in Table 14.2. In the case of Jonathan, Kristi had asked Jonathan to engage in an action strategy. In the following interchange, she changes direction as follows:

Jonathan: "Now that you know that I can't even write for 15 minutes, what are we going to do?"

Kristi: "After hearing this, I realize that solitary homework isn't going to work. I think that you instinctively knew this and that is why you didn't follow through. Instead, let us work on the writing here together. How does that sound?"

Summary

Demoralization, discouragement, and learned helplessness all refer to a condition that indicates lowered expectations, loss of hope, and a lack of motivation for change. At some point in the therapeutic relationship, helpers encounter these feelings in nearly everyone who comes for help. From the outset, one of the major tasks of helping is to help the client overcome demoralization, which can interfere with the client's willingness to enter into the therapeutic relationship.

The Adlerian concept of encouragement involves attitudes and behaviors that include a positive focus, a belief in equality, respect for the client, and enthusiastically challenging the client. Encouragement is an attitude, as well as a set of skills, that can be especially helpful with demoralized clients.

Resistance has traditionally been defined as any client behavior that interferes with the agreed-upon goals. Many experts now recognize that resistance is a natural part of any change process and that helpers must also look for sources of resistance in their own behavior and in the environment, including the client's family and friends. Traveling with the resistance is a simple method of accepting and defusing noncompliance by the client by accepting and normalizing the resistant behavior. Other methods for dealing with resistance include direct confrontation, contingency contracting, and finding ways to tip the balance by focusing on driving or restraining forces.

Clients vary in their readiness for change and a helper must learn to accept the client's current level of motivation, rather than becoming frustrated when progress is not achieved as quickly as hoped. One way of conceptualizing these differences comes from the work of Hanna and Ritchie, who identified precursors to change such as hope, effort, and social support. Prochaska and DiClemente suggest that a client's readiness determines which methods and techniques will be the most effective. de Shazer, on the other hand, simply identifies clients as either visitors, complainants, or customers to emphasize that a different approach is required for different amounts of client involvement.

Group Exercises

Role-Play—Traveling with the Resistance

Form groups of three consisting of a client, a helper, and an observer. The client chooses to enact one of the following scenarios. He or she can expand on the basic story to give it some scope for the helper to explore. The client should be slightly uncooperative at first to give the helper practice in dealing with a resistant client.

The helper's job is to follow the basic outline: (1) use the nonjudgmental listening cycle to explore the client's resistant behavior, (2) convey acceptance of the resistant behavior, and (3) devise a new strategy to accomplish the goal.

The observer writes down all helper statements in order.

Scenario 1   The client has been coming to the helper over the last few months for career counseling. The client has begun to make some progress and appears to be on the verge of identifying a new career field. Suddenly he or she has begun missing appointments. The client has shown some evidence about being fearful of impending change. When asked about the missed appointments, at first, the client says, "I just got busy."

Scenario 2   The client has been through an assertiveness training group to deal with an inability to say, "No." The client habitually becomes overloaded with extra responsibilities at work and at church and with family duties because of a tendency to agree to whatever is asked. During this session, the client tells the helper about a recent episode at work where the client reverted back to the nonassertive behavior. The client understands the problem, and the helper and client have covered this ground before. Still, the client cannot seem to apply the insights learned in assertiveness training or in the helping relationship.

Following the role-play, both observer and client give the helper feedback on the following issues:

- Did the helper convey any frustration or disappointment in the client? Don't forget to check nonverbals.
- Which statements by the helper conveyed acceptance of the resistant behavior?
- Was the helper able to devise a new strategy to accomplish the goal that was acceptable to the client?

Additional Exercises

Exercise 1

Following are three client statements. Indicate whether they are visitors, complainants, or customers according to Table 14.2. What interventions might you use to help each client address goals at his or her current level of motivation? Exchange your ideas with your classmates.

a. "You may be right, I do need to do something about my job. I am spending very little time with my wife and kids. She's upset. But at work, we are just about to start a very exciting project. It'll probably mean more time away, but what can you do?"
b. "My ex-girlfriend Verna keeps stopping at the house. I am starting to think it might be a problem. My present girlfriend gets a little annoyed, even though she knows I would never go back to Verna. Maybe I should do something about it because, to tell the truth, I don't really know why she keeps coming around. I guess we're just friends."

Client, helper, and observer then exchange roles so each has an opportunity to practice this technique.

Quick Tips: Traveling with the Resistance

- Be sure that you do not communicate disapproval nonverbally. As you are listening, stay nonjudgmental.
- Try to identify the positive aspects of the client's behavior. If a small step has been made, notice it.
- If the client mentions a favorite activity such as reading, journaling, or watching movies, see if you can use one of these interests when you devise a new strategy.
- If the client appears discouraged, use encouraging techniques.
- If the client appears angry or defensive, return to the nonjudgmental listening cycle.

c. "Last night, my boyfriend got drunk again. It wasn't just that it happened in front of my parents, it is just that I am always worried. I can't relax when we go out anymore. It used to be fun, but now it is boring and it makes me angry. The relationship is not worth what I have to go through every weekend."

Exercise 2: Practicing Encouragement

Following are a number of client responses that suggest pessimism and discouragement. Review the list of encouraging responses and make a statement that reflects feelings or meanings. Then write down one or more encouraging responses that (1) focus on the positive and the changeable, (2) communicate equality in the helping relationship and respect the individuality of the client, or (3) push or confront the client, adding energy and enthusiasm for the goal.

Example: "Our marriage is on the rocks. We just can't talk anymore. Anytime I try, she just starts an argument. I need some freedom to be alone once in a while, to work in my shop or on the computer, to read, or to go over to Jeff's house and watch the game. It wasn't like this when we were living together, but now she thinks she owns my time. Before, she would have her interests, I would have mine, and then we would spend some time together. I wish she had some hobbies or something. It's just too much pressure."

Reflecting: "You feel trapped and you don't know how to improve the situation."

Encouraging (focusing on the positive and the changeable):

"You say that you used to manage this issue pretty well before you were married. You were able to balance alone time and together time. It sounds like you two have the ability to communicate well at times. Is that something you might be able to do again?"

Now give both a reflecting and an encouraging response to the following client statements:

a. "I don't like talking about myself very much. For one thing, how will it really help? You just throw things out. That doesn't change them and, besides, I was taught never to air dirty laundry in public."
b. "My wife feels I have problems with drinking. But I don't. She says she's at the end of her rope and is going to leave me unless I get help. I'm working every day, I bring home my paycheck. Lots of people drink more than I do."
c. "I've tried everything to quit smoking in the past. Why, two years ago, I went to hypnosis. Once when I was younger, I went to a seminar. Somebody said I should try nicotine gum or patches. But I've tried before. I know it's bad for my health and the kids are always nagging me, but some people just can't quit."
d. "I'm in a dead-end job. I know I should look for a new job. But maybe I'm too old to go back to school, learn a whole new way of doing things. When I see these young people on computers, they already know so much. Could I really keep up?"

In a small group, discuss your answers to these exercises. Note that these helping responses are designed to increase the client's sense of optimism and hope, not to solve the client's problem for him or her. Evaluate both your reflecting and encouraging responses. When looking at your encouraging responses, think about whether the client might perceive these as patronizing, or not genuine, or whether the client might get the impression that you are ignoring the seriousness of the problem.

Homework

Homework 1: Functional Analysis

One obstacle to change is overcoming the force of habit. A bad habit can be frustrating because we seem to persist in it, even when we don't want to. One way of attacking bad habits is to scientifically identify what factors are supporting the behavior. This process is called *functional analysis*. Clients can learn functional analysis and then devise self-management strategies to eliminate bad habits by building in rewards (positive reinforcement) for new behaviors. To understand this process better, select a behavior of your own that you would like to change and follow the instructions:

a. Begin by identifying the behavior or bad habit you would like to change with as much objectivity, simplicity, and specificity as you can. Example: "I bite my fingernails."

_____

_____

_____

b. Indicate things that occur simultaneously with or around the same time as the problem behavior. Example: "I bite my fingernails when I am watching television or when I am reading a good book."

_____

_____

_____

c. List things that are consistently not associated with the bad habit. Example: "When I am biting my nails, I am not with anyone else."

_____

_____

_____

d. What happens right before the problem behavior? Example: "I am nervous."

_____

_____

_____

e. What are you experiencing when you are doing the problem behavior? Example: "When I am biting my nails, it seems to distract me and I feel less nervous."

_____

_____

_____

f. What happens right after the problem behavior? Do you get a reward or is something negative eliminated? Example: "I am angry at myself for biting my nails and I call myself an idiot." (no reinforcer found)

_____

_____

_____

g. Based on this exercise, what do you think is maintaining the problem behavior? Example: "Biting my nails makes me feel less anxious when I am alone watching television or reading a book."

_____

_____

h. How could you manipulate the environment to reduce the problem behavior? Example: "I could make an agreement with myself not to watch television by myself for a while. When I am reading, I could wear gloves. That way, I won't bite my nails without thinking."

_____

_____

i. How could you use rewards to change the behavior? Example: "If I can make it through one day without biting my nails, I will treat myself to an ice cream cone. If I can make it through a week, I will go and get a manicure."

_____

_____

_____

j. Devise a plan to manipulate the environment and to reward alternative behavior. Practice your plan on two occasions and note the results:

Trial 1:

_____

_____

Trial 2:

_____

_____

• If you feel comfortable discussing your plan with others, involve someone else in your plan so that he or she knows what you are trying to accomplish and can support and encourage you (social reinforcement).

- Discuss this homework with your instructor if you are having trouble devising techniques to manipulate the environment or you can't seem to identify suitable rewards. Refer to Bellack and Hersen's book, *Dictionary of Behavior Therapy Techniques* (1986), for other ideas.
- When applying these techniques with clients, how will you know which rewards will be the most effective? What kinds of clients and client problems might work best with a functional analysis and positive reinforcement?

Homework 2: Contracting

Use the guidelines given in this chapter and draw up a mock contract between a teenager and his or her parents. The parents want the client to improve grades, get a job, and join the basketball team. The teenager wants to spend time with friends, listen to music, watch television, and talk on the phone. Keep in mind that it is not necessary to accomplish everything in a contingency contract, but that greater successes can be built from a small accomplishment.

Homework 3

Recall the earlier dialogue between Jonathan and Kristi. Suppose that Kristi suggests a method for tipping the balance to motivate Jonathan. List five or six questions that you would use to get pertinent information from Jonathan that would help you implement this technique. Next, write a dialogue between Kristi and Jonathan in which Kristi confronts Jonathan's behavior. Of these two methods, which do you think would be the most effective for this client? Defend your answer.

Journal Starters

1. Go back to the Precursors Assessment Form (Figure 14.2) and the Driving and Restraining Forces Worksheet (Figure 14.3). Even if you did not complete these assignments or did them partially, reflect on your own resistance to change. What forces within you and in your environment spur you to grow and what sorts of things keep you in place?
2. There are ethical issues concerning treating clients who do not wish to change. Some helpers give their clients a little time before terminating them, even if they are ordered to counseling by the court. How would you feel about having a client who was forced to come to counseling but was unmotivated? What do you think about the whole issue of requiring counseling?

For more journal ideas, as well as more practice with activating client expectations, hope, and motivation, refer to Chapter 14 in *Exercises in the Art of Helping*.

References

Adler, A. (1954). *Understanding human nature.* New York: Fawcett Premier.

Amatea, E. S. (1988). Engaging the reluctant client: Some new strategies for the school counselor. *School Counselor, 36,* 34–40.

Bellack, A. S., & Hersen, M. (1986). *Dictionary of behavior therapy techniques.* New York: Pergamon.

Bergman, J. S. (1985). *Fishing for barracudas.* New York: Norton.

Blanck, G. (1976). Psychoanalytic technique. In B. B. Wolman (Ed.), *The therapist's handbook: Treatment methods of mental disorders* (pp. 61–86). New York: Van Nostrand Reinhold.

Brammer, L. M., Shostrom, E. L., & Abrego, P. J. (1989). *Therapeutic psychology: Fundamen-*

tals of counseling and psychotherapy. Upper Saddle River, NJ: Prentice Hall.

Bugental, J. F. T., & Bugental, E. K. (1986). A fate worse than death: The fear of changing. Psychotherapy, 21, 543–549.

Cormier, L. S., & Hackney, H. (1987). The professional counselor: A professional guide to helping. Upper Saddle River, NJ: Prentice Hall.

Cormier, W. H., & Cormier, L. S. (1991). Interviewing strategies for helpers: Fundamental skills and cognitive behavioral interventions (3rd ed.). Pacific Grove, CA: Brooks/Cole.

Davanloo, H. (Ed.). (1978). Basic principles and techniques in short term dynamic psychotherapy. New York: SP Medical and Scientific Books.

de Shazer, S. (1985). Keys to solution in brief therapy. New York: Norton.

de Shazer, S. (1988). Clues: Investigating solutions in brief therapy. New York: Norton.

de Shazer, S. (1989, October). Brief therapy. Symposium conducted at Stetson University, DeLand, FL.

Dinkmeyer, D., & Losoncy, L. E. (1980). The encouragement book. Upper Saddle River, NJ: Prentice Hall.

Dinkmeyer, D. Sr., & Losoncy, L. E. (1995). The skills of encouragement: Bringing out the best in yourself and others. Boca Raton, FL: St. Lucie Press.

Dowd, E. T., & Milne, C. R. (1986). Paradoxical interventions in counseling psychology. Counseling Psychologist, 14, 237–282.

Dowd, E. T., & Olson, D. H. (1985). Contingency contracting. In A. S. Bellack & M. Hersen (Eds.), Dictionary of behavior therapy techniques (pp. 70–73). New York: Pergamon.

Dowd, E. T., & Seibel, C. A. (1990). A cognitive theory of resistance and reactance: Implications for treatment. Journal of Mental Health Counseling, 12, 458–469.

Driscoll, R. (1984). Pragmatic psychotherapy. New York: Van Nostrand Reinhold.

Dyer, W. W., & Vriend, J. (1977). Counseling techniques that work. New York: Funk & Wagnalls.

Egan, G. (1990). The skilled helper: A systematic approach to effective helping. Pacific Grove, CA: Brooks/Cole.

Frank, J. D., & Frank, J. B. (1991). Persuasion and healing. Baltimore: Johns Hopkins University Press.

Frank, J. D., Nash, E. H., Stone, A. R., & Imber, S. D. (1963). Immediate and long-term symptomatic course of psychiatric outpatients. American Journal of Psychiatry, 120, 429–439.

Freud, S. (1900/1952). A general introduction to psychoanalysis. New York: Washington Square Press.

Guidano, V. F. (1988). A systems, process-oriented approach to cognitive therapy. In K. S. Dobson (Ed.), Handbook of cognitive-behavioral therapies (pp. 307–355). New York: Guilford.

Haley, J. (1976). Problem-solving therapy. San Francisco: Jossey-Bass.

Haley, J. (1989, May). Strategic family therapy. Symposium conducted at Stetson University, DeLand, FL.

Hanna, F. J. (1996). Precursors of change: Pivotal points of involvement and resistance in psychotherapy. Journal of Psychotherapy Integration, 6, 227–264.

Hanna, F. J., & Ritchie, M. H. (1995). Seeking the active ingredients of psychotherapeutic change: Within and outside the context of therapy. Professional Psychology: Research and Practice, 26, 176–183.

Harris, G. A., & Watkins, D. (1987). Counseling the involuntary and resistant client. Alexandria, VA: American Association for Counseling and Development.

Hart, J. T. (1986). Functional eclectic therapy. In J. C. Norcross (Ed.), Handbook of eclectic psychotherapy (pp. 221–225). New York: Brunner/Mazel.

Hitz, R., & Driscoll, A. (1988). Praise or encouragement? New insights into praise: Implications for early childhood teachers. Individual Psychology: Journal of Adlerian Theory, Research and Practice, 43, 138–141.

Jackson, D. (1968). Therapy, communication and change. Palo Alto, CA: Science and Behavior Books.

Kanfer, F. H. (1986). Implications of a self-regulation model of therapy for treatment of addictive behaviors. In W. R. Miller & N. Heather (Eds.), Treating addictive behaviors: Processes of change (pp. 29–47). New York: Plenum.

Kanfer, F. H. (1980). Self-management methods. In F. H. Kanfer & A. P. Goldstein (Eds.), Helping people change. New York: Pergamon.

Larke, J. (1985). Compulsory treatment: Some practical methods of treating the mandated client. Psychotherapy, 22, 262–268.

Larrabee, M. J. (1982). Working with reluctant clients through affirmation techniques. *Personnel and Guidance Journal, 6,* 105–109.

Lauver, P. J., Holiman, M. A., & Kazama, S. W. (1982). Counseling as battleground: Client as enemy. *Personnel and Guidance Journal, 61,* 105–109.

Lawson, D. M. (1986). Strategic directives with resistant clients. *American Mental Health Counselors Journal, 8,* 87–93.

Lerner, S., & Lerner, H. (1983). A systematic approach to resistance: Theoretical and technical considerations. *American Journal of Psychotherapy, 37,* 387–399.

Lewin, K. (1951). *Field theory in social science.* New York: Harper & Row.

Losoncy, L. E. (1977). *Turning people on: How to be an encouraging person.* Upper Saddle River, NJ: Prentice Hall.

Mahoney, M. J. (1988a). The cognitive sciences and psychotherapy: Patterns in a developing relationship. In K. S. Dobson (Ed.), *Handbook of cognitive-behavioral therapies* (pp. 358–386). New York: Guilford.

Mahoney, M. J. (1988b). Constructive meta-theory II: Implications for psychotherapy. *International Journal of Personal Construct Psychology, 1,* 299–316.

Marlatt, G. A. (1988). Matching clients to treatment: Treatment models and stages of change. In D. M. Donovan & G. A. Marlatt (Eds.), *Assessment of addictive behaviors* (pp. 474–483). New York: Guilford.

Martin, D. G. (1983). *Counseling and therapy skills.* Prospect Heights, IL: Waveland Press.

McMullin, R. E. (1986). *Handbook of cognitive therapy techniques.* New York: Norton.

Meichenbaum, D., & Turk, D. C. (1987). *Facilitating treatment adherence: A practitioner's guidebook.* New York: Plenum.

Mosak, H. H. (1987). *Ha ha and aha.* Muncie, IN: Accelerated Development.

O'Hanlon, W. H., & Weiner-Davis, M. (1989). *In search of solutions: A new direction psychotherapy.* New York: Norton.

Otani, A. (1989). Resistance management techniques of Milton H. Erickson, M.D.: An application to nonhypnotic mental health counseling. *Journal of Mental Health Counseling, 11,* 325–333.

Palazzoli, M. S., Boscolo, L., Cecchin, G., & Prata, G. (1978). *Paradox and counterparadox: A new model in the therapy of the family in schizophrenic transaction.* New York: Jason Aronson.

Patterson, C. H. (1973). *Theories of counseling and psychotherapy* (2nd ed.). New York: Harper & Row.

Perls, F. S. (1971). *Gestalt therapy verbatim.* New York: Bantam.

Pitsounis, N. D., & Dixon, P. N. (1988). Encouragement versus praise: Improving productivity of the mentally retarded. *Individual Psychology: Journal of Adlerian Theory, Research and Practice, 44,* 507–512.

Prochaska, J. O., & DiClemente, C. C. (1983). Stages and processes of self-change in smoking: Toward an integrative model of change. *Journal of Consulting and Clinical Psychology, 51,* 390–395.

Prochaska, J. O., & DiClemente, C. C. (1986). The transtheoretical approach. In J. C. Norcross (Ed.), *Handbook of eclectic psychotherapy* (pp. 163–200). New York: Brunner/Mazel.

Prochaska, J. O., & Norcross, J. C. (1994). *Systems of psychotherapy.* Pacific Grove, CA: Brooks/Cole.

Prochaska, J. O., Norcross, J. C., & DiClemente, C. C. (1994). *Changing for good.* New York: William Morrow.

Redl, F. (1966). *When we deal with children.* New York: Free Press.

Ritchie, M. H. (1996). Counseling involuntary clients. *Journal of Counseling & Development, 64,* 516–518.

Roloff, M. E., & Miller, G. R. (Eds.). (1980). *Persuasion: New directions in theory and research.* Beverly Hills, CA: Sage.

Sack, T. (1988). Counseling responses when the client says, "I don't know." *Journal of Mental Health Counseling, 10,* 179–187.

Seligman, M. E. P. (1975). *Helplessness.* San Francisco: Freeman.

Seligman, M. E. P. (1991). *Learned optimism.* New York: Alfred Knopf.

Siegel, B. S. (1986). *Love, medicine and miracles.* New York: Harper & Row.

Simonton, O. C., & Mathews-Simonton, S. (1978). *Getting well again.* Los Angeles: Tarcher.

Singer, E. (1970). *Key concepts in psychotherapy.* New York: Random House.

Stream, H. S. (1985). *Resolving resistance in psychotherapy.* New York: Wiley.

Sweeney, T. J. (1998). *Adlerian counseling* (4th ed.). Muncie, IN: Accelerated Development.

Walker, J. E., & Aycock, L. (1986). The counselor as "chicken." In W. P. Anderson (Ed.), *Innovative counseling: A handbook of readings* (pp. 22–23). Alexandria, VA: American Association for Counseling and Development.

Witmer, J. M. (1985). *Pathways to personal growth.* Muncie, IN: Accelerated Development.

Wolberg, L. R. (1954). *The technique of psychotherapy.* New York: Grune & Stratton.

Young, M. E., & Feiler, F. (1993). Trends in counseling: A national survey. *Guidance and Counselling, 9,* 4–11.

New Learning Experiences and Evaluating the Effectiveness of Helping

15

Education is not the filling of a pail, but the lighting of a fire.
William Butler Yeats

In this chapter, we want to do two things: (1) explore the techniques under the final therapeutic factor, new learning experiences (Figure 15.1), and (2) discuss the final step in the five-part stages of the helping process (see Figure 15.3). We begin

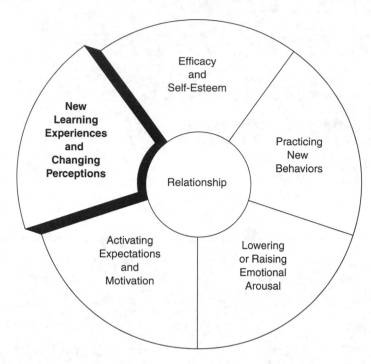

Figure 15.1
Curative Factors in the REPLAN System: New Learning Experiences and Changing Perceptions

by looking at the ways helpers educate clients and encourage them to see the world in a slightly more constructive way. This therapeutic factor refers to ways of teaching the client new skills or helping the client develop a new outlook. As the quote from Yeats suggests, though, teaching is not necessarily a classroom activity. New learning can be sparked through instruction or modeling, but it can also be stimulated indirectly through techniques such as humor, stories, metaphors, interpretation, and reframing.

One type of new learning experience occurs when a client leaves the helping situation, having changed his or her self-concept or philosophy of life. According to research, gaining a new perspective is one of the most frequently mentioned helpful experiences cited by therapy clients (Elliott, 1985). Clients have been able to recall insights and learning up to 6 months following therapy (Martin & Stelmaczonek, 1988). Yalom (1995) has also identified learning as a significant therapeutic factor consistently identified by group therapy participants. They learn from each other, through modeling, and by paying attention to their own verbalizations and feelings.

Definitions of New Learning

A number of different terms have been used to describe this therapeutic factor: changing the worldview, redefining personal mythology, developing insight, developing outlook skills, perception transformation, cognitive restructuring, reframing, meaning attribution, perception shifts, the "aha!" experience, relabeling, redecision, and many more. All of these terms seem to involve two basic helping techniques: (1) imparting to clients new information or skills and (2) persuading clients to change inappropriate beliefs, perceptions, and outlook. Let us look at a couple of client stories in order to demonstrate how these two types of new learning experiences are commonly embedded in a treatment plan.

- Rhonda is a 23-year-old woman who is admitted for substance abuse problems following her arrest on a charge of driving while intoxicated. On the first day, the goal of the staff is to introduce clients to a "disease concept" model of alcoholism. Rhonda attends a class where she learns that she is genetically predisposed to addiction based on her family history, and that she cannot help the effect alcohol has on her. The result of this information is that Rhonda begins to stop thinking of herself as "weak" or as morally unworthy. Instead, she starts to realize that she has a biological weakness. This new perspective has been stimulated by learning. It changes her attitude about herself and increases her hope for recovery.
- Dujuan is a 30-year-old man referred for help with panic attacks. During moments of high anxiety, he has been experiencing shortness of breath, rapid heart rate, and intense fear. At their first session, the helper identifies a core belief that seems to increase his anxiety, "I could lose control over myself and go crazy." During the next 3 weeks, the helper encourages Dujuan to examine and modify this core belief. The goal is to help him to focus on the evidence for and against this belief and to develop a more reasonable point of view. After a month, Dujuan is able to say, "Watching for danger actually increases my fear rather than reducing it. It is better to have a panic attack once a month than to spend every day worrying about it." Six months later Dujuan claims that he rarely finds himself falling into his old way of thinking. He feels that he has modified a core belief.

What Client Problems Are Helped Through New Learning?

A number of client problems are the result of inadequate training or lack of knowledge. In seminars and workshops, one can learn to cope with stress, learn alternatives to addictive behavior, as well as develop better interpersonal, marital communication, and parenting skills. Through new learning and by adopting new perspectives, clients can change their thinking about painful remembered events and rethink their sense of guilt and failure. They can see themselves and others in a new light and they can discover that many situations that they have feared and avoided are not really harmful.

Resistance to New Learning

"The truth will set you free, but *first,* it will make you miserable." This saying from a humorous poster summarizes the experience of a person who is undergoing a significant change. Change brought about by new information may ultimately bring about enlightenment, but it can be extremely unsettling at first. Change is not only disquieting to the changing individual, but also to those in the client's sphere of influence. The story of Copernicus is a good example. He taught that the earth revolved around the sun and not the other way around. This upset the existing worldview so much that he was forced to recant, and his student Bruno was put to death 50 years later for spreading the news (Bernard & Young, 1996).

On a much smaller scale, a helper tries to persuade a client to leave behind self-defeating ideas and teaches the client new skills and how to construct a slightly different worldview. The result is that both the client and those close to the client experience discomfort and may actually try to resist or slow down change. For example, a social worker at a hospice had a client, a 65-year-old Italian woman whose husband had died a year ago. The client was lonely and depressed but refused to go to social functions in her retirement community because going unaccompanied to such an event was, in her view, undignified and a sign to the world that she was looking for a new partner. She had grown up in a strictly religious, Italian community where such behavior was frowned upon. No external force prevented her from enjoying the company and support of others, only her outdated ideas of propriety. The social worker's attempts to get this client to change her behavior or think about this in a different way met stiff resistance bolstered by years of experience and cultural reinforcement.

The flip side of the coin is that when clients change their outmoded concepts and self-imprisoning ideas, enormous growth can occur. This chapter examines a few of the many tools helpers use to assist clients in seeing things in a different way and creating new visions of the future.

Common Methods Helpers Use to Provide New Learning Experiences for Clients

Interpretation

Interpretation, next to free association, is one of the oldest therapeutic techniques (Clark, 1995). Interpretation consists of encouraging the client to look at the problem in the context of the theoretical orientation of the practitioner. Once the helper explains the reason for the problem, a client develops insight and is then better able to change. For example, from a psychodynamic perspective, a client's reaction to his boss may be a carryover from his lifelong issues with his own father. Once this reaction is interpreted, confronted, and clarified, the client may start to see the unconscious motives behind his actions. Insight may occur suddenly ("aha!") or it may dawn gradually. Once insight occurs, that learning may be applied to other situations. In this example, the client may become aware of similar tendencies in his relationships with other authority figures.

Psychodynamic therapists are not the only practitioners to use interpretation. Virtually all theoretical systems induct clients into their theoretical system and teach them a new vocabulary (Frank & Frank, 1991). For example, clients of transactional analysis learn a new vocabulary for describing the human psyche and human interactions, which includes the words "strokes," "scripts," and "games." The psychodynamic technique of interpretation, described previously, is an advanced method that cannot be grasped in a few paragraphs and must be learned in an extended training program. Today, it is a controversial technique because it firmly places the helper in the role of expert and it is not entirely compatible with the current emphasis on brief therapy and constructivist approaches.

Modeling as New Learning

Another way that clients change through new learning is by copying the behavior of the helper or that of other models. Bandura (1971) is responsible for recognizing the potential power of modeling in the helping process. Modeling has been used extensively to help children learn prosocial behaviors, to assist developmentally delayed adults in skill development, to teach alcoholics methods of relapse prevention, to train helpers, to instruct parents, and to help clients deal with fearful situations (Perry & Furukawa, 1986).

In group therapy, it is common for members to copy the helper or other group members who are functioning more effectively. Clients learn to be more self-disclosing, assertive, and spontaneous by seeing examples of these behaviors and trying them in the safe environment of the group. In addition, clients have identified this as one of the most significant curative factors in group therapy (Yalom, 1995).

Modeling can take place in the helping arena, either as an intentional process or as an unexpected by-product. An example of the latter occurs when clients take on the therapeutic mannerisms or copy the clothing of the helper. Intentional modeling is exemplified by a helper's use of role-playing a specific behavior while the client watches or exposing clients to symbolic, biographical, or fictional models in books, tapes, and films (Milan, 1985). Through modeling, clients are able to see a successful performance of a skill. The client then attempts to reproduce the skill, getting feedback from the helper (Mitchell & Milan, 1983).

Stop and Reflect

Think about three of your favorite teachers. Write their names in the following chart and describe them as best you can according to the format shown:

Name	Personal Trait You Most Admired	Subject Taught	Values Held by Teacher	Most Important Thing You Learned	How Did Teacher Influence You?

- As you look over your answers, how do you think the teacher influenced or changed you? Was it primarily through modeling or was it through the subject matter that he or she taught?
- Look over the list of personal traits. Are these traits you have tried to develop in yourself?
- Which traits of your favorite teachers do you think would transfer well to the therapeutic relationship?

Using Metaphors and Stories

Metaphors, stories, parables, and tales are common means for stimulating new learning in clients (Barker, 1985; Gordon, 1978). For example, a helper once came up with this little aphorism for a client who was stewing about a situation over which he had no control, "You know, worry is like a rocking chair. It doesn't get you anywhere but it's something to do." A thought like this can gently suggest that the client think about his or her behavior.

Metaphors and stories engage the listener with imagery, suspense, and humor. Consequently, the client is not fully aware that he or she is learning something. A story bypasses some of a client's resistance to new ideas; they are too engaged to fight. This was true in the case of Judie, a 35-year-old woman living in New York City who had grown up on a farm. Judie had considered marriage to several different men while in her 20's. Each time she had ended the relationship when marriage seemed to be the next step. Judie was an only child and was close to her parents, whose marital relationship was quite poor. They had fought bitterly for years and she believed that they had stayed together for her sake. She admitted that she saw love as "chains."

Judie came for help because she had finally met a man whom she wanted to marry. She was filled with confusion and had changed the date of the wedding twice. In the first few counseling sessions, reflective listening uncovered her fears, thoughts, and feelings about marriage and relationships. She felt better about her decision to get married after these sessions, but one night (a week before the wedding), she telephoned the helper in a crisis of doubt about whether to go through with the ceremony. On the telephone, her helper told her the following story: "When I was a boy, we lived on a farm, and we had a very healthy and strong mare. She was high spirited, but gentle. She also had one peculiarity. She hated it when we closed the gate of the corral. In fact, she would run around in circles, rearing up, sometimes even hurting herself on the wooden fence. One day, we discovered by accident that if we left the gate open she calmed down. And she never ran away. She didn't mind being in the corral. She just wanted to make sure that she could leave at any time."

The helper credited this story as the turning point in Judie's treatment and in restoring her sense of control. Although no interpretation was made, she apparently grasped that she did not have to feel imprisoned by marriage, that she could retain a sense of freedom. The helper used the farm story because of his knowledge about Judie's background. He used the metaphor of the corral because she saw marriage as a form of bondage. Through the image of the open gate, he was telling her that she could retain the option of leaving. Knowing that she had this option would help her stop worrying about being trapped and enjoy her marriage. The story seemed to be much more effective than giving advice because it allowed her to decide for herself how to act.

Exposure to Avoided Stimuli

There is a story about a woman who sees a man rubbing a rabbit's foot furiously and asks what he is doing. "I am keeping the tigers away," he replies.

"But there aren't any tigers around here," she argues.

"See," he says, "it's working."

Many clients come for help because of avoidance of social situations, dogs, airplanes, or being far from home. Like the man in the story, they are not willing to risk their safe behavior, even when it is ineffective. Because a client has learned to reduce anxiety by avoidance, he or she must be taught that the feared object or situation is not really harmful.

Exposure is the technique of helping clients to gradually face feared stimuli (Emmelkamp, 1982; Foa & Goldstein, 1978). Exposure is an important treatment for all sorts of fears and phobias. Helpers set up hierarchies of feared situations and step by step encourage clients to face more and more difficult situations.

Clients learn important lessons from facing rather than avoiding. They learn that many of their fears are groundless and that their perception of how people will react to them may be erroneous. For example, many people fear that being more assertive will create worse relationships in their families. As they become more assertive, they learn that most of the feared consequences of assertiveness never occur and that their relationships actually improve.

Humor

We know that learning is facilitated in a light atmosphere (Gardner, 1971). Humor also offers a subtle way to shift a client's viewpoint (Ansbacher & Ansbacher, 1956; Mosak, 1987). Like a metaphor, a joke tells a story and sometimes contains a philosophical shift, interpretation, or message.

One of the most common ways that helpers use humor to get clients to think about a situation in a different way is to use exaggeration. By exaggerating a client's situation, sometimes it helps to put it into perspective. Once, when a client was stewing about the fact that her divorce would become public, it was clear that she was making a mountain out of a molehill. The helper made the following comments, "Yes, undoubtedly this will make the front page with a big headline: 'Woman gets divorce—friends abandon her.' Perhaps it will make the television news." The client laughed and was able to recognize her tendency to catastrophize.

Linguistic Changes

Linguistic changes are helper suggestions that the client use different language in talking about the problem. Since language mirrors thought, what we say is a reflection of our worldview. Helpers often suggest that clients use new jargon or use specific words that promote the ideas that the client is responsible for his or her own life, thoughts, and feelings. For example, when a client says, "I can't seem to get to work on time," the helper challenges the client's lack of responsibility by suggesting that the client rephrase as follows: "I won't go to work on time." Helpers also challenge clients when they engage in black-and-white thinking by using such terms as "always" and "never."

Direct Instruction

Direct instruction is one of the most often used methods in helping. Direct instruction involves lecturing, discussion groups, modeling, and the use of films and demonstrations to provide new information to clients. These psychoeducational seminars are the stock-in-trade of parent education programs, stress reduction groups, anxiety management training, cognitive therapy for depression, marriage enrichment seminars, substance abuse education, and a myriad of other programs. Besides the educational material that is presented, clients benefit from the support of others who are experiencing the problem and they learn vicariously from the experiences of fellow learners.

Direct instruction can just as easily take place in the helper's office. Marriage counseling may involve training in good communication skills, and helpers often assign books and other reading material to educate clients about specific problems such as stress, substance abuse, dealing with anxiety or depression, proper parenting procedures, and particular social skills that a client needs to acquire.

The Technique of Reframing

Many of us are familiar with an advertisement for the Peace Corps that ran on television during the 1960s. It challenged viewers to determine whether they saw a glass as half empty or half full. This commercial was constructed to show that there are two ways of looking at a situation: in terms of its assets or its deficits. Reframing is the therapeutic technique of persuading the client to view the positive or healthy viewpoint: to see the glass as half full.

An even better example of reframing comes from Mark Twain's story of Tom Sawyer, who convinces his friends that painting a fence is fun and a privilege, not work. A more contemporary illustration comes from the movie *Moonstruck*. The hero of the story is rejected by his fiancée when his hand is severed by a bread slicer. The hero had always blamed his brother for distracting him at the crucial moment when the accident occurred. The reframing takes place when his new girlfriend convinces him that the real reason for the accident was his unconscious wish to stay single. She elegantly uses the metaphor of a lone wolf and accuses the hero of gnawing off his own leg to avoid the trap of marriage.

Helpers use reframes like this to help the client see the problem in a more constructive and responsible way. They move clients from blaming to taking responsibility, from the victim's role to the survivor's role, by gently urging them to look at the world through a different lens.

Stop and Reflect

Figure 15.2 is a famous drawing you may have seen before. It can be seen as two separate portraits, one of a young woman wearing a feathered hat and a black neckband and another of an old woman with a long nose and head scarf. Typically, it is easy to see one figure or the other. If you have trouble finding one of these faces, ask a classmate or teacher to help you. Notice that you cannot see both portraits at once; you have to focus on each individually.

Figure 15.2
Old Woman/Young Woman

Looking at a drawing such as this is not unlike looking at a problem situation (McMullin, 1986). Every issue has its positive and negative sides, a solvable way of looking at it and a hopeless way of looking at it, depending on which you have been trained to focus on. By shifting your attention, you can pay attention to one side or the other. Drawings illustrate to clients that reframing is not just pretending that the negative issues are not there; rather, it is simply more useful to learn that every cloud also has a silver lining and it is more productive to change one's outlook and to see the sides of the problem that are solvable and changeable.

One easy way of understanding the idea of multiple viewpoints is a technique called *relabeling*. We use relabeling in career counseling to help clients recognize their personal strengths. Have you ever noticed it is easier to get people to identify their weaknesses than their positive qualities? In this exercise, clients make a list of their own undesirable traits and then of some undesirable traits of someone else they know. Then they try to think of another descriptor that puts a positive spin on the very same trait. Take a look at these examples and then make two lists of your own. First, make a list of personal qualities or traits about yourself that you do not like and then make a similar list of qualities you do not like about someone you know. Finally, relabel them by trying to reword the trait in a positive way.

Negative Viewpoint	*Positive Viewpoint*
Compulsive	Organized
Sloppy	Casual, relaxed
Loud	Enthusiastic

Now consider the following questions:

- Is reframing like this just putting a coat of paint on a negative trait, or does it really uncover something positive about the tendency?

- As you look over your own list, would you really want to lose this quality? What would you be giving up?
- Does your relabeling another person's traits help you to see that person differently?
- Discuss some of these issues and your own reactions with your classmates.

How to Reframe

According to Watzlawick, Weakland, and Fisch (1974), reframing means coming up with a new, more constructive definition of the problem that fits the facts just as accurately as the old definition. To reframe a client's problem, the helper must appreciate the client's worldview and then replace it with an acceptable alternative. Reframes fail when helpers do not take the time to make sure that the new definition is accurate and that it does not clash with the client's perspective. For these reasons, it is best to proceed as follows:

Step 1   Use the nonjudgmental listening cycle to fully understand the problem. The nonjudgmental listening cycle gives the helper a firm grasp of the details of the problem, including the individuals involved, their relationships, and the environment where the problem exists. Before reframing, it is especially helpful to reflect meaning to get at the client's worldview and values. In the following summary, the helper brings together a number of the feelings and meanings the client, Marlene, has expressed during the session.

Marlene: "So, that's the story, I have to move whether I like it or not. It's like being fired and I have no control over it. Either I move or I am out of work. I've never lost a job before. Sometimes I think it's their way of telling me they want me to quit."

Helper: "From what I have heard so far, what bothers you the most is the lack of control over the decision. That makes you mad. But sometimes you see this situation as your failure and, at the same time, a personal rejection."

Step 2   Build a bridge from the client's viewpoint to a new way of looking at the problem. Develop a reframe that bridges the client's old view of the problem with a new viewpoint that stresses the positive aspects of the problem or presents it as solvable. The important point is to acknowledge some aspect of the client's viewpoint while, at the same time, suggesting another way of looking at it.

Helper: "I wonder if you could start thinking about this move in a different way? You have always wanted to travel. A few months ago, you were even considering a new job or moving to another state. Although you feel uneasy about this because you don't like it when the decision is made for you, I wonder if this may not be a blessing in disguise. How might this job actually give you a little more freedom?"

Step 3   Reinforcing the bridge. A shift in perspective is often something that develops slowly. One way of sustaining the perspective shift is to assign homework that forces the client to see the problem in a new light. Marlene, for example, might be given a homework assignment to do more research on the positive aspects of the move.

Problems and Precautions of Reframing

Reframing is most likely to be successful if the client is able to relate the significant aspects of the new frame of reference to corresponding features in the old frame of reference. For example, an algebra teacher used to try to reframe her examinations as "sharing experiences." The analogy was not successful and everyone groaned because "sharing" is not a graded activity (an important feature). Unfortunately, it may be impossible to identify all aspects of a problem that might be important to the client; however, every effort should be made to imagine those that could be crucial. In a metaphor or story told by the helper, the basic elements of the tale must conform to the client's situation or the reframe may be rejected.

Poorly timed reframing can sometimes be worse than none at all. One example that comes to mind concerns the reframes often extended to persons grieving over the death of a family member. Well-meaning friends are apt to say such things as, "It is God's will," or, "She's gone to a better place." Because a person is dealing with strong emotions, these kindly offered phrases are perceived as platitudes. Later, such words may be comforting when emotions have subsided and the person tries to place the experience into perspective.

To summarize, reframing is a major technique in the art of helping. Many clients are overfocused on the hopelessness of their situations and need a different way to get a handle on a problem. The helper facilitates alternative ways of looking at a problem by listening to the client's point of view and forming a bridge between the old way of thinking and the new. Reframing is more than just gaining a positive attitude. It involves thinking about the problem in a completely new way and focusing on what is solvable and changeable. Reframing is also helpful in situations where direct action is not possible or advisable and a change of attitude or perspective is needed.

Stop and Reflect

One of the tenets of stress management is that solving a problem or acting is not always desirable or possible. Sometimes change is impossible; sometimes it is not the right time to act. In these situations, the best course is to deal with negative feelings by relaxation or by paying attention to the positive aspects of the situation. Consider the following example: Bob and Diane and their 5-year-old daughter live next to Diane's parents. For Bob, this is stressful at times because he thinks that his in-laws are around the house too much and that they take away from his own time with his family. On the other hand, for Bob, the benefits of living next to his in-laws outweigh these annoyances. The in-laws help with child care and provide help and support in many other ways. He likes his house, and his wife and daughter are happy to be near his in-laws. He does not want to move. In this situation, a helper might suggest that Bob change his outlook rather than his address. He or she might suggest that Bob pay more attention to the features of the situation that are positive and changeable, rather than the parts that are negative and not open to change. In other words, how can Bob find ways to be alone with his family without moving and to enjoy the benefits of living close to family?

- If you were helping Bob, how might you go about getting him to see the positive aspects of his situation? What aspects can you identify that put the situation in a different light?

- Is there a danger in being a Pollyanna, that is, just pretending everything is all right rather than dealing with problems? How might you avoid this?
- Do you think that showing Bob the old woman/young woman drawing might help him understand this concept? From what little you know about Bob, what other metaphors might you use to explain the concept of looking at a problem from different angles?
- Discuss your reactions to this exercise with your classmates.

Evaluating the Effectiveness of Helping

The first part of this chapter dealt with the final curative factor in the six-part RE-PLAN system. Now, let us turn our attention to the final issue of evaluation, which is the last of the five stages in the helping process (see Figure 15.3). Helping, as we have described it, moves from *relationship building* to *assessment,* to *goal setting* to *implementing techniques* and ends with *evaluation.* At the evaluation stage, the helper reflects with the client on the overall impact of the helping process. Were the helper and client able to reach the agreed-upon goals? If not, should the helper consider "replanning" and work with the client to set new goals? Even if the goals were reached, important new issues may have arisen; client and helper may wish to negotiate a new contract, and the cycle depicted in Figure 15.3 begins again.

If helper and client can agree that substantial progress has been made toward the goals, the helper may recommend *termination,* which is the discontinuation of the therapeutic relationship. Termination is not merely a process of leave-taking, but also a time to look back on the original goals and celebrate client success (Kramer, 1986, 1990). As the client and helper prepare to end the relationship, the helper encourages the client to focus on successes and also to become aware of other issues that have not yet been resolved and that may need work later on.

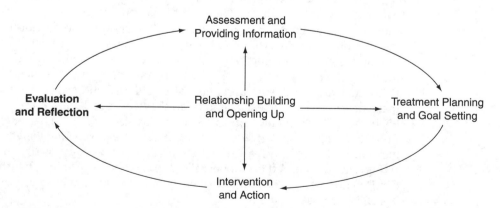

Figure 15.3
Stages of the Helping Relationship: Evaluation

How to Tell Whether Termination Is Needed

Clients should be terminated when they have attained their goals, when they have been receiving counseling or psychotherapy for some time and have not made progress, or when there are signs that they can handle their issues independently but have become dependent on the helpers. Most professional organizations, including the American Counseling Association, the American Psychological Association, the American Association for Marriage and Family Therapy, and the National Association of Social Workers, in their codes of ethics, state that a client should be terminated if he or she is not making progress. In such cases, the client should be made aware of alternate sources of help and a referral should be made. The decision as to whether a client is making progress is not always easy because some of the signs that suggest a client is ready for termination, such as missing sessions, coming late for sessions, or failing to do homework, can be signals of resistance or problems of motivation as well.

How exactly do we know when helping has been successful? Should we consider success from the standpoint of the client or from the standpoint of the helper? Should we define success in terms of societal standards (dangerousness, employment, school grades) or from some ideal of mental health advanced by theorists? Mathews (1989) suggests reviewing one's caseload and asking oneself, "If I had a waiting list right now, would I be seeing this client?" (p. 37). Based on Maholich and Turner (1979), Sciscoe (1990) identified five questions a helper might ask himself or herself to assess a client's readiness for termination:

1. Is the presenting problem under control?
2. Has the client reduced the initial level of distress by developing better coping skills?
3. Has the client achieved greater self-awareness and better relationships?
4. Are life and work more enjoyable for the client?
5. Does the client now feel capable of living without the therapeutic relationship?

The first four of Sciscoe's questions highlight improvements that have been made and goals that have been achieved. The last question is especially important, since it asks the helper whether or not the client is able to maintain the gains of helping without the therapeutic relationship. Answering these questions in a dialogue with the client and arriving at a mutual decision can help in working out the knotty question of termination.

How to Prepare a Client for Termination

Most experts agree that sudden termination is not advisable (Brammer, Shostrom, & Abrego, 1989), but how soon should the topic of termination be brought up? Dixon and Glover (1984) recommend that at least three sessions in advance of termination be devoted to issues of termination, while Lamb (1985) recommends at least seven sessions. As much time as was spent in relationship building in the beginning of the therapy should be devoted to termination, say Cormier and Cormier (1985); and one-sixth of the time spent in therapy should be devoted to termination, according to Shulman (1979). In other words, there should be a period of preparation. How long this should take is a matter of judgment and should be determined by the length and quality of the therapeutic relationship.

During the preparation period, the helper leads the client in a discussion that reviews the counseling process and progress made. In general, it is important to emphasize the client's strengths and to end on a positive note; however, areas left untreated or unresolved must also be discussed (Anderson & Stewart, 1983). One way to review is simply to compare before-and-after client functioning from the viewpoint of both helper and client. Also, an early session in counseling might be discussed, or case notes read to show progress. Finally, any unfinished business between client and helper should be addressed, and the client should be encouraged to think about how he or she will look back on the counseling experience in the future.

The general strategy to help clients deal with their feelings of loss at termination is to take time to prepare them and to ask them to identify both positive and negative feelings associated with the end of the relationship. Clients may be upset by termination because it is associated with other historical losses (Ward, 1984). Some suggestions to help prevent, explore, and resolve these feelings include (Cavanagh, 1982; Dixon & Glover, 1984; Hackney & Cormier, 1979; Munro & Bach, 1975):

1. Bring termination up early.
2. Reframe termination as an opportunity for the client to put new learning into practice.
3. Limit the number of counseling sessions at the beginning stages of helping.
4. Use a fading procedure; that is, space appointments over increasing lengths of time.
5. Avoid making the relationship the central feature of helping. Although relationship building is crucial, it may be unwise to employ only this curative factor. Help the client to see his or her own actions that led to success.
6. Play down the importance of termination; play up the sense of accomplishment and the value of independence.
7. Use reflective listening to allow the client to express feelings of loss.

The Helper's Reaction to Termination

Kanfer and Schefft (1988) suggest that the helper needs to learn to accept the fact that termination inevitably occurs at a point far short of perfection. Many clients leave with the counselor feeling that the solutions are still under construction. Helpers may also drag their feet on termination because of their own attachments and feelings of sadness and loss (Gladding, 2000).

Goodyear (1981, p. 348) lists several possible reasons that helpers have trouble letting go:

1. The relationship may be quite significant to the helper.
2. The helper may feel uncertain that the client will be able to function independently.
3. The helper may believe that he or she was not effective.
4. The helper may feel that his or her professional identity is challenged by the client's premature termination.
5. The termination may represent a loss of continued learning for the helper, who was looking forward to gaining experience from the client's peculiar problem.

6. The helper may miss the vicarious excitement of the client's exploits.
7. The termination may uncover historical events associated with loss in the counselor's life.
8. A helper's feelings of loss at termination may also be due to a reliance on helping relationships to meet needs for intimacy (friendship) as well as a conscious or unconscious sexual attraction.

Krantz and Lund (1979) feel that trainees may have special difficulty with termination. Beginning helpers may keep clients too long because they like the client or because of a hope that the client will accomplish even greater goals. They may also be unprepared for their own feelings or for the powerful loss experienced by the client, no matter how much they are intellectually informed. A supportive supervisory relationship (Sciscoe, 1990) can help trainees through difficult terminations.

How to Maintain Therapeutic Gains and Prevent Relapse Following Termination

The term *follow-up* refers to a brief contact the helper makes to determine how the client is progressing and to remind the client that the door is open if counseling is needed in the future (Wolberg, 1954). On the other hand, there are a number of activities that helpers employ that go beyond a brief reminder. They are designed to help maintain therapeutic gains and are actually means for extending help following termination. Here are some suggestions (Cavanagh, 1982; Perry & Paquin, 1987):

Fading
Fading means scheduling follow-up sessions with longer and longer intervals spaced over a 1-year period. For example, a 6-week, 6-month, and 1-year follow-up can be planned during the evaluation period. When clients are learning specific skills, such as assertiveness training, stress management, and communication, these follow-ups can be called "booster sessions" or "refreshers" with the stated aim of reviewing learning. One benefit of planning for follow-up as the relationship is winding down is that the client need not later feel a sense of failure if a return to counseling is needed. If the client decides to cancel the later visits, this can be reframed as a sign of success.

Home Visits or Observation
A possible follow-up to marriage or family counseling is to review helping progress later with the family at home. Observing the family in this setting can convey a great deal about progress, though it is not an ideal therapeutic setting because of the many distractions.

Contacts with Paraprofessionals
Many agencies provide follow-up services for clients on a free or inexpensive basis. Many mental health clinics, for example, provide home visiting to monitor and maintain progress of clients suffering from severe mental disorders.

Self-Help Groups
Self-help groups, if improperly conducted, can be a case of the blind leading the blind. The quality of such groups is quite variable, and so the helper must be familiar with

groups in the client's vicinity before making a recommendation. As an adjunct to individual, group, and family therapy, they can provide an important means of maintaining gains by providing regular peer support.

Self-Monitoring Activities

Clients can also be encouraged to engage in continued self-monitoring activities, which they report at follow-up sessions. A less formal way to encourage self-monitoring and self-reflection is teaching the client to use a personal journal to explore thoughts and feelings (Kalven, Rosen, & Taylor, 1981).

Self-Management Skills

Clients can learn to use behavioral principles to reward their own positive behaviors and to punish negative ones (Kanfer, 1975; Kazdin, 1980; Rudestam, 1980). For example, students can learn to make watching a one-hour television show contingent on completing several hours of study.

Audiovisual Material

Both printed and recorded materials can be sent by clients back to the helper as evidence of practice on helping goals following termination. Clients can send in monthly self-monitoring forms or tapes of communication practice. Likewise, helpers can send clients reminders of their goal statements. Young and Rosen (1985) describe a group activity in which clients write a letter to themselves during the last session before termination. The letter reminds the client of the helping goals. It also contains a list that the client drafts that predicts some of the excuses the client may use to try to avoid achieving the goals. The therapist mails the letters to clients about a month after the completion of group therapy.

Summary

The final topic in this chapter and in this book is the evaluation of the client-helper collaboration and dealing with the ending of the helping relationship. On the one hand, client and helper may decide to continue working on the stated goals or develop new ones. Alternately, a decision may be reached that the maximum benefit has been achieved. While the door may be left open for future help, termination can evoke feelings of loss for clients and helpers. Developing a positive ending for the helping relationship helps clients celebrate their successes and can shape their attitudes about receiving help in the future. One important issue during the evaluation stage is building in a follow-up system to help clients maintain change and prevent relapse.

Group Exercise

Reframing with a Reflecting Team

A recent innovation in family therapy is the reflecting team. A family therapist meets with a family and gets their perspective on the problem facing them. Midway through the session, the therapist stops and consults with a group of observers who have been watching through a one-way mirror or on video. The observers suggest alternate ways of looking at the family's problem. The therapist then returns to the family and presents a reframe of their problem based on the suggestions he or she has heard.

In the following exercise, a small group of learners form a reflecting team as a way to practice reframing. Form groups of six or eight students. One person is designated as the helper, one as the client, and the remaining members form the team.

Step 1   The client discusses a real or role-play situation with the helper who uses the nonjudgmental listening cycle to understand the problem as completely as possible in the 5–10 minutes allotted for this activity.

Step 2   Once the helper feels that he or she has a good grasp of the client's viewpoint, and has summarized his or her situation, the client is asked to move out of earshot or leave the room for approximately 5 minutes. During this time, the team conducts a group discussion about alternative ways in which the client's problem might be viewed. The team is encouraged to identify viewpoints that are consistent with the client's worldview and values, but which are more positive and change oriented than the client's current way of looking at the problem.

Step 3: Delivering the Reframe   The helper brings the client back into the presence of the reflecting team and delivers a reframe to the client. The helper chooses the best reframe for the client based on his or her own thinking and the thoughts of the reflecting team. The client is encouraged to respond to the reframe. When this has been completed, the role-play is over.

Step 4: Feedback   The client gives written feedback regarding the reframe that was presented by the helper and team using a five-point scale, as shown in the Feedback Checklist.

Feedback Checklist: Reframing
_____

Client Name _____   Helper Name _____
1 = Disagree
2 = Slightly Disagree
3 = Neutral
4 = Agree
5 = Strongly Agree
_____ 1. The helper understood my problem completely.
_____ 2. The reframe was a more positive viewpoint than the original statement of the problem.
_____ 3. The reframe was a more constructive way of looking at the problem.
_____ 4. The reframe fit with my own personal outlook and values.
_____

The exercise continues in order to allow several team members to have the opportunity to play the role of helper as time allows.

Additional Exercises

Exercise 1

Think of a problem situation in your own life. Suppose that you decided that drastic action on your part was unreasonable and you only wanted to change your outlook or attitude about it. When you have settled on a particular problem, answer the following questions:

- What are the things about the situation that make you feel uncomfortable?
- What other things about the situation are positive (not just bearable)?
- What keeps you focused on the negative aspects of the problem?
- Can you see this situation as an opportunity rather than as a problem?
- What points would you need to focus on to keep your view of the situation positive?
- When would it not be a good idea to encourage a client to change his or her perspective on a problem?

If you wish, discuss your answers with a small group.

Exercise 2: Role-Play a Termination Session

In a small group, two members role-play client and helper discussing termination, which is to take place in a week's time. Observers give the helper feedback on the following:

- Did the helper review the history of the helping process and the therapeutic relationship with the client?

- Did the helper help the client celebrate success in attaining the goals?
- Did the helper leave the door open while expressing confidence in the client's readiness to terminate?

Homework: A Final Tape and Transcript

Homework 1: Self-Evaluation

Before you record and transcribe a final session with a client, take some time to review the feedback you have received during group exercises and your individual practice. Think about each of the following building blocks and for each skill, rate your current level of mastery.

1 = I understand the concept
2 = I can identify it and give examples
3 = I can do it occasionally
4 = I can do it regularly
__ Eye contact
__ Body position
__ Attentive silence
__ Voice tone
__ Gestures and facial expressions
__ Door openers and minimal encouragers
__ Open and closed questions
__ Paraphrasing
__ Reflecting feelings
__ Reflecting meaning
__ Summarizing

Compare the scores with your answers in Chapter 6. Where have you improved? Where do you still need improvement?

Homework 2: Final Typescript

In Chapter 6, you recorded and transcribed a session with a client. Now, it is time to make a final tape in the same way. Make a final tape of 20 to 30 minutes with a classmate who is discussing

a real problem or who is role-playing. During the taping, your goal as a helper is to:

1. Demonstrate the nonjudgmental listening cycle
2. Demonstrate challenging skills
3. Demonstrate goal-setting skills
4. Discuss with the client a possible treatment plan and what techniques you might use in subsequent sessions

Step 1   Choose the best 15 minutes of the tape and transcribe every word of both client and helper, using the format of Table 6.2. It is important that the client's statements appear directly *below* your helping responses so that the connection between the two can be examined. Be sure you have permission to record from the client. You can do this aloud on the tape and in writing.

Step 2   Listen to the tape or read the transcript and make comments, naming each of the skills that your response exemplifies. Sometimes, students describe their responses rather than categorizing them. It is important to identify the skills you are using to determine their frequency and appropriateness. Use only the names of the building blocks and techniques you have learned. The comments section is a place for you to reflect on your responses. Do not just note weaknesses; identify strengths as well. In the comments section, you may also wish to identify any other issues that come to mind as you review the transcript.

Most important, reflect for a few minutes on your progress from the start of your training until now. Make some comments about your progress over the course of your training. What impact has it had on you personally or on your professional goals or your relationships with others? Learning the art of helping is a journey. What steps have you taken so far? What must you do now to go farther?

Homework 3: Videotape Evaluation Form

In some training situations, a final transcript may not be required. Some instructors like students to watch and evaluate the tapes exclusively. Use the videotape described in the previous assignment. Watch the video twice.

During the first viewing of the tape, use Table 15.1 to evaluate your basic skills:

- Make tally marks in column 2, next to the skill in each of the first five skill areas. A tally mark is made each time you see a particular skill demonstrated.
- Stop the tape and make any comments or reflections about "depth." How deeply have you been able to allow the client to explore?
- In column 4, make notes about any problems you are encountering.

During the second viewing of the video, use Table 15.2 to evaluate your ability to activate the curative factors:

- Identify anything you did to activate one of the curative factors in column 1.
- In column 2, list any questions or problems you wish to share with your instructor. Make note of the video counter number or a quotation that will help you find that spot again.
- In column 3, write any reflections about your ability to activate the curative factors with this client and any questions for your instructor.

Table 15.1

Skills	Tally	Comment and Reflect on Depth of Client's Exploration	Questions and Problems
Invitational Skills			
Reflecting Skills			
Advanced Reflecting Skills			
Challenging Skills			
Goal-Setting Skills			

Table 15.2

Curative Factor	Evidence on Tape (Counter Number or Quotation)	Comment and Reflection
(R) Relationship Issues		
(E) Enhancing Efficacy and Self-Esteem		
(P) Practicing New Behaviors		
(L) Lowering/Raising Emotional Arousal		
(A) Activating Expectations, Hope, and Motivation		
(N) New Learning Experiences		

Journal Starters

1. In the first "Stop and Reflect" section in Chapter 1, you filled out an inventory of your attitudes about helping. Reread that section and think about how you might answer those questions now. In general, how has this training experience affected you? Has your level of confidence fluctuated during the training? What events have been helpful and which have been difficult?

2. Reread a journal entry at the beginning and the middle of training. What do you notice about your development? Look again at Perry's stages in Chapter 1. They are dualistic, multiplistic, and relativistic. Have you noticed any changes in your thinking during training? Review Table 1.1, which shows the levels of expertise beginning with naivette and ending with master. Where do you place yourself on this chart? What training experiences will help you develop to the next level?

For more journal ideas, as well as more practice with new learning experiences and evaluating the effectiveness of helping, see Chapter 15 in *Exercises in the Art of Helping*.

References

Anderson, C. M., & Stewart, S. (1983). *Mastering resistance: A practical guide to family therapy.* New York: Guilford.

Ansbacher, H. L., & Ansbacher, R. R. (Eds.). (1956). *The individual psychology of Alfred Adler.* New York: Basic Books.

Bandura, A. (1971). Psychotherapy based on modeling principles. In A. E. Bergin & S. L. Garfield (Eds.), *Handbook of psychotherapy and behavior change: An empirical analysis* (pp. 653–708). New York: Wiley.

Barker, P. (1985). *Using metaphors in psychotherapy.* New York: Brunner/Mazel.

Bernard, T., & Young, J. M. (1996). *The ecology of hope.* Easthaven, CT: New Society Press.

Brammer, L. M., Shostrom, E. L., & Abrego, P. J. (1989). *Therapeutic psychology: Fundamentals of counseling and psychotherapy* (5th ed.). Upper Saddle River, NJ: Prentice Hall.

Cavanagh, M. E. (1982). *The counseling experience.* Monterey, CA: Brooks/Cole.

Clark, A. J. (1995). An examination of the technique of interpretation in counseling. *Journal of Counseling and Development, 73,* 483–490.

Cormier, W. H., & Cormier, S. L. (1985). *Interviewing strategies for helpers: Fundamental skills and cognitive behavioral interventions* (2nd ed.). Pacific Grove, CA: Brooks/Cole.

Dixon, D. N., & Glover, J. A. (1984). *Counseling: A problem-solving approach.* New York: Wiley.

Elliott, R. (1985). Helpful and nonhelpful events in brief counseling interviews: An empirical taxonomy. *Journal of Counseling Psychology, 32,* 307–322.

Emmelkamp, P. M. G. (1982). Exposure *in vivo* treatments. In A. Goldstein & D. Chambless (Eds.), *Agoraphobia: Multiple perspectives on theory and treatment.* New York: Wiley.

Foa, E. B., & Goldstein, A. (1978). Continuous exposure and complete response prevention in the treatment of obsessive compulsive neurosis. *Behavior Therapy, 9,* 821–829.

Framo, J. (1996). Personal communication.

Frank, J. D., & Frank, J. B. (1991). *Persuasion and healing. A comparative study of psychotherapy* (3rd ed.). Baltimore: Johns Hopkins University Press.

Gardner, R. A. (1971). *Therapeutic communication with children: Mutual story-telling technique.* New York: Science House.

Gladding, S. T. (2000). *Counseling: A comprehensive profession* (4th ed.). Upper Saddle River, NJ: Merrill/Prentice Hall.

Goodyear, R. (1981). Termination as a loss experience for the counselor. *Personnel and Guidance Journal, 59,* 347–350.

Gordon, D. (1978). *Therapeutic metaphors.* Cupertino, CA: Meta Publications.

Hackney, H., & Cormier, L. S. (1979). *Counseling strategies and objectives.* Upper Saddle River, NJ: Prentice Hall.

Kalven, J., Rosen, L., & Taylor, B. (1981). *Value development: A practical guide.* Ramsey, NJ: Paulist Press.

Kanfer, F. H. (1975). Self-management methods. In F. H. Kanfer & A. P. Goldstein (Eds.), *Helping people change* (pp. 309–355). New York: Pergamon.

Kanfer, F. H., & Schefft, B. K. (1988). *Guiding therapeutic change.* Champaign, IL: Research Press.

Kazdin, A. E. (1980). *Behavior modification in applied settings.* Homewood, IL: Dorsey Press.

Kramer, S. A. (1986). The termination process in open-ended psychotherapy: Guidelines for clinical practice. *Psychotherapy, 23,* 526–531.

Kramer, S. A. (1990). *Positive endings in psychotherapy.* San Francisco: Jossey-Bass.

Krantz, P. L., & Lund, N. L. (1979). A dilemma of play therapy: Termination anxiety in the therapist. *Teaching of Psychology, 6,* 108–110.

Lamb, D. H. (1985). A time frame model of termination in psychotherapy. *Psychotherapy, 22,* 604–609.

Maholich, L. T., & Turner, D. W. (1979). Termination: That difficult farewell. *American Journal of Psychotherapy, 33,* 583–591.

Martin, J., & Stelmaczonek, K. (1988). Participants' identification and recall of important events in counseling. *Journal of Counseling Psychology, 35,* 385–390.

Mathews, B. (1989). Terminating therapy: Implications for the private practitioner. *Psychotherapy in Private Practice, 7,* 29–39.

McKay, M., Davis, M., & Fanning, P. (1981). *Thoughts and feelings: The art of cognitive stress intervention.* Richmond, CA: New Harbinger.

McMullin, R. (1986). *Handbook of cognitive therapy techniques.* New York: Norton.

Milan, M. (1985). Symbolic modeling. In M. Hersen & A. S. Bellack (Eds.), *Dictionary of behavior therapy techniques* (pp. 212–215). New York: Pergamon.

Mitchell, Z. P., & Milan, M. (1983). Imitation of high-interest comic strip models' appropriate classroom behavior: Acquisition and generalization. *Child and Family Behavior Therapy, 5,* 25–30.

Morris, R. J. (1986). Fear reduction methods. In F. H. Kanfer & A. P. Goldstein (Eds.), *Helping people change* (pp. 145–190). New York: Pergamon.

Mosak, H. H. (1987). *Ha ha and aha.* Muncie, IN: Accelerated Development.

Munro, J. N., & Bach, T. R. (1975). Effect of time-limited counseling on client change. *Journal of Counseling Psychology, 22,* 395–398.

O'Hanlon, W. H., & Weiner-Davis, M. (1989). *In search of solutions.* New York: Norton.

Perry, M. A., & Furukawa, M. J. (1986). Modeling methods. In F. H. Kanfer & A. P. Goldstein (Eds.), *Helping people change* (pp. 66–110). New York: Pergamon.

Perry, G. P., & Paquin, J. J. (1987). Practical strategies for maintaining and generalizing improvements from psychotherapy. In P. A. Keller & S. R. Heyman (Eds.), *Innovations in clinical practice: A source book* (Vol. 6, pp. 151–164). Sarasota, FL: Professional Resource Exchange.

Rudestam, K. E. (1980). *Methods of self-change: An ABC primer.* Monterey, CA: Brooks/Cole.

Sciscoe, M. (1990). The termination of therapy. Unpublished manuscript.

Shulman, L. (1979). *The skills of helping individuals and groups.* Itasca, IL: Peacock Press.

Ward, D. E. (1984). Termination of individual counseling: Concepts and strategies. *Journal of Counseling and Development, 63,* 21–25.

Watzlawick, P., Weakland, J., & Fisch, R. (1974). *Change: Principles of problem formation and problem resolution.* New York: Norton.

Wolberg, L. R. (1954). *The technique of psychotherapy.* New York: Grune & Stratton.

Yalom, I. R. (1995). *Theory and practice of group psychotherapy* (4th ed.). New York: Basic Books.

Young, M. E., & Rosen, L. S. (1985). The retreat: An educational growth group. *Journal for Specialists in Group Work, 21,* 157–171.

Index